© 2002 Subway & Elevated Press
All rights reserved
ISBN 0-9666469-7-5
Distributed by New Mouth from the Dirty South
To order copies of this book, send $12 per book to:
New Mouth from the Dirty South
PO Box 19742
New Orleans, LA 70179

or order online at:
www.newmouthfromthedirtysouth.com
www.Future500.com

Printed in the United States of America on recycled paper
Book design by Tyler Askew (www.tyleraskew.com)

The Active Element Foundation presents

FUTURE500

Youth Organizing and Activism in the United States

SUBWAY⊕
ELEVATED

Introduction

When seeking justice becomes completely illegal, this book will be the star witness for the prosecution. Or less dramatically, the next time you see a news story about the slacker generation, the ultra-apathetic generations X, Y, and Z, or the woman-hating, platinum-champagne obsessed Hip Hop generation, simply refer to this book-- it's shouting that the mainstream media emperor is butt-naked. Or more practically, when you are tired of the madness on your block, in your community, city or world, and you feel like nobody else is fighting the good fight and building the just peace, flip through these pages and find where your talent, resources and passion can fit. This book is all about change-- learning about, documenting, admiring, being, making-- change.

Foundation-speak: It is with great excitement that we share this first-of-its-kind resource with you-- Active Element Foundation's Future 500. While there have been other directories of grassroots organizing, mappings of youth organizations working on particular issues, and regional youth organizing directories, this is the first published national directory of youth organizing in the US that cuts across issue, race and gender. We set out to find 500 youth organizations (see pg. 35 for the criteria) and 25 individuals who tell the largely untold story of a new generation's response to, among other issues, vast economic inequality and corporate abuse, relentless attacks on everything public from education to the arts, unprecedented rates of incarceration, irreversible environmental destruction and neighborhood pollution, the persistence of military, political, and community violence, and the resilience of sexism, racism, and heterosexism. After two years of research, we feel confident that this directory will reate a stronger understanding of youth organizing and its response to the daily realities and price of American hegemony.

AEF embarked on this project because we believed it would help us in our institutional mission, which is to create infrastructure for people who want to build a more just and equitable society. We strive to accomplish this by forging relationships between community organizers, professionals, artists, entrepreneurs, donors and young people nationwide through strategic collaborations, Hip Hop and youth culture-friendly spaces, technical assistance, and grant-making. A mapping like the Future 500 seemed like a logical and necessary internal project. Since its inception in 2000, AEF has granted over $250,000 in money and computers to 90 grassroots youth-led organizations. As we pursued this work, we realized that while we are the only foundation in the country that exclusively funds youth organizing nationally across issue area, we are not the only ones interested in these groups-- other foundations, progressive media outlets and, perhaps most importantly, other youth organizations and individuals kept calling us requesting information. So we decided that what began as in internal project should become this public networking and educational tool.

Part of the AEF family (clockwise from upper left): Gita Drury, Pablo Caraballo, Ibrahim Abdul-Matin, Kofi Taha (with Isa Taha), Jee Kim, Billy Wimsatt, Meghan Tauck, Mathilda de Dios, Manuela Arciniegas

The Future 500 marks beginnings, not the end of a project. We hope it's the beginning of www.Future500.com becoming the most useful and thorough database of youth organizations in the country. We know it'll be the start of a debate, over which groups were and were not included. It should also then be the start of a conversation about how much bigger and stronger the movement is than what's captured in this book, and how different yet like-minded many of these organizations are. So here it is. We deliver it with hopes that it will inspire **organizers** to network, to share victories and challenges, learn new strategies and gain new skills, be a model or find a role model; **individuals** to find an internship, volunteer, donate, begin a dialogue or do some research; **foundations** to recognize youth organizing as a critical area of youth development and as a field with necessary and specific social impacts; **educational institutions** to inform adolescents and young adults about the potential of civic engagement, non-profit employment and social justice work; and **media organizations** to find young people that correct the currently skewed view of this generation.

Let's get started.

Gita Drury & Kofi Taha / Co-Directors, Active Element Foundation

How to Use this Book

The book you hold in your hands is a snapshot of the movement put on paper. Like any snapshot, it will go out of date.

That's why it's all about **www.Future500.com**.

We expect Future500.com to become the most trafficked youth activist and organizing web site by the end of 2003. So if your group is already in here, get ready for a flood of media, money, volunteers, and random inquiries. Or at least random inquiries. If your group is not in here, and it does youth organizing and activism, please go on line to Future500.com and add it right away.

If you're not involved in any of this stuff, then Welcome to The Movement. Call up. Show up. Make yourself useful. Just because the first three groups you called are stuck up, that's no excuse for your lazy ass to sit around smokin weed and talkin bout the Illuminati (or sipping on Starbucks complaining about how apathetic people are). If you're down to put in work, somewhere some group needs you. This is a book about possibilities.

If this book has only confirmed there ain't shit in your town, then it appears it's up to you to start something (and make sure you list it on Future500.com). Also, do us all a big favor: Anytime you meet someone who's starting a new group or changing phone numbers-- tell them to add it. You will never have to lose their contact info again! And any time you travel, look at Future500.com. See what groups you want to connect with. Let's build with each other, learn from each other, support each other across our many differences, and get the Starbucks/Apathetic People/Illuminati in check.

We argued about whether to include international groups and ultimately decided it was too important to do a half-ass job. Corporations are global. Politics is global. Our struggle is global. The Future 500 will be global, next edition. Eventually we want it to become The Future 5000 and The Future 50,000 (seriously) as the Movement-- and our capacity to document and support it-- grows.

Now, about the structure. Prior to jumping into the 500, THE FUTURE 25 highlights some of the amazing young activists and the personal stories behind the organizations. THE FUTURE 500 is organized alphabetically by state. Then, a brief NATIONAL RESOURCES AND NETWORKS section charts over 130 organizations, followed by a listing of FOUNDATIONS relevant to the youth movement and a YOUTH ALLIES directory composed of organizations that are not youth groups but can provide support. Our CHARTS analyze some of the key data we've collected about the Future 500 and precedes the INDEX of the groups ordered alphabetically by name and by issue.

Finally, about the terms. Controversy, controversy, controversy. People define their work, themselves, and the issues differently. What we've tried to do is come up with a common language, not a final set of definitions. So use the GLOSSARY below as a key to this book and starting point for exploring an issue or term. The glossary covers acronyms, frequently used phrases, and the issue areas we used to describe the work of each group. The main objective is to make sure that a young person who looks up "gentrification" in the dictionary and finds nothing can still figure out that the group they are interested in deals with neighborhood politics. Activists can get acronym-crazy to the point where nobody really understands what's going on, so this glossary is also a decoder ring. Read with a salt-shaker and get over it if you don't like what our sampling of different sources has resulted in. No offense intended.

Eventually, we're planning to make Future500.com an interactive site that includes many more resources, such as listings of youth activist-friendly journalists, businesses, artists and their visuals, and much more. We want YOUR feedback! Please use the FEEDBACK FORM at the end of this book or hit us up online at... yeah, you know the place. Future500.com.

Acronyms and short-hand

9/11:	September 11, 2001
API:	Asian & Pacific Islander.
DIY:	Do It Yourself, an anarchist/punk motto & way of life.
DNC/RNC:	Democratic National Convention/Republican National Convention
FTAA:	The proposed Free Trade Area of the Americas (NAFTA pt 2)
IMC:	Independent Media Center (see Independent Media below)
IMF:	International Monetary Fund
LGBT:	Lesbian, Gay, Bi-Sexual, Transgendered
LGBTTSQ:	Lesbian, Gay, Bi-Sexual, Transgendered, Two-Spirited, Questioning
NAFTA:	North America Free Trade Agreement
WCAR:	World Conference Against Racism, held in Durban, South Africa in 2001
WEF:	World Economic Forum
WRC:	Worker's Rights Consortium
WTO:	World Trade Organization

Glossary

Below is a listing of frequently used phrases and terms used to describe Future 500 organizations, including the issues tackled and their racial make-up. Please note, organizations are limited to five issues and can have multiple race categories. For example, if "People of Color" and "Latina/o" are listed, the organization is made up of people of color but is largely Latina/o. If "Multi-Racial" and "White" are listed, then it is a mostly white yet multi-racial organization. For a distinction between constituency and leadership race, please see Future500.com.

Ageism: Descrimination based on age, weather against the young or against the elder. In this directory, mainly refers to exclusion of youth in decision making.

Alternatives to Incarceration: See prison industrial complex/criminal justice system. The idea is that US policymakers should explore alternatives to throwing people in jail, such as rehabilitation programs, re-allocating money spent on prisons to education programs, job creation, career development, youth spaces and community projects. With over 2 million prisoners, 70% of which are non-violent offenders, the US incarcerates more people than any other country in the world!

Arab/Arab American: Arab people have diverse nationalities and religions yet are connected by culture. The term Arab generally refers to someone who comes from an Arabic-speaking country in southwestern Asia or northern Africa, a region known from colonial times as the Middle East. Arabs can be of varying nationalities, like Yemeni or Lebanese or American. They belong to many religions, including Islam, Christianity, Druze and Judaism, or can not be religiously affiliated.

African American/Black/Afrikan: People of African descent whose ancestors were brought to this country mostly during the slave trade. African-descendents of other nationalities or ethnicities, like a dark-skinned Puerto Rican, are not identified as African Americans unless they expressly told us to. Also includes recent wave of immigrants from African countries like Senegal, Ghana, Nigeria, etc.

Arts/Culture: This issue area refers to people who organize using the arts or culture to teach political themes, affect positive social change, or organize around the preservation or expansion of culture.

Animal Rights: This issue includes, but is not limited to, vegan groups organizing against the killing of animals, their confinement and treatment in zoos and as pets, those bred for their skin/fur or other products for human consumption, and those used for medical testing.

Asian/Pacific Islander: People from East, South, or Southeast Asia (China, Korea, India, Tibet, Vietnam, Thailand, Burma, etc.) or the Asian-Pacific Island regions, like the Philippines or Hawaii.

Campaign Finance: The idea used to be that the best candidate would represent the people. Today, the candidate with the richest friends or the most corporate backing wins. Can a person represent the poor in public office, please? Campaign finance reform is about getting private money out of politics. If everybody has the same amount of money to campaign with and the same amount of media exposure, those who fight for campaign finance reform believe that the public would be more informed about issues, have more qualified candidates to choose from, and would be able to hold elected officials more accountable.

Collective: Flat organizational structure where the members of a group are responsible for or involved in making all decisions. There are no ranks or structures that make one person more powerful than another. Collectives in this book are particularly popular among art, organizing or media groups. Also see Consensus Model below.

Community-Based Organizations (CBOs): Organizations where the community directly affected by an issue organizes itself, identifies how it will address the issue, and then works in the community to create the changes it wishes to see.

Consensus Model: Decisions are made when everyone can arrive at a place of agreement or comfort with a decision. Unlike a majority-rules vote, the consensus model is designed to ensure group participation and cohesion, to be non-hierarchical, and to make sure everyone has a voice. The art of good consensus building is to create the space for all perspectives to be heard, yet still get things accomplished in a timely manner.

Corporate Accountability: Working to hold corporations responsible for the exploitation of human and natural resources. Demands include: fair pay for workers, environmental responsibility, community reinvestment and ending sweatshop labor. Activities include divesting from companies that contribute to human rights abuses and crimes, like Shell Oil, The Gap/Old Navy, or Nike.

Critical Mass: Enough folks to make a visible argument for a change. Strength in numbers. Also specifically used to refer to bicycle protests, usually to raise awareness about alternative forms of transportation and public space. A successful Critical Mass demonstration organizes enough bicycles to disrupt city traffic and "take back the streets."

Decentralization: Spread out with no one central decision-making body or focus of power. This often refers to organizations with many chapters and no national headquarters or committee making decisions for them. This allows for diverse strategies, ideologies and internal structures to emerge.

Differently-abled: Folks who walk, speak, move, think in extraordinary ways, fighting for equal access to facilities and resources. Raise awareness that different abilities do not mean a person is "disabled," "in-valid" or incapable of being successful.

Digital Divide: Gap in access to computers and the internet between communities of color and predominantly white communities, between mid to upper income neighborhoods and low income neighborhoods, between economically developed nations of the North and economically developing nations of the South. The communications boom has only gone down for some people.

Direct Action: A strategy to raise issues or injustices through an individual or group's physical presence or collective activity. Show up at the Mayor's office, boycott a product, occupy an administrative building, flood a company with calls, faxes or emails, create a mural without a permit, etc. Frequently involves a civil disobedience component, which entails breaking a law or an ordinance that is deemed unjust. An alternative to sending money for someone else to lobby the causes you believe in; instead you get on a bus and head to D.C. with some folks.

Drug Policy: The criminalization of youth of color, militarized policing in targeted communities, mandatory minimum sentencing even for first time offenders, supply-side emphasis instead of demand-side treatment, punishment instead of prevention through educational investment, and the overall focus on busting people dealing dime bags instead of the big and powerful profiteers are all features of US drug policy that activists are addressing. The 'war on drugs" has really manifested as a "war on communities." A legislative example is the Drug-Free Student Aid Provision, which prevents kids who have ever been arrested or convicted of some drug-related offense (like carrying a joint) from getting financial aid for college. This law mostly affects low income people and people of color. Also see Plan Columbia below.

Environment: Mainly wildlife and land preservation, seeking sustainable energy sources and clean air, and trying to address global warming. Human beings, through corporate entities and governments, have, in our arrogance, desire for convenience and rush to industrialize, chopped down forests, dirtied lakes, dumped garbage in the ocean and made animal species extinct or endangered.

Environmental Justice (EJ): Low-income communities and communities of color are fighting to live and work in healthy environments! Polluting manufacturing plants, cancer-causing power facilities, military weapons testing areas and garbage incinerators, asthma-inducing wood chip mills and bus depots are not only concentrated in low income neighborhoods but also target playgrounds, sacred spiritual grounds and parks! EJ directly addresses the results of corporate abuse and "not in my backyard" syndrome-- toxic waste dumps and other environmental hazards end up in low-income communities because the rich effectively lobby to make sure that none of these dangers end up in their neighborhoods. Folks ain't having it anymore.

Education: In this book, this issue refers to political education: workshops, trainings, and activities that build a person's analysis and skills, helping them to understand and choose to address issues affecting them and their community. For home-schooling and education reform, see Student Rights/Education Reform.

Fast Track Legislation: Politricks designed to give the President of the US power to bypass congress in making international trade agreements.

Gang Issues: For organizations whose constituency is gang-members, issues include mediation, prevention, violence prevention and creating educational and employment opportunities. Gangs here refer to street organizations, not other gangs like fraternities, corrupt police rings or athletic teams.

Gentrification: The process of displacing low-income residents and/or communities of color to make room for urban professionals or corporations. Rents get high, fancy stores move in, neighborhoods suddenly get fixed up, folks with money (usually white) move in until there's no more housing for folks without money (usually people of color, artists, small business owners, etc).

Globalization: After the fall of the Soviet Union and the communist bloc, the world's economic system began to follow the American model of capitalist growth-- cut social programs, remove trade barriers/protections and let the corporations do their thing without much regulation from governments, whether that means exchanging local union workers for exploited workers overseas, causing environmental destruction or ruining local economies. Big enforcers of globalization include the World Trade Organization, International Monetary Fund and World Bank. This is a very simplified explanation, for a more in depth analysis read **Global Village or Global Pillage** by Jeremy Brecher and Tim Costello.

Guerrilla Theater: A form of popular education that uses creative tactics to teach people about an issue. Pioneered by Cesar Chavez and the United Farmer's Workers, skits, plays, songs and art were used to illustrate the abuses of farm bosses and overseers. This fun and diverse type of work has been applied in many struggles over the last 30 years. A great alternative or addition to rallies, protests and demonstrations.

HIV/AIDS: Related to education about HIV/AIDS, treatment of patients and infected people, sex education and access to medicine and pharmaceutical products to fight it. Getting past the lies that AIDS is a "gay disease" or that Africa is the "AIDS continent," and starting to deal with the reality that young women of color bear the highest burden of HIV/AIDS and, that without serious work on this pandemic, 100 million people will be infected by 2010.

Hip Hop Activism: We use this category so that Hip Hop movement activists can find and connect with each other, not because we think Hip Hop activism is clearly distinct from other organizing. People who are Hip Hop teach it and use its elements (Breakdancing, MCing, DJing, and Graffiti) to educate and raise awareness for justice and social change. Hip Hop is a movement by and for young people of color speaking about the daily conditions of their oppression, and at this point, it is WORLDWIDE.

Healthcare: Fighting for universal healthcare, increased access to quality healthcare in low-income communities, protection of Medicaid, creating a universal patient Bill of Rights, and promoting nutrition in schools. Or fighting against exorbitant rates and biased health insurance companies.

Homelessness: People without stable places to live or in transitional housing situations such as shelters or group homes. Most homeless people are children under 18 years of age. How does the "richest nation in the world" account for the estimated 7 million homeless people? Or do we just not account for this population, pretend it doesn't exist or, better still, pass "quality of life" laws making it illegal for folks to ask for money on the train because it inconveniences us?

Hope VI: Pushes low-income people of color out of housing projects so that they can be renovated/torn down to create "mixed income" housing. It is currently creating severe gentrification in Seattle, WA and Roxbury, MA and other places across the country. Originally known as the Urban Revitalization Demonstration (URD), this is a federal housing program. Question is, where do folks go if they can no longer afford public housing? See Homelessness.

Human Rights: Traditionally used to refers to international efforts to stop violations of the Universal Declaration on Human Rights committed by governments and corporations, such as the use of military violence, unfair imprisonment, torture, denial of political expression and other basic civil or political rights. Increasingly, however, organizers connect labor, housing, immigration, sexuality, racial and gender issues to the human rights paradigm and call the US to task on its outrageous prison population, its own political prisoners and prisoners of war, and its military and economic interventions worldwide.

Independent Media: A call for news and information that is not controlled by the same four media corporations. Why wouldn't information be censored and tailored to the interests of these private companies, and why would a reporter expose information that could result in her/his unemployment? The Independent Media Center, now leading this call for truth in journalism, was formed by dozens of independent media groups covering the World Trade Organization protests in Seattle in 1999. Now there are more than 80 IMCs around the world from Nigeria to Colombia to Jerusalem.

Immigrant/Refugee: Issues associated with people who live in, but were not born in, the US, people who are children of immigrants, and people fleeing their countries or exiled from their countries due to violence, political repression, or other persecution. Refers to people organizing around the policies/laws that deny immigrants access to education and healthcare, and that create language barriers, deny civil liberties and foster hate crimes.

Indigenous Rights: Struggle for the sovereignty and self-determination of Indigenous people. The preservation of a healthy mother earth, honoring Indigenous sacred sites and culture, and rebuilding Indigenous economies while fighting off attempts by corporations and the US government to further violate treaties and exploit natural resources. What claim to justice does anyone in this country have without acknowledgement of and commitment to the struggle of the First Nations?

Institutional Racism: Racism is not only power exercised by individuals, it is embedded in laws, policies, and institutions meant to support and reinforce white supremacy. Examples include the disparity in sentencing in the criminal justice system, tracking in public schools, insurance and loan redlining, zoning for elections, locations of hospitals and schools, and placement of environmental hazards. Similar institutional barriers exist for other "-isms," like sexism.

Intergenerational: Yo' grandma, yo' father and yo' auntie too. Even yo' child! Elders, adults, youth, and children working together, sharing experiences and transferring knowledge so every new organizational effort doesn't start from scratch and so communities can see their collective goals. There is a rich history of struggle in the US and around the world to draw from, and any organizer who doesn't find a mentor and/or mentor someone else is doing this work a great disservice.

Labor/Economic Justice: For low-income, working class or non-working people. Includes living wage campaigns, labor law/reform and divestment strategies; unites unionized and un-unionized workers, sweatshop workers and farm workers in a fight against poverty and economic abuse. Draws a strong connection between other social issues-- from crime to health to education-- and economic opportunities.

Latina/o: Of Latin American and Caribbean, Spanish-speaking descent, drawing on a unique combination of Indigenous, African and European cultural influences. For our purposes, this term includes, for example, people living in the United States who consider themselves Chicana/Xicano, Mexican American, Afro-Boricua and/or white Brazilian.

LGBTTSQ/Queer Rights: Lesbian, Gay, Bi-sexual, Transgender, Two-spirited, Questioning folks fighting for equal protection and non-discrimination. Some people like Queer, others feel that there is nothing queer about loving who you love or being who you be. We use the two terms interchangeably, usually depending on what the group itself uses.

Lobbying: Groups of people with particular interests in mind go visit their state or congressional representatives to advance their interests. It costs a lot of money or a lot of community involvement to be able to lobby regularly and effectively. Companies with lots of money tend to push Congress or state legislatures to vote in their interests; community based organizations are starting to use lobbying as a strategy for social justice.

Media: This issue area covers both media watchdog work and independent/alternative media sources.

Militarism: This issue area includes fighting the effects of military testing and training on citizens, people organizing for peace and non-violence, and opposing JROTC-- army recruitment programs in high schools that frequently present themselves as the only viable alternatives for low-income youth of color to find work or get to college. Post-9/11, this has included resistance to "the war on terrorism," the war in Afghanistan, the deployment of the Israeli military against Palestinian civilians, and the "preemptive self-defense" policy of the Bush Administration.

Mobilizations: A show of organized, numeric strength towards a specific goal. When we use this term, we usually mean demonstrations, pickets, strikes, protests, anything where a community takes public action.

Multiculturalism: A model for how people of many different cultures can live, work and learn together through mutual respect, understanding and appreciation for diversity. This issue area refers to groups that are working to increase understanding between communities, not necessarily using culture as a political tool.

Multi-Racial: Encompassing people of many races working together. For the purposes of this book, we use the unscientific term "race" because that is the social reality that organizers are addressing. Multi-racial is used to be distinct from groups that have one main racial constituency and groups that are comprised of people of color only (see below). Multi-racial groups have white and people of color members.

Participatory Democracy: The idea that our governmental system is at its best when people vote, attend city council meetings, make their voices heard, and are aggressive about presenting the issues they care about to their representatives. This also refers to organizational systems that operate like a government where everyone is participating and actively involved. A number of youth organizations try to create an environment wherein all members are encouraged to implement their ideas (as opposed to just talking about it in terms of larger government structures).

People of Color: People whose cultural/ethnic/racial heritage is African, Indigenous, Asian/Pacific-Islander, Arab, Latino, or any other race/ethnicity that is not white/Caucasian. This distinction is made largely to understand the organizing efforts of groups that strive to understand the long-term social, political and psychological impacts of white supremacy, genocide, slavery, colonialism and imperialism. If a majority of the people in the world are people of color, who are "minorities?" Some find people of color clumsy and unspecific; others love it for its unifying implications.

Plan Columbia: An example of US drug policy— a $4 million "aid package" to the Colombian military to fight the drug war that has been linked with paramilitary death squads, torture and indiscriminate fumigation of crops. Not only has the crop spraying destroyed banana farms and other legal food sources, workers are reporting life-threatening health problems connected to inhaling or being directly sprayed by the toxic substances used.

Police Accountability: Holding police responsible for abusing their authority, excessive force harassment and corruption. People organizing around this issue deal with police brutality, establishing civilian complaint review boards, enacting residency requirements, training truancy officers, ending racial profiling and improving police-community relations.

Political Education: Through workshops, lectures, in-the-field experience and learning about power and how it plays out in our lives, political education raises awareness about social and political issues, develops leadership skills, and teaches effective organizational development. The goal is to educate peoples on the REAL DEAL about our collective situation in the world and to teach us how to fight oppression.

Political Prisoners, POWs, and the related term, Self-Determination: There are an estimated 100 political prisoners/POWs in the US, mainly political folks working in their communities in the 60's and 70's. We'll use the definitions from international human rights organizations. Political Prisoner: a person incarcerated for actions carried out in support of legitimate struggles for self-determination or for opposing the illegal policies of the United States government and/or its political sub-divisions. Prisoner of War: those combatants struggling against colonial and alien domination and racist regimes captured as prisoners and whose treatment should be in accordance with the provisions of the Geneva Conventions. Self -Determination: the right by which all peoples are entitled to determine their political status, pursue their economic, social and cultural development, freely dispose of their natural wealth and in no case be deprived of its own means of subsistence. See www.prisonactivist.org for more info.

Prisons/Criminal Justice: This issue refers to groups fighting the expansion of the prison industrial complex (see below) and the criminal justice system, a.k.a., the criminal injustice system. What does it say about a society if it spend more money on putting folks in jail than it does on schools?

Prop 21/No Prop 21 Campaign: Proposition 21 was a ballot initiative in California that aimed to try 14 year olds as adults, put 16 year olds in adult prison facilities, and create a special "gang related" capital punishment. Though the initiative passed state-wide, a historic youth movement came together in opposition, such that every county in which youth were actively organizing, the initiative did not win a majority of votes. This campaign was the spark for the national Schools Not Jails/Education Not Incarceration/Books Not Bars campaigns.

Public Space: This issue refers to people interested in preserving community space or creating new spaces for youth, for art and for non-profit endeavors. It also includes organizing against governmentally imposed curfews. In this book, this issue area does not refer to actual community centers but rather organizing efforts for the existence of such centers.

Prison Industrial Complex: Prisons are businesses and many are owned and run like corporations. To make sure business keeps growing, you gotta have more and more workers, i.e., prisoners, so policy-makers, politicians, and the media work with corporations to create laws and conditions that will incarcerate more and more people. And surprise, most of the people incarcerated tend to be low income and/or people of color. Even though crime rates have not changed or have slightly decreased since 1970, the prison population has increased from 200,000 to 2 million over the same period. In that time, 700 new prisons have been built and there are now 7 times more women in prison then there were in 1980. To learn more, check out **No More Prisons** by William Upski Wimsatt or **Lockdown America** by Christian Parenti.

Racial Justice: This issue refers to those fighting against injustices driven largely by racism, e.g., gentrification, police brutality, living and working conditions, etc. Includes the movement for reparations for slavery.

Reproductive Rights: Protecting the right to choose, keeping abortions affordable and safe, and providing access to accurate and respectful information and services for young women and girls concerning their own bodies.

School of the Americas: US Military sponsored training ground for assassins and torturers who, after graduation, serve oppressive regimes throughout the Western hemisphere. Located at Fort Benning in Columbus, GA.

Squats/Squatter: If you don't have a place to live and you decide to take over and live in an abandoned or unused property, you are a squatter, and the spot you are in is a squat. Your presence makes that space a home and can improve the overall well being of your family and community. Challenges morality of traditional notions of property rights.

Student Rights/Education Reform: Curriculum reform, campus organizing, home-schooling, fighting truancy policies and school policies (like "No Braids"), and working for systemic change. Are students in school to learn how to think or what to think? To become whole people or parts in the American economic machine?

Superfund Site: US government designation for many toxic waste sites.

Sustainability: Refers to exploring alternative energy sources, recycling technology, organic food production methods and other ways for human societies to develop without depleting the earth's natural resources. In the context of an organization, this refers to building a healthy structure that honors the involvement of its members, develops and transfers leadership, and avoids individual burnout in order to do effective work in the community over time.

Sweatshops: Sweatshops are factories where mostly people of color work long hours in unsafe working environments, make little or no money, and suffer harassment, abuse, and intimidation. Companies like Nike contract with an abusive sweatshop company overseas to make their sneakers and then sell them for 100 times the price it costs to make them (including the wages of the workers). Sweatshops are not limited to the apparel industry or to factories in developing countries. They exist right here in major US cities, in prisons, and many places where working class people try to make an honest living. Most of what Americans buy is made in sweatshops! Watch what you buy...

Tenant Rights: Refers to the basic rights of people who rent their homes. This term usually comes up when we speak about unfair, unhealthy, or dangerous housing conditions and the everyday people who organize themselves against these conditions.

Third World People's Movements: Again, the Third World is one of those terms some folks love and other's don't, but it refers to people living in or originating from formerly colonized nations, largely comprised of People of Color, and their unified efforts towards dismantling white supremacy and Euro-American domination. The concept of the Third World is designed to unify people, communities and nations against racism, exploitation and multiple forms of oppression. Historic and contemporary Third World People's Movements tell the story of resistance against slavery, colonialism, imperialism and neo-colonialism, a.k.a., globalization, from India to Cuba, the Philippines to South Africa.

Violence Prevention/Abuse: Domestic violence, youth-on-youth violence, hate crimes, street violence, gang related violence.

Welfare Deform/Reform: In 1996, former president Clinton launched "welfare reform" (now commonly called welfare deform), a system that has forced thousands of families (mostly single women with children) off welfare and into extreme and isolating poverty. Time limits were imposed, putting caps on how long people were allowed to receive assistance. States were also given financial incentives to cut their welfare rolls, putting pressure on case workers and welfare offices to deny benefits to those who are eligible. Welfare recipients are often forced to work jobs once performed by union employees for a fraction of the wages (often as little as a $1.35/hr.) with no benefits, no protections, and no opportunity for permanent employment. Welfare rights activists are fighting the legislation and its effects, educating people about their rights and eligibility, and battling media and policy attacks on low-income communities.

Welfare/Poverty: See welfare deform. Also includes women, children, and families living on or fighting against the injustices caused by welfare and the conditions of poverty.

White: For the purposes of this book, European American, Caucasian, Anglo American, Appalachian, Jewish (although we know many folks don't see it this way).

Women's Rights: This issue refers to those organizing against sexual discrimination, oppression and violence against women, and fighting for women's power in all areas of society.

Youth Development: This issue refers to community centers, schools, and organizing where young people are flourishing, learning leadership skills, developing their political analysis and their understanding of themselves, their creative potential, and their power. It often includes tutoring and mentoring components.

Zine: Self-published, underground photocopies-turned-magazines that are creative and political and speak to the REAL DEAL of what youth are experiencing. Not controlled by mainstream media.

Table of Contents

State of the Movement

by William Upski Wimsatt

I will never forget the way I felt in 1984 when Hip Hop hit my elementary school. It was the greatest feeling ever. Suddenly I wasn't just a 12-year-old kid anymore. I was a breaker and a graffiti writer. I had a reputation and a mission: to paint my school, my neighborhood, and the whole city (Chicago) until it looked like the photos we'd seen of the South Bronx. I was hooked on Hip Hop. It took over my life. I had so much to learn: running subway tunnels, racking paint, rocking styles. I couldn't get enough. I had friends in every neighborhood and we would sneak out and paint every night. We thought we could do anything. There was so much excitement, so many discoveries, so much to do!

That's how I feel about the movement right now. Which movement? All of them. The youth movement. The prison movement. The global justice movement. All of the mini movements which add up to the one big Movement which is about people respecting each other, respecting the Earth, and taking away the guns from the big bad monsters who are destroying and disrespecting everything we hold sacred.

Until recently, there wasn't much of a youth movement. During the 1980s and '90s, college students consistently polled as the most conservative segment of the voting public. We were said to be reacting against our absent, divorced parents, rejecting the idealism of the '60s. We were hypnotized by turbo-capitalism, video games, and shock TV. The political Hip Hop of the late '80s turned into the hyper-consumerism of the late '90s. We created great art about how alienated, angry, and escapist we were: Kurt Cobain, Biggie, Rage, the entire techno genre. We medicated ourselves with 40s, weed, ecstasy, and status symbols bought on credit. Nineties style campus activism was lampooned as political correctness and identity politics.

In the past three years, all that changed. Students have organized more protests on college campuses since 1999 than any period since the 1960s-- and they're winning major victories: living wages, sweatshops, ethnic studies, recruitment and retention of students and faculty of color, Native American mascots, divestment from companies crushing the people of Burma and Tibet, cafeteria companies which own for-profit prisons, oil companies drilling on indigenous lands. Three years ago, few people had heard of the WTO. Now, after tens of thousands of young people locked arms in Seattle, Washington, Quebec City, Prague, and Genoa, it feels compelled to change its name (and supposedly its mission-- yeah, right) in response to a worldwide movement. Started three years ago, Independent Media Centers (indymedia.org) are now in more than 90 cities from Venezuela to Nigeria-- a global network rivaling CNN. April 20, 2002 was the largest protest against US foreign policy since the Vietnam War with an estimated 100,000 people in DC and 30,000 in San Francisco. Polls now show the college class of 2005 is the most progressive in at least 30 years, according to the American Freshman Survey.

The same thing is happening in communities of color. Blatant institutionalized racism in prisons, sentencing laws, police brutality, schools, immigration, environmental violence, gentrification, media, voter disenfranchisement, and welfare reform have forced a level of organizing not seen since the Panthers and the Young Lords. The fight against Prop 21 in Cali (charging 14-year-olds as adults) galvanized a generation of young people who staged statewide high school walk-outs and Hip Hop-based sit-ins at corporations who funded Prop 21, winning major victories with Chevron and Pacific Gas & Electric. As word spread about the politically sophisticated multiracial young organizers in California, it emboldened youth nationwide, who began to see themselves as part of a growing movement with the rallying cry: "Schools Not Jails" and "Educate Don't Incarcerate." Suddenly, all across the country, Hip Hop heads had heard of "Third Eye Movement" (now called "Let's Get Free"). The first Hip Hop political organization with national name recognition, it captured the imagination of groups like Critical Breakdown in Boston, SYPP (Seattle Young People's Project) in Seattle, and University of Hip Hop in Chicago.

It's hard to comprehend how big a development this was. Ten years ago in Chicago, there were literally no political youth organizations of any kind (except for the occasional sectarian front group). Now count them: 14 progressive youth groups in Chicago alone. Even in conservative suburbs where I never dreamed anything progressive could happen, I hear shocking reports: 200 anti-war demonstrators in Wheaton. Reclaim the Streets Naperville draws 300 young people. Could this really be true?

Yes, and it's spreading all over the country. One of the big surprises for all of us who worked on the Future 500 is that none of us, myself included, had any clue how much was going on. Who knew there were young people organizing for social change in Machias, Maine or Tifton, Georgia or Boise, Idaho? The Future 500 started out as a six month project. Two years and dozens of researchers later, here we are. Far from finished, but at a certain point, you just need to put the book out.

Union Square, NYC, April 30, 2002
©ramona photo

Washington DC, April 20, 2002
©ramona photo

I first realized something was happening when I got hired by Rock the Vote in 1998 as a talent scout to find youth activists to profile on MTV. So there I was in Louisville, Kentucky interviewing some kids from The Brat, an underground paper whose tagline reads "because your school paper sucks." They didn't just publish the magazine; they used it to organize campaigns. When a high school banned books by E. Lynn Harris, a gay Black writer, they fought it and won. When the City of Louisville instituted a curfew, The Brat organized a concert called "Screw the Curfew," a punk rock/Hip Hop concert on the steps of city hall. 400 kids came. They didn't beat the curfew but they attracted the attention of a civil rights lawyer Bill Allison who was running for City Council. He asked them for help. They went door to door and helped him win. He helped them build their own youth center, the Brycchouse.

I was like: Damn, we never did anything like that in Chicago. I never even knew I could talk to my city council person.

Then I went to Albuquerque. There I was sitting in a Mexican diner, as three people my own age told me how they had organized against the most powerful developer in New Mexico, John Black. Black had gained permission to build a highway over the Petroglyphs, a national monument and a Native sacred site. The young people sitting across from me, eating rice and beans like me, had educated and mobilized voters and forced the Petroglyph issue to the top of the city's agenda. Because of their organizing, voters had already tossed out two Albuquerque city council members and the mayor over this issue. (As we go to press, they've won two more city council votes but they lost the mayor so they still need one more vote to win. See story pg. 12).

Who knew all this was happening in Albuquerque and Louisville? The State of the Movement is that almost no one in the Movement, let alone anyone outside of it, has any idea how much is going on. Sometimes we're so busy responding to the terrifying rise of the Corporate/Rightwing/Military Agenda that we forget to notice how much better our little movement looks now than five years ago. Today's young organizers are light years ahead of where I was at their age. They change government policies, win concessions from multinational companies. World leaders seem scared of them. They have well-researched targets, and specific, winnable demands.

Right now, it's almost becoming cool for young people to be political. We've got major recording artists going to Cuba for Mumia benefit shows and Russell Simmons and Def Jam's roster mobilizing tens of thousands of high school students in NYC to protest education cuts. In part, activism is cool now because there's nothing else interesting to do. Everything that used to be cool, underground, spiritual or revolutionary (from Punk and Hip Hop to Indigenous cultures and feminism) have been exploited to sell everything from sweatshop clothes to the "war on terrorism." Young people are noticing that the only thing that can't be bought, sold, co-opted or marketed anymore is substantive political organizing and dissent.

This is a ripe time to expand the movement. Bush's beast-like policies are an eloquent recruiter. According to the US Census, there are more than 80 million teens and twenty somethings in the US today. All 500 organizations in this book put together aren't even close to organizing 1% of them. Millions of young people are critical of the current system and want to get involved. Most are disconnected from any organized movement. One of our biggest jobs now is simply to be good volunteer coordinators: to welcome kids into the movement and help them find their place.

It's also high time to step up our game organizationally. A few of the major challenges/ opportunities we face are: leadership development, funding, government repression, and coalition-building.

Leadership Development

We were overextended before September 11. And we've been working on overdrive ever since-- at great personal sacrifice. Many of us are getting burned out. We're getting repetitive strain injuries and other health problems (20–30 year-olds are the least likely age group to be insured). Movement journalist Daniel Burton-Rose, 24, who co-edited The Battle of Seattle can barely sign his name anymore. He has become a yoga teacher and is recovering slowly. I'm getting wrist pains right now as I type this. People like me need to pass the torch. And I think we often underestimate how much work it takes. Raquel Lavina at Ella Baker Center opened my eyes to this. Two and a half years ago, she identified six skill sets she had acquired, and five younger people she wanted to train. So, for example, she decided to train one young woman in meeting facilitation. They would go to meetings together. An hour in the car each way. On the way up they would plan the meeting. On the way back they would debrief. Every week for eight months. That's leadership development.

Funding

Funding is a double-edged sword. Even under the best circumstances, it often entails subtle compromises and dependency. It's also necessary for long-term, large-scale success. Three organizations I care about died this month in part for lack of funding. One of them is the Brycchouse mentioned above. More and more of us are learning fundraising (the single best introductory resource is Grassroots Fundraising with Kim Klein: www.chardonpress.org).

Looking at the movement as a whole, it costs roughly $25-30 million a year for us to pay our bills. That sounds like a lot of money until you realize that's only enough to pay about 500 people in the entire country (figuring $27,000 salaries plus benefits and office overhead) or the cost of running two floors of one office building in corporate America. Yes, it's true, we as a movement do an unbelievable amount of work for next to no money. We should feel very proud of ourselves. What could our movement do if we had more money?

Education budget cut
demonstration,
NYC City Hall, April 30, 2002
©ramona photo

That's why we started Active Element. Active Element is the only foundation that exclusively funds youth organizing and activism across all issues and constituencies across the country. You can imagine how many requests we get. Part of the reason we published the Future 500 is to encourage more people to give more money to the movement. If you know anyone who works at a foundation or is planning to start one, tell them it's not crowded over here at all. There's plenty of room. We like neighbors. And while you're at it, why not pledge 10% of your income to supporting your favorite local youth groups? That's what the right-wing does. That's part of why they kick our ass. So make your next event or party a fundraiser!

Government Repression

So many people have gotten phony felony charges for protesting. Our very own Bernadette Moreno, the 18-year-old organizing whiz who's coordinating the Future 500 & Liberation Drive-in Tour got hit with two bogus felonies for participating in Reclaim the Streets. The good thing is that most of these cases get pleaded down to misdemeanors or thrown out but only after sapping resources and energy from the accused and their supporters.

People always ask: Aren't the FBI going to use your database to target the movement? Right-wing corporate maniacs are already trying to bring the environmental groups like Ruckus before Congress, painting them as "eco-terrorists." Aren't you scared, people ask, that the Future 500 will make their jobs easier?

First of all, as far as we know, no organization in the Future 500 is involved in illegal activity, other than a few well-considered acts of civil disobedience (for which they are planning to be arrested). Second, the FBI already has our information. They have already confiscated cell phones, palm pilots, laptops, computers, and address books. So what? We are not criminals. If we are prepared with lawyers, media, and community organizing, their attempts to mess with us will ultimately make them look bad.

Third, everyone I've talked to who experienced COINTELPRO and other highly-unethical government attempts to illegally undermine legitimate political dissent, has told me that the paranoia and infighting created by the fear of FBI infiltration damaged the movement more than the FBI itself. For tips, there's an excellent article, "Dealing with Government Repression," at the back of the Slingshot Organizer available from radical infoshops (see Long Haul Infoshop, pg. 159). A global movement based on Internet communication is always vulnerable. Anyone could infiltrate anyone's email and send divisive messages, sowing seeds of mistrust. The only real protection we have is our integrity and our relationships.

Coalition-Building

The dark forces give us an important reminder: No matter how big and real our differences with each other, we do not have the luxury to hate on each other. We do not have the luxury to not support each other. And we do not have the luxury to not work on untangling our own internalized issues. Forget the FBI, how many of our organizations have imploded because we couldn't work through our own race, class, ideology, power, gender, sex, culture, personality, ego, and clique dynamics?

It may be too ambitious and probably unwise to imagine we can all just "work together" and smush ourselves into one giant coalition. That will probably take years of mending and relationship-building. In the mean time, we can strive for a smaller good thing: learn from each other, compare notes, share strategies, skills and resources, show up for each other's events and actions, try to not step on toes, and try our best to communicate across the chasms that separate us.

The best coalition story I've heard lately is from Alejandro "Blu" Cantagallo at the Prison Moratorium Project in Brooklyn. PMP heard that the New York State Legislature had allocated $73 million to build a new Juvi Super-Prison upstate and that it was to be located in one of two all-white towns, one affluent, one poor. So PMP sent an organizer upstate to build relationships with people in each of the towns, introduced the people in each town to each other, and organized a joint lobby day with them in Albany, the state capital.

"It was an unbelievable day," explained Blu. "It was a big sharing experience. Legislators told us: 'You really rocked the house today.' No one had ever thought that young people from cities and upstate rural communities would get together on the same issue. It made a hell of an impact. We got a lot of press. The Albany Times-Union called it the '$73 Million Question.' We brought so much heat that in May the news came: the $73 million was withdrawn from the state budget."

I was talking to a kid who went to my high school the other day. He was telling me he wished he "grew up in the '80s because Hip Hop seemed so much better back then." I told him I wished I was growing up now. Think how jealous kids 15 years from now will feel of him-- to be alive at such a moment!

There are plenty of reasons to feel discouraged about the world right now. But nobody can say that the movement we've built in the past three years is anything short of a miracle. Along with all the other feelings we may have about the state of the movement-- the anger, the frustration, the exhaustion, the sense of isolation, of being stretched too thin-- all of us also have the right to feel another way: Proud.

Democratic National Convention,
Downtown LA, August 2000
©ramona photo

©Jee Mee Kim

The Future 25,000

by Jee Kim

The debate over creating a Future 25 was as difficult as pulling together the profiles with limited resources.
It went something like this:

Point: We're gonna rank 25 individuals as the top young activists in the country?!
Counterpoint: We have to make sure people understand it's not a ranking or comprehensive list of any kind. It's not **the** 25 dopest, it's 25 **of the** dopest.
Point: So why are we calling it **the** Future 25? And what's the point of it anyway?
Counterpoint: Well, it's the same answer to both. It's about creating points of entry, and not just for us and our "enlightened" activist friends. People love rankings, people love personal, human stories. For magazines, top 50 whatever issues always do well, and one of the first sections looked at is the faces in the crowd part in the back. Maybe it won't gain points on an analytical political integrity scale, but it's a marketing decision. It's easier to get non-activist high school students, drop-outs, people glancing over your shoulder on trains, and cousins who work retail open to The Future 25 versus Faces in the Movement, or some other less hierarchical, aggressive title. So we offer a list, **the 25,** and show as many interesting human stories as possible to get as many people open as possible. It's about prioritizing reaching and inspiring people, potential youth activists, ahead of not catching shit from some of our friends.
Point: Well, as long as the selection process is careful.

Unfortunately, our selection process was not the most careful. Final decisions were much too often made by a few individuals (and sometimes a single person) because of extreme time constraints. The pool of candidates was generated through outreach to limited networks. Diverse backgrounds and dynamic stories were important criteria, at times, placed before leadership qualities, political analysis, or "successful" movement building.

Despite these limitations, our hopes were met and the results are amazing. Dynamic and diverse? Flip through and look at people's faces. Then consider these fragments of their stories: Native American tribal chief and "African American trans boy queer fag bisexual young future karaoke star." Single mothers,fathers with 3 kids and a wife, Demon Killers and Big Sisters of Little Palestines. White kids with money and Native Americans from reservations. Bushwick, Brooklyn and Boulder, Colorado. Louisville and Milwaukee. MAs in Engineering Management and high school drop-outs. Gay Black Muslims and Puerto Ricans in the Nation of Islam. Vegans and cheesesteak eaters. Cambodia and Guatemala. Poets, promoters, performers, and pastel hustlers who listen to Riot Grrrl, Jill Scott, No Doubt, Alanis Morissette, Meshell Ndegeoceollo, and Public Enemy.

And our other priority, inspiring people? Put next to each other, the Future 25, reflect and refract difference without end. But the inspiration comes in their commonalities, the qualities and beliefs that repeat throughout like they were pre-requisite criteria. Indigenous leadership, activists coming from within the communities they serve. An understanding of the interconnectedness of issues. A foundational passion, inherent knowledge that injustice is a wrong that must be righted. A faith, persistence, and patience that defy each person's chronological age.

Point: But it should be The Future 250, not 25.
Counterpoint: And we should do all we can to guarantee that the 250 **stays** growing to 2500, 250000, and more.
Point: As long as you make the process better the next time and open our networks up.
Counterpoint: We'll tell everyone to email info@future500.com with suggestions and nominations to make it even tighter the next time.

Gabriel Foster: It's Not Unusual

by Amy Sonnie

When I called Gabriel Foster to tell him that he's among 25 of the dopest young folks doing work for social justice today, he stammered into the phone: "Wait. What!? Who!? Are you sure?" His humility was not unexpected. I've known Gabriel since 1998 when he was living in Oakland, CA, and he's certainly not one to talk himself up. It took three conversations and two rounds of e-mails to get the full run down on all the work he's involved in, in addition to being program assistant for GLBTQ youth programs at AFSC: his participation in last summer's WCAR in Durban, South Africa, his leadership in the National Youth Advocacy Coalition in DC, his work with the Trans Youth Service project in Seattle, and his role in the revival of Queer Youth Rights, an organizing project of Seattle Young People's Project (SYPP, pg. 146). Oh, and there's more. But what's most unique about Gabriel is not his long list of affiliations and titles. It's the way he approaches his work-- with insight, humor and a rare modest charisma. In Gabriel's own words, he does most of his work "behind-the-scenes." But, contrary to his own opinion, he is a national leader-- committed to building a movement where advocacy and activism are seen as equal players and a political, anti-oppression approach to "service" lays a foundation for young folks to rise up and make change.

The identity question:
I will always be figuring out my identity. Today my laundry list is African American trans boy queer fag bisexual young future karaoke star.

Favorite song to sing at a karaoke bar?
"It's Not Unusual" by Tom Jones.

Where did you grow up and how did it shape you as an activist and as a person?
I'm a survivor of the 'burbs. I grew up in a seriously white suburb called Federal Way outside Seattle. For anyone who's not white, who's queer/trans and has any kind of political conscience, growing up in Fed Way... may god have mercy on your soul! I always felt really awkward and out of place. But I believe that everything happens for a reason. In some weird way I figured out who I was because I lived in Fed Way. Not being white, but not being Black enough. I had to really figure out who I was, and it's helped the work I've done. But it's a struggle I'm still dealing with, just trying to find that space that I belong in.

What do you see as the biggest challenges to organizing queer youth for social justice?
Money is always an issue. Stability is another. I work with young people who are dealing with issues like homelessness or folks who have never had stability in their life. It hard to do social justice work when you're thinking about where to sleep for the next week or how you're going to eat.

Do you feel a part of a "youth movement"?
I'm familiar with national queer youth organizing around police harassment, racism, school safety, religious right, and a whole bunch of other issues. Out at queer youth conferences, I feel a part of something bigger. A large part of me wishes that I felt a part of a larger youth movement but I'm not really plugged into the national youth movements. Lots of times it's intimidating in any space to be the only trans person of color there.

What gives you hope?
I think hearing people's laughter gives me hope. I like to people watch, have a smoke and drink some coffee and just watch people interacting with people. Sometimes those interactions can be so beautiful, so simple.

How are you trying to change this country over the next decade?
Gawd! You make me feel like Miss America! I'm just tryin' to do the best that I can and inspire others to do the same, to make change in myself and in others.

If you had 5 minutes alone in a room with the president, and there were no consequences for your actions, what would you do?
Flash em my tits...why not!? I figure that should get his attention.

Gabriel Foster is 22 years old.

Chhaya Choum: Organizing Asian Communities

by Chhaya Choum (with assistance from Chisun Lee)

After 9/11

"September 11 made work that much tougher. We've provided political background on the relationship between the US and Afghanistan. We've advocated for domestic and hotel workers who lost their jobs and given support to Chinatown residents who live near the World Trade Center and have been harassed by the police there. But there isn't only more work, it's also harder to do it. Since 9/11, there's been an atmosphere of fear, which has made it more difficult to do activist work and speak out against social injustices. Our funding resources, as with many non-profits, are dwindling. But we're trying our best to continue on, just more creatively. It's more important than ever for people to join and support grassroots organizations in the anti-war movement. The world won't get better if we just let it be."

I was born in Battambang, Cambodia on April 1, 1978. The US had bombed our country "by mistake," and Vietnam and the Khmer Rouge were fighting. My parents had fled through the jungle to refugee camps along the Thai border. I lived in the camps for a few years then moved to the Philippines before coming to The Bronx, New York City in 1985. I have no memory of my country and have never returned.

Growing up in the US is hard enough with parents who have different values and traditions. But as an immigrant and young woman of color, it's been that much harder. I often wondered why my life was nothing like what I saw on TV: my father worked long hours in a factory for over 10 years without a raise and my aunts were always at the factory too. One day when I was in elementary school, I came home to see coverage of the Gulf War on TV. Without thought, I said, "Why don't the Iraqis do what the US asks?" My uncle responded, "You have no idea what the US is doing to people around the world."

This was the turning point. After that, I felt like I was being cheated in school with a one-sided version of history. I was lied to about the history of this country, the history of people of color-- the people in my school and neighborhood. I was angry.

Joining CAAAV (see pg. 107) helped me learned more about the truth. When I was 16, I applied there for a tutoring job. One interview question was, "Do you call yourself American or Asian American?" I responded, "Cambodian." I was hired. I got a political education on issues like systems of inequality and patriarchy, and I learned to be a community organizer.

My parents were afraid at first about my political work. Under the Khmer Rouge, they learned to fear speaking out against anything. Then I got them involved in community meetings and rallies and their views changed. They became very supportive of my work and activism brought us closer together. My mother is one of my biggest mentors. I learned she was committed to true justice and is an activist at heart. She taught me to love myself, as a woman. I respect and love the importance she places on family and friends. Growing up with 11 brothers and sisters and marrying at 17 put her on the fast track to tremendous responsibility.

Being a mother is the hardest job I've ever had. But having a daughter hasn't stopped me from doing what I love. In fact, it's inspired me more. Work cuts back on my time with her, which hurts. But I am fighting for us both. I never want her to experience a world where violence is used against women of color for someone else's gain. I want her to know how to fight. I don't want her to be lost, without both her mother's Cambodian and father's Puerto Rican cultures. I love her so much I could almost swallow her (a Cambodian expression).

There are times when I want to just burrow in my bed and be with family and forget about work. That's when I know I need to take a break for a few days and recuperate. But I love work and the people I work with, like 2 of my mentors, Eric Tang and Jane Bai. They are always honest with me, support my work and life, and have helped me develop skills, like speaking in public. In school I was the kid who sat hoping not to be called on, not because I didn't have anything to say, but because I didn't want to feel stupid or have people make fun of my accent and pronunciation.

From my own experience, I know how hard it is to be young and political. It takes years to unlearn what's been taught by schools and other institutions; I am still struggling with this. But it's important to remember that activism is fun, especially if you use your own culture and express your individuality. And it's powerful. We have to realize the conditions we live under were shaped by those in power, yet we have the power to change them.

Chhaya Choum is 24 years old.

Lester Garcia: Swallow the Red Pill

by Lester Garcia

Some folks think I must be crazy for doing what I do. To dedicate so much of my time and energy to some abstract thing called Liberation. A family member once asked me with a look of confusion: "Why do you what you do?" I've often asked myself the same thing.

When I first became active about three years ago, my parents didn't exactly know what I was getting into and being from Guatemala, where student organizations suffer extreme repression, they didn't want me getting involved with anything similar. But a few conversations later they realized the vision I am trying to bring into being, and that this is something I will fight for until it comes to be. I'm very fortunate; my family may not always agree with my point of view but they completely support everything I do. It is their support that keeps me from ripping out my hair and motivates me to keep going and not give up. And that's why between being a full-time student at California State University Long Beach, a Youth Organizing Communities (YOC, pg. 60) staff member, meetings with staff, teachers, students, and school administrators, constant trips to Office Depot and the taco stand down the street, and at least a million other things, I always make time for friends and family.

Describe your work

"I coordinate the organizing that takes place at Roosevelt High School. Most of the organizing I do centers around educational justice, which cannot be understood without an analysis of how our educational system is in the shape it is because of this nation's prioritization of the military and prison system. Therefore, in addition to training students in organizing skills, we also run political education sessions every week that cover topics from understanding oppression to the military industrial complex."

I try to look back and pinpoint exactly when I decided to become an organizer. Then I realize I didn't. As stupid, unoriginal, and cheesy as it sounds, organizing chose me. I remember growing up always having this... yearning to change things. I don't know where it came from but I know that shit was fucked up in my neighborhood. I remember riding the bus with my mom over to the Westside, where she cleaned the houses of rich white folks, and noticing the difference between their hood and my own. I remember going to sleep listening to the gunshot, ghetto bird orchestra giving its nightly performance in the skies above. I didn't know exactly why things were the way they were, I just knew they were happening and needed to change.

As I got into high school, organizing wasn't exactly on my list of things I wanted to do with my life. We had a M.E.Ch.A (pg. 137) club on campus but it never really drew my attention. Until this girl I had a crush on asked me to go to one of the meetings. Of course, I went. Little did I know it would change my life forever. Though the girl that asked me to that first meeting stopped going, I remained consistent in M.E.Ch.A for the next two years.

I was a senior in high school when Proposition 21 came around and I began to truly organize. This is when I became involved with Youth Organizing Communities, which gave me the knowledge and the skills to organize my community. The more politicized I became, the more my sense of personal responsibility to change the current social situation grew. The more I learned, the more I knew I couldn't just sit by and allow things to happen. People think that because I'm young, being political and active are just a phase; I'll get over it. And sometimes I wonder why can't I be a normal person and just live my life and not worry about anything just like everyone else? I quickly snap back into reality and ask myself, why would I want to? What folks don't realize is that I've taken that red pill, and I can never go back. Me and an entire generation of young organizers have made a lifelong commitment to the people of the world; we will not rest until all our sisters and brothers are free, until there is justice. Organizing is like no other work because it's more than just work. It's your heart and soul. It's thinking back to all the injustice you've lived and witnessed and doing everything in your power to ensure it doesn't happen in the future. Why do we do what we do? I've got a better question: How can you not?

Lester Garcia is 19 years old.

Lyn Bluehouse Wilson: Self and Community

by Jamel Brinkley

Lyn Bluehouse Wilson grew up partly on a reservation and partly in a reservation border town. Until she was 14, all she had known were the mesas and canyons that surrounded her grandmother's house. Despite her love of home, she knew that many resources and opportunities would not be available to her there. So like many other young Navajos she started on the path to becoming an "urban Indian."

Lyn's path took her to the city of Albuquerque, which was an unfamiliar world and pace. "I got so caught up in trying to keep up," she says, "that I began to get involved in all the things that I had been running from back home, all the things that I wanted to leave behind." Getting involved in and confronting alcoholism, poverty, and depression wasn't something Lyn feared-- instead, she saw it as destiny.

Describe your work

"I am a community organizer with SAGE Council, a people of color-led community organization building self-determination through organizing, education, and leadership development. We are committed to impacting the social, economic, and political decisions affecting our communities, and using the teachings of our ancestors to prepare for future generations. We maintain spiritual and political values that respect Mother Earth and all People with truth, honesty, respect, compassion, generosity, humility and prayer."

Lyn learned how to embrace her destiny and create her own outcome when the Albuquerque Public School system tried to tell its Native American students that they couldn't wear traditional dress at graduation. She had planned to wear a squash blossom that her uncle had worked on for weeks, a concho belt handed down from her grandfather (who had used it as collateral for his first head of sheep), a traditional rug dress made by her mother, and her first pair of turquoise bracelets that her father had saved up for. Instead, the sanctioned uniform was a $30 mass-produced cap and gown with black shoes, white shirts, and black pants or dresses. For Lyn, "that meant that after 12 years of Euro-centric education and school systems, I still couldn't be free to represent my people at graduation." The graduation, "awakened a fire in my belly that I had never experienced," she says. "I wanted to stand up and shout." She began a proactive political education campaign, going to school board meetings, reading books, and talking to people who were fighting for change. Soon she was going to city council meetings and local actions, as well as speaking out in class. "I was empowered. I had never realized before that I could create my own destiny and not run from reality."

She became involved in the dress code issue and followed it up to its climax in the spring of 1997. A school board meeting was held where it was decided that Native American students could wear traditional dress but with the school's cap and gown. Lyn describes this as, "a disappointing decision," but that it was nonetheless, "a step forward." She learned one of her most important lessons as an organizer that day: "To win, you must have several small victories."

Lyn took those lessons to the SAGE Council (Sacred Alliances for Grassroots Equality pg. 104) when she became active in 1997. She organizes to increase the visibility of their campaigns, like the fight to stop the proposed extension of Paseo del Norte through the Petroglyph National Monument, a sacred and holy place for Native Americans that holds over 17,000 Petroglyphs, many over 2,000 years old. The Paseo would cut directly through it and primarily benefit John Black, a local real estate developer. As Lyn explains, "Albuquerque does not need poorly planned roads at the expense of a sacred site." The struggle means meetings with elected officials, doorknocking, phonebanking, and strategizing in order to push a vote on the Paseo and gain the majority 6 City Council votes needed to block it.

Lyn's experiences have taught her many things, including accepting fear as part of an activist's life, as long as it doesn't induce paralysis. She holds herseld accountable to her, "people, community, ancestors and family." Maintaining the balance between the self as individual and self as part of the community is foremost in Lyn's mind: "I think the most important thing is the realization that work needs to be done in your community and that it begins with you. A strong foundation begins with you... then take it from there."

Lyn Bluehouse Wilson is 22 years old.

Nahed Freij: Big Sister of Little Palestine

by rashid kwame shabazz

Palestine Rally, NYC 2002

Nahed Freij describes herself as a resource to young people, not a youth organizer, a label she avoids like a virus. She prefers to think of her work as listening to and helping young people with their goals. "I listen to the young people. They make the decisions. I'm more like a big sister." An independent thinker and fearless in her opinions, Nahed would love the opportunity to tell George Bush that he's a failure as a leader and believes that Arafat does not represent the majority of Palestinians or their best interests.

An Arab Christian, Nahed's story begins in the West Bank, the center of an unbalanced war of suicide bombers vs. tanks, rocks vs. grenades that the media misrepresents daily. Her opinions are rooted in her first-hand experience and knowledge that her people are not terrorists, but victims of occupation fighting for self-determination. Nahed fears that if the occupation and the war continues, her people could lose their culture, the only thing Palestinians have not been robbed of. But today Nahed is far from the cries of families losing their children in the conflict she describes as a national liberation struggle.

Nahed came to the United States to study at North Park University in Chicago, majoring in International Business. After graduating she found a corporate job that left her unfulfilled, feeling the need to do something for her community and nation. She remembered the youth volunteer work she participated in while living in the West Bank and decided to apply her skills to her community in the United States.

On August 15th, Nahed began working with the Arab American Action Network (pg. 77) as a community organizer. It was like home, working in an Arab community that's 70% Palestinian. Initially, her work focused on helping youth develop leadership skills and an awareness of their Palestinian heritage. But within a month two planes were flown into the World Trade Center and everything changed for those who identify as Arab, Middle-Eastern, or Muslim. Led by mainstream media, the American public came to view the Arab community as a terrorism incubator. An atmosphere of fear, backed with hate crimes like assault, murder, and arson, settled on populations and communities across the country.

Nahed and the youth she worked with were made to feel the fear first hand when the Arab American Action Network was burned to the ground shortly after 9-11, the result of arson. "On all levels, the youth were targeted and affected by 9-11. It was very hard for some of the youth and their mothers to let them come to an organizing project. They felt like it was not the time for our youth to meet all at the same time at the same location," Nahed explains. Out of fear came a silencing period. But young people still wanted to speak out; they wouldn't let fear turn into paralysis.

The youth wanted to convince their classmates that Palestinians, that Arab-Americans were not terrorists. So Nahed listened, as she always does, and began helping them to develop educational materials to debunk the idea that all terrorists are Arab and that Israel was justified in its attack on Palestinians. "Many of the youth felt that we needed not to be scared, we needed not to be silenced. They felt we had to go out there, we had to do workshops, we had to do presentations at school and explain to people who are Arabs, who are Muslims, or Arab-Christian. Explain what exactly it is like to be a Palestinian living in the United States."

Nahed loves eating Greek salads and reading books by her favorite authors Mina and Ghaffam Kanafani, but she has little time for either. "It's like a seven day job," she says with a laugh. "Sometimes you come in at 8:00 and leave at 2:00 a.m." But sustaining Palestinian culture and identity are worth the long hours. Nahed's plans involve more organizing in the US, including changing racist school curricula that portray Arab Americans through negative stereotypes, but also a return to her home. She sees her future in the West Bank, where she hopes to start a youth organization and provide resources to help fear become action.

Nahed Freij is 23 years old.

Bryan Proffitt: White Boy Curriculum

by Jamie Schweser

What's your approach to activism?
As a privileged white person in this country, trying to understand issues of community accountability and responsibility is not an easy process. We white males tend to be really reactionary; there's just a lack of understanding as to what real relationships are about, a lack of understanding of power and privilege. So I'm trying to understand how to be anti-racist, anti-sexist, anti-heterosexist. I think it's about being real open and having a lot of integrity, as far as how decisions are made and processes, and being willing to hear difficult things about myself.

What kind of work are you doing, and how does this relate to your work?
I've been doing this work with The North Carolina Network for Popular Democracy (NCNPD), which includes education, networking, and direct action. It's a movement-building organization focused on building really strong local orgs that are working on local issues in order to build power bases... The statewide organization is not defining local issues, instead, it's hooking people up. We're starting a local Raleigh working group and I've taken some of the lead on pulling that together.

I'm trying to write a book called **The White Boy Curriculum** for people who came up like I did, class privileged, straight white boys, to get an idea of how we help perpetuate those oppressions, how to break down those oppressions, understanding how being a dominant group affects us, and how it basically kills our souls and isn't really anything that serves us.

We really want to bring people together and form community and relationships first before we start trying to identify any "real work." I think taking the time to get to know people and share space is "real work." The powers that be in this country, or wherever, have done a really good job of individualizing us and isolating us and making us not understand community or collective energy or collective creativity. So for me, a group of folks coming together and eating dinner is a revolutionary act right now. Taking time to share our stories with each other and really grow with each other as people is the most foundational basis for good work.

A lot of this really intense, in-your-face direct action work that doesn't have a foundation in community and integrity and collectivity feels really reactionary to me. We spend all this time, money and energy reacting to whatever is put forward, whereas if we develop relationships and community-based, long-term revolutionary strategy, we won't be getting caught on our heels so much and fighting just to maintain the shitty conditions that people are in. Every now and then we got to throw a punch and step forward.

The idea that having dinner with people is revolutionary isn't the most popular approach to activism.
All these things are not my original ideas. I've had a lot of really good teachers-- not just in school-- a lot of really strong mentors, people who have really supported and pushed me. Like Catilla Everette, a bad-ass organizer who happened to be down in NC when a lot of my really intense changes were going on. And Easter Maynard from Reciprocity who has been able to get deep into my space and see where I need the most intense challenge and the most support. Also my relationship with Angela, my partner, has been really revolutionary because we've kind of grown through this process together and been each others' biggest challenge and biggest support, and stuck with each other through some really intense shit. My relationship with her is really foundational in terms of my activism and my spirituality. Also my friend Erica Smiley, who y'all should probably have on your 25 list, cuz she's amazing. I could probably name fifty more people. I'll run into someone on the street and get into a conversation and learn ten new things. I've just been really into trying to learn, and that opens up a lot.

So, what have you learned?
We need really diligent processes that we're willing to engage in with each other, and we need to create new models for doing that. To me, principled organizing looks like people having strong relationships with each other where they're really, really ready to challenge and be challenged and ready to be down for each other in a really long-term way.

Bryan Proffitt is 23 years old.

walidah imarisha: Bad Sista

by walidah imarisha

Walidah grew up on military bases and attended college in Portland until she got tired of what she calls "translation activism" ("translating everything for white people"), eventually moving to Philly. A spoken word artist, poet, essayist, journalist, historian, and general rabble-rouser, Walidah Imarisha is the author of children of ex-slaves: the unfinished revolution and co-editor of Another World is Possible. She is the bad sista part of the dynamic poetry duo Good Sista/Bad Sista, with her better half Turiya Autry.

My tattoos take me back to a day when parents had more
than words to leave their unborn children,
when the only scars I carried were those from playground fights
and botched bike lessons.
Now
I tattoo rooster trees on my back
and run across the naked limbs,
because I will be my own bridge.

be all that you can be...
in this army of hypocrisy
with policies like shoot before they/don't ask don't tell
about the whites of their eyes
and their lies.
do all that you can do...
to disrupt this institutionality
where nations are built on the backs of slaves
and children are the fuel the furnaces crave.

I take this space and time to issue a proclamation:
Mumia must be set free
Our voice must be allowed to breathe without the stench of
death in the air.
If not, we will give this nation something to truly fear...

Families separated by land and barbed wire and iron bars
And fifteen minutes phone calls that are interrupted every three
minutes
Just so some automated voice can tell you
"you're talking to an inmate"
just to remind you constantly who has the power...
and that it isn't you.

burrowing down into the belly of the beast,
ripping from the inside out
until I can breathe,
finally understanding the powers that be
are terrified
because we be the power
and if I play this track backwards,
voices scream for more than
apple pie or a cabin in the sky
but I decide to just let it drop.
and the record is not over yet
the record is not over yet
the revolution is not over yet.

My newest collection of political poetry is called "this back called bridge," an understanding that as a mixed black young conscious activist women of color in this world, there is no designated box for me. Fuck a box. The activism I do is all about binding all parts of me together. Whether with AWOL Magazine (pg. 126), where revolutionary artists can make conscious music and educate youth about the military industrial complex, or with my poetry group Good Sista/Bad Sista, where we explicitly talk about everything from big hair to being bi-racial to Mumia to the prison industrial complex, it's all related and relevant.

We are feeling the pressure worldwide these days, as we got an endless war on "terrorism," a war on immigrants and people of color, fueled by young Black and Brown bodies. They are also coming after dissidents, rebels, revolutionaries, guerrillas, fighters, poets, writers, thinkers, dreamers.

The case of Mumia Abu-Jamal, political prisoner and uncompromising journalist, helped to politicize me. My first protest was for Mumia when I was 14 years old, living in a small, mean Oregon town. I had already decided I wanted to be a journalist. This brotha used his relentless words to lay naked government corruption and brutality and was handed a death sentence for the truth. Through Mumia's case, I learned how interconnected all the issues are: the prison industrial complex, racism, patriarchy, imperialism, poverty, all of it.

I have always been extremely interested in the growth of the prison industrial complex, which steals life disproportionately from young people of color. In AWOL we focus on the military and prisons, because these are increasingly the only two options left for youth of color; in a downsized economy, we have become expendable. My work with the Human Rights Coalition, a group that empowers prisoners' families (founded by political prisoner Russell "Maroon" Shoats), has reinforced my belief that people know what's going on, they don't need to be "educated," as so much activism focuses on. Oppressed peoples don't need to be told they're oppressed, they just need access to resources and battle plans to end that oppression.

walidah imarisha is 22 years old.

Satya: Stressing the Connections

by Jee Kim

Satya is all over the place geographically, networking and making connections, a reflection of one of the main focuses of his work: "I think it is important to see the interconnectedness of all issues of oppression." I imagine being his tour manager and keeping a journal that would look something like this:

Life's Road Tour (selected notes):

1995: Just outside Houston, Texas
Home is Sugarland, a wealthy 'burb and home to many Enronites. Roots of activism can be traced back to debating in high school, becoming a vegetarian, and listening to punk with edge (Minor Threat, Youth of Today, Propagandhi).

1997: Durham, North Carolina
College years at Duke start. Becomes active with the vegetarian club and the food coop. Free Tibet cause catalyzes him into world of political activism. Major in biomedical engineering, under family pressure to be good "doctor/ engineer." Graduates with MA in Engineering Management. Fortunately, all hope is not lost to a six-figure salary job offer working at Monsanto. Academic knowledge gained here later becomes ammunition for fight against corporate power (especially the biotechnology industry).

MAY/JUNE 2001: BioJustice, San Diego, CA
"Preparing and organizing for the demonstrations was quite a task. Television reports were warning San Diegans about the upcoming protests and riot, saying how the city was going to be the next Seattle with lots of violent protestors. The city spent $4.7 MILLION in riot gear, overtime pay for cops, hiring new cops. On the first day of the Biotech Industry conference, hundreds of people showed up on the streets. A festive event!!! It was quite amusing to see these cops all decked out with riot gear and rifles when we were dressed as butterflies!!! $4.7 million. We even saw cops putting on black bloc garb-- huge 250 pound linebacker-type cops trying to go undercover as black bloc anarchists. People were dressed as giant ears of corn, killer tomatoes, a big puppet of 'MonSatan,' and George W. Bush clones to show the horrors of genetic engineering and cloning. We informed people and started dialogue about the dangers of genetic engineering: how corporations are patenting genes, driving up the cost of medicines, and contaminating our food with unsafe, untested, genetically-engineered products."

AUGUST 2001: Chautaqua, Sonoma County, CA
Trains people on how to climb trees, do tree sits, sleep in trees, and build an Ewok village at Ruckus Society's Global Justice Action Camp in preparation for protests of the World Bank/IMF meetings.

SEPTEMBER 2001: Washington, DC
Drives across country from Oakland, CA. And then, September 11 happens. Stays around DC for next several weeks, organizing against the war, racial profiling, and attack on civil liberties.

DECEMBER 2001/JANUARY 2002: TX
"The American Correctional Association was having its semiannual meeting in San Antonio. We worked hard to put together protests, teach-ins, and a counter-conference. Most of our efforts were directed at outreach, informing the residents of San Antonio, Houston, Dallas, and Austin about the atrocities of the Prison Industrial Complex. We wanted to educate them and work on larger movement building, not necessarily get lots of people out just for one event. My friends and I created and hung this huge banner that said 'Their Prisons, Their Profit, We All Pay.'"

MARCH/APRIL 2002: Washington, DC
Back in DC helping coordinate April 20th Mobilization for Peace and Justice. 75,000 to 100,000 people turn out and march to oppose many connected issues, including Bush's plan for "endless war" at home and abroad, US backed Israeli occupation of Palestine, and World Bank/IMF meetings.

MAY 2002: Florida
Travels around the state for press conferences with a huge inflatable prop of a power plant in order to put pressure on Senator Graham to endorse the "Clean Smokestacks Act" and the "Clean Power Act," which would require older power plants to meet new reduced emissions regulations.

PRESENT DAY AND THE FUTURE: Washington DC
Recently moved to DC. Frustrated with the lack of support as a person of color working in a predominantly white, upper-middle class global justice movement. Plans to work on integrating anti-oppression analysis/principles into organizations. Along with Jia-Ching Chen and others, pushing activists in the global justice movement hard on the challenges/limitations of working with oppressed communities. Dream is to organize and spotlight the connections between biotech, race, and class, so that anti-biotech work helps the communities directly affected (the poor, people of color, local farmers), not just white upper-middle class who can afford expensive pharmaceutical drugs and want organic food at the supermarket.

Satya is 23 years old

Venus Rodriguez: Joy and Pain

by Malachi Larrabee-Garza

My good friend Venus Rodriguez, the sweetest and most incredible organizer I know under 25. Astounding political clarity. Irresistible smiles, wit, and charm that can capture the mind and heart. Carries herself with the joy and pain that only life can grant you. When I asked Venus to tell me about when she first came into consciousness she sighed like the grandmother she is often accused of being and asked, "how far back you want me to go?" I didn't really know so I said, "give me everything."

Everything: Beginnings. Venus was born in Buffalo, NY to parents who had love and were trying to get the rest together. She moved around a lot: 11 schools, family and friends to stay with here and there. Venus's father was in and out of jail for abusing her mother and both were fighting drug addictions. One day Venus's mother saw a Juicy Fruit TV commercial with some guys surfing in the sun and decided to move to California.

Welcome to California. "The first time I went to California, I didn't go for a family vacation to see Disneyland or check out Hollywood. Instead, I stepped off the bus with my mom, a few garbage bags filled with everything we owned, and $20." Venus's mom found them a shelter to sleep in. "I experienced a different class. I had always been poor but now I was beyond poor-- I was homeless," which opened Venus's eyes to a different reality and sense of survival. She found an escape in school. "I went to school every day, I got into my studies, joined school activities, study groups, and became a peer counselor. It was a place I could forget about all my problems, like the mice and the plumbing at the shelter, not to mention sleeping with my shoes on so they'd be there in the morning." Venus would tell friends that her mother didn't like company and catch the school bus blocks away so no one would see her coming from the shelter. Her cover was eventually blown when she was sent by her shelter as a representative for homeless kids to the White House. When she came back, the local and national media attention meant that everyone knew. But instead of ridicule, to her surprise, Venus found support.

Child Protection Services. The shelter threatened to call CPS when they peeped that her mom was still using. Venus and her mom left the shelter and were able to get into the Gateway Program, which houses families and teaches mothers computer skills. But when her mother left once and didn't return for three days a squad car pulled up to her school to let her know she would have to go to foster care. Her mother enrolled in a drug rehab program but wasn't allowed to see Venus, who was scared they'd never be together again. Eventually, her mother turned things around and reunited with Venus when she turned 18, moving in together. "I knew then that I wanted to start a non-profit organization to help others. I know first hand what can happen out there. I saw the importance of being a young woman who had been through the system and from the streets to be working with people in need and with my own community." Venus went on to study non-profit organization in college and started fulfilling her dream. Her community work beginnings include being teen liaison at the YWCA, San Francisco Youth commissioner under Mayor Willie Brown, and working for the domestic violence and statutory rape unit of the DA's office, creating youth curriculums presented in group homes and drug rehabilitation centers.

Realizing A Dream. Venus went on to become Director of Young Women United for Oakland, "an organization comprised of and run by young women who live and work in the street economies. Taking street knowledge and survivor skills and transferring them into marketable skills." At We Interrupt This Message (pg. 58), Venus worked on the YMC (Youth Media Council) where she conducted media trainings, offered technical support, and helped conduct Speaking for Ourselves, an assessment of KTVU's coverage of young people (especially poor and of color). Venus is presently at PUEBLO (pg. 60) directing the YOU (Youth of Oakland United) program and preparing to take on the role of lead organizer in its next, yet-to-be-determined issue/campaign, following a recently produced film about gentrification in Oakland. "This is exactly what I want to be doing. Working with young people, especially poor young people of color, everyday, organizing."

And More Dreams. Venus and a close friend are busy planning a community house in Oakland, a house in the cut, in the "ghetto," for youth, single mothers, street youth, young revolutionaries, grandmothers, and anyone else who walks through the door with good intentions. "A self sustaining house with a bookstore and offering free classes in self-healing, political education and healthy cooking." Damn Venus, always keep dreaming.

Venus Rodriguez is 21 years old

Reggie Moore for Mayor

by Supriya Pillai

If you ask Reggie Moore for a written bio on himself, he'll tell you he doesn't keep one. Instead, he defers to a letter of nomination for Youth Worker of the Year from a mentor at the University of Wisconsin that paints a picture of a tirelessly dedicated youth advocate whose career started at the North Central YMCA. Reggie then served as a Program Director of Community Youth Assets and went on to work at Public Allies. Now, at 25, Reggie has helped birth a youth movement in Milwaukee through his organization, Urban Underground (pg. 149), co-founded by Charlen Bowen. An impressive resume. But if you ask Reggie if this is a career, he answers, "No, this is a life. It's not a job. The stressful stuff for me is all administrative. If one day I'm a politician or if I'm just raising my kids at home, I'll always be committed to this work."

> "The Underground Railroad helped people get out of slavery. Urban Underground does the same thing for young people who are up against a system where white people control the economy. Any person of color not for the empowerment of young people is part of the problem."

It's judgment day and you are watching your life as a movie. How would it begin?

I was born in Milwaukee and raised in the Waico Apartments housing development. Even at a young age, I was always a loner-- by choice. Once, when I was 5, I left kindergarten and walked across the way to the Hillside Projects. I'd always go places as a kid that most people's parents would tell them not to go. I was a wanderer and I met people that helped shape who I am. I wasn't one of those kids who didn't leave the block.

Turning points?

In middle school, I was bussed to Audobon, a predominantly white school. I remember around the second day I passed by a group of white kids on the concrete playground and they said, "No niggers back here." This was the first time anyone had said that to me and I began realizing that life just wasn't about getting good grades or hanging out. This was my first real introduction to racism and division. I didn't let that jar me. In high school, I worked with other students in creating drama, art, and literature; I wrote and directed two of my own plays. I ended up going on to college at a private catholic college (Cardinal Stritch University). While I was there, I realized it wasn't my fight to diversify the school as some of the other students of color felt. I felt that the real battle was in my community; some kids can't even get to college to think about fighting to diversify. So I started contacting schools and mentoring students, which is how I met Charlen Bowen and started Urban Underground.

Who are the good guys?

My mother raised us on our own. She introduced me to God before I even knew my name. Through faith and prayer, she helped me learn resilience. My family, in general, has been supportive. And Charlen.

What's the future of Milwaukee? For young people of color there?

Milwaukee is going through a lot of changes. It's becoming a city predominantly populated by people of color. We may soon have a Black mayor. Other politicians of color are coming up. In comparison with other cities, usually when politics starts to be run by people of color, it is in a time of crisis. It's like Milwaukee is being set up so that people will say, "That's what happens when you have a Black mayor." But we have the organizations in place... that are preparing to groom leadership among the youth.

Top issues, priorities for Urban Underground?

Right now the issue is zero tolerance policies and drug offenses that lead to expulsion in MPS (Milwaukee Public Schools). Research has found that drug offenses committed by suburban school students are treated differently than those in MPS. Suburban school students are offered treatment, while public school students are shown the door-- not only to the school but the door to the system. Our youth are working on giving schools more discretion when dealing with these cases instead of having a system wide policy of automatic expulsion.

Reggie Moore for Mayor?

Maybe Public School Board.

Any regrets?

I regret times I didn't believe in myself. There were times when I didn't think I was skilled enough to start an organization. People made me believe that I had to get my degree first. I value college for me, but it's not for everyone... I think that there may have been some lost opportunities.

Reggie Moore is 25 years old.

Ebony Barley: Southern Girl

by rashid kwame shabazz

Well, I'm from the south
I'm a Southern Girl
Home of the burnin' church....
Southern Girl I'll rock your world
Fly as a bumble-bee
Can't nobody fuck with me....
-- Erykah Badu

The South conjures up images of burning churches, Black folk hanging from trees by their necks, confederate flag waving Klu Klux Klan members. The South also conjures up images of struggle and African Americans organizing for civil rights, like Fannie Lou Hamer in Mississippi, Ella Baker, and Rosa Parks sitting adamantly on a bus in Alabama.

Ebony Barley is Director of Communications and Community Outreach and Women of Color Leadership Project Coordinator for Georgia Abortion and Reproductive Action League (GARAL), pg. 163.
"My work is outreach and message development, to let women know it's not just abortion we're talking about. We're talking reproductive health: contraception, and the infant mortality rate, especially in low-income communities, undeserved communities, communities of color. My job is to educate women on what is going on and continue to educate myself."

Ebony Barley is Southern. You hear it in her voice-- the drawl. It seeps out like juice from a ripe Georgia peach. "I've always had something to say, always... always been an advocate for people. Reproductive health was just something I cared deeply about; I know what it's like not to have health care or insurance, I know what it's like to go to the doctor and not be able to pay for it." Originally from Miami, the Howard University graduate migrated to Atlanta after working for Catholics for a Free Choice in Washington, DC, Ebony wanted to return to her roots and work more with people who shared her experiences.

When she returned, she found a community willing to listen with open ears, but she also found men who felt that other issues, e.g., racial profiling and affirmative action, were more important than reproductive rights and that she shouldn't be organizing around some "white women's issue." When she hears this, she gets angry but remains calm; it's that southern hospitality non-violent approach. Fight with kindness and respect. "I explain to them about Roe v. Wade, how we've struggled to retain this right, how many women of color cannot celebrate Roe v. Wade because they are on government assistance and couldn't afford an abortion even if they had health coverage because federal funds do not cover it. We've been celebrating Roe v. Wade but many women of color, low-income women, young women, immigrant women, they're really celebrating in vain."

Ebony is concerned that women of color, especially the poor, will have no options. She describes the programs and legislation that requires low-income women who are addicted to drugs not to have children-- forced sterilization-- with an undertone of mixed emotions. Sadness, anger, pain, frustration, hope, and sincerity. "Tubaligation without consent, that's coercive, that's sterilization, that's moving us back to the eugenics movement." Determination. Ebony ain't going to stand for it. She's committed to preventing her sisters from suffering needlessly because she knows what it's like to have an abortion, to be scared and worried, ashamed. She knows what it's like not to have anyone to talk to and having her mother, a teacher, find out by mistake. Her religious faith helped her through those challenges and she hopes her experiences can empower the young women in her workshops in the same way.

"It's about having access to all the types of contraception that are available, having the option of abortion if that is what you choose to do, just having all options. Not going to the doctor and the doctor telling you what your health care will and won't pay for, "They'll pay for a Norplant shot and Depo-Provera shot." And a lot of the women don't understand the serious implications that go along with the contraception offered through Medicaid." Ebony wants the government to require medical professionals to provide all patients with the full range of facts, considerations, and coverages available. Ultimately, it's bigger than abortion, it's an issue of education, self-esteem, and access.

The child of the South, Ebony likes macaroni and cheese and grew up near Luke Campbell of the 2 Live Crew, the father of commercial booty music. Her father named a chain of record stores "Ochea," after her middle name. She runs and loves reading. Elaine Brown's **A Taste of Power** is on her nightstand. Listens to No Doubt, Alanis Morissette, Mary J.Blige, Lena, Jill Scott and Erykah Badu. The South, Atlanta, is a place to plant her roots. She anticipates tremendous growth; maybe one day she will hold a position that is not "racially coded," maybe as Executive Director of GARAL. For now she enjoys where she is, educating and organizing.

Ebony Barley is 25 years old.

Antonio Torres: Trabajo de Hormigas

by Manuela Arciniegas

Life story?

My parents were farm workers when they first arrived in the US from Michoacan, Mexico. They planted and took out trees. I remember going with them at 5 o'clock in the morning to help. They used to do this same work in Mexico, but in Mexico it was even harder to do. My parents always told me when they'd get home from a long day's work, "When you get older, I don't want you coming home muddy and wet like me!" That was eye opening 'cause I would look up to them working trying to do the best for us. When they first said it I didn't receive the message, but when I got older I saw what they meant.

We eventually moved to Hillsboro where there wasn't much to do there for youth my age, 13-14 years old. I got involved with the gangs and started to see things that were going on in the community, how people would stereotype young people, whether or not in a gang. Sometimes parents don't believe in our young people, the communities don't believe in them, the Three Strikes and You're Out! Measure doesn't believe in them, so sometimes the only thing that's left is gangs. It was the only place I saw for support. The relationship between me and my younger brother had been getting worse and he had started getting involved in a gang. The only way I saw to be closer to him and make sure he wasn't doing anything bad was to join the gang too. Thankfully there was only little things that had happened, nothing major, and I was able to watch out for him. Ironically, only after I joined a gang and began cooling off some tensions is when people started seeing my leadership abilities.

I left Hillsboro in 1996 and I went to a small public university in Monument, Oregon. It was a different experience and opened me open up about the Chicano Civil Rights movement in the 1960's. Being one of about 15-20 Mexicanos at Western Oregon College brought all of us together. We eventually started organizing and opened a MEChA chapter (see pg. 137). Then I started getting involved in supporting a farmworkers' boycott in Woodward, which was the start of organizing for me.

Lessons in organizing?

When I first started organizing, out there on the field talking to the workers and seeing how close-minded they had been trained to be, I got so frustrated... and then I realized that there are scare tactics the growers use that prevent the farm workers from organizing. My supervisor and my mentor told me organizing is trabajo de hormigas (ants' work), and I need to patiently wait to support them when they're finally ready to do it.

You recently left LUS (pg. 125) and moved to Cali? Why?

I thought it was time to go back to labor organizing. So I'm now working with the healthcare workers alliance-- United Skills Workers of America and the California Nurses Association. I'm also trying to reach out to Californians for Justice and beginning to volunteer on some youth work. My main issues have always been labor, immigration, and youth.

Can you tell be about non-organizing stuff?

Umm... I can't! Organizing is my whole life! I have children, Antonio is 5, Cesar Emiliano is 3, and Natalia, my spoiled little brat, is 1. I give my wife so much credit. For my first 2 children she's been the mother and father to both of them. With my first kid, I was in college, and she was still in Hillsboro. She was raising my kid, finishing up high school, and just doing it all alone, as an "illegal." She was supportive of me going to college too, cause she knew it would be something better for our future. Really, she has made me who I am today.

What are the characteristics people love you for?

Outspoken, passionate, and a good organizer. I've been thru a lot of the stuff I organize around... I've been there. I remember growing up picking at 5 in the morning with my parents, I can relate to the farm workers I helped organize in college, I can relate to the young people that deserve a second chance.

Antonio Torres is 24 years old.

Nell Geiser: Take Control

By Brooke Lehman and Nell Geiser

Nell Geiser is the interim Co-News Director at KGNU Community Radio in Boulder, Colorado. She sits on the board of the Center for Commercial Free Public Education, helped to found Student Worker, an activist high school student union, and formerly sat on Boulder's Youth Opportunities Advisory Board. Nell, a high school senior, has been involved in organizing and media activism since she was a freshman.

"Unless young people seriously rise up and take control of the media, we're screwed. Most of our elders have comfortably adjusted to the constricted flow of information in our globalized world, so it's up to us to create space for our voices and the voices of all those left out of the sound-bites on network TV... Kids like me from Portland to New York are taking the media by storm and challenging the idea that teens can't wield power. We can and we must prove it."

Young people, I believe, must decide between two futures. We can remain in the thrall of consumer culture and let our lives and the future of our communities slip through our fingers in a blur of value-added products and invisible oppressions, or we can stand up and fight. But it's often hard to make that leap and join a movement for global justice that is intangible and imperfect. I'm not an expert on activism, I just try to speak my own truth as much as I can.

I live in Boulder, Colorado, a town founded on racist, exclusionary policies that keep people of color and working class people out by design. There is a strong "activist community" here but I can hardly wait to get out of this town because as a white person who wants to be an ally to people of color and an anti-racist activist, it's hard to stomach a town that sits in insulated, blissful privilege. Once someone asked me to describe what type of activist I am. I don't really know yet. I'm only 17 but there are a few things I'm sure of. Being an activist is about knowing what your aims are and, if you're stuck in a town like Boulder, shaking things up. I am the type of activist who believes unconditionally in the interconnection of struggles and the power of solidarity. I am the type of activist who shamelessly promotes how fun and powerful activism is so that other kids will raise their fists and join the fight. I am the type of activist who looks to the past and the legacy of social justice struggles in this country and the world for inspiration and strategies to instruct our work today. I am the type of activist who recognizes the immense amount of privilege I have as a white, middle-class kid, and who desires greatly to "own" my privilege and to work towards dismantling all systems in which privilege and power are unequally distributed.

The main thing that fills my time these days is independent media, through my work at KGNU community radio. Independent media is about challenging the degeneration of communication and, as Amy Goodman, host of "Democracy Now!" says, "going to where the silence is and saying something." Underground media has long been a way for rebellious youth to metaphorically, "fuck shit up!" Since I began volunteering at KGNU, I've gotten to cover fascinating news stories, from the history of Black women in my mostly-white county, to a struggle for land rights in Southern Colorado. I love the wide-open airwaves that characterize community radio because we are able to create radio that people identify with through awkward pauses and moments of real clarity. But stations like mine are an endangered species in a country where six media corporations control the majority of everything we read, watch, and hear.

It may sound trite to say, but unless young people seriously rise up and take control of the media, we're screwed. Most of our elders have comfortably adjusted to the constricted flow of information in our globalized world, so it's up to us to create space for our voices and the voices of all those left out of the sound-bites on network TV. One way to claim that space is to join the Indymedia movement, which was spawned in 1999 at the anti-World Trade Organization protests in Seattle, and now includes dozens of Independent Media Centers around the world. But taking back the media has got to happen at every level. When you're out in the street at a protest or organizing your community or sitting through another boring class in school, realize that your voice is as powerful as you make it. I walked into a radio station as a freshman in high school and got on the air through dumb luck. Kids like me from Portland to New York are taking the media by storm and challenging the idea that teens can't wield power. We can and we must prove it.

Nell Geiser is 17 years old.

Ada Rivera: Life, Liberty, and the Pursuit of Hip Hop

by Jennifer "J-Love" Calderon

She came to me from the back of the room. We were at the Hip Hop as a Movement Conference in Wisconsin, after a panel discussion focusing on women in Hip Hop. I saw her make her way through the crowd with determination in her stride and fiery passion in her eyes. "Make way for me!" her spirit was screaming. She stepped to me and although she spoke calmly with a smile on her face, I heard pain in her voice. "Hip Hop don't respect women, and society don't have respect for women period. How can you not have respect for women if that's the originator? Women are the originator of everything." That's how I first met Ada Rivera, an 18 year old that outshined all the big names on the women in Hip Hop panel.

The fire behind her piercing questions and passionate relationship to Hip Hop was undoubtedly sparked by a childhood in Humboldt Park (Chicago), marked by dodging blows from a father who eventually bounced, fighting off cruel kids who made fun of her prosthetic leg, and helping her mother hustle pastelitos to make ends meet. "She would tell me and my brother, 'you ain't going no where until you roll 100 pastelles!'" Ada turned to Hip Hop to find love. "What is Hip Hop? It's an escape; it's my security blanket, something I can do and feel good about. I can put my love into Hip Hop and it won't hurt me or smack me up." And when she switched high schools and became politicized through learning about herself - culturally and historically - at Pedro Albizu Campos Alternative High School, she started to bring her passion for Hip Hop together with her desire to become an organizer/activist. Since then, she's done work around voter registration, repping Blu Magazine, Puerto Rican political prisoners, creating summer programs for kids, and using Hip Hop to get young people involved in positive activities: "Hip Hop is like vegetables, it is important to eat a healthy meal everyday."

Ada Rivera is 19 years old.

In her own words:
I grew up around pure negative energy, seeing my father beating up on my mom every day. The way I viewed women and myself became so distorted. It wasn't until my mother started to fight back, started to say no, that I started to say to myself, "that's never gonna happen to me." As a young child, I would counsel my mother that she should get away from him. It kinda took away from my Barbie time.

I went to Prosser Vocational High School. And I was getting kicked out. I didn't have any credits. It was completely ghetto. I never fit in there. Even though I had friends and was popular, people knew me but they didn't really know me. I was depressed all the time.

I started to write. I started to write poetry and do poetry slams. And people were just like, "whoa." And I started to gain respect for myself. I started to like myself and said, "I need to transfer to a school where I can learn about myself," so I went to Campos. I would spit in front of the whole class. I loved having the attention. I loved having the family. When my house burned down, these people raised money for us. The director, Marvin, I grabbed him like he was my adopted father. And he came to me with $700 cash. My mother cried. No one had ever given her anything before. And that showed me who my family was.

I know everybody in Humboldt Park and everybody knows me. I was never in a gang but we still had our people we loved and respected. We'd go hang out with people just to keep them off the street. It'd be 2 and 3 in the morning and I'd be sitting on someone's front stairs to hold them back to keep them from shooting somebody. And we wouldn't care if our mothers would snap on us because in our minds we were stopping our friends from going out and shooting someone or getting shot or going to prison. Because I might need someone to stop me one day.

Omana Imani: Power, Hip Hop, and Youth

by Jamel Brinkley

Born and raised in San Francisco, a child of mixed heritage (South Asian, French, German, and Irish), Omana grew up in the North Beach Housing Projects with her mother and two brothers. She realized at a young age the harsh realities of being poor. "Living in a community where poor people had to struggle and hustle daily to have their basic needs met affected me deeply," she says. "It was very clear to me growing up that my community didn't have a lot of opportunities to succeed." At 15, she began working with youth and homeless people in her neighborhood.

"As time passed I became more sophisticated in my political beliefs and developed my skills as a leader." She also found her commitment to community-centered activism: "One of the keys to building a movement is to ensure that the leadership and direction comes from the communities most impacted by the injustices of our world. My job as an organizer is to go out and talk with people about their issues/conditions, put the issues into a political context, dialogue about real solutions, and push people to become involved to fight for those real solutions."

As an artist and founding member of Underground Railroad (pg. 57) struggling to address such complex and challenging issues, Omana has come to understand the significance of art and culture and the role it plays in the movement for social change. Through Underground Railroad, she has been able to work collectively with others to inspire people to work against all forms of oppression by promoting art and culture that celebrates a vision of a society built on freedom, justice, and equality. "Art is an expression of culture and culture is what gives meaning to people's lives. For instance, Hip Hop. Hip Hop makes sense to young folks and is often what inspires them to get involved."

In addition to her work as an organizer and artist, Omana is the dedicated mother of her six-year-old daughter, Jael. "Having to raise a young woman of color in this society in a healthy way can be incredibly challenging. What I've come to realize is that being a mother has helped bring political clarity to my work as an activist. The principles I use when raising my daughter to be a strong, healthy woman, are the same principles I apply to building capable leaders within the movement."

What's a highlight?

"The Superjail fight in Alameda County. In March 2001, the Oakland Tribune did an article about how the Probation Department and Board of Supervisors had been trying to get a new youth jail built. What caught our attention was that one of their main reasons for requesting the money was that youth crime had gone up 71%, when really it had fallen drastically by 24%. We were outraged at how the County could put this in a grant proposal when what we need is more alternatives and services for young people in Oakland. So Youth Force Coalition (pg. 60) and Books Not Bars called them on it. They claimed it was an accident, a misprint.
That prompted us to look into it more. We discovered that Alameda County had paid a company $6 million to do a study showing that juvenile crime was going up. And we found out that the study was done by the same architecture firm that was going to profit from building the jail!

"The grant proposal was going up for review at the State Board of Corrections. We went to their meeting and demanded that they hear from the people. Instead of respecting our message they kicked us out of their meeting. They were planning to make their decision in Sacramento on April 17, 2001. They said we'd be able to voice our opinion then so we started mobilizing people. Then they moved the meeting from Sacramento to San Diego but we weren't going to let that stop us from fighting the expansion so we fundraised and sent 25 people to San Diego to the Board of Corrections meeting. We met up with 50 people from YOC in San Diego and LA. A bunch of young people and allies spoke. I sung a spiritual about freedom. We were packed in there with sheriffs, probation departments from all over California, and the State Board of Corrections. We publicly challenged the legitimacy of the proposed expansion and got their $20 million grant taken away. It was a major victory. But they still tried to build it. Fortunately, we were able to get the number of beds down to 330 beds from the original number of 540."

What are you doing now?

"I recently finished an internship organizing with POWER (People Organized to Win Employment Rights, pg. 53) in San Francisco and am currently the Director of Underground Railroad. I'm planning to go back to school to finish college. For the first time I'm prioritizing myself which feels good."

Omana Imani is 25 years old.

Salih Abdul-Haqq Watts: Walking the Talk

by Ibrahim Abdul-Matin

It's a hawkish February late afternoon in Philadelphia but the wind is nothing to Salih. No hat, a leather jacket that fits nicely, jeans, and he tends to smile. Salih does not have a car so we walk through the winding back alleyways of Philadelphia en route to his office at the Youth Health Empowerment Project (pg. 130), talking politics, family, and drama. Literally walking the talk.

YHEP is under the umbrella of Philadelphia FIGHT (Field Initiated Group HIV Trials), which houses the nations oldest AIDS library, in operation since 1987. The AIDS research that comes through FIGHT is some of the most extensive in the world. But the majority of Salih's research is in the streets of neighborhoods like Kensington, which, "is known for its potent heroin," he explains.

As we begin to cross a busy street, two young men dressed in puffy jackets and with skull caps call out, "Salih!" Both of our heads turn sharply into the sunlight. My middle name is also Salih. We stop and talk to the men. Salih keeps the conversation silent and hushed. I find out later that these men are homeless heroin addicts, a dangerously high AIDS at-risk group. This is the population that Salih is immersed in, addicts between 13-25 years old, and this is where Salih does most of his work, on the streets. We keep walking.

Explaining why he doesn't have a car, Salih says, "it's not some clean-air thing... I don't even know how to drive!" But that's not to say he doesn't think cross-issue. Though his main work is as a youth advocate specializing in HIV/AIDS prevention, Salih is involved in youth issues across the board from gentrification and the Prison Industrial Complex to the abuse facing queer youth and the growing anti-war movement to racial profiling. Salih is also a founding member of the Brown Collective (pg. 126), a group of progressive Philly people of color developed during the Republican National Convention. They established a safe space in a downtown church to support people of color coming in for the demonstrations. Eventually, they formed an affinity group and staged one of the more successful direct actions during those protests. They are now actively engaged in the fight against Edison controlling the Philadelphia schools because, as Salih explains, "people are dropping out of schools and dropping into prisons. We want to keep the Prison Industrial Complex from sucking in all the youth of color."

We pass by a building that is slightly taller than all the other buildings. "My mother works there" he says pointing upwards. A big figure in his life, Salih's mother juggled numerous roles: mother to 5, wife of an Imam (religious community leader) and a CPI analyst. "Mother provided for us. We never had to struggle, never had to worry about being cold or hungry," he explains. Salih's family converted to Islam after having been a part of the nation of Islam. It was a common transition for many African-American Muslims, including my parents, in the late '60s. We are a generation of American born Muslims that did not grow up celebrating Christmas, Halloween, or Easter. In many ways he has always been on the outside of the spectrum in this country but also an outsider to his family. Salih left home soon after coming out.

"How do you identify?" I ask him, "queer or gay?"
"I grew up in a strongly homophobic home," he explains. "My wali (stepfather) often called people in the streets 'those f#!king queers.' Those words are like poison to me."

So Salih prefers using "gay" and has managed to find an international community of Gay Muslims. At a 1999 Conference in London, he unexpectedly met contingents from traditionally Muslim countries like Saudi Arabia, Yemen, and Pakistan. Salih plans on bringing a Philly contingent to the next one. In addition to political education and direct action, his work in the local gay community includes helping people get IDs, access to health care, and clothing. His work is vital, especially in his own demographic: 1/3 of young, Black, gay, urban men are HIV positive. "The message is not getting out enough," he says. Which prompts him to want to reach out to even more people. He has been taking a sign language class.

A setting sun and chilled wind don't even evoke a shiver from Salih. He's comfortable out here in the streets, walking the talk. "I'm good in crisis situations," he says. "They happen all the time."

Salih Abdul-Haqq Watts is 21 years old.

Evelyn Zepeda: All Flavors

by Mattie Weiss

Evelyn's organizing strength comes from her devilish sense of humor, her openness, and her contagious enthusiasm. Her strength is also in her political savvy. With unpretentious personal politics, she is able to negotiate egos and agendas, and provoke other activists to think harder and smarter. Believing in the empowering capacity of activism and the ability of organized groups of people to change the world they live in, Evelyn works to stoke the passion and bring out the analytical and organizing skills of everyone around her. This includes her own mom, young organizers just getting their feet wet, and more experienced organizers, like those at USAS (pg. 69) whom she has pushed to broaden their international solidarity efforts.

The activist spirit in Evelyn was awoken at 16, when she became involved in a city-wide campaign to tackle corporate corruption in the construction of one of Los Angeles' new public high schools. The campaign target was a Japanese corporation implicated in the use of Chinese slave labor and union busting. This organizing taught her about the interconnection of struggles across race and border lines. But her organizing really took root at Pitzer College, after her best friend dragged her along to a meeting of the Workers Support Committee, a group backing campus employees' fight against subcontracting. She became deeply involved with this campaign and committed to activism in general, soon branching out into work with the Women's Center's rape crisis hotline, farmworker solidarity work, and the protests at the Democratic National Convention in Los Angeles.

Evelyn Zepeda works with USAS (national coordinating and international solidarity committee) and Jobs with Justice (steering committee). "I try to build bridges between workers and students. I work really hard to understand, confront and acknowledge the oppressive dynamics at play, even within progressive circles. I've learned that revolution is a state of mind, and actively working against all forms of oppression while doing this work is what is revolutionary."

Evelyn eventually focused her organizing efforts on United Students Against Sweatshops. She was drawn to USAS' sophisticated identification and targeting of the larger systems and institutions of oppressive power. Not being afraid to go after "the big guys," USAS has amassed a number of major victories on the national and international levels. As much as she values USAS' agenda and tactics, as one of the only people of color in leadership in a primarily white organization, Evelyn has at times felt burnt out and tokenized, but she remains committed; she is known by USAS members around the country for actively confronting and working to change the organization's racial dynamics from within.

Evelyn knows that the passion and love of life that drives her fight for change is the same thing that sustains her as a person. So her commitment to the long haul has taught her to savor, not deny, her own whims, impulses, and contradictions. Evelyn loves to party, and has a weakness for nice clothes and pedicures. "I'm not one of those hard-line, super-vegan, straight-edge activists. I want to be accessible, not alienating; I want people to see themselves in me and know that activists come in all flavors. Being accessible means having a good sense of humor, a few obvious contradictions, and a whole lot of love for the people around you."

What are 5 things you want to personally do before you die?
1. Spend a few months with my grandparents in Guatemala
2. Fall in love
3. Work in coalition with activists in Africa
4. Learn to play the guitar
5. Write something IMPORTANT and lasting.

When was the last time you really felt like a hypocrite?
When I worked as a teller for Wells Fargo last year.

A guilty pleasure? Freaky secret?
I've eaten dirt (literally) before...

Your most embarrassing shortcomings?
I am controlling and impatient at times and then I rationalize it by saying that that is what being an organizer is all about.

Evelyn Zepeda is 19 years old.

David Muhammed: Hip Hop Generation

By Juan Pablo

On growing up a Puerto Rican Muslim in Madison Wisconsin...

We were one of the few Boricua families in Madison and I grew up mainly with Blacks and Mexicans, so I was sort of an outcast. I was always the only Puerto Rican in school and my racial identity was always in question from Blacks and Latinos, while to whites I was just a nigger. I drew strength from my parents lessons; my father stressed our "Afro-Caribbean" identity and he would always tell me, "Si no tienes Dinga, tienes Mandiga," which forced me to identify with Black youth and the more African elements of Puerto Rican culture. My parents guided me politically because they were Puerto Rican nationalists. My father was from New York and had been involved in a lot of organizations, from the Young Lords to the United Farm Workers. My mother was a social worker and she grew up in an Independentista family in Puerto Rico. They taught me a lot about my culture and gave me a political worldview while allowing me to form my own opinions about life.

Describe your work

"Getting the National Hip Hop Activist Network started and running the Hip Hop Generation (HHG, pg. 147), which hosts community events, a radio program on WSUM 91.7, teach-ins, in addition to our national conference, Hip Hop as a Movement. I follow the Honorable Louis Farrakhan and am active in the Nation of Islam. I have done coalition work with the National Council of La Raza, United States Student Association, and other organizations. I am preparing HHG's new leadership to carry on these events and vision after I graduate the University of Wisconson in 2003."

On Hip Hop and the Nation...

What hurt more than white people's hate was the amount of disunity I saw among people of color and the lack of knowledge of self. Hip Hop became my outlet for identity and expression and it became the talking piece for me to explain myself to others. My parents bought me my first Rap tapes. Once, my father took me to the store and bought "It Takes A Nation of Millions." We listened to the record together. My father put me onto Islam but PE was a huge influence and one of the main reasons I joined the Nation, along with my mentor, a local DJ who was the NOI Study Group Coordinator in Madison. I joined the NOI at the age of 13 and fell in love with the teachings of the Honorable Elijah Muhammad, specifically with the concept of Allah in the person of Master Fard Muhammad. The NOI made me more serious about the study of my culture and nurtured my love for Hip Hop since there were always rappers at NOI events. It was the one spiritual home that accepted, embraced, and celebrated Hip Hop as a divine tool.

On the organizing effectiveness of the Hip Hop as a Movement conferences...

Conferences and gatherings have never saved anybody; it is the experience gained and the work carried out afterwards that produces change. Our work must be both cultural and economic because these are the two guiding realities that shape our condition. There always has to be efforts to deal with the immediate need to negotiate power within this society as well as organizing and preparations for independent support systems on a cultural level at the same time.

On white people in the movement and their place...

It's essential that our work includes whites of conscience but we have to tailor our approach to them very carefully. Too many white people want to work with people of color from a position of privilege, like it's the urban Peace Corps. They have to be dedicated to anti-racist work among their own in cooperation with people of color organizations first. It is our duty to check whites that work on these issues; nothing is more annoying than a white person who thinks they "get it" or are "down." We are responsible for teaching those who are committed to the work, but coalition building between Black, Indigenous, and Asian communities must be the top priority. We have to stop abusing ourselves through drugs and alcohol as well as gossip and low behavior. Conscious folks of color need to tighten up our ranks; the challenge of unity and improving our conditions begins with us.

On the future, David Muhammed in 10 years...

I want to be involved in the ministry (NOI), which almost directly conflicts with my desire to work with Hip Hop and the Rap music industry. If there is some reconciliation between the two then I'll be at peace, though there is less need for entertainment than for passionate voices for truth. Whatever my contributions, I want to continue working with young people and expressing my love for music. Aside from that, I think my greatest role will be as a husband and father. I look most forward to family life, the most important aspect of community building.

David Muhammed is 24 years old.

Crystal Haveland: Life Ain't No Crystal Stair

by Jennifer "J-Love" Calderon

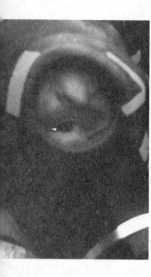

When listening to Crystal tell her story one can't help thinking that out of every necessary evil comes a hint of goodness, light, and truth. Born to a white working class family, Crystal spent her younger years living what appeared to be a "normal" life - going to a culturally diverse school, dealing with the regular ups and downs of growing up. But what wasn't apparent to school counselors and other adults in power positions was the violence in Crystal's home. Surviving an abusive childhood, Crystal had an early life lesson in self-preservation, which led to self-determination. At 16 she left her house and never went back. From her teens on, her blatant repulsion of anything representing authority grew from her feeling that her every attempt to be a good person was met with opposition. She went from blindly hating the system, to articulating her disgust of it, then organizing to change it.

Her skill at organizing quickly became apparent. Crystal's ability to mobilize and connect a broad base of organizers in Connecticut set a precedent during a time when activism was largely on college campuses. "While in Connecticut I started Connecticut Global Action Network (CGAN, pg. 64), an anti-capitalist group that organized over 500 people to go to the IMF protest in Washington D.C. in April of 2000. I also helped organize 500 for the September 26 day of solidarity for the protests in Prague. Our event was phenomenal because we teamed up with local 531 janitors in Hartford and demanded living wages, drawing attention to two important issues and getting fabulous news coverage. We also did other smaller actions around the state around wage issues, race issues, FTAA, and sweatshops, among others. I also helped start a radical feminist group that had a march on June 3 for reproductive freedom, was part of the newly formed ARA (anti-racist action), and participated in demonstrations against local racists in the KKK and the World Church of the Creator. Overall I would say that the majority of what I did was successful grassroots organizing and direct action."

Crystal will be applying the same power and skill to Community Works when she moves to California. Community Works is a non-profit organization based out of Berkeley that focuses on art, education, and social justice projects through programs in schools and jails. Regardless of where she is, Crystal will always be, "educating people, learning, smiling, loving, and fighting for rEVOLUTION."

Editor's note: In summer 2001, Crystal moved to Berkeley. We asked Adam Hurter, still active in CGAN, to reflect on Crystal's role and what CGAN has been doing since she left:

Crystal got into organizing when she worked with our friend Jen in a coffee shop. Jen told her, "You have all these views. I think that you would be an awesome political activist." Crystal was like, "Really?" She dove in headfirst and picked up skills really fast. She had no hesitation. She just DID it. I remember the first meeting of CGAN. There were 60 people. I was like "Wow." I didn't know there were this many radicals in Connecticut. CGAN started with all the other GANs because after Seattle, people wanted to organize for April 16 in DC. There were about a dozen of us at the core and CGAN was our baby. Crystal's energy and effort was one of the main reasons that the project got off the ground.

Our biggest recent action was after September 11 when we marched through the heart of downtown Hartford going to Senator Lieberman's office (the first Democrat who said we should bomb Iraq) to present our demands to his aide with 200 people. We turned the corner and that's when the cops ambushed us. They pushed us on each sidewalk and then this guy Vic who's a 61 year old Vietnam veteran, they severely beat him because he was making noise on a tambourine. Broke his ribs and pepper sprayed him, even though he has asthma and was screaming, "I have asthma! I have asthma!" They arrested 17 people.

Afterwards, the corporate media coverage was horrendous but the local weekly paper did a cover story "Free Speech R.I.P." that made the connection about civil liberties and dissent being squelched after September 11. We ended up receiving tremendous support and solidarity from all over the country. Student Peace Action Network put out a call to send letters to the Mayor and the judge. A Sunday School class sent letters to the Mayor of Hartford. Dozens of people from around the state came out to support us in court. We were $30,000 in debt but raised about $25,000. I felt psyched that people were supporting us from all over the place for breaking the silence of post-September 11.

Evon Peter: Graceful Balance

by Jee Kim

In every sense of the word, Evon is an activist. As the chief of his tribe, he is responsible for its well-being on an individual and collective level, which includes navigating an ongoing colonial relationship with the US government, bringing justice and empowerment to his people, serving as mediator in local disputes, and building an indigenous movement on a local and global level. How does a 26 year old bear this type of weight? By not being an "activist."

The distance often associated between "activists" and "constituents" is why Evon wouldn't immediately label himself an "activist." As Evon explains, "I wasn't used to being referred to as an activist until recently." Because in his tribe, he is no different from anyone else; Evon was a high school drop out, hung out in pool halls, drank and smoked, faced the criminal injustice system, hunts for his own food, packs the water for his home, and has a 5 year-old son. He just happens to occupy the position that he does, along with all its responsibilities. "My people believe that everyone has a role that they're good at and are meant to fill." And since his role entails a broad responsibility to whatever his people face, it's hard to pinpoint a singular issue area or struggle for Evon. It may be environment, food, and indigenous land rights one day or youth, drugs, and education the next. The graceful balance needed to be both community member and leader translates clearly in his personality as well.

Evon carries a passion that fuels him and a faith that stays him: "With all the pressures and responsibilities on me, all I have is faith sometimes." A stoic confidence necessary as a mediator that will, occasionally, break out into a sick rhyme about empowerment. An intensely focused brow that opens, among trusted company, into a growing and infectious laugh built on a quiet sarcasm. A sense of spiritual calm that, from time to time, warms into an excited glow when talking about his son. At a recent retreat, he asked everyone to sing "Happy Birthday" on the phone to his son, leaving smiles all-around. I asked him later what his son looked like and he replied, "nothing special." We both broke out laughing for what seemed like forever.

I used to joke with Evon that I got my cynical, urban, sarcastic sense of humor from him. He'd acknowledge with a slight smile. When I emailed him a list of questions, including a few obnoxious, light-hearted ones, he diplomatically declined responses to the less serious ones. But he did answer others:

Where do you see your hometown in 20 years?

I see my village functioning as a truly self-determined community, free of the oppression of corporations and western government. I believe that small quasi-sovereign communities with a global set of standards for relations to one another, the land, and animals is potentially a foundation for how we are to relate to each other as a global family.

Where do white people with money fit into the activist community?

From a tribal perspective we look at the world and its resources and say, "we should only take what we need." For us, to take more than what we need would mean to oppress and create an imbalance in the relationships we have with each other as humans, with the land, with the animals, and spiritually. So, innately I feel that people who possess a great deal of wealth are oppressing others and creating an imbalance, but in the case of our activities to promote positive change I feel that those people must be respected and are often helpful with what they have to contribute.

A guilty pleasure? Freaky secret?

N/A (I imagine a slight smile, maintaining his balance.)

Evon Peter is 26 years old.

Describe your work

"My community is a small tribe in the Brooks Range of Alaska, 300 miles from the nearest city and only accessible by small plane or river. There are about 150 Neetsaii Gwich'in who live here. We seek to find balance and good relations with other peoples and the earth as the process of globalization occurs. We fight to make amendments to and create new legislation that recognizes our inherent right to our way of life and get funding to initiate local programs that facilitate the recovery and maintenance of our language and culture, as well as develop sustainable energy. One of our greatest challenges at the moment is the protection of the birthing grounds of the porcupine caribou herd from oil drilling. This effort is focused on keeping the Arctic National Wildlife Refuge closed to the oil industry, which has, so far, been successful."

Isabel Gonzalez: What It Is

By Jee Kim (with help from Gina Arias)

When I was asked to make a few New York City Future 25 nominations, I turned to my long-time activist friends for suggestions. As soon as I heard Isabel's name, I thought, "oooh shit, of course." Why "of course?"

Well, first is because Isa's been doing the work for a loooong time. Active since 1996, Isa's track record starts with teaching video production and media literacy to young people and includes being a long time member of the Escuela Popular Nortena (EPN), a national popular education school, and volunteer in queer organizations of color, like the Audre Lorde Project. Before her current position as co-coordinator for organizing and outreach for Sista II Sista (SIIS, pg. 114), which she started last fall, she worked at El Puente (an alternative high school, pg. 109) for a few years and then at Make the Road by Walking (see pg. 119), organizing immigrant women in Bushwick around welfare rights.

Second is because I met Isa in a smoky room full of Hip Hop heads, some Stress Magazine folks, empty bottles and nicks, and real loud music. I don't remember one political word being exchanged; Isa was just another regular Brooklyn cat at a party, not part of the college educated, middle-class crowd I associated with activists. Seven years later, Isa is part of a growing wave of indigenous leadership. Activists that fight the Prison Industrial Complex and the welfare state and go home to friends on welfare and family (specifically for Isa, a brother) locked up. People who fight out of necessity, not with the luxury of calculated choice: "This organizing shit comes natural to me because I grew up in these fucked conditions and analyzed my surroundings with my companeros around me and decided to work with my folks and make a change. I didn't learn any of this stuff in books or in college or by traveling to Cuba or Nicaragua or any other 'exotic revolutionary places.'"

Third is because of how unafraid Isa is to pull a card and call it for what it is. Despite pierced ears, eyebrow, and lower lip, on first glance, Isabel fits the quiet type profile: soft-spoken and careful with the words she chooses, pausing often to drop a "you know" into conversations. But put her around some friends with good music and drink, and Isa is anything but. The last time we linked, at a CAAAV party with the DJ playing Brand Nubian and the bar serving $4 Skyy, Isa and I talked straight and honest about everything from old friends who front on rallies and being hooked on Newports, to accountability and white activists who occupy leadership positions in people of color organizations.

And the last reason is the same as the first; she's been active for a loooong time. And is still doing it. At SIIS, an organization for and by women of color, Isa's work is guided by the member's desires, which is integral to giving members ownership and developing future generations of indigenous leadership. Isa's current work fighting sexual harassment by cops, part of SIIS's anti-violence against women initiative, came out of a survey of 400 young neighborhood women which revealed how prevalent the problem is. Isa is helping create a video, "Cop Watch," that includes interviews with young sisters and catching cops harassing them on tape. The video and survey results will be part of a media campaign and help tackle the bigger issue of how to deal with violence against women in households and communities without relying on the police, who are too often agents of even greater violence. Isa is also incorporating her gender analysis as SIIS's representative in two coalitions, Third World Within and the Coalition Against Police Brutality, challenging the deeply embedded idea that police brutality victims are only young men of color. Like I said, never afraid to call it for what it is.

Isabel Gonzalez is 23 years old.

Charles "Nook" Byrd: Demon Killer

by Juan Pablo

In 1995, some high school kids were hanging out at a Valentine's Day party. Then suddenly, 83 officers ran up, wilin' on the teenagers, macing people, and arresting older relatives. For the kids, it was nothing new, but the case got widespread media exposure and led to the Austin police getting smacked with a lawsuit. The mayor asked for a meeting with young people from the community in order to negotiate an out-of-court settlement; Charles "Nook" Byrd was one of the negotiators. After a grueling 70-hour session, the city coughed up $750,000 to start First Step, a fund for scholarships and grants for the youth of East Austin. But Nook wasn't completely satisfied with the settlement because it offered nothing to kids who didn't want to go the college route. Fortunately, the youth were able to push the city council to vote unanimously on instituting an annual reporting program that tracks the number of complaints made and civil or criminal cases filed against officers, the race/ethnicity/sex of complainants, witnesses, and officers, and the outcome of complaints broken down demographically. Out of all this was born the Demon Killer Committee (pg. 136).

In addition to outreach and education, the Demon Killer's main push to organize their community around police brutality has been the annual summer Hip Hop concert series, Jump On It (JOI). Maybe the most impressive thing about JOI, on top of the diverse MCs that educate and perform for the 8,000 fans that turn out every year, is the $38,000 Nook fundraised from the Austin police. The same police that got hit with a lawsuit, the same police that Nook "uninvited" after getting the $38,000 from them. Knowing that chances of a violent incident are far greater with a police presence at JOI, Nook wisely assured them that JOI's own security was sufficient and that their services would not be needed. But if anything did happen, Nook knew that the police would shut down JOI and blame Nook and his community for not being able to "control themselves." But Nook had faith and sure enough, 5 years later, JOI keeps running smoothly, without any incidents on its track record. What's more impressive is that the Demon Killers have always insisted that no one be searched for weapons as they enter the concert grounds. Can you imagine? 8,000 heads and everything is peace.

When was the last time you had a run in with the beast?
Christmas Day, 1999. We were eating BBQ at a restaurant, laughing and carrying on. Some bum was in there and went outside and told the cops something. The cops ran inside asking us for ID and with no explanation, grabbed up our friend. They kept asking us for ID but we felt we ain't do anything wrong so we didn't want to give it to them. Finally I gave him my ID and as they did the warrant check they had me straddled on the hood of their cruiser, handcuffed. Then the cop started frisking me, groping my crotch for like 2 or 3 minutes and then going in my pants. So now I'm trying to turn around to see their badge numbers but they keep my face on the hood of the car. I was on the verge of tears. Finally they let us go. We filed a complaint but because we didn't have badge numbers it wasn't much help.

What are some parts of your game that need improvement?
Right now, obtaining more financial backing to reach more people.

True or False: Cash Rules Everything Around Me
In a way, it's true 'cause money and power do run the world. But for me personally, they don't. God rules everything around me.

That "24 Hours to Live" song. How would it go for you?
If I had one day to live, first thing would be to take the time to make sure my spiritual relationship with God was intact. Second, ask for forgiveness from anybody I wasn't at peace with. Third would be to give everybody a phone call and let them know I'm aight and everything is going be alright, and I'm going to a better place to be at one with my creator. The last thing would be to pick up my moms and take her to the studio and hold her hand and record as many songs as I can before my time is up. My last moments would be with the person that I love the most doing the thing that I love the most.

Nook is 22 years old.

Jackie Vélez: "We," not "I"

by Jackie Vélez and Natalie Avery

Born in the Bronx, New York, Jackie Vélez spent her childhood in Puerto Rico and teen years in Washington, DC. In high school she began writing poetry and plays about all her intersecting worlds-- family, neighborhoods, and homelands. Jackie's activism emerges from her sensitivity as a poet and a writer who listens to and documents the stories of her neighbors, friends and families. As both an artist and organizer Jackie brings humor, humanity, love and passion to her work.

In 1998, as a senior in high school, she joined the Youth Action Research Group (pg. 69), a DC based organization of young people who do research and activism around social justice issues in their neighborhood. The experience changed her: "The previous years, I just lived, adapted and accepted injustice in my community as 'just the way things are.' But my experience in YARG changed me. I began to connect the dots between people's daily struggle to live a decent human life and the barriers set up by a system that deprives many of their humanity. From that summer on I knew I would be an activist and organizer." That fall, as a freshman at Trinity College, Jackie became a key leader in YARG and 4 years later continues as the program's co-director. In this capacity, she works with young people and adults to help build awareness and organizing around human rights issues in DC, particularly around issues of equitable development and affordable housing.

Jackie's leadership is about opening up spaces for people to find their voices and come up with their own analysis. It is rooted in the message of one of her most important mentors, the late Lisa Sullivan: "We are the leaders we've been looking for."

If you had 5 minutes alone in a room with the president, and there were no consequences for your actions, what would you do?

One minute. I would bring a tape recorder with me and multiple pictures. When I enter his office I would greet him and place the recorder in the center of table. The recorder would contain a cassette with stories of the poor and working class people in DC and other states; it would contain their needs, struggles, love, and beliefs in different languages with no translation provided because it would take away from their true experience.

Two minutes. As the recorder plays I would decorate the table with pictures from the lives of the poor: homeless, DC Public School classrooms, boarded-up buildings, overcrowded apartments, work conditions, children's drawings, graffiti, hospitals, birthday parties, and churches.

Three Minutes. I would sit in front of him in silence. I would hand him a note: "Listen to the Stories. Look at the pictures. Reflect. These are the human lives you have ignored. These are the realities of those left behind by the system. Reflect and share with other colleagues in power."

Four Minutes. "I am a young Latina woman, raised in poverty and working towards social change. I'm liberal because I seek liberation. I believe in 'We' not 'I.' The recorder and pictures are evidence of the humanity of this country. It's up to you whether to value it and conserve it. In the meantime, while you decide, we will continue to rise and fight for what we have been robbed of."

Five Minutes. I would hand him a map of the world as a symbol, to show him that there is a broader world to consider and not just one nation.

A typical Friday night looks like...

A chill-out sleep-in morning, cash my Resident Assistant check, get a steak and cheese from the corner store. Get ready to meet Natalie for a meeting, come back to campus and start receiving or making phone calls about what's popping for the night: usually a girls night out at my best friend's house, a club, bowling, or on campus chilling in someone's room. If lucky, a date might come through, though not usually the case because they are driven away by my busy schedule during the week and by Friday they have given up.

Jackie Vélez is 21 years old.

Netta Brooks: Whupping Ass

By Mangala Manju Rajendran

Underneath her quiet, tough attitude, Netta Brooks is snarky and determinedly playful. She cusses like a sailor, laughs easily, and opens herself like we are making a meal of candor. A queer African-American 19 year old activist from Louisville, Netta is Southern civil rights organizer meets poet Saul Williams plus her own secret riot grrl sauce. She hates her hometown for being so big you can't know everybody while loving it for being diverse and progressive. Netta's work with the Fairness Campaign (pg. 84), a broad-based civil rights organization with an emphasis on the struggles of lesbian, gay, bisexual and transgender people, has helped establish Fairness Laws to prohibit discrimination based on sexual orientation or gender identity. On the board of Fairness Campaign, Netta participates in executive decision-making and works on the community-building committee, as well as volunteering her time stuffing envelopes, making phone calls, and knocking on doors. She has also been active around police brutality and youth liberation. Netta has published a small collection of poetry, but she couldn't be squeezed for poetry in time for this interview because she's grappling in a headlock with writer's block.

What do you love about the South?
I like that the South is progressive in its own way, that it goes at its own pace, that it's not trendy. The work that we do here is difficult, and I like that. In the General Assembly, we're pushing for state Fairness Ordinance laws. As shitty as it is, we fight for the Fairness Ordinance to get the same basic rights as everyone, like prohibiting discrimination in housing and public accommodations (hotels, taxis, restaurants, and public transportation). It doesn't make sense that we should have to struggle for the mundane things other people take for granted. We won Fairness at the city and county level, and now we're fighting for the laws at the state level.

Work outside of Fairness Campaign?
Carla Wallace, Angelyn Rudd, and three other activist-delegates just returned from Palestine. A thousand delegates from all over the world were part of this peace delegation. I want to support their efforts, participating in meetings or demonstrations. Recently I helped organize an International Women's Day celebration film festival with films about women in Palestine, Arab feminists, and women in prison. There were different films about contraception, including one about Norplant and how its use and availability is shaped by race and class. I recently did a workshop with Sheila Sutton of Kentucky Reproductive Health Network, Natalie Reteneller of Louisville Youth Group, and other young activists on safe sex and safe relationships for youth at Liberty High School, a public alternative school in Louisville. Me, my partner Tanisha Johnson, Darnell Johnson, Keisha Sanders, Akiba Timoya, and others from Southerners On New Ground (see pg. 121) are discussing having SONG's next LGBT people of color retreat in Louisville and having some kind of black pride celebration.

Beginnings?
I've been involved in movement work since I was 14. I started out by writing for Brat magazine, a youth-run zine here in Louisville. Brat covered political things like police brutality, poverty, schooling, homophobia, sexism, racism, sweatshop labor, the struggle to free Mumia, Critical Mass, domestic violence, and pollution. Our writing was a tool for social change. I believe in writing whatever's on the heart and reading it to people.

What do you listen to?
I listen to riot grrl. Bikini Kill, the Red Aunts, the Slits, Le Tigre. I just got a new CD, the Smears. I would recommend it but it's out of print. I like Hip Hop and this stuff people call neo-soul: Jill Scott, D'Angelo, Meshell N'degeocello, and even this white dude from Canada named Remy Shand.

Do you want to have kids?
Yes, I want to have kids, but no, I don't want to birth anything. I don't want to waddle around and I don't want to push something big outta my crotch.

If you could be alone in a room with George W. Bush for five minutes, what would you do?
Whup his ass. I know I should say I want to hand him a long list of plights but in honesty I would like to just kick his head. The FBI's going to be knocking on my door in five minutes for saying this, 'cuz you know they're tapping our phones...

Netta Brooks is 19 years old.

Ravi Krishna Dixit: People and Land

by Manuela Arciniegas

Describe your work
"Helping others take control of their situation. Whether people take control, fight for it, or create it. Whatever it takes: the people of South Africa holding their governments and employers accountable or helping the brothers in the prisons take control of their thoughts and what they want to learn."

"Naw. Just get on the bus." He said in his mild, yet stone-firm steady way when I suggested I postpone my arrival into Boston because I was running late. Ravi instantly dismissed all of my indecisions and attempts at politeness. "Just come, it's cool. I'll be waiting for you right outside the station, okay?" and his word was all I needed.

Fluidly ready to go with the flow in any situation, Ravi has dedication the strength of a tidal wave without asking for a raindrop's worth of credit or thanks. Incredibly humble about his contributions, I would have never known about all of his organizing and support work had I not seen him in other people's pictures building with activists in Jackson, Mississippi, South Africa, Cuba and more. Whether teaching a Black studies course to men in Suffolk County Jail, serving as the Chairperson for the Board of Project Hip Hop (pg. 91), doing fundraising and program development for DRUM (pg. 107), this brother is constantly busy working for and building coalitions with the Latino, African-American, Southeast Asian AND Palestinian communities. The motivation and stamina to do all this work? A deep spiritual connection and identification with all peoples. With a chuckle as pure as a child's, Ravi explains, "when I was a little boy, everyone thought I belonged to their racial or ethnic group!" Which is why he can both help instructing Chinese Kung-Fu and catch the meaning of any outburst in high-speed Caribbean Spanish.

While growing up in Egelston Square, a low-income neighborhood in Jamaica Plain, Boston, Ravi thought of himself as, "a regular American kid. My dad's friends were these two older Irish guys who sat around drinking beer, smoking cigarettes and watching baseball. They taught me how to play stickball and helped make me 'American.'" Ravi did not realize he was "different" until he went to a predominantly white Catholic school in Dorchester, Boston, where he got into fights for being brown-skinned and from Jamaica Plain. He learned how being "normal" meant access to wealth and belonging to pre-defined racial and ethnic groups. It echoed his experiences of grade school, where young Black and Latino kids accused him of killing the pilgrims because he was "an Indian," to which he would scream back, "Yeah and I'd kill them again dammit!"

At least a decade wiser now, Ravi no longer gets angry at people who don't respect or share his intense sense of global social justice. "I just don't believe most people are the enemy, and purposely want this world to be horrible place. They just need help thinking and learning about what's really happening. It's important to think that all people have value; getting angry and alienating others gets in the way. This is exactly how the few people in power who set up these systems want us to think."

However, Ravi's humanism, mobility, and chameleon-like abilities do not betray a lack of groundedness. In fact, his easy-going, cool-headed manner momentarily disappears when he speaks about the severed connection to land and place he saw in a recent trip to Palestine: "It's unbelievable seeing refugee camps where you could see the tanks a few paces away... Being with people who were shot at and had to flee their homes, seeing whole families physically shaking, entire areas just destroyed for no good reason! These folks knowing they can't live on the land they feel is theirs and have invested a deep connection to that very soil!"

The same concerns are echoed when Ravi speaks on the, "cheap, plastic sh*t houses," being built in the gentrification of his home neighborhood. "One day I want a strong, sturdy, brick house big enough to accommodate a community center and a small section in it for my own family. In India people make their houses out of stone, because they are supposed to last a long time. As the youngest child of an immigrant in the US, it's important to know you have a place. The most amazing place I've ever been was this small city in India because everyone in this community knew each other, knew everyone's stories. A place where there was community love and togetherness and human connectedness which is hard to find in this g*dd*mn country." But Ravi's anger does not translate into becoming an ex-pat or capitalizing on his privilege and abandoning his home for an idyllic small village to quietly live out his days: "I'm staying around here for a little while though. A lot of time people think America's a lost cause, an evil empire to destroy. But if we change our country, the US, I don't need to go to another country to do work! Those countries will benefit most if we become more connected to each other and our own humanity."

Ravi Krishna Dixit is 22 years old.

FUTURE500

www.Future500.com

Virtual Spinal Cord: The Future 500 Process

by Ibrahim Abdul-Matin

It is 2 am on a Friday night. I have no illusions about what I'm doing at the Active Element Foundation (AEF) office, still scanning a computer screen after 12 hours. I come from a historic people. Mom and Dad are fond of telling stories of those who have come before us, our ancestors, as if they were second cousins we would see at the next family reunion. My mother always says that we are ancestors in training. One day our descendents will be curious about where they have come from. This is how I came to view the Future 500 (F500), as a labor of necessity filled with highs, lows, uncertainty and joy, and plenty of workdays ending at 2 am. Standing on the tradition of struggle that has changed the course of this country before, this feels like another critical period in history. No time for half-stepping.

With an assortment of researchers (ten over two years) coming from various socio-political-sexual-economic-cultural backgrounds, and a movement to document that neither has a traditional figurehead nor wants one, we set out to provide a backbone for a future network, a virtual spinal cord if you will, that can carry messages, ideas, strategies and dreams to and from many limbs. The Future 500. I have always operated under the premise that what we are doing has not been attempted before. Honestly, I have no idea. The fact remains that there now exists an attempt. We have put forth, in spite of all the horrible things that take place everyday, a list of folks that still strive to take ownership of their communities and who are not afraid to step outside of their comfort zones to do so.

The process of making this directory has brought us closer to answering many questions, including: How did we choose? We dove into our own lists of friends, organizers, artists, community workers, youth workers, educators, and their friends. Then we grabbed existing directories and phone books, searched the web, checked into issue-specific networks and worked backwards from other foundation's grantee lists. Though calling all over the country to find people that were progressive in their politics and had a critical analysis of power was our primary tactic, researchers have also traversed the country on various organizing projects and speaking engagements, to attend conferences and convenings, or simply in the sway of their lives, but at all times, as "talent scouts" for the F500. Over time, we developed the following 16 criteria, and we aimed for groups that possessed at least 12 of these characteristics:

Our 16 criteria aimed at finding groups that...

1. are recommended by other organizing peers
2. are led by young people (under 30, but the younger the better)
3. working with young people in a manner where young folks have a voice in defining, designing and leading the work being done.
4. have a track record of effectiveness (no time minimum)
5. have a progressive political analysis
6. use innovative or original strategies
7. work with low-income/communities of color
8. are led by low-income/people of color
9. are connectors with a movement-building vision
10. are deomocratic or run by consensus
11. are not well known and deserve more support
12. give the F500 geographic diversity (we aimed for at least two from each state)
13. give the F500 diversity in the spectrum of issues young people face and are organizing around
14. give the F500 diversity in a range of ideologies, strategies and organizing styles
15. are a good group to call if someone wanted to get involved, write an article, or build a campaign.
16. are sustainable, provided the proper resources and technical assistance.

Ibrahim is a dreamer. Prior to working on the F500 he was a mover, production assistant with the International African Arts Festival, Outward Bound Instructor, organizer on corporate accountability issues with INFACT, and worked behind the counter at a local coffee shop. He is an aspiring creative writer with a novel and a collection of short stories in development. Now 24, he was raised a Muslim with 6 brothers and sisters and a fierce extended family. Reared in the Brooklyn activist tradition of his strong mother and later in upstate NY by his father and step-mother, he earned a football scholar-ship and spent his college years trying to throw off the "black athlete = machine" stereotype. In the world, Ibrahim grav-itates towards live music, poetry, and human expression of all types. Having lived in cities, rural areas, and near the ocean, he has come to prefer natural beauty to man-made things.

What did we do when we found a group? We interviewed as many people in the group as possible by phone or email, using a standard protocol of questions that we designed based upon feedback from groups and our own subjective research objectives. An average initial interview would take an hour, we would then ask for groups to send us some of their materials; upon receipt we would check them out and call back with more specific questions. We asked things like what resources are needed, what are the greatest challenges faced, what size is the operating budget, how are decisions made, who makes them, and what campaigns are being worked on? All of these questions were turned into fields in our database, but all of these fields do not appear in this book. Why? Given the number of groups we are surveying, including a full interview on each organization would result in a directory over 1000 pages. So we had to make some hard choices and we cut down the amount of information for each group so as to make this book as usable as possible. More detailed information is at: www.Future500.com.

Have we been scientific? Only partially, so no. There are many more checks and balances that need to be in place next time to ensure that all groups answer all the same questions, that these questions can be translated into both quantitative and qualitative data sets, that the differences in interviewing and profiling styles of researches are accounted for, and that groups have an opportunity to present themselves in a more thorough manner (through multiple interviews, written surveys and/or site visits). Furthermore, in selecting groups, it would be more scientific to establish a single set of criteria that all included organizations conform to, rather than have our small collective discuss (albeit democratically) whether exceptions should be made in order to balance geographic or issue coverage. In short, we know how we could have made this a more comprehensive and scientific study, but the fact is, this is a directory, a tool, one that is needed now, if not yesterday, and a resource that could not wait for additional funds to become available.

So here we are in a brownstone in Harlem, 2 am, with neither the money nor the time to go about this comprehensive national search for youth organizations in any other way than the let's-just-make-it-happen way. We already acknowledge that we will not get everyone; that's good news as far as we are concerned, the more the better! We already know that there will be some groups that some people don't think should be in here; that's fine by us as constructive critical dialogue always makes things better. We know there are some obvious groups that should have been here but aren't; usually that happened when organizers were out doing their thing and didn't have time to participate, which is great-- keep on doing the real work! We knew our efforts, like much of the organizing going on, would be concentrated in the large urban centers and the coast; but we have much love for all the strugglers and strivers! To say the very least, this book is a first draft of a much larger effort that will have to continue with you.

This brings me to another important question. Who are we to decide who the Future 500 are? We're nobody but a bunch of passionate justice-workaholics. Researchers in a bling-bling foundation palace looking down on the masses from our fourth floor perch? No, this directory uses a pedagogy of the popularly educated with a "learn by doing" sensibility. It has come about with the concentrated efforts of a cadre of organizer/researchers and volunteers that walk the talk. Between our other organizing efforts, foundation responsibilities, family commitments, run-ins with the police and love for all things cultural, we put in the work that high paid consultants get multiple-hundred thousand dollar grants to do. We are the folks that flocked to the Muslim sections of the city after 9/11 to offer ourselves as witnesses or human shields if necessary. We are the folks that stop on the way home from a 10 hour work day to monitor an arrest in the subway. No slackers or wannabes here. We are young, far from perfect, and have probably created double work on this project out of inexperience-- but we have put in the work. This is a by and for the people directory in every sense of the phrase.

The day I joined the F500 team, I could barely grasp the gravity of what I was setting out to do. I did not consider the political implications of connecting grassroots organizers all over the country. This is some revolutionary stuff! But beyond a book or a website, it is a grand attempt to let our descendents know (given we are ancestors in training) that just as every German was not a Nazi, every young person in this country is not a car-obsessesed, war mongering, over-consumptive cultural imperialist. We are letting it be known that at the turn off the 21st century there was the Future 500, that we could see past all this talk of being the "greatest nation on earth," and were instead focused on our responsibility to generations to come.

Nobody Told Me

by Manuela Arciniegas

It was around 6:30 pm on a Tuesday when I surreptitiously walked to the bathroom at the far end of our one-room office, sat on the toilet and cried. Tears flowed, bathing my neck and slicking my stomach, where racks of pain forcibly flexed my abdomen. I was ashamed to cry in front of my co-workers. Not in front of my friends, Ibrahim, Pablo, Emily, Kofi, Gita, and Billy, but my "co-workers," fellow researchers, career peers in our workplace, with phones and computers and stationary and maps with hundreds of push pins on the wall.

When I was hired, no one told me that on some Tuesday night I would be inquiring about one of the youngest, most influential leaders in an intergenerational independence movement, and that the response on the other side of the phone line-- transmitting from an island misnamed a "US territory"-- would cut into me deep. "Mana is not involved so much anymore. Her boyfriend is... abusive. He hits her, and screams and fights with her; intimidates her. She's not so involved in the movement anymore. We've done everything we can except beat him up and there's so much violence here it doesn't seem like an alternative. Mana's got to choose on her own." After reading inspiring speeches this 18-year-old organizer had published, I took it personally that a man was pounding into her face regularly. I was hurt, scared, angry, prodding the older woman on the line to continue reaching out to the young woman. The world needs Mana to continue her powerful organizing and writing, needs her to continue her life's work. I need Mana to do this. I didn't even know her, but I knew her intimately, and I hurt because she was hurting.

No one told me I would develop an emotional relationship to all the people I would call and meet and email and visit-- Mana, Kiko, Heather, Marquita, Nohelia, 'Naro, Anita-- that I would call and hear their stories and feel and listen, like a friend listens and feels, and quickly begin feeling about folks as if they were my friends. And drown, and feel some more, and go home and break other plans and sit in my room and think about a woman I never met, and dream about her crying. Looking back, the connecting roots that sprouted from my soul were inevitable.

Only now am I realizing that when I got the opportunity to sit and listen, I was hearing myself in the Southern lilts and mid-western twangs and island melodies of young organizers battling the same institutions and schemes for their oppression that I battle, bouncing back against these forces with the same hope I try to muster each day. The reason we are so powerful, and frightening to many people, is that we share a vision for how this society needs to grow. Like true brothers and sisters, we recognize what's always been there-- the umbilical cord tying all of us together, tugging masses towards transformation. A lifetime's work was slowly crystallizing in my mind.

I'm about a year farther along in this crystallization process. I decided that to best serve youth organizers, I need to be one, so I'm off to California to intern with some dope community organizations. One year out of Harvard College with a BA in Government, I have a deep-rooted sense that the lens through which I was taught to see success, the world, and justice needs to get windshield wiped fast-- by a squeegie wielding young wo-man with a black/brown hand and a pocketful of organizing plans that all lead to action, the kind of action that isn't afraid of the personal bonds and the pain and the tears that make this hope so real. I can hear the timber of our voices and actions getting louder and louder, if only in my head and the heads of other fresh minds awaiting a black-hole expansion of universal proportions-- a massive meltdown of injustice-- all from these phone calls and interviews I conducted this last year. Bite-size tasks with cosmic proportions.

Manuela Arciniegas. 22 years old raised in the Southeast Bronx, graduated from Harvard College with a BA in government, of African and Indigenous ancestry, parents born in Quisqueya, has three strong sisters, an appetite for drums, good spices, and youth organizing against environmental racism and police brutality. Believes in making art, organizing, and being free.

Shape Shifting Movement Builders

by Mathilda de Dios

Rewind: I first go to Active Element's office in August 2001 after I run into Billy Wimsatt on the street at a book fair. I had seen him at different events in Chicago, but this time I press him to bring me to AEF's space so I can dig through their files for youth organizing efforts happening in NYC. I want to continue the national campaign and campus work I had done in Colorado, but now with local struggles, so I need to know who is hitting the streets and making moves. Our conversation about race, class, privilege and philanthropy gets me even more hyped and inspired.

Fast forward: I help start a community organizing program through the Center for Third World Organizing focusing on the NYC education crisis and I become involved with the No More Youth Jails campaign (we just won a huge victory-- see Justice 4 Youth Coalition, pg. 110). When the program ends, I go to Cali and Colorado to visit my people and come back thirsty for a rest from organizing, but I still want to contribute to movement building.

Play: My partner and I are working on a project about youth organizing so we go to AEF to get some leads. Folks there are working on the Future 500 project and soon I get hyped and inspired to do something besides talk about how wack foundations are. Shortly thereafter I'm on the phones interviewing complete strangers about their campaigns.

Listen: Through this research, the fire to organize returned full strength. I felt odd asking questions-- an organizer asking other organizers if they qualify as the "future"-- but generally people are very real in their analysis and reflection. I learned so much just listening; tactics for issue development courtesy of the youth organizers from AYPAL who do a "fashion show" of campaigns before they choose their new projects; how organizers managed to beat their own participation record for a high school walk-out in protest of privatization; or the idea of cross-issue coalition building when an unlikely relationship between Youth Build Immigrant Power in Cali and SMYAL (Sexual Minority Youth Assistance League) in DC emerged.

The most amazing part about this project is that I realized, despite all the drama and hating that folks can fall into (including myself), that many of us are on the same page, working in solidarity alongside each other, trying to understand each other, and challenging each other in order to implement a common vision. Respect to the people who aren't afraid to be honest about the challenges they face in their daily struggle for social justice! I've had the honor of meeting many of the groups in the F500, and these beautiful shape shifting movement builders cannot be fairly represented in a handful of glittering words. But this was the only way we could get folks to know about them and knowing, as they say, is half the battle; the other half is to rise up! Makibaka! Huwag Matakot! means Dare to Struggle! Don't be Afraid!

Math is a 22 year old pansexual NYC-born Filipina German mixblood. She started organizing in college against institutional racism through anti-police brutality/street law education and eventually with the Not with Our Money campaign. After graduating from college she went through the MAAP program and the Community Partnership Program facilitated by the Center for Third World Organizing. She is a volunteer with the Justice 4 Youth coalition and works with NY Jobs with Justice and Philippine Forum. She is trying to relearn the cello and Tagolog.

Connecting Work

by Emily Kramer

I am very eager to be alive right now. Working on the Future 500 project the past few months has sparked many questions for me about who I am in a political context, and most importantly, what I can do. Following September 11th, I found myself needing to do some type of connecting work because, in a sort of urgency I had not experienced before, I also began to find my own ability to speak, to challenge. Shortly thereafter, I came into this project with a renewed sense of searching: for coalition, for empowerment, for new definitions of freedom-- not the co-opted George Bush freedom, but one that demands that no one can be free until we all are. I need to live for this reality, and right here, in this book alone are 500 organizations fighting to do the same.

Despite the violence and terrorizing that occurs daily for so many of us, there is a strong undercurrent mobilizing passion, vigilance, and critical love toward social justice, toward new patterns of freedom. While working on the F500, which for me meant interviewing and profiling over 70 groups, my voice has been met over and over by other voices seeking a vision much like mine. This is exciting and amazing to experience. Yet, there are many penetrating distances in this kind of work which I have felt strongly and have been questioning throughout this process. How does my location (white, middle-income, queer, young, student, etc.) affect the way I portray groups? How does who I am and how I speak influence the way I interact with people? How do my words (which are necessarily "translating" only a small piece of the actions, difficulties, goals and experiences of dynamic individuals) actually speak to who these organizations are? Can I possibly represent the spirit of the groups I am summarizing in 80 word profiles?

There were times when I felt limited by these realities, but I quickly became immersed in people's stories and aspirations, which are both moving and inspiring to me. Call after call, overwhelmingly, I felt a mutual willingness to share about our work, to discuss strategies, opportunities and connections to further the movement of progressive social organizing in all its configurations. This has had incredible value for me, expanding possibilities in terms of building solidarity across all kinds of borders at a time when that is exactly what is needed.

Where and how I go from here are loosely woven questions in the fabric of my life-- the Future 500 project has become an important thread leading me in many different, connected directions. My hope is that as a living, imperfect resource, the F500 can function the same way for others. I believe that none of these groups can or should be fully represented here-- instead, this book is intended to light a spark, feed the fire that fuels us, begin conversations, inspire self-inquiry and hold out the possibility of honest communication.

Emily Kramer, 19, grew up in Ithaca, NY and now lives in New York City where she's a student at the New School. She focuses in Cultural Studies, as well as various student organizing efforts to create spaces for libratory teaching and learning at the institution she's going into debt at. A major source of strength and inspiration for her is playing music with The Syndicate, a project rooted in anti-white supremacist, anti-capitalist, queer political and spiritual art activism.

Bout It Bout It Organizers

by Pablo Caraballo

I love living in New York City for many reasons; the way I met Upski is one of them. I had just picked up a check (always on the paper chase) and was riding the uptown A train. This kid came into my car selling books, which is illegal without a vending license.
When I saw that he was selling No More Prisons, I asked him if he knew the guy Upski who wrote it.
"I am Upski."
"Word? I'm Pablo from Blu Magazine."
"Oh word!" We exchanged a pound.
We had spoken briefly on the phone earlier that week through a mutual friend who thought we should work together. After we talked a bit, he invited me to the Active Element office. See? In what other city can you build with a critically acclaimed author and activist just by riding the train?

Anyway, when I got there the next day I was hired on the spot as a researcher for the Future 500. Though I kept an optimistic, interested front, I wasn't the least bit fond of the idea of sitting in a crowded office space all summer making phone calls and searching the Internet. Nope, not this kid. I'd rather be politicking by way of running the streets all day and hitting up parties every night. Plus, I was already a bit turned off by "organizing" from experiences with open-mic-pointless-meeting-having-never-doing-any-thing-for-the-people type of groups. Even though folks at AEF seemed different, I didn't know exactly what they wanted from me. Once I accepted the job, I was already thinking of ways to get out of the commitment. But all that changed with one phone call to Mike 360.

Mike was the first activist I had to call up and we spoke for damn near an hour. This kid told me about everything-- from the Tortuga Project, to the child he and his wife were expecting, to the gardens they were cultivating in the hood. Mike's commitment is what grabbed me; he'd lose me at times as I furiously scribbled my notes because he was so passionate about everything he spoke about. After I hung up the phone I had a clearer idea of why I needed to do this project, and I became amped to get to it. Not that my task seemed any easier or more appealing (hot office, phone, and computer... nope) but it just seemed clearer. I knew that we had to get youth like my man Mike 360 into the nation's spotlight if only to inspire kids like me who want to do right but don't always know how to go about doing it; to inspire everyone who feels they can't make a difference.

Over the next year, Mike and I spoke from time to time. He would fill me in on his progress and that would reaffirm my commitment to getting these 'bout it 'bout it type of organizers some positive attention and some funds. Especially funds because a lot of us knuckleheads out here would be doing positive, self determination type shit like Mike if we could eat while doing it (always on the paper chase). Mike and his gardens, his art, his family, his community and passion inspire me to think about the whole concept of making a difference and self determination every day.

Juan Pablo. Jp. Ablo. Average kid. Loves to read. Loves to write. Crumbles urb and guzzles alcohol and invests too much time and money into both. Often puts off his work until the last minute because he's off with a love interest. "Get money" is his credo, but so is "If I got it, you got it." Teaches reading/writing workshop for hooky players. Published freelance writer. High school drop out. Somehow still managed to get his high school diploma (not a GED, but an actual diploma). College drop out. Never had an actual 9 to 5. Loves his momma. Wasn't much of a team player until he hooked up with Active Element. They gave the kid a chance to bring something to the table. Still not exactly sure what that something is. Time will tell.

ALABAMA

21st Century Youth Leadership

Contact: Malika Sanders
Address: PO Box 2516, Selma, AL 36702
Phone: 334-874-0065
Email: youth421c@aol.com
Founded: 1985
Budget: under 500k
Constituency Age: 13-25
Issues: Youth Development, Racial Justice, Labor/Economic Justice, Environmental Justice
Race: African-American/Black
Profile: With 35 chapters, including 3 in West Africa, 21st Century works to empower African-American youth through social, economic and political justice work and leadership training. Their work is wide-ranging and creative, including registering voters with "Super-Birthday Tuesdays" celebrating 18th birthdays at Selma High monthly. Played a major role in electing the first Black mayor in Selma, led a remarkable turnaround in educational performance at a rural junior high school and won a campaign rejecting a major landfill slated for Tuskegee.

Southern Girls Convention

Contact: Claire Rumore
Address: 5025 Tenth Court South, Birmingham, AL 35222
Phone: 205-595-3142
Email: clairedeviva@onebox.com
Website: www.infoshop.org/southerngirls
Founded: 1999
Budget: out of pocket
Constituency Age: 13-30
Issues: LGBTTSQ/Queer, Women's Rights
Race: White, Multi-Racial
Profile: The largest political gathering of its kind, SGC brings thousands of young women together to convene, receive workshops and to organize around multiple issues, though with focus on gender, sexuality, and reproductive rights. Four conventions-- in Memphis, TN, Louisville, KY, Auburn, AL and Athens, GA-- have been held thus far and each has been twice the size as the previous one. The Birmingham Arts Collective was spun off from SGC.

The Pan Afrikan Alliance

Contact: Marcus Sims
Address: 2809 Academy Drive, Huntsville, AL 35811
Phone: 256-852-1520
Email: afrikanlife@hotmail.com
Website: www.naturalmysticpaa.freeservers.com
Founded: 1992
Budget: out of pocket
Constituency Age: 19-25
Issues: Education, Youth Development
Race: African-American/Black
Profile: Stressing love for community and culture, the Alliance supports political prisoners and other human rights campaigns through speaking tours and community events. Issue and campaign development is led by young people, as are local fundraising efforts. While remaining focused on education and cultural pride as a vehicle for skill development, the Alliance provides important political education opportunities in a relatively isolated area.

ALASKA

Alaska Action Center

Contact: Soren Weurth
Address: 308 G St, Suite 218, Anchorage, AK 99501
Phone: 907-563-2784
Email: akaction@alaska.com
Website: www.alaskaactioncenter.org
Founded: 1998
Budget: out of pocket
Constituency Age: 13-30 and over
Issues: Militarism, Indigenous Rights, Environmental Justice, Globalization
Race: Multi-Racial, White, Native American
Profile: AAC has organized local communities to stop land development, used memorials and vigils to raise consciousness about oil spills, and ingeniously linked 9/11 peace protests to an educational campaign about national missile defense and testing in Alaska. Continue to be on the front lines resisting federal government plans to open Alaskan reserves for oil drilling. Primarily university students, they are beginning a campaign with high school students focused on supporting the traditional culture and economy of indigenous communities.

Alaska Youth for Environmental Action

Contact: Polly Carr
Address: 750 West Second Ave, Suite 200, Anchorage, AK 99501
Phone: 907-258-4825
Email: ayea@nwf.org
Website: www.nwf.org
Founded: 1998
Budget: under 100k
Constituency Age: 13-18
Issues: Corporate Accountability, Environmental Justice
Race: Multi-Racial, White, Native American, Asian/Pacific Islander
Profile: AYEA is the National Wildlife Federation's state-wide, multi-cultural network of high school environmental education and leadership clubs for teens. They've addressed issues around clean air and water, protection of the Arctic National Wildlife Refuge and the Copper River Delta, cruise ship pollution, and pesticide use. Youth gain project planning and environmental assessment skills through workshops, attend

local governmental meetings, show political education videos in their communities, and promote pro-environment legislation.

ARCTIC VILLAGE COUNCIL

Contact: Evon Peter
Address: PO Box 48, Artic Village, AK 99722
Phone: 907-587-5523
Email: nativemovement@hotmail.com
Budget: out of pocket
Constituency Age: 13-30 and over
Issues: Youth Development, Indigenous Rights, Environmental Justice, Globalization
Race: Native American
Profile: This tribal government is in the daily trenches of struggles for environmental justice and indigenous sovereignty. AVC is at the forefront of the campaign to prevent oil drilling in the Arctic National Wildlife Refuge, not simply because it is against the principle, but because it has to be-- it is their people who will feel the direct impact of hazardous waste and potential spills. AVC has wisely linked its local struggle for survival to international campaigns against corporate and governmental abuse. (see pg. 28)

ARIZONA

BLACK MESA TRUST

Contact: Vernon Masayesva
Address: PO Box 30456, Flagstaff, AZ 86003
Phone: 928-734-9255
Email: kuuyi@aol.com
Website: www.blackmesatrust.org
Budget: out of pocket
Issues: Indigenous Rights, Environment
Race: Native American
Profile: This intergenerational organization addresses sustainable development issues, with focus on the depleting water supply and its long range implications for the Black Mesa people (Hopi and Dineh). Its members strive to bring back traditional ethics of water use and water healing and are currently fighting for the conservation and preservation of the underground Navajo aquifer in northeastern Arizona.
They are working to create, "a community characterized by vast open spaces with a healthy ecosystem and habitat for all living things."

BORDER ACTION NETWORK (BAN)

Contact: Jennifer Allen
Address: PO Box 384, Tucson, AZ 85702
Phone: 520-623-4944
Email: swarm@resistmilitarization.org
Website: www.resistmilitarization.org
Founded: 1999
Budget: under 100k
Constituency Age: 12 and under-30 and over

Issues: Racial Justice, Militarism, Immigrant/Refugee, Environmental Justice
Race: White, Latina/o
Profile: Focuses on exposing and ending the militarization of the US-Mexico border as well as ending ongoing police abuse and environmental violations by corporations in the surrounding communities. Current campaigns exist to cease privatization of jails in the area and to provide education and advocacy for people in border and new immigrant communities. BAN helped form the Arizona Prison Moratorium Coalition, which has worked to build leadership from within communities targeted for prison placement.

BRIGADA JUVENIL

Contact: Jose Matus
Address: PO Box 1286, Tucson, AZ 85701
Phone: 520-770-1373
Email: azbrp@aol.com
Website: www.afsc.org/az/derechos.htm
Budget: under 250k
Constituency Age: 13-21
Issues: Youth Development, Police Accountability, Militarism, Immigrant/Refugee, Environmental Justice
Race: People of Color, Native American, Latina/o
Profile: A project of Derechos Humanos, which promotes civil and human rights on the US-Mexico border, Brigada Juvenil is a group of Indigenous and Chicano youth, ages 15-21, who explore each other's cultures and work together to combat the racial and social injustices in border communities. Through leadership training and political education, youth learn about and research local issues in order to educate their communities by giving Know Your Rights presentations in their high schools and colleges.

CENTRO ADELANTE CAMPESINO

Contact: Lisa Miranda-Lintz
Address: PO Box 1338, Surprise, AZ 85374
Phone: 623-583-9830
Email: centro_campesino@yahoo.com
Founded: 1978
Budget: under 500k
Constituency Age: 19-30 and over
Issues: Immigrant/Refugee
Race: Latina/o
Profile: CAC (translated: Center for Progress of Farm Workers) is an intergenerational advocacy group serving documented and undocumented Latino workers. Because the community is severely under-served and an easy target for abuse, CAC uses a combined organizing and service strategy, tackling workplace rights, youth employment and tutoring, ESL and GED courses, bi-lingual legal representation, and the operation of a food-bank for low-income residents. Currently creating a documentary about the history of campesinos in the U.S. from the 50s to the present.

CHILDREN FOR A SAFE ENVIRONMENT

Contact: Keri Johnson
Address: 7733 North 13th Place #2, Phoenix, AZ 85020
Phone: 602-279-5001
Email: children4asafeenviro@prodigy.net
Website: www.cfsenvironment.org
Founded: 1988
Budget: out of pocket
Constituency Age: 12 and under-18
Issues: Indigenous Rights, Environment, Health Care,
Environmental Justice
Race: Multi-Racial
Profile: A multicultural organization composed of Native
American, Latino, African-American, and Anglo youth, CSE
supports Indigenous and other low-income communities
affected by industrial waste contamination by providing
information and resources. They are currently organizing to
shut down a medical waste incinerator on the Heelah River
(located on Indigenous land) and providing information for
community members about asthma, diabetes, high birth defect
rates, and other health issues connected to dioxins and other
toxins linked to industrial waste.

INDIGENOUS ACTION MEDIA (IAM)

Contact: Klee Benally
Address: 6680 Columbine Blvd, Flagstaff, AZ 86004
Phone: 928-527-3791
Email: indigenous_action_media@yahoo.com
Founded: 2001
Budget: out of pocket
Constituency Age: 19-30
Issues: Indigenous Rights, Media
Race: Native American
Profile: IAM produces videos and documentaries designed to
highlight issues impacting indigenous communities.
Intergenerational, but with focus on supporting young leaders,
IAM offers training in media relations and documentary
videography to other grassroots organizations and community
members working on indigenous rights. Media ready elements
and political education tools are created to support campaigns
around issues such as land use and rights, education, poverty,
health care, cultural preservation, environmental justice and
sovereignty.

PHOENIX COP WATCH 602

Contact: Pat Schwind
Address: PO Box 1543, Phoenix, AZ 85001
Phone: 602-241-6353
Email: copwatch602@hotmail.com
Website: www.phoenixcopwatch.org
Founded: 1998
Budget: out of pocket
Constituency Age: 19-30 and over
Issues: Racial Justice, Police Accountability, Human Rights
Race: White, Latina/o, Asian/Pacific Islander

Profile: Copwatch 602 is a citizen's group formed to combat
police harassment and brutality, including police shootings of
unarmed citizens. 602 uses direct action strategies such as
videotaping stop-and-frisks or arrests, starting community
patrols, holding forums and protests. Public education
campaigns link police brutality with racism, demonstrating the
prevalence of police violence in communities of color. Specific
campaigns have formed around changing the "Shoot to Kill" and
"Shoot First, Ask Questions Later" training and instruction that
police officers receive.

TOHONO O'ODHAM COMMUNITY ACTION (TOCA)

Contact: Tristan Reader
Address: PO Box 1790, Sells, AZ 85634
Phone: 520-383-4966
Email: wynread@earthlink.net
Founded: 1996
Budget: under 250k
Constituency Age: 12 and under-21
Issues: Youth Development, Indigenous Rights, Arts/Culture,
Environment
Race: Native American
Profile: TOCA works to build cultural pride and political strength
among indigenous people through traditional arts and cultural
practices. They focus on learning traditional farming methods,
viewed as a remedy for the alarming rate of diabetes in the
community. TOCA is deliberately multigenerational, with a core
group of 20 youth in positions of leadership. Specific youth
projects include a traditional food systems program, a basket
weaving cooperative, poetry nights, a youth video
project, and a youth and elders outreach initiative.

TONATIERRA

Contact: Tupac Enrique
Address: PO Box 24009, Phoenix, AZ 85074
Phone: 602-254-5230
Email: tonal@tonatierra.org
Website: www.tonatierra.org
Founded: 1994
Budget: under 250k
Constituency Age: 12 and under-30 and over
Issues: Immigrant/Refugee, Environmental Justice,
Indigenous Rights
Race: Native American, Latina/o
Profile: Tonatierra is an intergenerational human rights and
indigenous peoples advocacy organization. Ongoing campaigns
include fighting the desecration of Native sacred sites,
organizing day laborers, and working with gangs and youth.
Community programs include intergenerational and
Native/Chicano cultural events, ESL classes, a correspondence
program with inmates, a health clinic, a food bank, and
teaching organizing tactics derived from indigenous traditions.
Tonatierra also is an organizer of the Peace and Dignity
Journey, an intercontinental spiritual run that takes place
every four years.

ARKANSAS

180 MOVEMENT FOR DEMOCRACY AND EDUCATION

Contact: Andy Burns
Address: PO Box 251701, Little Rock, AR 72225
Phone: 501-244-2439
Email: clearinghouse@tao.ca
Website: www.corporations.org/180mde
Founded: 1996
Budget: out of pocket
Constituency Age: 19-30
Issues: Student Rights/Education Reform, Globalization, Corporate Accountability
Race: White
Profile: A national network with 15 chapters linking hundreds of active students working to promote democratic participation while fighting corporate control over educational institutions. Locally determined organizing has included anti-sweatshop, anti-death penalty, human rights, environmental, electoral, LGBT and living wage campaigns. The 180 MDE Clearinghouse is a volunteer central coordinating office that publishes a national newsletter and houses archives and organizing resources.

CAMPUS DEMOCRACY COLLECTIVE

Contact: Daniel Vot
Address: A665 Arkansas Union, 6th Floor, University of Arkansas, Fayetteville, AR 72701
Phone: 501-575-2275
Email: cdemcol@uark.edu
Founded: 1998
Budget: out of pocket
Constituency Age: 13-30
Issues: Student Rights/Education Reform, Militarism, Labor/Economic Justice, Globalization
Race: Multi-Racial, White
Profile: Working on campus democracy issues at the University of Arkansas, a.k.a. Walmart University (the Waltons gave $300 million to the university-- all for corporate research). Consistently organizing to end the influence of corporations on their university and educational experience, CDC is actively involved in the election process of university trustees. Current campaign focuses on post 9/11 peace and the protection of civil rights.

COMMUNITY HEALTH OF PEOPLE AND ENVIRONMENT (C-HOPE)

Contact: Tina Blue
Address: 1308 West Second St, Little Rock, AR, 72201
Phone: 501-376-7913 x16
Website: www.arpanel.org
Budget: under 500k
Constituency Age: 13-18
Issues: Environmental Justice, Education
Race: Multi-Racial, White, African-American/Black, Latina/o
Profile: Based in El Dorado, C-HOPE is an intergenerational group organizing against toxic contamination caused by the El Dorado Chemical Company. Aided by the Arkansas Public Policy Panel, which supports over 50 organizations in the region, C-HOPE is implementing a political strategy to have environmental regulations enforced at the plant, to mobilize and educate community members, and to specifically organize young people in schools directly affected by the industrial plants.

STUDENTS TRANSFORMING AND RESISTING CORPORATIONS (STARC 180 MDE)

Contact: Seth Baldy
Address: PO Box 251701, Little Rock, AR 72225
Phone: 501-244-2439
Email: clearinghouse@tao.ca
Website: www.hendrix.edu/starc
Founded: 1996
Budget: out of pocket
Constituency Age: 19-21
Issues: Student Rights/Education Reform, Globalization, Corporate Accountability
Race: White
Profile: Creating a book exchange so students can have an alternative to their Barnes & Noble owned bookstore. Organized a number of protests around Citibank, participated at protests at the School of Americas in Fort Benning, Georgia, and boycotted Staples until they increased their stock of recycled paper. Organized 200 letters from students, faculties, and administration to the Democratic Senators about drilling in the Artic Wildlife Refuge and are looking into starting up a slew of other activities and campaigns!

WOMEN'S PROJECT

Contact: Angeline Echeverria
Address: 2224 Main St, Little Rock, AR 72206
Phone: 501-372-5113
Email: amewproject@aol.com
Website: www.womens-project.org
Founded: 1981
Budget: under 500k
Constituency Age: 13-30 and over
Issues: Youth Development, Women's Rights, Violence Prevention, Racial Justice, Prisons/Criminal Justice
Race: Multi-Racial
Profile: A central node of activism in Arkansas, WP combats violence and discrimination against women and girls, with focus on issues from domestic violence to incarceration. Coordinates myriad innovative state-wide projects such as the Sister2Sister program, which recruits young recipients of services from other non-profit organizations and trains them to become effective activists, leaders, and organizers.

CALIFORNIA

ACTION FOR LOCAL/GLOBAL JUSTICE (ALGJ)
Contact: David Solnit
Address: 611 32nd St, Oakland, CA 94609
Phone: 510-601-8116
Email: dsolnit@riseup.net
Founded: 2001
Budget: out of pocket
Constituency Age: 13-30 and over
Issues: Environmental Justice, Globalization
Race: Multi-Racial, White
Profile: A coalition formed in the wake of the Seattle WTO protests, ALGJ coordinates grassroots organizations for actions addressing corporate abuses and globalization. Staged two major actions with local environmental justice groups to coincide with global WTO and IMF/World Bank protests. A vital hub for anti-globalization work in the Bay Area.

ART AND REVOLUTION
Contact: Alli Starr
Address: c/o Agape Foundation, 1095 Market St #303, San Francisco, CA 94103
Phone: 415-339-7801
Email: alli@riseup.net
Website: www.artandrevolution.org
Founded: 1997
Budget: under 25k
Constituency Age: 19-30 and over
Issues: Arts/Culture, Globalization, Human Rights, Militarism, Public Space, Racial Justice
Race: White, Multi-Racial
Profile: Known for making the giant puppets that have become so prominent at anti-globalization campaigns, A&R does all kinds of creative actions and guerilla theater. A prime example of the value of culture in politics, A&R is known for visually integrating fun, humor and critical analysis. With chapters in seven cities, definitely the most active national network of artists in the social justice movement.

ASIAN PACIFIC ENVIRONMENTAL NETWORK (APEN)/ASIAN YOUTH ADVOCATES
Contact: Grace Kong
Address: 220 25th St, Richmond, CA 94804
Phone: 510-236-4616
Email: apen@apen4ej.org
Website: www.apen4ej.org
Founded: 1995
Budget: under 250k
Constituency Age: 13-21
Issues: Youth Development, Women's Rights, Environmental Justice
Race: Asian/Pacific Islander
Profile: Working to represent the environmental justice interests of Asian/Pacific Islanders in California, APEN houses Asian Youth Advocates, a project prioritizing youth leadership and training for Laotian young women organizing around environmental and economic justice in Contra Costa County. Educating the community on local toxic assaults, i.e., daily emissions, workplace exposures and lead poisoning, the young women from AYA played a critical role in the successful fight to shut down a Chevron chemical fertilizer incinerator in Richmond.

ASIAN PACIFIC ISLANDER YOUTH PROMOTING ADVOCACY AND LEADERSHIP (AYPAL)
Contact: Kawal Ulanday
Address: 310 8th St, Suite 306, Oakland, CA 94607
Phone: 510-465-9876 x309
Email: m3fontan@aol.com
Website: www.filipinos4action.org
Founded: 1998
Budget: under 100k
Constituency Age: 13-18
Issues: Racial Justice, Prisons/Criminal Justice, Labor/Economic Justice, Arts/Culture, Student Rights/Education Reform
Race: Multi-Racial, Asian/Pacific Islander
Profile: A project of Filipinos for Affirmative Action, AYPAL is a collaborative of Filipino, Cambodian, Chinese, Vietnamese, Korean, Mien and Polynesian high school students organizing around a range of social justice issues. A recent campaign included actions at four airports in support of Filipino workers, while students at three different sites engage in AYPAL's ongoing organizing around racism within schools and the "Books Not Bars" campaign. Through a youth-to-youth-grants project, AYPAL organizers dialogue with their peers and re-grant $10,000 each year.

ASIAN PACIFIC ISLANDERS FOR HUMAN RIGHTS (APIHR)
Contact: Patrick Mangto
Address: PO Box 461671, Los Angeles, CA 90046
Phone: 323-860-8775
Email: pmangto@apihr.org
Website: www.apihr.org
Founded: 2000
Budget: under 100k
Constituency Age: 13-25
Issues: Youth Development, LGBTTSQ/Queer, Immigrant/Refugee, Health Care, HIV/AIDS
Race: Asian/Pacific Islander
Profile: APIHR's broad goal is to create safe spaces for and promote acceptance and understanding of the Asian/Pacific Islander LGBTQ population. It conducts leadership training for youth and provides mentoring services, as well as culturally relevant 'coming-out' materials for Asian/Pacific Islanders. APIHR also has a media program promoting tolerance and political education.

BARRIOS UNIDOS

Contact: Daniel "Nane" Alejandrez
Address: 1817 Soquel Ave, Santa Cruz, CA 95062
Phone: 831-457-8208
Email: barrios@cruzio.net
Website: www.barriosunidos.net
Founded: 1997
Budget: over 1 million
Constituency Age: 12 and under-30 and over
Issues: Youth Development, Violence Prevention, Gang Issues, Prisons/Criminal Justice, Education
Race: People of Color, Latina/o
Profile: Barrios Unidos is a pioneering national umbrella organization of Latino gang truce efforts. Work areas include truce negotiation, crisis intervention, and silk-screen micro-enterprising. Its Cesar E. Chavez School for Social Change and Community Economic Development provides teens with education in history, art, computer literacy, cultural dance, video production, creative writing and political organizing. A powerful example of young people identifying a problem and building an institution designed to address that issue.

C-BEYOND

Contact: Malachi Larabee-Garza
Address: 1846 B Grant St, Concord, CA 94520
Phone: 925-676-6556
Email: cbeyond@igc.org
Website: www.youthec.org/cbeyond
Founded: 1996
Budget: under 250k
Constituency Age: 13-18
Issues: Student Rights/Education Reform, Prisons/Criminal Justice, Youth Development
Race: Multi-Racial
Profile: A youth-led organization focused on leadership development, C-Beyond offers internships training young people in public speaking, campaign development and political analysis. Putting theory into practice, C-Beyond was the first group in the Bay Area to specifically target corporations in the No Prop 21 Campaign. Using non-violent direct action protests, Chevron and later Pacific Gas & Electric agreed to stop funding Prop 21. Currently publish the Voice of Youth newsletter and working in a coalition to stop the Alameda County Super-Jail.

CALIFORNIANS FOR JUSTICE

Contact: Emmanuelle Regis (San Diego)
Address: 1611 Telegraph Ave, Suite 1550, Oakland, CA 94612
Phone: 510-452-2728, 562-951-1015
Email: sanjose@caljustice.org
Website: www.caljustice.org
Founded: 1996
Budget: under 1 million
Constituency Age: 12 and under-30 and over
Issues: Racial Justice, Immigrant/Refugee
Race: Multi-Racial, People of Color
Profile: CfJ is focused on strengthening the political base of communities of color across California. It works on statewide public policy campaigns with an emphasis on educational access, policing and prisons, and living wages. Past campaigns include the fight against Prop 209, 21, and 22, increasing the state minimum wage to $6.75, and the passing of Bill 540 (tuition exemptions for undocumented students). An intergenerational organization, Californians for Justice also offers training on lobbying, public speaking, community organizing, and alliance building.

CENTER FOR YOUNG WOMEN'S DEVELOPMENT

Contact: Lateefah Simon
Address: 1426 Fillmore St, Suite 205, San Francisco, CA 94115
Phone: 415-345-0260
Email: cywd@cywd.org
Website: www.cywd.org
Founded: 1993
Budget: under 500k
Constituency Age: 13-25
Issues: Women's Rights, Gang Issues, Prisons/Criminal Justice, LGBTTSQ/Queer
Race: People of Color, Latina/o, African-American/Black
Profile: Run almost entirely by young women who have been released from juvenile detention centers, each year the Center recruits and hires 10-15 young women for a 15 month job-training and youth leadership program. Offer advocacy workshops for incarcerated young women and are involved in community building activities with low and no income LGBTQ young women. Currently working on a "Know Your Rights" handbook teaching incarcerated young people to advocate for themselves.

CHALLENGING WHITE SUPREMACY

Contact: Sharon Martinas
Address: 2440 16th St, PMB #275, San Francisco, CA 94103
Email: chriscrass1886@hotmail.com
Founded: 1993
Budget: under 50k
Constituency Age: 13-30 and over
Issues: Racial Justice, Education
Race: Multi-Racial, White
Profile: An intergenerational organization that views racism as the major barrier to fundamental social change in this country, CWS provides anti-racist trainings for white social justice activists. The objective is to strengthen political organizations and increase effectiveness by teaching white organizers how to support social justice work in communities of color. CWS offers a thirty week training program in San Francisco as well as a four-hour traveling workshop designed for activist gatherings and conferences.

CIRCLE OF LIFE FOUNDATION

Contact: Julia Butterfly Hill
Address: PO Box 3764, Oakland, CA 94609
Phone: 510-601-9790
Email: info@circleoflifefoundation.org
Website: www.circleoflifefoundation.org
Founded: 1999
Budget: under 250k
Constituency Age: 12 and under-30 and over
Issues: Environmental Justice, Genetic Engineering, Environment
Race: White
Profile: Created by visionary tree sitter and author Julia Butterfly Hill, COL travels the world inspiring people to make a difference. With specific focus on the environment and sustainable growth, the goal is to support and connect, "a spiritual activation movement." May sound vague, but they back it up, channeling Julia's "rock star" status to support myriad concrete local grassroots struggles.

COALITION FOR EDUCATIONAL JUSTICE

Contact: Kirti Baranwal
Address: 939 S. St Andrew's Place #3, Los Angeles, CA 90010
Phone: 310-452-3310
Email: caputoprl@aol.com
Founded: 1999
Budget: under 25k
Constituency Age: 13-30 and over
Issues: Immigrant/Refugee, Student Rights/Education Reform, Racial Justice
Race: Multi-Racial, People of Color
Profile: CEJ is an intergenerational membership organization of students, parents, and teachers engaged in a city-wide campaign against the high stakes testing (like the high school exit exam) that determines whether or not a public school gets funding. It supports the expansion of bilingual education programs and is pushing for more investment in class size caps instead of school police. Young people in CEJ participate at all levels, making decisions on policy and strategy, implementation of tactics and member recruitment.

CONSCIOUS ROOTS

Contact: Jinee Kim
Address: 178 B Montana St, San Francisco, CA 94112
Phone: 415-709-9719
Email: troobloojk@lycos.com
Founded: 2001
Budget: out of pocket
Constituency Age: 13-30
Issues: Education, Hip Hop Activism
Race: Multi-Racial
Profile: CR bridges culture and politics through events, workshops, creative non-violent direct action, and popular education for social change. They train high school students to conduct workshops on gentrification, ethnic studies, interacting with police and sexism. Involved in the statewide Schools Not Jails campaign to reprioritize budgetary expenditures from incarceration to education and fighting for ethnic studies in public high schools.

CULTURAL LINKS

Contact: Alli Starr, Holly Roach, Erika Zarco
Address: c/o Agape Foundation, 1095 Market St, Suite 304, San Francisco, 94103
Phone: 415-339-7801
Email: alli@riseup.net
Website: www.cultural-links.org
Founded: 2000
Budget: under 25k
Constituency Age: 13-30
Issues: Arts/Culture, Globalization, Racial Justice
Race: Multi-Racial
Profile: Cultural Links is focused on making connections between arts and activism, between young people and tools of empowerment, between different communities. Youth led projects include: Art in Action Summer Camps (30-40 youth, mostly of color), socially conscious road shows (the last one traveled through schools and community centers in the Southwest, linking prisons, immigrant rights, and environmental racism through arts and issue-based workshops), and art festivals like Radical Performance Fest, which showcases young women, people of color, and the differently-abled.

DESTINY ARTS YOUTH CENTER

Contact: Naomi Bragin
Address: 5688 San Pablo Ave, Oakland, CA 94608
Phone: 510-597-1619
Email: info@destinyarts.org
Website: www.destinyarts.org
Founded: 1988
Budget: under 250k
Constituency Age: 12 and under-18
Issues: Arts/Culture, Violence Prevention
Race: Multi-Racial
Profile: Destiny Arts is a dynamic collective of young people who creatively address social and political issues through self-produced performances. Combining martial arts, dance, theater, spoken word, spiritual traditions and music, performers explore the issues impacting their communities, including racism, homophobia, poverty, violence, and education. Martial arts training and artistic expression are used to build self-confidence, strengthen leadership skills and inspire community involvement; the traveling repertory company reaches young people throughout the state. Leadership development with flavor.

ELLA BAKER CENTER FOR HUMAN RIGHTS

Contact: Raquel Lavina
Address: 1230 Market St #409, San Francisco, CA 94102
Phone: 415-951-4844
Email: raquel@ellabakercenter.org
Website: www.ellabakercenter.org
Founded: 1996
Budget: under 500k
Constituency Age: 13-30 and over
Issues: Racial Justice, Prisons/Criminal Justice, Police Accountability, Human Rights, Arts/Culture
Race: Multi-Racial
Profile: Founded as Bay Area Police Watch, it now hosts seven innovative youth and intergenerational organizations: Let's Get Free (Bay Area youth/ Hip Hop-based organizing around prisons), Books Not Bars, Freedom Fighter Music, New York City Police Watch, INS Watch, Transaction (challenging the unique harassment of transgendered folks by police), and FIERCE. Hella pioneering, leaders in the Hip Hop sit-in movement around Prop 21. Probably the most influential human rights organizations of our generation.

ENVIRONMENTAL HEALTH COALITION

Contact: Nohelia Ramos
Address: 1717 Kettner Blvd #100, San Diego, CA 92101
Phone: 619-235-0281
Email: noheliar@environmentalhealth.org
Website: www.environmentalhealth.org
Budget: under 100k
Constituency Age: 13-21
Issues: Youth Development, Environmental Justice, Corporate Accountability
Race: Latina/o, Asian/Pacific Islander
Profile: EHC recently incorporated youth organizing into their ongoing political education campaigns on toxics and environmental sustainability. The 20 member youth group canvasses high schools and colleges, does presentations on the harmful environmental impact of the nearby South Bay Power Plant, and educates local communities about the highly toxic naval presence in San Diego Bay. Currently networking with youth-led organizations in preparation for focused lobbying campaigns for stronger environmental legislation.

ESTACION LIBRE

Contact: Miguel Rodriguez
Address: PO Box 226758, Los Angeles, CA 90022
Phone: 323-273-5724
Email: e-libre@tao.ca
Founded: 1997
Budget: under 25k
Constituency Age: 19-30 and over
Issues: Indigenous Rights, Globalization, Multi-Culturalism, Education
Race: People of Color

Profile: EL takes delegations of young people of color to Chiapas, Mexico to learn from the organizing strategies and practices of the Zapatistas. Participants gain hands-on experience with community organizing and direct democracy by working in a community fighting daily for indigenous rights and sovereignty. EL also organizes protests and petitions in solidarity with organizations like La Red Defensores who fight for indigenous and human rights. Currently exploring the application of indigenous organizing models to communities of color in the U.S.

FREEDOM FIGHTER MUSIC

Contact: Jakada Imani
Address: 1230 Market St, PMB 409, San Francisco, CA 94102
Phone: 510-381-1595
Email: hello@freedomfighter.ws
Website: www.freedomfighter.ws
Founded: 2001
Budget: under 25k
Constituency Age: 13-25
Issues: Militarism, Racial Justice, Prisons/Criminal Justice, Hip Hop Activism
Race: People of Color
Profile: Hip Hop-based political label that created "Shame the Devil: Hip Hop Tells the Truth About the Prison Industrial-Complex" and an anti-war album (soon to be released). A program of the Ella Baker Center, Freedom Fighter Music uses art and culture as a political tool through albums, shows and support for progressive local artists like Zion I, Company of Prophets, and Prophets of Rage. FFM folks are fixtures in the broader cultural and political scene in the Bay Area.

FREEDOM TRAINERS

Contact: YK Hong
Address: 2416 Potter St, Oakland, CA 94601
Phone: 415-305-9045
Email: yk@freedomtrainers.org
Website: www.freedomtrainers.org
Founded: 2001
Budget: under 50k
Issues: Women's Rights, Racial Justice, Globalization, LGBTTSQ/Queer
Race: Multi-Racial
Profile: Using popular education methods, FT workshops integrate an analysis of oppression, strategic planning for non-profits, and planning skills for cultural and political events, all in an effort to provide leadership tools for self-empowerment. FT has been active in attempts to defeat racist and ageist California ballot initiatives, and provides a consistent presence of youth, LGBTQ people and people of color at conferences and demonstrations.

Destiny Arts, May 10-12, 2002. From "The Beat on Both Sides: a cry for freedom." The pieces detect the heartbeat of urban youth living on both sides of the juvenile injustice system. "The Beat On Both Sides" is a quest for solidarity, honoring all young people whose bodies may be locked down but whose voices remain. © Steve Meslemka

GROUNDWORK BOOKS

Contact: Lori Gutierrez
Address: 0323 Student Center, La Jolla, CA 92037
Phone: 858-452-9625
Email: groundwork@libertad.ucsd.edu
Founded: 1974
Budget: out of pocket
Constituency Age: 13-30 and over
Issues: Youth Development, Prisons/Criminal Justice, Arts/Culture
Race: Multi-Racial
Profile: This collectively run bookstore sells left-oriented political books, hosts and sponsors trainings and study groups, and does tabling at local cultural and political events. The collective also runs educational programs for grassroots groups, including organizational development and how to effectively use consensus decision making. Operates a books for prisoners program, works with local food co-ops, and participates in UCSD university organizing. An important intergenerational activist hub that demonstrates why Barnes & Noble is wack.

GUERRILLA NEWS NETWORK

Contact: Ian Inaba, Anthony Lappe
Address: 2732 Claremont Blvd, Berkeley, CA 94705
Phone: 510-940-2600
Email: ian@gnn.tv
Website: www.gnn.tv
Founded: 2000
Budget: out of pocket
Constituency Age: 13-30 and over
Issues: Prisons/Criminal Justice, Human Rights, Media
Race: White, Asian/Pacific Islander
Profile: Started by ex-MTV employees, GNN provides alternative news and political commentary via the internet. Through insightful documentary-style pieces and reportage, GNN explores the impact the "war on drugs" is having on communities, the post-9/11 "war on terror" and the accompanying assault on civil liberties, as well as militarization, globalization and corporate crime. As a fundraiser for their new film on 9/11, they created a DVD of GNN videos, one of which won at the 2002 Sundance On-Line Film Festival.

HOMIES ORGANIZING THE MISSION TO EMPOWER YOUTH (HOMEY)

Contact: Julia Sabatori
Address: San Francisco, CA
Phone: 415-863-1100
Email: homeysf@earthlink.net
Website: www.homeysf.org
Budget: under 250k
Constituency Age: 12 and under-21
Issues: Youth Development, Gang Issues, Arts/Culture
Race: Multi-Racial

Profile: Youth-led organization providing arts-oriented violence prevention and political education workshops in the Mission District. High school and drop-out kids participate in leadership development trainings, silk screening and business workshops. Produce Listen Up, a newsletter written by teens covering issues such as the criminalization of young people, the prison industry, education, teen homelessness, gang violence and Hip Hop culture. Participate in the annual Youth 2k Festival, an interactive arts/culture/job fair event, and were very active in the No Prop 21 campaign.

HOMIES UNIDOS

Contact: Sylvia Beltran
Address: 1605 West Olympic Blvd, Suite 1040, Los Angeles, CA 90015
Phone: 213-383-7484
Email: homiesunidos@yahoo.com
Website: www.homiesunidos.org
Founded: 1996
Budget: under 250k
Constituency Age: 13-25
Issues: Youth Development, Gang Issues, Prisons/Criminal Justice, Immigrant/Refugee, Human Rights
Race: Latina/o
Profile: Though it states that it is apolitical, HU's organized campaign against INS/LAPD collusion in criminalizing and deporting Latino youth is highly political! Because death squads in El Salvador are known to kill tattooed gang members, deportation can be a life or death matter, so taking its gang truce work one step further, HU sends informed legal counsel into the courts when necessary. They run coping and leadership training, arts and "Know Your Rights" programs in San Salvador, El Salvador and LA.

IMIX BOOKS/DIVINE FORCES

Contact: Sol & Fidel Rodriguez
Address: 3655 S. Grand Ave, Los Angeles, CA 90007
Phone: 213-765-0827
Email: kinan2012@earthlink.net
Website: www.divineforces.org
Founded: 2001
Budget: out of pocket
Constituency Age: 12 and under-30 and over
Issues: Media, Hip Hop Activism, Arts/Culture
Race: People of Color, Multi-Racial, Latina/o
Profile: This husband-wife team has created possibly the hottest Hip Hop spiritual & political bookstore and cultural center on the planet (Imix) and the most important political and spiritual radio show in LA (Divine Forces Radio: "Escape the Matrix.This is real Hip Hop!") on KPFK (90.7 in LA, 98.7 in Santa Barbara). Imix sells Zapatista coffee and indigenous creations while providing a hub for youth organizing activity; Divine Forces keeps folks in the know about global developments as well as local grassroots mobilizations.

INDIGENOUS AND NON-INDIGENOUS YOUTH ALLIANCE (INIYA)

Contact: Sarah Ghiorse
Address: 1148 Stanford Ave, Oakland, CA 94608
Phone: 415-648-0908
Email: sarahg@igc.org
Website: www.iniya.org
Founded: 2000
Budget: out of pocket
Issues: Indigenous Rights, Multi-Culturalism
Race: Multi-Racial
Profile: Youth-founded and led coalition of young people both indigenous and non-indigenous to the Americas. Works to foster intercultural exchange and healing by creating international and regional gatherings for participants to share experiences, beliefs, information, and resources on computer technology, ancient ritual technologies, political and ecological literacy, governance and intercultural legal models.

INNER FIRE PROJECT OF GREENACTION

Contact: Natalia Bernal
Address: 1 Hallidie Plaza, Suite 760, San Francisco, CA 94102
Phone: 415-248-5010
Email: innerfire@greenaction.org
Website: www.greenaction.org
Budget: under 100k
Constituency Age: 13-21
Issues: Indigenous Rights, Housing/Gentrification, Environmental Justice
Race: People of Color
Profile: Seeking to strengthen the presence of young people in the environmental justice movement, Greenaction's new Inner Fire project provides opportunities for young people to create personal, informed pieces of art designed to support grassroots environmental justice campaigns. The young people engage in leadership camps and political art-making sessions, and participate in direct action and community organizing. The Inner Fire Project is currently focused in the Central Valley and West Oakland.

JEWISH YOUTH FOR COMMUNITY ACTION (JYCA)

Contact: Miriam Grant
Address: 2484 Shattuck Ave, Suite 210, Berkeley, CA 94704
Phone: 510-704-7475 x500
Email: jycajustice@hotmail.com
Founded: 1995
Budget: under 100k
Constituency Age: 13-21
Issues: Youth Development, Racial Justice, Prisons/Criminal Justice, LGBTTSQ/Queer
Race: Multi-Racial, White
Profile: Founded by high school students seeking to empower Jewish youth, JYCA runs a leadership training program on community organizing and racial justice. A main JYCA objective is to serve and organize unaffiliated Jewish youth, largely people of color, low-income and queer communities, who are alienated in traditional Jewish spaces. JYCA has developed workshops on education and juvenile jails, publishes a zine on queer inclusion and identity, and participates in local political activity such as police accountability campaigns and anti-war protests.

JUSTACT: YOUTH ACTION FOR GLOBAL JUSTICE

Contact: Colin Rajah
Address: 333 Valencia St #325, San Francisco, CA 94103
Phone: 415-431-4204
Email: info@justact.org
Website: www.justact.org
Founded: 1983
Budget: under 500k
Constituency Age: 13-25
Issues: Youth Development, Racial Justice, Labor/Economic Justice, Environmental Justice, Globalization
Race: People of Color, Multi-Racial
Profile: Through its education and movement-building efforts, JustAct works to inform and engage students and young people (especially youth of color, working class students, and other historically marginalized youth) in grassroots movements for social, economic, and environmental justice. Through training camps, workshops, and experiential learning opportunities, JustAct develops political and economic literacy, leadership and organizing skills to enhance young people's critical analysis of global issues and their relationship to their own lives and communities. A central, active Bay Area organization.

LATE NIGHT COALITION (SFLNC)

Contact: Leslie Ayres
Address: 268 Bush St #2931, San Francisco, CA 94104
Phone: 415-820-3256
Email: info@sflnc.com
Website: www.sflnc.com
Founded: 1999
Budget: out of pocket
Constituency Age: 19-30 and over
Issues: Drug Policy, Public Space, Prisons/Criminal Justice
Race: White
Profile: Clubs are closing, party permits denied; raves and other parties are being targeted by police and politicians. SFLNC is a volunteer-run Political Action Committee that fights for the right to party through protests, legislation, and voter registration/education drives. SFLNC is made up of an intergenerational mix of DJs, musicians, retail store owners and employees, visual artists, groovers, clubbers and ravers, venue owners and employees; it has spawned autonomous affiliates in five other cities.

LET'S GET FREE

Contact: Nicole Lee
Address: 1357A 5th St, Oakland, CA 94607
Phone: 510-451-5466 x311
Email: nicole@ellabakercenter.org
Website: www.ellabakercenter.org
Founded: 2001
Budget: under 250k
Constituency Age: 13-25
Issues: Racial Justice, Prisons/Criminal Justice, Police Accountability
Race: People of Color
Profile: LGF (formerly Third Eye Movement 510) plays a central role in organizing young people of color around prison expansion and police accountability in the Bay Area. Combining Hip Hop culture, community organizing and direct action, LGF was at the forefront of the state-wide No Prop 21 campaign and, more locally, has succeeded in getting a few infamous cops reassigned to desk jobs. A project of the Ella Baker Center, LGF is currently fighting against the Alameda County juvenile Super Jail.

LITERACY FOR ENVIRONMENTAL JUSTICE

Contact: Jenn Sramek
Address: 6220 Third St, San Francisco, CA 94124
Phone: 415-508-0575
Email: livingclassroom@mindspring.com
Website: www.lejyouth.org
Budget: under 1 million
Constituency Age: 12 and under-21
Issues: Youth Development, Environmental Justice
Race: Multi-Racial
Profile: LEJ young people address the environmental problems affecting their communities in Bay View/Hunters Point and surrounding neighborhoods-- due to continual dumping, their low-income communities have double the breast cancer rates and quadruple the asthma rates of other Bay Area communities. LEJ conducts leadership workshops, runs wetlands restoration and neighborhood air quality projects, trains youth in research analysis and environmental public policy, as well as grassroots campaigning skills. LEJ youth are the primary stewards of a local restored park and marsh.

LOS ANGELES INDIGENOUS PEOPLE'S ALLIANCE/ XINACHTLI LEADERSHIP

Contact: Sara Mendoza
Address: 5930 N. Figueroa Blvd #42118, Los Angeles, CA 90031
Phone: 323-221-0712
Email: info@laipa.net
Website: www.laipa.net
Founded: 1992
Budget: under 100k
Constituency Age: 12 and under-21
Issues: Indigenous Rights, Youth Development, Women's Rights, Violence Prevention, Arts/Culture
Race: Latina/o, People of Color, Native American
Profile: Sponsor several programs emphasizing the history of the Indigenous in the Americas and promoting cultural strength and solidarity. Run human and women's rights trainings and rites of passage programs for young women based on indigenous cultures. Mural projects by children are up in several neighborhoods as part of the Violence Prevention Mural Project. Run reproductive and alternative health workshops for women of all ages. All programs are designed by members.

LUNA TIERRA SOL CAFE

Contact: Robert Lopez
Address: 2501 West 6th St, Los Angeles, CA 90057
Phone: 213-380-4754
Email: xipotl@lunatierrasolcafe.com
Website: www.lunatierrasol.com
Founded: 1995
Budget: out of pocket
Constituency Age: 12 and under-30 and over
Issues: Racial Justice, Arts/Culture
Race: Latina/o
Profile: A cooperatively-owned cafe, Luna Tierra Sol serves up affordable healthy food, provides a venue for local artists and serves as a meeting place for community organizers and activists in Los Angeles. They hold open mics, yoga classes, film screenings, discussions and organizing meetings. A lot of planning for the DNC protests happened here. Opened a new East LA location. "One of the only places in LA where you can express yourself, eat a vegetarian meal and be part of social change."

MANDELA ARTS CENTER (MAC)

Contact: Nikki Byers
Address: c/o Youth Empowerment Center, 1357 Fifth St, Oakland, CA 94607
Phone: 510-451-5466 x316
Email: nikki@youthec.org
Founded: 2001
Budget: under 100k
Constituency Age: 12 and under-25
Issues: Youth Development, Racial Justice, Hip Hop Activism, Arts/Culture, Education
Race: Multi-Racial
Profile: MAC is a large space used to meet the artistic and cultural needs of Oakland's youth with Hip Hop and other urban expressions as the driving force for politicization and community involvement. Integrating artistic expression with community issues, MAC's youth-led programming helps young people become politically aware agents for social change. MAC course offerings include political activism, dance, DJing, and mural painting. Currently developing a summer program focused on the affects of environmental racism.

NONCHALANCE COLLECTIVE

Contact: Jeff Hull
Address: 1346 El Centro Ave, Oakland, CA 94602
Phone: 510-531-6200
Email: info@nonchalance.org
Website: www.nonchalance.org
Founded: 2000
Budget: out of pocket
Constituency Age: 13-30 and over
Issues: Public Space, Media, Hip Hop Activism, Arts/Culture
Race: Multi-Racial
Profile: Mysterious movies and posters appear on a wall. Who's behind it? A loose-knit collective of political artists and pranksters including: Oaktown Underground, The Bay Area Aerosol Heritage Society, Properganda, Lentil Village, and the Liberation Drive-in. They create subversive art in public spaces honoring the socio-political heritage of the East Bay.

OLIN

Contact: Nancy Hernandez
Address: 528 20th St, Oakland, CA 94612
Email: Olin@schoolsnotjails.com
Founded: 1997
Budget: under 250k
Constituency Age: 13-25
Issues: Youth Development, Racial Justice, Environmental Justice, Student Rights/Education Reform
Race: Multi-Racial, Latina/o, African-American/Black
Profile: Though it focuses on creating ethnic studies programs in high schools and colleges, Olin also organizes for access to education and against prison construction. It has a successful history of organizing all-city high school student walk-outs, the most recent involving upt to 3000 students. Has been an important training ground for some of California's best young organizers. Currently, Olin is restructuring, but members are working with Schools Not Jails and organizing around Indigenous Peoples Day (October 12th, a.k.a., Columbus Day).

PEOPLE ORGANIZED TO WIN EMPLOYMENT RIGHTS (POWER)

Contact: Steve Williams
Address: 32 7th St, San Francisco, CA 94103
Phone: 415-864-8372
Email: steve@fairwork.org
Website: www.fairwork.org
Founded: 1997
Budget: under 250k
Constituency Age: 19-30 and over
Issues: Welfare/Poverty, Labor/Economic Justice
Race: Multi-Racial
Profile: Young low and no wage workers-- largely women and people of color-- leading a grassroots campaign for employment, worker rights and living wages. Work includes benefits advocacy, community education, lobbying, direct action and coalition building. Currently organizing Workfare Workers to win permanent jobs paying a living wage instead of the temporary, menial sweatshop-wage jobs created in the wake of welfare deform.

PEOPLE'S CORE

Contact: Cory Jung
Address: 300 West Cesar Chavez, Los Angeles, CA 90012
Phone: 213-625-7705
Email: coryjung@yahoo.com
Website: www.geocities.com/kmb_usa
Founded: 2000
Budget: out of pocket
Issues: Militarism, Welfare/Poverty, Racial Justice, Police Accountability, Student Rights/Education Reform
Race: Asian/Pacific Islander
Profile: A tri-chapter high school alliance that is currently focused on police brutality, welfare deform, neighborhood cleanup, access to education and the relevancy of education to their lives. They have also formed a coalition against the war in Afghanistan. By arousing, mobilizing and organizing, this group of Asian/Pacific Islander youth fights local police and global military intervention with Hip Hop culture. They strengthen their organization by engaging in critical self-evaluations and in the last two years they have doubled in size.

PEOPLE'S GROCERY

Contact: Malaika Edwards
Address: 820 Wood St, Oakland, CA 94607
Phone: 510-504-0323
Email: peoplesgrocery@hotmail.com
Website: www.peoplesgrocery.org
Founded: 2002
Budget: under 50k
Constituency Age: 12 and under-30 and over
Issues: Racial Justice, Environmental Justice, Education, Environment
Race: People of Color, Multi-Racial
Profile: Bought an ice cream truck and now drive around West Oakland (which has no quality grocery stores) blasting Hip Hop music and selling affordable organic produce. Trains and employs neighborhood youth and supports local organic farmers of color in its mission to build food security, community self-reliance and economic justice. Innovative and creative, PG participants are also active in environmental justice and other coalitions in the Bay Area.

Drumming during ArtsCore mural project, Highland Park, LA
© Rhea Vedro

Attica surviver at anti-police brutality rally in NYC 2001
© Rhea Vedro

PODER: People Organizing to Demand Environmental and Economic Rights

Contact: Teresa Almaguer

Address: 474 Valencia St #125, San Francisco, CA 94103

Phone: 415-431-4210

Email: poder@igc.org

Budget: under 250k

Constituency Age: 13-18

Issues: Youth Development, Public Space, Housing/Gentrification, Environmental Justice

Race: People of Color, Latina/o, Asian/Pacific Islander

Profile: PODER trains low-income Latino/a youth to organize around their urban environment and to integrate themselves into environmental and economic justice campaigns. Collaborating with the Chinese Progressive Organization on a summer program called Common Roots, 10 youth organizers run joint campaigns on neighborhood displacement and housing issues, community planning and re-zoning, lead poisoning and public space. Youth dialogue with community members, network with other youth organizers, do summer street theater and are working on an EJ curriculum for elementary school youth.

POWER/Concerned Citizens of South Central LA

Contact: Syntyche Jenkins

Address: 4707 South Central Ave, Los Angeles, CA 90011

Phone: 323-846-2505

Website: www.ccscla.org

Founded: 1998

Budget: out of pocket

Constituency Age: 13-21

Issues: Youth Development, Environmental Justice

Race: People of Color, Latina/o, African-American/Black

Profile: POWER, a project of the highly effective CCSCLA, is a grassroots, environmental justice effort led by young people of color in the freeway, incinerator and toxic waste plagued South Central community. POWER orchestrates weekly community clean-ups, leads various environmental hazard education projects (such as air quality testing and asthma prevention), educates and mobilizes through community mural projects, and is working to strengthen grassroots environmental coalitions in the southwest. With mentors at CCSCLA, POWER is beginning to tackle legislative lobbying.

Prison Activist Resource Center (PARC)

Contact: Trinh Le

Address: PO Box 339, Berkeley, CA 94701

Phone: 510-893-4648

Email: parc@prisonactivist.org

Website: www.prisonactivist.org

Founded: 1996

Budget: under 250k

Constituency Age: 12 and under-30 and over

Issues: Racial Justice, Prisons/Criminal Justice, Police Accountability, Human Rights

Race: Multi-Racial

Profile: With a national scope, PARC offers a resource directory of organizations addressing various aspects of the prison crisis. The Curriculum Project sends materials to high school teachers so they can run their own workshops about the prison system, and PARC also has a project that responds to inmate requests for health care, legal help, family visitation rights, books, pens and more. A vital resource run by young folks for the population (young folks) most impacted by the prison crisis.

Project Underground

Address: 1916A MLK Jr. Way, Berkeley, CA 94704

Phone: 510-705-8981

Email: project_underground@moles.org

Website: www.moles.org

Founded: 1996

Budget: under 500k

Constituency Age: 26-30 and over

Issues: Corporate Accountability, Human Rights, Environmental Justice

Race: People of Color, Multi-Racial

Profile: PU is an intergenerational vehicle for environmental, human rights and indigenous rights activists to carry out focused campaigns against abusive extractive resource industries. Pursue non-violent direct action, lobbying and media strategies to raise public awareness about the destructive impact of the mining and oil industries. While exposure of environmental and human rights abuses by corporations and governments is central to their work, PU also focuses on building capacity within encroached upon Indigenous communities to protect and advocate for themselves.

Rainforest Action Network

Contact: Ilyse Hogue

Address: 221 Pine St, Suite 500, San Francisco, CA 94104

Phone: 415-398-4404

Email: rainforest@ran.org

Website: www.ran.org

Founded: 1985

Budget: under 1 million

Constituency Age: 26-30 and over

Issues: Corporate Accountability, Environment

Race: White

Profile: RAN works to protect the Earth's rainforests and support the rights of their inhabitants through education, grass-roots organizing, and nonviolent direct action. RAN accomplishes its mission through dynamic, hard-hitting campaigns that work to bring corporate and governmental policies into alignment with popular support for rainforest conservation. RAN works in alliance with environmental and human rights groups around the world, including Indigenous forest communities and non-governmental organizations in rainforest countries.

SCHOOL OF UNITY AND LIBERATION (SOUL)

Contact: Genevieve Gonzales
Address: 1357A 5th St, Oakland, CA 94607
Phone: 510-451-5466
Email: soulschool@hotmail.com
Website: www.youthec.org/soul
Founded: 1996
Budget: under 500k
Constituency Age: 13-25
Issues: Women's Rights, Welfare/Poverty, Racial Justice, Prisons/Criminal Justice, Education
Race: Multi-Racial
Profile: The nation's premier youth-led political education and organizer training center, SOUL's emphasis is developing young organizers, particularly young women and people of color. SOUL has designed sophisticated curricula that break down, among other things, systems of oppression, the legacy of colonialism and white supremacy, Globalization, revolutionary struggles worldwide, community organizing and leadership skills. The training and education pillar of the youth movement in California, SOUL recently extended its programmatic focus to include national trainings and workshops.

SILICON VALLEY DE-BUG

Contact: Raj Jayadev
Address: 48 S. 7th St, Rm 101, San Jose, CA 95112
Phone: 408-295-4424
Email: svdebug@pacificnews.org
Website: www.siliconvalleydebug.org
Founded: 2001
Budget: under 100k
Constituency Age: 13-25
Issues: Racial Justice, Labor/Economic Justice, Immigrant/Refugee, Media
Race: People of Color, Multi-Racial
Profile: Fresh website and bi-lingual, bi-monthly magazine subtitled, "The Voice of the Young and Temporary." De-Bug publishes the art and stories of low-wage workers in high tech industry, fostering a culture of political organizing in an area sold on its own prosperity. Conduct Know Your Rights workshops focused on the workplace (wages & hours, health & safety, discrimination), writing/art workshops and a critical thinking discussion group. Part of a campaign supporting two Palestinian workers fired from Macy's without cause. Average age=21!

SOLCITY

Contact: Brahm Ahmadi, Koren Giesbiecht
Address: 1148 Stanford Ave, Oakland, CA 94608
Phone: 510-420-8622
Email: solciti@riseup.net
Website: www.solcity.org
Founded: 2002
Budget: under 50k
Constituency Age: 13-21
Issues: Youth Development, Education, Prisons/Criminal Justice, Environmental Justice
Race: Multi-Racial, People of Color
Profile: Newly formed, SolCity runs environmental justice camps for young people of color from low-income communities. The camps are grounded in an arts-based anti-oppression and environmental justice curriculum, in addition to organizing and leadership training. Its first two camps (June and July of 2002) consisted of youth from the Mission district in San Francisco and from the East Bay. Issues explored included brown fields, gentrification, the prison industry, and superfund sites. Camp graduates are preparing to lead local organizing campaigns.

SOUTH CENTRAL YOUTH EMPOWERMENT THRU ACTION (SCYEA)/COMMUNITY COALITION

Contact: Alberto Retana
Address: 8101 South Vermont Ave, Los Angeles, CA 90044
Phone: 323-750-9087
Website: www.ccsapt.org
Budget: under 250k
Constituency Age: 13-18
Issues: Youth Development, Student Rights/Education Reform
Race: Multi-Racial
Profile: Based in five South Central high schools, SCYEA began by using disposable cameras to document their dilapidated schools and lack of books and computers. The resulting campaign successfully reclaimed $153 million that had been allocated to improve LA's worst schools but was being used on the more affluent West Side to fix pools filters and scoreboards. Students run demonstrations, letter writing campaigns and consciousness raising events. Starting a middle school outreach program. Very active in the No Prop 21 campaign.

THE BEAT WITHIN (TBW)/YOUTH OUTLOOK (YO!)

Contact: David Inocencio
Address: 660 Market St #210, San Francisco, CA 94104
Phone: 415-438-4755
Email: mmelamed@pacificnews.org
Website: www.pacificnews.org/yo/beat
Founded: 1996
Budget: under 1 million
Constituency Age: 12 and under-18
Issues: Youth Development, Prisons/Criminal Justice, Media
Race: Multi-Racial
Profile: TBW publishes two weekly 40-100 page newsletters, an eight page monthly and a monthly website, all written by incarcerated youth participating in forty weekly workshops spread between six juvenile hall facilities throughout the Bay Area. YO! is an award-winning literary monthly for youth in the Bay that features reporting, first person essays, comics and poetry. Both are powerful vehicles for self-expression and self-transformation as well as compelling resources for campaigns against the expanding prison industry and criminalization of young people.

THE RUCKUS SOCIETY

Contact: John Sellers
Address: 511 Telegraph Ave #523, Oakland, CA, 94609
Phone: 510-763-7078
Email: ruckus@ruckus.org
Website: www.ruckus.org
Founded: 1995
Budget: under 500k
Constituency Age: 22-30 and over
Issues: Human Rights, Environment
Race: White
Profile: Ruckus provides grassroots environmental and human rights organizers with the tools, and training needed to wage successful non-violent direct action campaigns. Working with a broad range of organizations and movements-- from high school students to workers, from the Bay Area to the Bronx-- Ruckus facilitators share expertise that strengthens the capacity of organizations to challenge corporate and governmental abuse. Projects include regular Action Camps, a Tech ToolBox Action Camp and a ten-city micro-RUCKUS tour with focus on blocking the FTAA.

THIRD WORLD MAJORITY

Contact: Thenmozhi Soundararajan
Address: 1916A Martin Luther King Jr. Way, Berkeley, CA 94709
Phone: 510-465-6941
Email: hellagetto@hotmail.com
Website: www.cultureasaweapon.org
Founded: 2001
Budget: under 100k
Constituency Age: 12 and under-30 and over
Issues: Women's Rights, Violence Prevention, Racial Justice, Media, Arts/Culture
Race: People of Color
Profile: A new media training and production resource center dedicated to global justice run by a collective of young women of color. Programs train participants in the production of politicized new media materials using digital video, the web, graphic design, sound engineering, and animation. TWM's principal organizing focus is the community digital storytelling workshop, which assists people in telling their own stories as short digital videos based on everyday materials in their lives (like photographs, personal drawings, letters, newspaper clippings, etc.).

TURD-FILLED DONUT

Contact: Iggy Scam
Address: PO Box 40272, San Francisco, CA, 94140
Founded: 1997
Budget: out of pocket
Constituency Age: 19-31 and over
Issues: Welfare/Poverty, Public Space, Media, Housing/Gentrification, Homelessness
Race: Multi-Racial, White
Profile: A free newspaper from San Francisco's skid row covering, "6th Street, The Tenderloin and all parts of The City the mayor wishes would just disappear." News by homeless youth and adults examining shelters, gentrification, city hall meetings, law changes, police crackdowns, protests and social services. Throws major political parties in squats, embarrassed the mayor, and confronted the editorial board of the SF Examiner. In the face of sugarcoated discourse on the economy and American democracy, TFD keeps it super real.

UNDERGROUND RAILROAD

Contact: Omana Imani
Address: c/o Youth Empowerment Center, 1357 5th St, Oakland 94607
Phone: 510-451-5466 x313
Email: omana@youthec.org
Website: www.underground-railroad.org
Founded: 1997
Budget: under 250k
Constituency Age: 13-30
Issues: Women's Rights, Racial Justice, Prisons/Criminal Justice, Arts/Culture
Race: Multi-Racial
Profile: UR aims to politicize people through the integration of culture, spirituality and revolutionary politics. The group has evolved from a small collective producing "edutainment" cultural events to a membership organization through which young Bay Area artists are politically active and can collectively produce projects that promote social change. Their training and production workshops inspire and further participation, and their politically oriented art has been most visible in the No Prop 21! and Education Not Incarceration campaigns.

UNITING COMMUNITIES AGAINST WAR & RACISM (UCAWAR)

Contact: Nisha Anand
Address: 1357 5th St, West Oakland, CA, 94612
Phone: 510-763-7078 x303
Founded: 2001
Budget: out of pocket
Constituency Age: 13-30 and over
Issues: Youth Development, Welfare/Poverty, Racial Justice, Militarism, Immigrant/Refugee
Race: Multi-Racial, People of Color
Profile: UCaWAR is a multi-racial volunteer organization fighting for racial and economic justice for low income people and communities of color in the aftermath of 9/11. The group, which calls for an end to US-led international and domestic wars, organizes among immigrant (documented and undocumented) and citizen communities to build opposition to the current war on terrorism. UCaWAR community outreach activities include a tax-day event designed to increase awareness about the military's disproportionate use of government funds.

U'WA DEFENSE PROJECT

Contact: Ana Maria Murrillo
Address: 850 Talbot Ave, Albany, CA 94706
Phone: 510-524-7027
Email: anamaria@mindspring.com
Founded: 1997
Budget: out of pocket
Constituency Age: 12 and under-30 and over
Issues: Corporate Accountability, Indigenous Rights, Environmental Justice
Race: Native American
Profile: UDP provides legal, community development, research and advocacy support to the U'wa people of Colombia as they work to defend their land and culture against the effects of oil exploitation. UDP was founded in 1997 by Terence Freitas after U'wa leaders sent representatives to Los Angeles, CA to seek help from the international community. Freitas was killed in 1999 with two other American activists in Colombia. An intergenerational and Colombian led organization, UDP created and launched leadership trainings in 2001.

WE INTERRUPT THIS MESSAGE

Contact: Malkia Cyril
Address: 2588 Mission St #212, San Francisco, CA 94110
Phone: 415-621-3302
Email: info@interrupt.org
Website: www.interrupt.org
Founded: 1996
Budget: under 500k
Constituency Age: 13-30 and over
Issues: Welfare/Poverty, Racial Justice, Prisons/Criminal Justice, Media
Race: People of Color, Multi-Racial
Profile: A key bi-coastal media training organization, WITM partnered with dozens of groups to publish landmark exposés of NY Times and Bay Area media coverage criminalizing youth of color. Formed a Bay Area Youth Media Council (YMC) and trained mothers how to reframe the debate on welfare reform. Trained thousands in media/PR strategy-- most recently in response to 9/11. WITM closed its doors in June 2002 for a year to restructure. YMC can be contacted via Movement Strategy Center (pg. 60 and pg. 159.)

WHISPERED MEDIA/VIDEO ACTIVIST NETWORK

Contact: Adams, Francine, Jeff & Mark
Address: PO Box 40130, San Francisco, CA 94140
Phone: 415-789-8484
Email: wm@videoactivism.org
Website: www.whisperedmedia.org
Founded: 2000
Budget: under 25k
Constituency Age: 13-30 and over
Issues: Globalization, Housing/Gentrification, Arts/Culture, Media
Race: Multi-Racial, White

Profile: Whispered Media was founded as an intergenerational collective that promotes the use of video and other alternative media tools in progressive grassroots movements. Whispered Media offers video training, collects archival political footage, and produces video works about specific grassroots campaigns and organizations. Recently produced "Boom:The Sound of Eviction," which explores the relationships between the dot-com boom (and bust) and community displacement and gentrification in the San Francisco Bay Area, particularly in the largely working class and Latina/o Mission District.

WIRETAP MAGAZINE

Contact: Twilight Greenaway
Address: 77 Federal St, San Francisco, CA 94107
Phone: 415-284-1420 x310
Email: info@wiretapmag.org
Website: www.wiretapmag.org
Founded: 1999
Budget: under 250k
Constituency Age: 13-25
Issues: Media
Race: Multi-Racial
Profile: A youth-led project of Alternet and the Independent Media Institute, Wiretap is a weekly magazine geared towards socially conscious youth, shedding light on issues neglected by the mainstream media. Wiretap is an important outlet for young writers and artists, showcasing their investigative pieces, essays, opinions and artwork. Facilitating networking between activists, Wiretap serves as a portal that directs its audience to other activist publications, resources and organizations. As per their subtitle, these are, "youth in pursuit of the dirty truth."

WISE UP!/CHIRLA (COALITION FOR HUMANE IMMIGRANT RIGHTS OF LA)

Contact: Ana Chaidez
Address: 1521 Wilshire Blvd, Los Angeles, CA 90017
Phone: 213-353-1333 x228
Email: wiseup_la@yahoo.com
Website: www.geocities.com/wiseup_la
Founded: 2000
Budget: out of pocket
Constituency Age: 13-25
Issues: Student Rights/Education Reform, Racial Justice, Immigrant/Refugee
Race: Latina/o
Profile: A project of the immigrant rights organization CHIRLA, Wise Up focuses on issues of immigrant youth in higher education. They won a recent victory with the passing of California's AB 540 legislation, which allows immigrant students the opportunity to pay in-state tuition vs. out of state tuition. They hold forums on educational injustice and discrimination at high schools and universities, and are actively engaged in a legalization campaign which, if passed, would grant college students citizenship upon graduation.

YOUNG WOMEN UNITED FOR OAKLAND
Contact: O'Shen Turman
Address: PO Box 23802, Oakland, CA 94623
Phone: 510-452-0185
Email: ywufo@earthlink.net
Founded: 1998
Budget: under 250k
Constituency Age: 13-21
Issues: Youth Development, Women's Rights, Violence
Prevention, Health Care, Homelessness
Race: People of Color
Profile: Run by and for young women from 14 to 21, YWUO
reaches out to young women working in the street economy
and living on the street, providing free condoms, hygiene kits,
and educational materials on drug treatment using the harm
reduction philosophy. In addition to providing leadership and
social change workshops, YWUO also recruits women from the
streets to work for the agency after intensive empowerment
training. A unique and successful combination of youth service,
development and activism.

YOUTH BUILD IMMIGRANT POWER PROJECT
Contact: Lily Wang
Address: 310 8th St #301, Oakland, CA 94607
Phone: 510-268-0192
Email: lilywang@igc.org
Founded: 1997
Budget: under 250k
Issues: Youth Development, Women's Rights, Welfare/Poverty,
Racial Justice, Labor/Economic Justice
Race: Asian/Pacific Islander
Profile: Youth identified campaigns address the language
barrier, low wage jobs, poverty, and insufficient resources in
public schools. YBIP brings together young Asian immigrants
for paid multimedia and organizing training programs. They
conduct an ageism workshop to strengthen their intergenera-
tional organizing. When AIWA Asian Immigrant Workers Clinic
found that 99% of garment workers have work related injuries,
YBIP participants connected this fact to their own families and
launched an inspired campaign to improve factory conditions.

YOUTH EMPOWERMENT CENTER (YEC)
Contact: Rona Fernandez
Address: 1357 Fifth St, Oakland, CA 94607
Phone: 510-451-5466
Email: info@youthec.org
Website: www.youthec.org
Founded: 2000
Budget: out of pocket
Constituency Age: 13-25
Issues: Youth Development, Racial Justice, Prisons/Criminal
Justice, Hip Hop Activism, Arts/Culture
Race: Multi-Racial, Latina/o, Asian/Pacific Islander,
African-American/Black
Profile: YEC brought together several of the Bay Area's

strongest youth-led organizations (SOUL, Youth Force Coalition,
Underground Railroad, C-Beyond, Mandela Arts Center) to
create a support center for the development of other youth
projects. YEC serves a broad range of youth projects with
technical assistance, training and organizational development
programs. YEC also fiscally sponsors grassroots youth projects
that do exciting work but lack non-profit status. This just might
be the most potent youth organizing hub and intermediary in
the US.

YOUTH FOR ENVIRONMENTAL JUSTICE PROJECT
Contact: Yuki Kidokoro
Address: 5610 Pacific Boulevard #203, Huntington Park, CA
90255
Phone: 323-826-9771 x105
Email: yuki@cbecal.org
Website: www.cbecal.org
Founded: 1997
Budget: under 100k
Constituency Age: 13-21
Issues: Youth Development, Environmental Justice
Race: People of Color
Profile: A project of Communities for a Better Environment,
Youth for EJ is a serious crew of environmental organizers
coming out of predominantly Latino communities in Southeast
LA. They just won a campaign to stop the Nueva Azalea power
plant from being built in their community despite all the media
hype on the recent California energy crisis. They are now
engaged in researching oil and energy industries, zoning and
land use issues. They also co-convene the important Youth In
Action Conference.

YOUTH FOR ENVIRONMENTAL SANITY! (YES!)
Contact: Ocean & Michelle Robbins
Address: 420 Bronco Rd, Soquel, CA 95073
Phone: 831-465-1091
Email: info@yesworld.org
Website: www.yesworld.org
Founded: 1990
Budget: under 500k
Constituency Age: 12 and under-30
Issues: Environment, Education, Multi-Culturalism,
Globalization, Genetic Engineering
Race: White, Multi-Racial
Profile: Founded to inspire high school students to confront the
environmental crisis, YES! grew into a perpetual speaker's
bureau that has now reached more than 600,000 young people
worldwide. In between political education tours, YES! Youth
Leadership JAMS bring together young visionaries from all over
the world for restful reflection, networking and cross-cultural,
cross-issue dialogue. A highly visible organization in the
emerging youth movement that emphasizes process and
discussion as a means of both raising awareness and
preventing activist burn-out.

YOUTH FORCE COALITION

Contact: Khadine Bennett
Address: 1357 5th St, Oakland, CA 94607
Phone: 510-451-5466
Email: khadine@youthec.org
Website: www.youthec.org
Founded: 1998
Budget: under 250k
Constituency Age: 13-30
Issues: Student Rights/Education Reform, Labor/Economic Justice, Prisons/Criminal Justice, Youth Development
Race: Latina/o, African-American/Black, Multi-Racial
Profile: Emerging out of the first Critical Resistance: Beyond the Prison Industrial Complex conference, YFC connects Bay area youth activists for focused campaigns against the expanding prison industry and its impact on youth of color. As part of the Youth Empowerment Center, provides technical assistance, publicizes events and enables organizations to support each other's work. Leaders in the No Prop 21 fight, YFC is currently working against expansion of Alameda County's super-jail. A great example of the power of coalition work.

YOUTH MAKING A CHANGE (YMAC)

Contact: Jose Luis Pavon
Address: 459 Vienna St, San Francisco, CA 94112
Phone: 415-239-0161
Email: ymac@colemanadvocates.org
Website: www.colemanadvocates.org
Founded: 1991
Budget: under 250k
Constituency Age: 13-21
Issues: Youth Development, Student Rights/Education Reform, Public Space, Prisons/Criminal Justice
Race: Multi-Racial
Profile: Y-MAC is a youth-led training and action group of teens organizing for education and school reform, healthy school environments and access to public space. Y-MAC is a project of Coleman Advocates, a pioneering community advocacy project that spearheaded the successful 1% for youth campaigns in Oakland and San Francisco. Students hold mock elections in city schools, run leadership training and organizing workshops, publish a newsletter, sponsor teen events and actively research critical local issues as part of their campaign development.

YOUTH MEDIA COUNCIL

Contact: Malkia Cyril
Address: 1611 Telegraph Ave #510, Oakland, CA 94612
Phone: 510-444-0640
Founded: 2001
Budget: under 250k
Constituency Age: 13-21
Issues: Media, Police Accountability, Prisons/Criminal Justice, Youth Development
Race: People of Color

Profile: Currently housed by the Movement Strategy Center, YMC works to improve the media effectiveness of Bay Area grassroots youth organizations. Publish a media watchdog newsletter, produce public service announcements regarding local and national youth issues, and are setting up a media school to teach media strategy and offer on-site PR and communications support. Recently released a groundbreaking report about the representation of youth in the media highlighting the dominance of racist and criminal portrayals of youth of color.

YOUTH OF OAKLAND UNITED (YOU)

Contact: Venus Rodriguez
Address: 1920 Park Blvd, Oakland, CA 94606
Phone: 510-452-2010 x22
Email: dphillips@peopleunited.org
Website: www.peopleunited.org
Founded: 1994
Budget: under 50k
Constituency Age: 13-18
Issues: Youth Development, Welfare/Poverty, Racial Justice, Prisons/Criminal Justice, Housing/Gentrification
Race: People of Color
Profile: YOU, a project of the pioneering PUEBLO, is a youth-led organizing training and action group working to address the concerns of Oakland youth. Have produced documentaries on issues such as gentrification, unfair suspensions and their campaign to increase city funding for youth programs. Participate in the Youth Media Council, which challenges the media's negative portrayal of youth. Spearheaded the Kids First coalition which successfully won the allocation of $72 million for youth development programs.

YOUTH ORGANIZING COMMUNITIES (LOS ANGELES)

Contact: Luis Sanchez
Address: 2811 Whittier Blvd, Los Angeles, CA 90023
Phone: 323-780-7606
Email: yoc@schoolsnotjails.com
Website: www.schoolsnotjails.com
Founded: 1998
Budget: under 100k
Constituency Age: 13-30
Issues: Youth Development, Student Rights/Education Reform, Racial Justice, Prisons/Criminal Justice, Militarism
Race: People of Color, Multi-Racial
Profile: YOC is a direct action network of youth in Southern California focusing on educational and environmental justice, multicultural curricula and social change. YOC identifies racism, sexism and class discrimination reinforced through testing and tracking as the historical roots of the current educational crisis. Their coalition played an instrumental role in the "No on Prop 21" campaign by hosting the movement's website, organizing a state-wide summit of youth organizers, and organizing banner drops on freeways. Conducts media activism summer trainings.

Concert protesting the building of new youth Super-Jail, Oakland City Hall
© Hans Bennet

Youth Organizing Communities (San Diego)

Contact: Tommy Ramirez
Address: 3727 Camino Del Rio S, San Diego, CA 92108
Phone: 619-203-3714
Email: tvalentino@yahoo.com
Website: www.schoolsnotjails.com
Founded: 1999
Budget: out of pocket
Constituency Age: 13-30 and over
Issues: Welfare/Poverty, Student Rights/Education Reform, Racial Justice, Prisons/Criminal Justice
Race: People of Color, Multi-Racial
Profile: This youth-led branch of YOC was founded to educate citizens about the ways Proposition 21 criminalizes and imprisons youth of color in CA. Among YOC-SD's campaigns is a movement to end standardized testing and to increase the budget for public schools in low-income areas deemed "failures" by state educational standards. YOC is building community support for the Schools Not Jails movement through political education presentations and trainings given in schools and other local organizations.

Youth Radio

Contact: Jaime Talley
Address: 1809 University Ave, Berkeley, CA 94703
Phone: 510-841-5123
Email: youthradio@youthradio.org
Website: www.youthradio.org
Founded: 1992
Budget: over 1 million
Constituency Age: 12 and under-18
Issues: Youth Development, Media, Arts/Culture
Race: Multi-Racial
Profile: Outstanding national after-school and summer programs in three states that produce shows for National Public Radio and other outlets. Led by peer and adult teachers, programs are youth produced. Stories range from police violence against youth to 9/11, senior prom experiences to environmental justice, personal journeys to investigative reporting; recent programs done in partnership with Afghani and Israeli youth. The Bay Area chapter remains focused on radio production but is now doing television and web design training as well.

Youth Speaks

Contact: James Cass
Address: c/o The Writing Center, 2169 Folsom St, Suite 100, San Francisco, CA 94110
Phone: 415-255-9035
Email: info@youthspeaks.org
Website: www.youthspeaks.org
Founded: 1996
Budget: under 500k
Constituency Age: 13-21
Issues: Youth Development, Arts/Culture
Race: Multi-Racial
Profile: Youth Speaks works to build a generation of leaders through the spoken and written word, believing that creativity and self-expression is essential to developing youth leadership. Through peer-to-peer outreach in public middle and high schools, YS runs a youth leadership program for 13-19 year olds and promotes internal leadership development through their Youth Advisory Board. They offer performance and publication opportunities for spoken word, slam poetry, and creative writing.

Youth United for Community Action (YUCA)

Contact: Oscar Flores
Address: 1836A Bay Rd, East Palo Alto, CA 94303
Phone: 650-322-9165
Email: ncyuca@igc.org
Founded: 1993
Budget: under 1 million
Constituency Age: 13-21
Issues: Youth Development, Multi-Culturalism, Education, Environment
Race: People of Color
Profile: Run entirely by young people of color under 30, YUCA conducts "toxic tours" and intensive political education workshops, promotes high school organizing and places youth in environmental justice/social justice paid internships throughout the Bay Area and LA. A powerful model of youth-led organizing, YUCA successfully campaigned to prevent the placement of a polluting plant in East Palo Alto and regularly fights hazardous industrial development in California. LA chapter is campaigning for appropriate use of city funds to improve school conditions.

COLORADO

Barrio Warriors de Aztlan

Contact: Rudy Balles
Address: 701 Logan St, Suite 109, Denver, CO 80209
Phone: 303-777-3117
Email: graspgang@yahoo.com
Website: www.barriowarriors.net
Founded: 1992
Budget: out of pocket
Constituency Age: 12 and under-30 and over
Issues: Youth Development, Violence Prevention, Racial Justice, Police Accountability, Indigenous Rights
Race: Multi-Racial, People of Color
Profile: Barrio Warriors is an organization led by Chicano youth committed to promoting Indigenous culture, creating alternative educational opportunities, and mobilizing for Indigenous self-determination. The organization grew from a popular zine called Todos Somos Raza (TMS), which uses art and culture to

unify Chicano youth, and later a second, more political and satirical zine, Con Safos. Dedicated to Chicano Power and the liberation of Aztlan, Barrio Warriors also works to build alliances with other Indigenous nations.

STEPSTONE CENTER

Contact: Felicia Trevor Gallo
Address: PO Box 2044, Carbondale, CO 81623
Phone: 970-963-3483
Email: stepstone@discovercompass.org
Founded: 1998
Budget: under 50k
Constituency Age: 13-18
Issues: Racial Justice, Housing/Gentrification, Globalization, Environment
Race: Multi-Racial, White, Native America, Latina/o
Profile: Modeled after the Highlander Center in Tennessee, Stepstone was conceived of as a training ground for social justice activists in the West. It has since become an epicenter of progressive activity in the greater Aspen area, halting a planned INS holding center through non-violent protests and lobbying, hosting symposiums on sustainable energy sources and land use, taking young people to Cuba to study development models, and collaborating with local LGBT and Latino organizations in anti-discrimination mobilizations and campaigns.

STUDENT WORKER

Contact: Max Holleran
Address: c/o Boulder High School, 1604 Arapahoe Ave, Boulder, CO 80302
Phone: 303-444-2042
Email: maxholleran@hotmail.com
Website: www.studentworker.org
Founded: 1999
Budget: under 25k
Constituency Age: 13-18
Issues: Media, LGBTTSQ/Queer, Education, Student Rights/Education Reform
Race: Multi-Racial, White
Profile: Active in 3 public high schools, this youth-led organization works to involve peers in local and international issues through their monthly newspaper, teach-ins and actions. Issues covered range from mandatory testing in public schools to discrimination, from globalization to the post 9/11 climate. Through these efforts, SW has greatly increased youth participation in local activism. Energetic and creative, when confronted with homophobic high school administrators, SW led their own non-violent direct action-- a "kiss in" on the school's lawn.

STUDENTS 4 JUSTICE

Contact: Yuriana DeLuna
Address: c/o Colorado Progressive Coalition, 1420 Ogden St, 1st Fl, Denver, CO 80218
Phone: 303-866-0908
Email: coprogressive@aol.com
Website: www.progressivecoalition.org
Founded: 1995
Budget: under 250k
Constituency Age: 13-18
Issues: Student Rights/Education Reform, Racial Justice, Labor/Economic Justice, Globalization
Race: Multi-Racial
Profile: A program of the Colorado Progressive Coalition, S4J is a nationally recognized, youth-led organizing effort to build a new generation of student leaders in the African-American, Mexicano and Chicano, Native American, and Asian/Pacific-Islander communities. S4J works in Denver public high schools to expose and end racial tracking and discriminatory disciplinary action. They also work to end child labor, Nike sweatshops and corporate welfare. S4J provides a strong youth presence in all components of CPC's civil rights and economic justice work.

THE SPOT

Contact: Dave DeForest-Stalls
Address: 2100 Stout St, Denver, CO 80205
Phone: 303-295-3700
Email: dave@thespot.org
Website: www.thespot.org
Founded: 1994
Budget: under 1 million
Constituency Age: 13-25
Issues: Youth Development, Violence Prevention, Gang Issues, Arts/Culture
Race: Multi-Racial
Profile: The hot spot for Denver youth; where else can you find a breakdancing studio, music recording studios, computers for graphic and web design, a dark room and graffitti space? A night-time drop-in center, The Spot provides job training, GED classes, and computer training. Also fights for the issues its youth find important, including criminalization of young people of color in public spaces like malls, public funding for youth services, and police harassment of artists selling their music without vendor licenses.

WESTERN COLORADO ACTION NETWORK (WeCAN)

Contact: Deanna Woolston
Address: PO Box 1931, Grand Junction, CO 81502
Phone: 970-256-7650
Website: www.wccongress.org/wecan.cfm
Founded: 2001
Budget: under 50k
Constituency Age: 13-21
Issues: Environmental Justice, Environment

Race: White

Profile: Led by college and high school students, WeCAN organizes to protect the Mesa Valley. Through press conferences, radio spots, lobbying trips to Washington, D.C. and campus organizing, they promote environmental protection, recycling and energy efficiency. Currently waging a campaign against extractive industries targeting local lands for oil and gas drilling. A project of the Western Colorado Congress, WeCAN runs hikes throughout the Mesa Valley to foster community stewardship and is the lead sponsor for a proposed wilderness area.

CONNECTICUT

CONNECTICUT GLOBAL ACTION NETWORK (CGAN)

Contact: Adam Hurter, Cliff Thornton
Address: 19 Kenneth Circle, Windsor, CT 06095
Phone: 860-343-9318
Email: cgan@topica.com
Website: www.efficacy-online.org
Founded: 2000
Budget: out of pocket
Constituency Age: 13-30 and over
Issues: Militarism, Labor/Economic Justice, Globalization, Corporate Accountability, Drug Policy
Race: Multi-Racial, White
Profile: CGAN was started after the anti-globalization protests in Seattle. It continues to mobilize participation for IMF/World Bank/WTO demonstrations worldwide. In an exciting example of local/global action, CGAN organized a rally with janitors in Hartford in solidarity with the global justice demonstration in Prague; the overall local campaign won important living wage gains. CGAN is currently connected to Efficacy, Connecticut's leading grassroots drug policy group. The group's current focus is on rejecting the FTAA.

NATIONAL YOUTH AND STUDENT PEACE COALITION (NYSPC)

Contact: Adam Hurter
Address: 19 Kenneth Circle, Windsor, CT 06095
Phone: 860-285-8831
Email: ahurter@wesleyan.edu
Website: www.nyspc.net
Founded: 2001
Budget: out of pocket
Constituency Age: 19-25
Issues: Student Rights/Education Reform, Militarism, Globalization
Race: Multi-Racial
Profile: NYSPC united 17 national youth and student groups with different missions for the purpose of mounting opposition to the "War on Terrorism." Through workshops, teach-ins and

peace protests, the Coalition is raising awareness about the Patriot Act, post –9/11 civil liberties violations, racial profiling, civilian casualties in Afghanistan and other aspects of foreign and domestic policy that go unreported in mainstream media. The Coalition is providing necessary communication between national organizations and is working to build long-term infrastructure for continued coordination.

DELAWARE

CAMPUS GREENS

Contact: Laura Devorak
Address: University of Delaware, Newark, DE 19716
Phone: 804-359-4880
Email: odyssey@udel.edu
Website: www.gpde.org/~udgreens
Founded: 2000
Budget: out of pocket
Constituency Age: 18-25
Issues: Environment, Student Rights/Education Reform, Globalization, Women's Rights
Race: White, Multi-Racial
Profile: Active on campus around enviromental issues, political education, globalization, women's rights and student rights. Organizes U Del's EarthJam and Greenfest, as well as ongoing campaigns to ban credit card solicitation on campus and to replace Starbucks with Fair Trade coffee. Host wide range of speakers, participate in an annual debate with the College Republicans and Democrats, and support other campus groups (e.g. Amenesty International, Muslim Student Union). Serves as the DE hub for marches and conferences in Philly and DC.

DISTRICT OF COLUMBIA

ANTI-CAPITALIST CONVERGENCE (ACC)

Address: Washington, DC
Phone: 703-276-9768
Email: info@abolishthebank.org
Website: www.abolishthebank.org
Budget: out of pocket
Constituency Age: 13-25
Issues: Globalization
Race: White
Profile: Organizes non-violent direct actions against meetings of the World Bank/IMF, WTO, and other such global institutions. Incredibly well organized, with fliers, organizer packets, local contacts, directions, and clear action plans for each protest posted on their website. These folks even have info about where to eat and stay when you come to march! Dedicated to social change both internationally and locally, ACC is involved in Critical Mass, a campaign against the closing of DC General Hospital and broader privitization issues.

ASIAN AMERICAN LEAD

Contact: Sandy Dang
Address: 3045 15th St NW, Washington, DC 20009
Phone: 202-884-0322
Budget: out of pocket
Constituency Age: 19-30 and over
Issues: Housing/Gentrification, Education
Race: Asian/Pacific Islander
Profile: Asian American Lead serves, empowers, and organizes Asian youth, especially those from the Vietnamese community, many of whom are "at-risk" low-income immigrants or refugees facing language barriers. AAL's approach to empowerment is holistic and comprehensive, employing a combination of services, leadership development and actvism in order to develop and strengthen ties between youth, families, and the community. It also builds coalitions with Latino and African-American groups to fight gentrification and other shared issues and struggles.

BLACK YOUTH VOTE!

Contact: Nnena Nchege
Address: 1025 Vermont Ave NW, Suite 1010, Washington, DC 20005
Phone: 202-659-4929
Email: ncbcp@ncbcp.org
Website: www.bigvote.org
Founded: 1976
Budget: under 100k
Constituency Age: 19-30 and over
Issues: Youth Development
Race: People of Color
Profile: A new initiative of the National Coalition on Black Civic Participation, Black Youth Vote! identifies and trains campus and street youth coordinators who work to build local coalitions to increase voter education and participation. Run by an advisory board of 35 young people drawn from the Coalition's member organizations, Black Youth Vote! seeks to register, organize, and mobilize young African-Americans ages 14-30 to become politically educated and to affect public policy.

CENTRAL AMERICAN RESOURCE CENTER (CARE-CEN)

Contact: Saul Solorzano
Address: 1459 Columbia Rd, Washington, DC 20009
Phone: 202-328-9799
Email: rina.reyes@cacerendc.org
Website: www.carecendc.org
Founded: 1981
Budget: under 500k
Constituency Age: 12 and under-30 and over
Issues: Racial Justice, Immigrant/Refugee, Housing/Gentrification, Globalization
Race: Latina/o
Profile: A multigenerational organization supporting Latino immigrants in DC's exploding Central American (primarily Salvadoran and primarily young) community. Works with tenants to fight gentrification and to protect tenant rights, advocates for and educates undocumented workers, offers citizenship and ESL classes, and provides translation and legal aid services. CARECEN also actively lobbies, organizes and participates in protests for immigrant rights. Has a second office in Arlington, VA.

CIVIL RIGHTS SUMMER

Contact: Donna Wilson
Address: 1629 K St NW, Suite 1000, Washington, DC 20006
Phone: 202-466-3311
Email: lccr@civilrights.org
Website: www.civilrights.org
Founded: 2000
Budget: over 1 million
Constituency Age: 19-21
Issues: Student Rights/Education Reform, Racial Justice, Labor/Economic Justice
Race: Multi-Racial
Profile: Civil Rights Summer (CRS) is a project of the Leadership Conference on Civil Rights, an organization that has led the fight for equal opportunity and social justice for half a century. CRS is a program for first and second year college students that propels youth into action and broadens their understanding of social justice through workshops, panels, group projects, speakers, mentoring and local actions. An important incubator for young organizers as well as an excellent example of the power of intergenerational efforts.

DEMOCRACY ACTION PROJECT/DEMOCRACY SUMMER

Contact: Amy Quinn
Address: 733 15th St NW, Suite 1020, Washington, DC 20005
Phone: 202-234-9382 x238
Email: nicksuplina@yahoo.com
Website: www.democracysummer.org
Founded: 2001
Budget: under 100k
Constituency Age: 13-25
Issues: Racial Justice, Corporate Accountability
Race: Multi-Racial
Profile: Inspired by the great presidential election theft of 2000, DAP exposes the role of corporations in the electoral process and advocates for the restoration of American democracy. Through its Democracy Summer, DAP trains young people how to organize for electoral reform, voting rights and accountability for elected officials. Housed at the Institute for Policy Studies (the nation's oldest progressive think tank), DAP is a partnership of USSA, Black Youth Vote, Interfaith Alliance, Public Campaign and other electoral politics organizations.

Voices of Color, Faces of Hope: Peace for People before Politics
© Christine Wong and Mandela Arts Center/Underground Railroad, 2001

Companeras: Honoring Revolutionary Women Cultural Workers
© Christine Wong and Underground Railroad

FREE BURMA COALITION

Contact: Jeremy Woodrum
Address: 1101 Pennsylvania Ave SE, Suite 204, Washington, DC 20003
Phone: 202-547-5985
Email: info@freeburmacoalition.org
Website: www.freeburmacoalition.org
Founded: 1995
Budget: under 100k
Constituency Age: 13-25
Issues: Human Rights, Corporate Accountability
Race: White, People of Color
Profile: Free Burma Coalition is an intergenerational organization with member groups and affiliates in 28 countries. Through internet organizing, public education, policy advocacy, consumer boycotts and divestment campaigns, FBC works to raise awareness about the human rights violations occurring daily under Burma's military dictatorship. The coalition works to build international support for the National League for Democracy, the people-supported political party led by 1991 Nobel Peace Prize winner Aung San Suu Kyi.

LISTEN, INC.

Contact: Ditra Edwards
Address: 1436 U St NW, Suite 201, Washington, DC 20009
Phone: 202-483-4494 x14
Email: nburrowes@lisn.org
Website: www.lisn.org
Founded: 1998
Budget: under 1 million
Constituency Age: 13-25
Issues: Arts/Culture, Youth Development, Student Rights/Education Reform
Race: Multi-Racial
Profile: LISTEN incubates the Youth Education Alliance-- a group of youth and young adults organizing to improve DC public high schools and build power for young people. Nationally, LISTEN is spearheading a mapping project on the experiences of youth organizers in twelve U.S. cities. Through its Global Exchange Leadership Program LISTEN has provided urban activists the opportunity to meet and strategize with their counterparts in other countries. LISTEN also convenes and provides intense technical assistance and training to youth organizations.

MIDNIGHT FORUM

Contact: Daniel Berry
Address: 3426 16th St NW #T-1, Washington, DC 20010
Phone: 202-276-5632
Email: akadino@aol.com
Website: www.metroteenaids.org
Founded: 2000
Budget: under 25k
Constituency Age: 13-25
Issues: Hip Hop Activism, Environment Justice, Police Accountability
Race: Multi-Racial
Profile: Midnight Forum trains young leaders, organizers, and entrepreneurs to develop their own campaigns and projects. Most recent efforts have focused on using youth culture and Hip Hop as tools for political education and outreach. A project fiscally-sponsored by Metro TeenAIDS (a peer HIV education network), Midnight Forum is tackling issues relevant to DC communities, such as the environment and harrasssment by the police.

NATIONAL ORGANIZERS ALLIANCE

Contact: Ron Garcia
Address: 715 G St SE, Washington, DC 20003
Phone: 202-543-6603
Email: info@noacentral.org
Website: www.noacentral.org
Budget: under 500k
Constituency Age: 19-30 and over
Issues: Environmental Justice, Immigrant/Refugee, Labor/Economic Justice, Prisons/Criminal Justice, Racial Justice
Race: Multi-Racial
Profile: A dynamic, intergenerational switchboard of community organizers. NOA holds a 600 person annual conference (which every young organizer should go to), disseminates a national events calendar and has created an excellent job bank. Offers health and retirment benefits as well as zillions of other creative and important resources that feisty, experienced NOA members have initiated.

SEXUAL MINORITY YOUTH ASSISTANCE LEAGUE (SMYAL)

Contact: Tracee Ford
Address: 410 7th St SE, Washington, DC 20003
Phone: 202-546-5940
Email: margaux.db@smyal.org
Website: www.smyal.org/activism.htm
Budget: under 1 million
Constituency Age: 13-21
Issues: Youth Development, Racial Justice, LGBTTSQ/Queer, Health Care, HIV/AIDS
Race: Multi-Racial
Profile: An excellent LGBTQ youth service org that increasingly has an activist edge through its Queer Youth for Social Justice (QYSJ) project. Serve as a regional support base for LGBTQ youth through their community center, offering job opportunities, HIV/AIDS outreach, job training and service referrals. QYSJ's focus has ranged from the boy scouts to exlusionary policies to the "war on terrorism." Campaigns involve letter writing, community service projects, political education forums and non-violent protests.

SIERRA STUDENT COALITION

Contact: Myke Bybee
Address: 408 C St NE, Washington, DC 20002
Phone: 888-JOIN-SSC
Email: ssc-info@sierraclub.org
Website: www.ssc.org
Founded: 1995
Budget: under 500k
Constituency Age: 13-25
Issues: Environment
Race: Multi-Racial, White
Profile: Campaigns include protecting wild lands (think oil drilling in Alaska Wilderness), international trade issues (fighting fast track trade legislation), as well focusing on clean cities and suburban sprawl. They have an organizing skills training for high school and college youth, and also sponsor backpacking outings in endangered wilderness areas. SSC is the largest network of student environmental organizers in the country.

STUDENT LABOR ACTION PROJECT (SLAP)/ JOBS WITH JUSTICE

Contact: Treston Faulkner
Address: 501 Third St NW, Washington, DC 20001
Phone: 202-434-1106
Email: treston@jwj.org
Website: www.jwj.org/SLAP/slap.htm
Founded: 2000
Budget: under 100k
Issues: Labor/Economic Justice, Immigrant/Refugee
Race: Multi-Racial
Profile: SLAP is builiding a nationwide coalition of college groups fighting for living wages, immigrant rights and an end to sweatshops. In partnership with Jobs With Justice, SLAP has become a clearinghouse for information on workers rights, an organizing training center and a virtual switchboard for campus organizing taking place in more than twenty states. Wisely, SLAP actively seeks intergenerational organizing opportunities with local unions, adult activists and community leaders.

STUDENT PEACE ACTION NETWORK (SPAN)

Contact: Jamie Gooley
Address: 1819 H St #425, Washington, DC 20006
Phone: 202-862-9740 x3051
Website: www.gospan.org
Budget: under 50k
Constituency Age: 13-25
Issues: Militarism, Corporate Accountability
Race: Multi-Racial, White
Profile: SPAN moved into high gear after 9/11 and convened one of the major strategy sessions for the emerging campus peace movement. Part of the National Youth and Students Peace Coalition, SPAN challenges the links between military spending and cuts in education and social services, while actively opposing an open-ended "war on terrorism." Coordinates student peace efforts mainly on college campuses, but involves youth off-campus as well.

STUDENTS FOR SENSIBLE DRUG POLICY (SSDP)

Contact: Shawn Heller
Address: 2000 P St NW, Suite 210, Washington, DC 20036
Phone: 202-293-4414
Email: ssdp@ssdp.org
Website: www.ssdp.org
Founded: 1998
Budget: under 50k
Constituency Age: 13-25
Issues: Prisons/Criminal Justice, Drug Policy
Race: Multi-Racial, White
Profile: With 156 chapters, SSDP is the fastest growing student organization on college campuses. Moving beyond the legalization of marijuana, SSDP fights racist drug policing and sentencing and is actively resisting Plan Colombia, the US funded crop fumigation and military aid "strategy" implemented as part of the "war on drugs." Major campaigns include protecting the right to use medical marijuana, supporting harm reduction initiatives and eliminating provisions in the Higher Education Act that cut financial aid for students caught with drugs.

THE EMPOWER PROGRAM

Contact: Rosalind Wiseman
Address: 1312 8th St NW, Washington, DC 20001
Phone: 202-882-2800
Email: empower@empowered.org
Website: www.empowered.org
Founded: 1994
Budget: under 500k
Constituency Age: 13-21
Issues: LGBTTSQ/Queer, Youth Development, Violence Prevention, Student Rights/Education Reform
Race: Multi-Racial
Profile: Working locally with youth to end the culture of violence in America. Workshops and trainings with high school and middle school youth deconstruct the fundamentals of violence, including issues of power and privilege, social dynamics, and cultural expectations of men and women. There is active youth participation in program development and policy through the Girls' Advisory Board (GAB), made up of young women across the country ages 14-18. A former GAB member recently received a MTV Youth Hero Award.

THE MOVEMENT FOUNDATION

Contact: Matthew Payne
Address: 813 Tuckerman St NW, Washington, DC 20011
Phone: 202-291-8363
Email: themove2k@hotmail.com

Website: www.divinecipher.com
Founded: 1997
Budget: out of pocket
Constituency Age: 13-30 and over
Issues: Racial Justice, Hip Hop Activism, Arts/Culture
Race: People of Color, African-American/Black
Profile: Not a movement or a foundation, but the oldest, most popular and politically infused Black youth arts organization in Washington, DC. Entirely youth-led, the Movement Foundation hosts 8-10 open mic spoken word events each month (including the Black L.U.V. Festival and the One Common Unity Alternatives to Violence Rally), creating a cultural space for political engagement among urban youth. It also provides reading materials, encourages Black youth to express themselves in creative expression workshops and has started high school chapters.

UNITED STATES STUDENT ORGANIZATION (USSA)

Contact: Julia Beatty
Address: 1413 K St NW, 10th Fl, Washington, DC 20005
Phone: 202-347-3319
Email: comm@usstudents.org
Website: www.usstudents.org
Founded: 1947
Budget: under 250k
Constituency Age: 13-25
Issues: Youth Development, Student Rights/Education Reform, Racial Justice, LGBTTSQ/Queer, Labor/Economic Justice
Race: Multi-Racial
Profile: The oldest student-led organization in the country, and one of few national, member-controlled, youth-led organizations, USSA operates as a lobby in DC and as a national network fighting to guarantee public access to higher education. Other campaigns include eliminating racist school mascots and the National Student Day of Action. Caucuses include National GLBT, the National Women's Student Coalition, and the National People of Color Student Coalition.

UNITED STUDENTS AGAINST SWEATSHOPS (USAS)

Address: 888 16th St NW #303, Washington, DC 20006
Phone: 202-NO-SWEAT
Email: emailusas@yahoo.com
Website: www.usasnet.org
Founded: 1997
Budget: under 100k
Constituency Age: 13-25
Issues: Labor/Economic Justice, Immigrant/Refugee, Human Rights, Globalization, Corporate Accountability
Race: Multi-Racial, White, Latina/o
Profile: Central in the most groundbreaking campus organizing movement of the '90s, USAS successfully pressured many universities to adopt ethical codes of conduct in the production

of school apparel. Later helped create the Worker's Rights Consortium as an alternative to governmental and corporate monitoring of labor practices. Now working with a broader definition of "sweatshops," USAS's 250 plus chapters have connected the dots, taking on issues like living wages, prisons, democratization of unions, farm labor organizing, and corporate presence on campuses.

YOUNG WOMEN'S PROJECT

Contact: Nadia Moritz
Address: 1328 Florida Ave, Suite 2000, Washington, DC 20009
Phone: 202-332-3399
Email: nadiamoritz@youngwomensproject.org
Website: www.youngwomensproject.org
Founded: 1994
Budget: under 500k
Constituency Age: 13-18
Issues: Women's Rights, Violence Prevention, Reproductive Rights, Health Care
Race: Multi-Racial, Latina/o, African-American/Black
Profile: Committed to self-empowerment of young women through the development of leadership and community organizing skills. Teen staff define and run several campaigns on multiple issues, including creation of a sexual harassment policy in their school district and implementing foster care regulations that truly protect young people. Their after school program runs in 3 high schools, providing peer-led workshops on sexual and mental health, violence, body-image, conflict resolution and oppression. Community outreach programs include support and leadership training for young mothers.

YOUTH ACTION RESEARCH GROUP (YARG)

Contact: Natalie Avery
Address: c/o Manna CDC, PO Box 26049, Washington, DC 20001
Phone: 202-232-2915
Email: dhaiman@mannadc.com
Founded: 1998
Budget: out of pocket
Constituency Age: 13-25
Issues: Youth Development, Welfare/Poverty, Racial Justice, Housing/Gentrification
Race: Multi-Racial, People of Color, Latina/o, Asian/Pacific Islander
Profile: YARG trains young people from Mt. Pleasant & Columbia Heights how to research, critically analyze and then define campaigns addressing key issues in their low-income communities. Emphasis is placed on developing skills needed to document voices excluded from governmental or mass media accounts of urban neighborhoods. The group's curriculum development project is based on popular education models, interviewing local residents as a means of including everyone in the community building process. Campaigns include gentrification, welfare deform, employment and education.

YOUTH ADVOCACY INSTITUTE

Contact: James Forman
Address: 1851 9th St NW, Washington, DC 20001
Phone: 202-939-9080
Website: www.seeforever.org
Founded: 2002
Budget: under 100k
Constituency Age: 13-25
Issues: Youth Development, Violence Prevention, Student Rights/Education Reform, Racial Justice, Prisons/Criminal Justice
Race: Latino/a, African-American/Black
Profile: Institute focus groups identify key issues, engage in trainings on legislative analysis, organizing and media strategies, and then collaborate with adult organizers and policy advocates to take action. Strategies have ranged from lobbying at legislative hearings to non-violent direct actions. Participate in the Justice for DC Youth Coalition working for juvenile system reform and youth sensitive policing. The Institute is a project of See Forever, which runs programs for court-involved youth and is recognized as a model alternative to incarceration.

FLORIDA

ARISE

Contact: Luke Dutch
Address: 439D W. Gaines St, Tallahassee, FL 32301
Phone: 850-577-0700
Email: ariseinfocenter@yahoo.com
Website: www.tallytown.com/arise
Founded: 2002
Budget: out of pocket
Constituency Age: 13-25
Issues: Public Space, Education
Race: White
Profile: A new info center that houses a library (books, zines, films), runs a free store (food, art supplies, clothes, bicycle parts), and sponsors an open forum community magazine. Conducts workshops in graffiti, racism trainings, organic gardening, self defense, alternative energy sources and bike repair. Houses Food not Bombs and Radical Cheerleaders. Staffed primarily by volunteers, the center is a good activist hub and an excellent starting place to find out what's going on in Tallahassee.

CENTER FOR PARTICIPANT EDUCATION – FREE SCHOOL (CPE)

Contact: Karma Bennett, Tony Williams
Address: A 303K Oglesby Union, Tallahassee, FL 32304
Phone: 850-644-6577
Email: sgacpe@admin.fsu.edu
Website: www.fsu.edu/~sga/cpe
Founded: 1970
Budget: under 50k
Constituency Age: 13-30 and over
Issues: Student Rights/Education Reform, Education, Environment
Race: White, Multi-Racial
Profile: Active in multiple campaigns both on and off-campus, CPE is in intergenerational but largely youth-led organization that has created a free school based on its participatory curriculum and alternative information sources. Housing a library and offering classes on social change, environmental justice and physical/spiritual well-being, the center also connects a variety of smaller focus groups such as Pax Christi and the National Organization for the Reformation of Marijuana Laws. Among the most consistent progressive campus organizations in the country.

CIVIC MEDIA CENTER

Contact: Sheila Bishop
Address: 1021 W. University Ave, Gainesville, FL 32601
Phone: 352-373-0010
Website: www.civicmediacenter.org
Founded: 1993
Budget: under 25k
Constituency Age: 13-30 and over
Issues: Media, Arts/Culture
Race: White, Multi-Racial
Profile: Started by a group of local publishers (including those responsible for the Gainesville Iguana, Counterpoise and the now defunct Moon Magazine) and inaugurated by Noam Chomsky in 1993, Civic Media Center is a library of the "non-corporate press," advocate of alternative media nationally and a nexus of local organizing in Florida. CMC hosts poetry jams, shows, skill-shares, office spaces for other grassroots groups, and an incredible film, book and periodicals library. An important intergenerational hub in a largely conservative area.

JACKSONVILLE AREA SEXUAL MINORITY YOUTH NETWORK (JASMYN)

Contact: Ernie Selorio, Daneisha Queen
Address: PO Box 380103, Jacksonville, FL 32205
Phone: 904-389-3857
Email: eselorio@jasmyn.org
Website: www.jasmyn.org
Founded: 1993
Budget: under 250k
Constituency Age: 13-21
Issues: Youth Development, Racial Justice, LGBTTSQ/Queer
Race: Multi-Racial
Profile: The best thing we have found in Jacksonville, JASMYN is mainly a service oriented, safe space for LGBTQ youth, but increasingly is involved in local organizing initiatives. Led protests against Winn-Dixie, Inc. headquarters for their discrimination against transgendered employees, and, following

youth testimony, forced the school board to add sexual orientation to the harrassment policy. Currently lobbying in Tallahassee for the Dignity for All Students Act. Intergenerational, but youth have major power in the organization.

RADICAL CHEERLEADERS
Contact: Aimee, Cara & Coleen Jennings
Address: PO Box 961, Lake Worth, FL 33460
Phone: not a chance buddy!
Email: eh_mee@yahoo.com
Website: www.radicalcheers.org
Founded: 1997
Budget: out of pocket
Constituency Age: 12 and under-30 and over
Issues: Prisons/Criminal Justice, Arts/Culture, Women's Rights
Race: White
Profile: "It's getting pretty quiet, I think we need a riot!" With dozens of chapters worldwide from Poland to Portland, the Radical Cheerleaders combine humor with critical analysis, using guerrilla theater to spice up protests on issues ranging from body image to globalization, queer politics to police accountability, education to sweatshops. Highly creative and adaptable, this strategy has become very popular.
Each autonomous squad is networked through the website; order your cheer books and get your pompoms out.

RADICAL STUDENT UNION
Contact: Peter Tsolkas
Address: PO Box 961, Lake Worth, FL 33460
Phone: 561-547-6686
Email: littleprince1@juno.com
Founded: 2000
Budget: out of pocket
Constituency Age: 13-25
Issues: Student Rights/Education Reform
Race: White
Profile: Founded during an anti-globalization teach-in, RSU uses creative direct action to confront the education system. Plastered OBEDIENCE TRAINING CLASSES banners and posters at local high schools, have opened a lending library and reading room, offer alternative information to military recruitment, and have distributed thousands of copies of their newsletters at more than a dozen schools (dodging security guards and administrators in the process). Includes participants from Vero Beach, Ocala, Orlando, St. Augustine, Naples, Miami, West Palm & Gainesville.

SOUTHERN POWER UNIVERSITY
Contact: Denise Perry
Address: 11625 NE 2nd Ave, Miami Shores, FL 33161
Phone: 305-576-8779
Founded: 2000
Budget: under 250k

Constituency Age: 13-30 and over
Issues: Environmental Justice, Housing/Gentrification
Race: Multi-Racial, People of Color, African-American/Black, Latina/o
Profile: A key multi-racial organizing hub of Southern Florida, SPU won a major campaign for low-income housing (which included defeating a HOPE VI proposal), and continues to focus on workers rights, education and environmental justice. Lead primarily by young women of color, SPU uses traditional grass-roots strategies, from petitioning and flyering, to lobbying and direct action. Making coalition work a priority, SPU is networked with most groups in Florida working on racial and economic justice.

STONE SOUP COLLECTIVE
Contact: Hugh Webber
Address: 1020 S. Orange Ave, Orlando, FL 32806
Phone: 407-999-7700
Email: richbully@aol.com
Website: www.stonesoupcollective.org
Founded: 1999
Budget: out of pocket
Constituency Age: 13-30 and under
Issues: Prisons/Criminal Justice, Militarism, LGBTTSQ/Queer, Environment
Race: Multi-Racial
Profile: The creative, activist hub of Central Florida, regularly attracting people from Daytona to Pensacola. Runs the Central Florida IMC and local manifestations of other national ideas such as a political education "stitch and bitch" sewing circle, Food Not Bombs, Critical Mass and the women-led Clitical Mass. Organizes the cultural/political Buckwild Fest (14 workshops, 21 bands), guerilla gardening, and a Book through Bars program for prisoners in Florida. House an infoshop of thousands of books, zines, and videos. Steady making moves.

STUDENT FARMWORKER ALLIANCE
Contact: Brian Payne
Address: c/o Coalition of Immokalee Workers, PO Box 603, Immokalee, FL 34143
Phone: 941-657-8311
Email: sfw_alliance@hotmail.com
Website: www.ciw-online.org
Founded: 2000
Budget: out of pocket
Constituency Age: 13-30
Issues: Education, Labor/Economic Justice, Immigrant/Refugee
Race: White, African-American/Black, Latina/o
Profile: SFA involves students in the movement against labor exploitation, particularly in association with the Coalition of Immokalee Workers and the Taco Bell boycott campaign (advocating for better working conditions for tomato farmworkers). The Alliance coordinates networks of students at 90

colleges to create local boycotts and alternative Spring Break programs where students work in the fields for a week. In March 2001, SFA organized a month-long series of nationwide protests, including on-campus workshops and local Taco Bell demonstrations.

TEEN DREAM TEAM OF FARMWORKERS SELF-HELP

Contact: Felicitia Morales, Youth Leader
Address: 14848 Porter St, Dade City, FL 33523
Phone: 352-567-1432
Budget: out of pocket
Constituency Age: 12 and under-21
Issues: Youth Development, Immigrant/Refugee, Environmental Justice, Health Care
Race: Latina/o
Profile: The Teen Dream Team is a group of over 60 middle and high school students dedicated to addressing the social and environmental problems facing their communities. The Team advocates for and participates in community clean-ups, as well as provides tutoring, counseling, political education, and bi-lingual assistance in schools within farm worker communities. They've hosted community gatherings with school officials and police to explore solutions to discriminatory policing, crime, drugs, and local gang isues.

GEORGIA

ASIAN PACIFIC LESBIAN BISEXUAL TRANSGENDER NETWORK

Contact: Ami Mattison
Address: PO Box 5683, Atlanta, GA 31107
Phone: 866-206-9069 x2321
Email: aplbtn@yahoogroups.com
Founded: 1993
Budget: out of pocket
Constituency Age: 19-30
Issues: LGBTTSQ/Queer, Women's Rights
Race: Asian/Pacific Islander
Profile: Sought out by women from all over the Southeast as a social center for the Asian/Pacific LBT community, the Network hosts monthly potluck dinners, participates in direct actions, holds community educational forums and conducts research projects. Current focus is a capital campaign to expand their resources, generate educational materials and create a substantial web presence. Political campaigns shift with membership but they remain a consistent support base in an under-resourced region.

BLACK YOUTH LEADERSHIP DEVELOPMENT INSTITUTE

Contact: Torkwase Karame
Address: 1115 Habersham St, Savannah, GA 31401
Phone: 912-233-0907

Email: karametorkwase@hotmail.com
Founded: 1992
Budget: under 25k
Constituency Age: 13-25
Issues: Youth Development, Environmental Justice, Arts/Culture, Education
Race: African-American/Black
Profile: BYLDI, an intergenerational project of Citizens for Equality, hosts three annual conferences, each gathering approximately 60 African-American youth from the Southeast. Provide organizing training and leadership skills, teach water sampling and how to create health surveys, discuss decision-making and risk-taking, learn about African history, conflict resolution, entrepreneurship, freedom songs and Tai-Chi! Graduates work in their own communities and also travel to work with West and South African youth on environmental justice issues and entrepreneurial projects. Developing a national institute.

CRIMETHINC EX-WORKERS COLLECTIVE

Contact: various made-up names
Address: 2695 Rangewood Dr, Atlanta, GA 30345
Email: info@crimethinc.com
Website: www.crimethinc.com
Founded: Mid 1990s
Budget: out of pocket
Constituency Age: 12 and under-30 and over
Issues: Globalization, Arts/Culture, Corporate Accountability, Media, Militarism
Race: Multi-Racial
Profile: A network of witty, unidentified people that have produced some of the most provocative books (Days of War, Nights of Love & Evasion) and one of the most compelling underground arts and social scenes for a generation of punks, radicals, and other people not satisfied with the current system. The collective finds creative ways to oppose globalization and gentrification; also sells Harbinger Magazine.

EMPTY THE SHELTERS (ETS)

Contact: Nasreen Jilani
Address: PO Box 6019, Atlanta, GA 31107
Phone: 404-371-8834
Email: etsatlanta@riseup.net
Website: www.etsatlanta.8m.net
Founded: 1995
Budget: under 25k
Constituency Age: 13-25
Issues: Welfare/Poverty, Labor/Economic Justice, Housing/Gentrification, Homelessness
Race: Multi-Racial
Profile: During the summer, ETS members live together in cheap communal housing, working on local and national homelessness, health-care, labor, and human rights issues. ETSers participate in workshops ranging from ecofeminism and media relations to art for social change. Caucuses based on

race, class, sexual orientation, and gender ensure that all voices are heard and valued in their own right. ETS also coordinates an "alternative" Spring Break program to introduce new students to the work and issues they take on.

SistaSpace

Contact: Candace Jones Meadows
Address: 5412 Trumpet Vine Trail, Mableton, GA 30126
Phone: 404-484-1098
Email: mscandacejones@yahoo.com
Website: www.sistaspace.org
Founded: 2000
Budget: out of pocket
Constituency Age: 12 and under-18
Issues: Women's Rights, Education, Arts/Culture, Youth Development
Race: African-American/Black
Profile: A unique program offering both one-on-one and group mentoring for 6th through 12th graders. Offers "whole-being" development with programs ranging from museum trips to sexual health workshops to book clubs to service-projects to political education. SistaSpace is all about empowering young women to transform themselves and their communities.

VOX– Youth Communication

Contact: Rachel Wallack
Address: 145 Nassau St, Suite A, Atlanta, GA 30303
Phone: 404-614-0040
Email: dear_vox@mindspring.com
Website: www.youthcommunication-vox.org
Founded: 1993
Budget: under 500k
Constituency Age: 13-21
Issues: Media
Race: Multi-Racial
Profile: A by teens, for teens newspaper reaching 80,000 young people in the Metro Atlanta area with full-length features, interviews, resource boxes, personal essays and editorials covering issues from racial justice to educational reform to poverty. Recent articles include an account of a young woman's experience with anti-Afgani sentiment, and a powerful editorial on sexism in advertising. Provides a space for activist, incarcerated and homeless youth to communicate their viewpoints to each other without fear of censorship.

Youth Pride

Contact: Ron Hidalgo
Address: 302 East Howard Ave, Decatur, GA 30030
Phone: 404-378-7722
Email: ron@youthpride.org
Website: www.youthpride.org
Founded: 1999
Budget: under 500k
Constituency Age: 13-25
Issues: Youth Development, LGBTTSQ/Queer

Race: Multi-Racial
Profile: Only support organization for GLBT and questioning community in Metro-Atlanta area. Hosts support and discussion groups for young women, older women, young men, older men, and Latinos. Provide confidential HIV testing and safer sex education programs. Social activities include karaoke, poetry slams, and pool competitions. Most programs are facilitated and planned by a young person and an adult in collaborative partnership.

Youth Task Force

Contact: Angela Brown
Address: PO Box 11078, Atlanta, GA 30310
Phone: 404-752-8275
Email: youthtaskforce@msn.com
Founded: 1992
Budget: under 500k
Constituency Age: 13-30 and over
Issues: Education, Environmental Justice, Labor/Economic Justice, Youth Development
Race: African-American/Black, Latina/o
Profile: Among the oldest black youth founded and led organizations in the country, this South-wide group takes on issues facing young people of all races: massive imprisonment, inadequate school funding, racism in communities and schools, and joblessness. Campaigns include the case of Lacresha Murray, a 14-year-old Black child wrongfully accused and tried for murder as an adult. YTF educates, trains, mobilizes and networks young people, often on campuses of historically Black colleges, working to improve their schools, colleges and communities.

HAWAII

Haiku Tea Party

Contact: Vangie Jones
Address: 331 Haloa Rd, Haiku, HI 96708
Phone: 808-572-0804
Email: cliffburton64@hotmail.com
Website: www.geocities.com/haiku_tea_party
Founded: 2001
Budget: out of pocket
Constituency Age: 13-30 and over
Issues: Indigenous Rights, Environmental Justice, Racial Justice, Media, Arts/Culture
Race: White
Profile: Dealing with issues of globalization, indigenous rights, and militarism, HTP's motto is Emma Goldman's saying "If I can't dance at your revolution, I don't want to be a part of it." Their work includes screening political videos, hosting performances and the revolutionary spinnings of Mirth the Mad DJ. They meet monthly and have eight working groups including "Making Maui a Self-sustaining Community," "Sovereignty and the Non-Native question," "Truth and lies in the media," and "Floating Hub of Information."

Hui Ho'oulo

Contact: Adrian Kamali'i
Address: 1682 Kalakaua Ave, Honolulu, HI 96826
Phone: 808-945-9953
Email: akamalii@hawaii.rr.com
Budget: out of pocket
Constituency Age: 19-25
Issues: Indigenous Rights, Youth Development, Environmental Justice, Education
Race: Multi-Racial, People of Color, Native American
Profile: Hui Ho'oulo has three divisions-- educational, political, and environmental-- with its programs for high school students based in "Hawaiian Homesteads," which are essentially reservations/housing projects. Programs include environmental field trips that are part youth development, part political education, part physical labor as planting and clean-up work is also done. Participants learn about traditional Hawaiian methods of economic production and are lobbying before the state legislature to protect and restore the environment.

Malama Makua

Contact: Sparky Rodrigues
Address: 86–222 Puhawai Rd., Wai'anae, HI 96792
Phone: 808-696-2823
Email: srodrigues@olelo.org
Budget: under 25k
Constituency Age: 12 and under-30 and over
Issues: Environmental Justice, Arts/Culture, Education, Militarism, Indigenous Rights
Race: White, Native American
Profile: Organizing intergenerationally since 1992, Malama Makua works to get the US military to clean up its military training sites in Makua Valley, Oahu, site of Makua Military Reservation, through litigation and political/cultural education. To re-educate their community about native history and culture, the young people of Makua have made films focusing on the legacy of the Makua Valley, run community environmental tours through the sites, engage in Makua's legal actions, and work on environmental impact studies.

Refuse and Resist Hawaii

Contact: Lis Rees
Address: PO Box 521, Honolulu, HI 96809
Phone: 808-598-4653
Email: rnrhawaii@aol.com
Website: www.refuseandresist.org
Founded: 1987
Budget: out of pocket
Constituency Age: 13-30 and over
Issues: Prisons/Criminal Justice, LGBTTSQ/Queer, Human Rights, Corporate Accountability
Race: Multi-Racial
Profile: "The island is a floating aircraft carrier, one of the most repressive and difficult places to do political work," says Lis,

a long-time organizer. R&R Hawaii's work includes combatting the Asian Development Bank (sister of the World Bank), supporting local effort to pass laws allowing for same-sex marriages, and pro-choice protesting and lobbying. Recently hosted a festival at the University of Hawaii bringing together anti-war, pro-choice and pro-speech artivists to build coalitions around other issues that affect the Hawaiian community.

IDAHO

Bisexual Gay Lesbian Alliance for Diversity (BGLAD)

Contact: Lindsey Vandenberg
Address: Boise State University, 1910 University Drive, Boise, ID 83725
Phone: 208-426-3171
Email: bsubglad@hotmail.com
Website: www.progressionproject.org
Founded: 1998
Budget: under 25k
Constituency Age: 13-30
Issues: Women's Rights, LGBTTSQ/Queer, Arts/Culture
Race: White, Multi-Racial
Profile: BGLAD promotes awareness and advocates for the LGBTQ community at Idaho State University. The only organization of its kind on campus, this group provides counseling, hosts conferences and organizes events to create dialogue and raise consciousness. The Progression Project is one of their annual activities highlighting music and poetry performances, anti-oppression workshops and art activism. BGLAD is very connected to the broader Boise/Pocatello community and is open to off-campus membership.

Idaho Community Action Network (ICAN)

Contact: Jessica Fry
Address: 1311 West Jefferson, Boise, ID 83702
Phone: 208-385-9146
Email: jfry_ican@hotmail.com
Website: www.nwfco.org
Founded: 1982
Budget: under 500k
Constituency Age: 13-30 and over
Issues: Labor/Economic Justice, Youth Development, Welfare/Poverty
Race: Native American, Latina/o, White
Profile: The largest grassroots organization for low-income families in the state, ICAN is an intergenerational group that mobilizes and organizes low-income families to take actions for social and economic justice. Run a youth organizing training institute and host a youth conference; increasingly have younger activists in decision-making roles. ICAN successfully campaigned to raise the state minimum wage for farm workers.

World Economic Forum demonstration, NYC 2002
© Bryan Iler

IDAHO PROGRESSIVE STUDENT ALLIANCE

Contact: Devin Kelly
Address: 1412 West Idaho, Boise, ID 83702
Phone: 208-331-7028
Email: ipsa_moderator@hotmail.com
Website: www.idahopsa.org
Founded: 1998
Budget: under 25k
Constituency Age: 13-30 and over
Issues: Labor/Economic Justice, Environmental Justice, Globalization, Campaign Finance, Corporate Accountability
Race: Multi-Racial
Profile: Known as one of the most radical groups in the state, IPSA is based on four campuses (Boise State, University of Idaho, Idaho State and Albertsons College). Focused on environmental justice, worker rights, globalization and corporate accountability issues. Organize an annual Progressive Advocacy Training conference, and recently campaigned against the National Governors Conference held in Idaho for its acceptance of corporate sponsorship and support of the "war OF terror."

ILLINOIS

A-ZONE

Contact: Rob Ebright
Address: 2129 N. Milwaukee Ave, Chicago, IL 60647
Phone: 312-494-3455
Email: azone@azone.org
Website: www.azone.org
Founded: 1993
Budget: out of pocket
Constituency Age: 13-30 and over
Issues: Corporate Accountability, Prisons/Criminal Justice, LGBTTSQ/Queer, Housing/Gentrification, Globalization
Race: Multi-Racial
Profile: A major organizing hub in Chicago which provides space for The Bike Collective, Freeware (computer collective), Food Not Bombs, Matches of Mahem (festival), Queerzone, Blackmarket Records, Chicago Radical Ananchist Youth Organizing Network, Animal Defense League, and Trans/Action. Houses a huge radical lending library, a huge zine archive and an art space. Hosts a variety of radical events, workshops, and performances-- everything from Thunderpussy and the Queer Family Circus to the 4th of July Unamerikkan Picnic. Organizing a suburban chapter in Aurora.

ANTI-RACIST ACTION (ARA) CHICAGO

Contact: Alex
Address: 1573 N. Milwaukee #420, Chicago, IL 60622
Phone: 312-409-1432
Email: ara_chicago@ziplip.com
Website: www.azone.org/ara

Founded: 1996
Budget: out of pocket
Constituency Age: 13-30 and over
Issues: Immigrant/Refugee, Racial Justice, Militarism, LGBTTSQ/Queer
Race: Multi-Racial, African-American/Black, Latina/o
Profile: Among the strongest ARA chapters, ARA-Chicago conducts research on the right wing, publishes the ARA Research Bulletin, runs community workshops, and wages direct actions against the KKK, The Steel Front and World Church of the Creator (WCC), a white supremacist group which has been increasingly active since WCC member Benjamin Smith went on a shooting spree in downstate Illinois in 1999. ARA is unique among anti-racist organizations nationally because it is almost entirely run and funded by folks under 25.

ARAB-AMERICAN ACTION NETWORK

Contact: Hatem Abudeyyeh
Address: 6400 S. Kedzie, Chicago, IL 60629
Phone: 773-436-6060 x61
Email: aaan@aaan.org
Website: www.aaan.org
Founded: 1995
Budget: under 250k
Constituency Age: 12 and under-30 and over
Issues: Violence Prevention, Youth Development, Racial Justice, Immigrant/Refugee, Human Rights
Race: Multi-Racial, Middle Eastern
Profile: The Arab-American Action Network has been an unshakeable support base for Chicago's Arab communities in the aftermath of 9/11. AAAN works to address issues common to most immigrant communities-- language, employment, discrimination-- but now increasingly tackles repression and violence. Its office at the 20-year-old Arab Community Center was destroyed by arson shortly after 9/11. AAAN continues to educate and advocate for citizen and immigrant communities, organize against racial and religious profiling, and to participate in city-wide coalitions promoting solidarity.

BATEY URBANO

Contact: Michael Reyes
Address: 2647 W. Division, Chicago, IL 60622
Phone: 989-714-1774
Email: chibateyurbano@hotmail.com
Website: www.bateyurbano.com
Founded: 2002
Budget: out of pocket
Constituency Age: 12 and under-30 and over
Issues: Arts/Culture, Racial Justice, Education
Race: Latina/o, People of Color
Profile: BU is a for-youth-by youth arts and political space incubated by the Puerto Rican Cultural Center. Campaigns strive to embrace issues facing all Latinos, whether it is Vieques, amnesty for undocumented workers or discrimination.

Art, lectures, music and discussion of local issues occur on designated nights-- Poetry with Purpose, All High-School, All Women, Conscious 4 Elements of Hip Hop and more. Batey means "sacred space" in Taino (Puerto Rican Indigenous culture).

BLOCKS TOGETHER YOUTH COUNCIL
Contact: Jennifer Dillon
Address: 3914 West North Ave, Chicago, IL 60647
Phone: 773-276-2194
Email: btogether@aol.com
Website: www.blockstogether.org
Founded: 1993
Budget: under 500k
Constituency Age: 12 and under-30 and over
Issues: Police Accountability, Student Rights/Education Reform, Youth Development
Race: Latina/o, White, African-American/Black
Profile: Blocks Together is a neighborhood-based organization working on issues of crime and safety, police brutality and the criminalization of young people. Its youth organizing component focuses on harassment of students within schools by the administration and security guards. Two young people sit on the board (out of 10) and the Youth Council's campaigns are all determined by youth between the ages of 11 and 17.

CHI-TOWN LOW DOWN
Contact: Anton Miglietta
Address: PO Box 804728, Chicago, IL 60680-4108
Phone: 773-334-8287
Founded: 1993
Budget: out of pocket
Constituency Age: 13-30 and over
Issues: Prisons/Criminal Justice, Housing/Gentrification, Welfare/Poverty, Media
Race: Multi-Racial
Profile: A major nerve center of sophisticated multi-racial youth activism in Chicago, Chi-Town Low Down has published 11 issues of a bilingual, full color, 20,000 circulation newspaper educating and organizing young people about local political issues from gentrification to Chicago's infamous anti-gang loitering ordinance. Organizing around affordable housing, Chi-Town Low Down produced their first educational documentary called Stop the Land Grab and hosts a weekly television call-in show. They also throw Hip Hop benefit parties and hold political discussion groups.

CHICAGO DIRECT ACTION NETWORK
Contact: Ted Cain
Address: Chicago, IL
Phone: 773-704-8515
Email: chicagodan@yahoogroups.com
Website: www.chicagodan.org
Founded: 2000
Budget: out of pocket

Constituency Age: 13-30 and over
Issues: Human Rights, Racial Justice, Globalization, Arts/Culture, Education
Race: Multi-Racial, White, Latina/o, Asian/Pacific Islander
Profile: Brilliant solidarity actions from Taco Bell Boycotts to a May Day "Carnival Against Capitalism" where they create a mobile art project out of collected neighborhood trash. Fought to build a school in their overcrowded Chicano neighborhood. Helped win a $5 million allocation from the city after staging a direct action with 80 people at Mayor Daley's house (!). Organize a summit to create a Midwest radical network and skill shares on direct actions, media workshops, legal briefings, and medical trainings.

DEPARTMENT OF SPACE AND LAND RECLAMATION
Contact: Josh MacPhee
Address: PO Box 476971, Chicago, IL 60647
Email: spaceandland@hotmail.com
Website: www.counterproductiveindustries.com
Founded: 2001
Budget: out of pocket
Constituency Age: 13-30 and over
Issues: Media, Housing/Gentrification, Arts/Culture, Prisons/Criminal Justice
Race: White, Multi-Racial
Profile: "An autonomous City department devoted to returning Chicago to those that work, live, and play in it," this free-floating creative action team stages imaginative interventions and art shows that promote dialogue about public space, gentrification and the urban environment's many racial and economic politics. Hosts gatherings, runs a vibrant on-line community and organizes targeted protests, e.g., brought 500 people to jam up MTV's Real World when it came to further gentrify Wicker Park. Also known as Autonomous Territories of Chicago.

INSIGHT ARTS
Contact: Craig Harshaw
Address: 1545 W. Morse, Chicago, IL 60626
Phone: 773-973-1521
Email: chiaia65@aol.com
Founded: 1995
Budget: under 250k
Constituency Age: 13-21
Issues: Arts/Culture, Education, Youth Development
Race: Multi-Racial
Profile: Located in the Rogers Park neighborhood of Chicago, Insight Arts is one of the most politically sophisticated youth arts organizations in the US. Fending off gentrification, IA succeeding in stopping state and local governments from placing a TIF (tax rebate for corporations) on their neighborhood. Community based, they give free arts education and activism classes to youth and adults, teach in schools, and present regular youth performances, exhibitions and art actions on local issues.

INTERFAITH YOUTH CORE (IFYC)

Contact: Eboo Patel
Address: 4844 N. Monticello, Chicago, IL 60625
Phone: 773-960-0854
Email: eboopatel@hotmail.com
Website: www.ifyc.org
Founded: 1998
Budget: under 50k
Constituency Age: 13-30 and over
Issues: Media, Human Rights, Globalization, Multi-Culturalism
Race: White, Asian/Pacific Islander, Multi-Racial
Profile: IFYC's pilot project in Chicago serves as model for interfaith youth coalitions worldwide, aiming to bring youth leaders of different faiths together to strategize and build an international network. Projects include an Action Exchange, a Sacred Stories Project (connecting personal histories to current political issues), and ongoing interfaith reflection. In 1999, IFYC created a successful program for 8000 youth attending the World Parliament on Religions in South Africa. Post-9/11 campaigns have addressed anti-immigrant and religious discrimination.

INTERNATIONAL PEOPLE'S DEMOCRATIC UHURU MOVEMENT (InPDUM)

Contact: Banio Carpenter
Address: PO Box 377603, Chicago, IL 60637
Phone: 773-913-2843
Email: INPDUM_Chicago@yahoo.com
Website: www.inpdumchicago.com
Budget: under 25k
Constituency Age: 12 and under-30 and over
Issues: Militarism, Racial Justice, Prisons/Criminal Justice
Race: African-American/Black, Multi-Racial
Profile: InPDUM fought for the freedom of the unjustly incarcerated Fred Hampton, Jr. for 10 years, ultimately winning his release in 2002. Dedicated to exposing, "the government's use of prisons as a tool of genocidal, colonial repression and a key weapon in the US war against African people." Active in the Free Mumia campaign and working both within the system organizing incarcerated individuals and outside the system with community activists to oppose police violence and the expanding prison industry.

SOUTHWEST YOUTH COLLABORATIVE (SWYC)/GENERATION Y

Contact: Jeremy Lahoud, Monica Avery
Address: 6400 S. Kedzie, Chicago, IL 60629
Phone: 773-476-3534
Email: swyouth@igc.org
Website: www.swyc.org
Founded: 1992
Budget: under 1 million
Constituency Age: 13-25
Issues: Gang Issues, Racial Justice, Public Space, Student Rights/Education Reform, Prisons/Criminal Justice
Race: Multi-Racial, People of Color
Profile: The most active and consistent hub of multi-issue youth organizing in Chicago, the intergenerational SWYC's innovative programs organize around Hip Hop leadership, school funding equity, reproductive freedoms, and the criminalization of youth of color. The youth-led Generation-Y project fights tracking and school issues in addition to lobbying city hall for more educational alternatives and leadership opportunities. They have organized major city-wide protests for multicultural education and mobilized 500 youth to protest at city hall to save summer jobs.

STONE SOUP COLLECTIVE

Contact: Dan Scheid
Address: 4637 N. Ashland, Chicago, IL 60640
Phone: 773-561-5131
Email: zawszesophie@yahoo.com
Founded: 1997
Budget: out of pocket
Constituency Age: 12 and under-30 and over
Issues: Public Space
Race: Multi-Racial, White
Profile: Three joy and social justice filled co-op houses (with 18, 11 and 7 people respectively living in each) forming a key hub for progressive and radical activists in Chicago. They are a magnet for political/cultural events and visiting groups from out of town, hold infamous Tuesday night potluck dinners, and host several groups such as Food Not Bombs, Green Party, Kovler Center (human rights refugees) and Colombia Vive.

STREET LEVEL YOUTH MEDIA

Contact: Shinae Yoon
Address: 1856 W. Chicago Ave, Chicago, IL 60622
Phone: 773-862-5331
Email: admin@street-level.org
Website: www.street-level.org
Founded: 1993
Budget: under 1 million
Constituency Age: 12 and under-21
Issues: Youth Development, Media
Race: Multi-Racial, Latina/o, African-American/Black
Profile: Reaching 1800 youth city-wide, Street-Level Youth Media (SYM) trains young folks to use technology and arts for social change. Innovative projects include: The Chiapas Youth Media Project, Cyber Block Parties (with dozens of TV sets on the street playing videos), How Boys Treat Girls, and Neutral Ground, which brokers gang truces using video. SYM also goes into public schools to help integrate media into the curriculum.

UNIVERSITY OF HIP HOP

Contact: Lavie Raven
Address: 6400 S. Kedzie, Chicago, IL 60629
Phone: 773-476-3534 x59
Email: university_of_hiphop@yahoo.com,
hekter1@yahoo.com, xanga79@msn.
Website: www.universityofhiphop.org
Founded: 1997
Budget: out of pocket
Constituency Age: 13-25
Issues: Women's Rights, Hip Hop Activism,
Student Rights/Education Reform, Arts/Culture, Education
Race: Multi-Racial
Profile: Created by and for the Chicago Hip Hop community, the
UoHH teaches breaking, DJing, MCing, graf, and political
education citywide through high school chapters at Kenwood,
Hubbard, Brother Rice, Curie, Revere (elementary school), and
Prolog. UoHH also reaches youth who aren't in school,
reconnecting Hip Hop to activism and community organizing. A
project of the Southwest Youth Collaborative, UoHH has painted
more than 100 public murals and is strongly focused on
developing girls and women in Hip Hop.

VIDEO MACHETE

Contact: Cesar Sanchez, Davida Ingram
Address: 1180 N. Milwaukee, Chicago, IL 60622
Phone: 773-645-1272
Email: info@videomachete.org, videomachete@hotmail.com
Website: www.videomachete.org
Founded: 1994
Budget: under 250k
Constituency Age: 13-21
Issues: Youth Development, Media, LGBTTSQ/Queer,
Racial Justice, Prisons/Criminal Justice
Race: Multi-Racial
Profile: Video Machete works with young people in four public
schools and the juvenile justice system. It runs programs like
Global Youth, Experimental TV, Latino Chicago, MAGIK for
queer girls, and Route Doctors. Recent videos produced include
one about immigrants after September 11th and the Patriot Act.
In addition to creating a national video and organizing
distribution network, Video Machete is leading an intensive
six-week workshop called the Media Activism Institute.

YOUTH FIRST!

Contact: David Thibault-Rodriguez
Address: 6400 S. Kedezie, Chicago, IL 60629
Phone: 773-476-3534
Email: debi@cjiyouthfirStorg
Website: www.cjiyouthfirst.org
Founded: 1997
Budget: out of pocket
Constituency Age: 12 and under-21
Issues: Education, Violence Prevention,
Student Rights/Education Reform, Racial Justice,
Prisons/Criminal Justice
Race: People of Color
Profile: Launched by the Community Justice Initiative in
response to an "anti-gang loitering ordinance," Youth First! is a
dynamic organization run primarily by young women of color.
Youth First! is campaigning for a permanent allocation of the
city's budget for a wide range of programs that promote power,
justice and equity for all youth, including summer jobs, free
youth clinics, and alternatives to incarceration. They offer
youth-led workshops on grassroots fundraising and research,
power analysis, media, networking, and direct action.

INDIANA

HIP HOP CONGRESS

Contact: Alex Fruchter
Address: Bloomington, IN
Email: contact@hiphopcongress.com
Website: www.hiphopcongress.org
Founded: 2000
Budget: under 25k
Constituency Age: 13-25
Issues: Hip Hop Activism, Arts/Culture
Race: Multi-Racial
Profile: One of the most active campus chapters of the
California-based HHC is at Indiana University. Long-term goal:
network campus Hip Hop groups with the off campus and
on-line Hip Hop communities, building a multi-racial political
power base. Short-term goal: throw live, socially conscious
Hip Hop events. They have organized shows in the most
unlikely places such as Urbana, IL and Salt Lake City, Utah.
The Bloomington chapter also has a Sons and Daughters of the
Nile Spoken Word troupe. Check the mind-expanding website.

UNITED STUDENTS AGAINST SWEATSHOPS
(USAS) – PURDUE UNIVERSITY

Contact: Elizabeth Gattman
Address: Purdue University, 1001 Stewart Center, Box 649,
West Lafayette, IN 47907
Phone: 765-743-1564
Email: nosweat@expert.cc.purdue.edu
Website: www.purdue.edu/nosweat
Founded: 1999
Budget: out of pocket
Constituency Age: 13-30 and over
Issues: Labor/Economic Justice, Globalization, Corporate
Accountability
Race: Multi-Racial
Profile: A particularly strong chapter of the national
organization, USAS-Purdue puts consistent pressure on the
university, which takes in roughly $600,000 a year from sales of
apparel largely manufactured in sweatshop conditions over-

seas. Through their organizing, members now serve on a joint student/administration committee to review monitoring agency reports of the corporations that manufacture Purdue's apparel. USAS-Purdue also supports janitorial and secretarial staff around issues of work conditions, living wages and job security.

IOWA

CORNFED HUSSIES: A RURAL REVOLUTION
Contact: Collective
Address: c/o Ruby's Pearl, 13 S. Linn #3, Iowa City, IA 52240
Phone: 319-248-0032
Email: lcarman@blue.weeg.uiowa.edu
Founded: 2001
Budget: out of pocket
Constituency Age: 19-25
Issues: Arts/Culture, Women's Rights
Race: White
Profile: With pompons made from sliced trash bags and duct tape, and mismatched red & black sequined costumes, these aren't typical cheerleaders. "You've got anger, soul and more! Take it to the street and let it roar!" they shout before arranging themselves into a wobbly pyramid. Iowa City's radical cheerleaders branch is a group of 11 women and one man out to effect social change around issues of sex equity, women's rights and body image-- one cheer at a time.

GARLIC PRESS
Contact: Michael Antonucci
Address: PO Box 10051, Iowa City, IA 52240
Phone: 319-354-0132
Email: garlicpress@graffiti.net
Website: www.kickme.to/garlicpress
Founded: 2002
Budget: out of pocket
Constituency Age: 19-30
Issues: Arts/Culture, Media
Race: White
Profile: Run collectively, GP is the only fully independent source of radical journalism in Iowa City. A bi-monthly zine style paper, it supplies coverage of area artists, galleries and events, and only accepts ads from locally owed businesses and organizations. It notoriously pushes the envelope on speech and taste issues. In the past, GP has focused on such topics as women's self defense, the effects of the "war on drugs" in Iowa City, GLBT issues and animal rights.

GRAFFITI THEATRE
Contact: Mara McCann
Address: PO Box 2177, Iowa City, IA 52244
Phone: 319-621-3234
Email: mara@graffiti-theatre.com

Website: www.graffiti-theatre.com
Founded: 1998
Budget: out of pocket
Constituency Age: 13-30 and over
Issues: Education, Youth Development, Racial Justice, Women's Rights
Race: White
Profile: Graffiti Theatre is a small traveling theatre group that uses interactive plays to educate and engage audiences in discussions about social justice and equality, with focus on women's rights and racial justice. It provides an outlet for teenagers who are (or want to be) socially and politically active and who enjoy the performing arts. An intergenerational organization comprised mostly of young people under 20, GT works to bring messages that might not otherwise be heard to small communities.

IOWA CITIZENS FOR COMMUNITY IMPROVEMENT/YOUTH WORKING FOR POSITIVE CHANGE
Contact: Joe Fagan
Address: 1607 East Grand Ave, Des Moines, IA 50316
Phone: 515-282-0484
Email: iowacci@dwx.com
Website: iowacci.org
Founded: 1976
Budget: under 250k
Constituency Age: 26-30 and over
Issues: Labor/Economic Justice, Welfare/Poverty, Environmental Justice
Race: Multi-Racial
Profile: With both rural and urban chapters, CCI tackles a wide range of issues including predatory lending, illegal dumping, production of methanphetamines, federal farm policy, tenants rights and violence prevention. Youth Working for Positive Change (YWPC) is CCI's youth organizing project, made up of youth who identify and address issues that affect them. YWPC has launched focused campaigns on abandoned houses, gun violence, crime, education and drug activity.

RAPE VICTIM ADVOCACY PROGRAM
Contact: Michael Shaw
Address: 320 South Lynn, Iowa City, IA 52240
Phone: 319-335-6001
Email: michael-shaw@uiowa.edu
Website: www.uiowa.edu/~rvap
Founded: 1997
Budget: out of pocket
Constituency Age: 13-30 and over
Issues: Youth Development, Women's Rights, Violence Prevention, Education
Race: Multi-Racial
Profile: RVAP is a proactive rape crisis center that offers support and advocacy for surviving victims of sexual abuse as

well as educates about issues of violence, sexual violence, and the mechanisms of interlocking oppressions. They maintain as flat a hierarchy as possible, holding one another accountable and making decisions with collective input. Everyone, directors, volunteers and staff, is trained in both education and crisis support so that everyone can offer the same services equally.

UNITED ACTION FOR YOUTH

Contact: Stu Mullins
Address: 410 Iowa Ave, Iowa City, IA 52240
Phone: 319-338-7518
Email: uaystu@aol.com
Website: www.unitedactionforyouth.org
Founded: 1972
Budget: over 1 million
Constituency Age: 12 and under-18
Issues: Media, Youth Development, Arts/Culture
Race: Multi-Racial, White
Profile: UAY is THE place in Iowa City for teens to get involved. Teens publish a zine (Alternative Shapes of Reality) and have discussion and action groups such as LGBTQ Youth and Gearl Jam (young women addressing the representation of women in the music industry). UAY also provides services for homeless kids and teen parents, have a teen-run hotline, and are planning a radio station that will be run by teens and will play music created in the UAY recording studio.

WOMEN, FOOD AND AGRICULTURE NETWORK

Contact: Denise O'Brien
Address: 59624 Chicago Road, Atlantic, IA 50022
Phone: 712-243-3264
Email: wfan@metc.net
Website: www.wfan.org
Founded: 1997
Budget: out of pocket
Constituency Age: 19-30 and over
Issues: Women's Rights, Education, Genetic Engineering, Globalization, Environment
Race: White
Profile: WFAN is a small, member-based, intergenerational women's organization that practices and educates their community about sustainable agriculture. Through economic and environmental literacy training, leadership development, international networking, internships, mentoring, participatory research, and activist training, WFAN works to build self-sufficient community structures as well as social, economic and ecological justice. Though many young people are involved in all aspects of the collective, WFAN is currently developing a component specific to youth.

KANSAS

CENTER FOR COMMUNITY OUTREACH

Contact: Margaret Perkins-McGuinness
Address: 405 Kansas Union, Lawrence, KS 66045
Phone: 785-864-4073
Email: cco@ku.edu
Website: www.ku.edu/~cco/
Founded: 1992
Budget: under 100k
Constituency Age: 12 and under-30 and over
Issues: Labor/Economic Justice, Education, Environment, Youth Development, Welfare/Poverty
Race: White, Multi-Racial
Profile: A student-run, student-funded volunteer placement and resource center; an excellent resource for anyone interested in volunteer opportunities. Hooked up to large variety of organizations (some political, some straight service-oriented) in Lawrence. Runs eleven programs and two service partnerships. Programs range from after school mentoring, to community gardens, to a breakfast restaurant for the homeless, to food delivery for the homebound. Bridging community service with community activism.

DELTA FORCE

Contact: Kit Brauer
Address: 400 Kansas Union, Lawrence, KS 66045
Phone: 785-218-5376
Email: kitb@ku.edu
Website: www.ukans.edu/~dforce
Founded: 1996
Budget: under 25k
Constituency Age: 19-25
Issues: Student Rights/Education Reform, Labor/Economic Justice, Racial Justice, Corporate Accountability, Environment
Race: White
Profile: A major University of Kansas student government party in the unusually powerful student government. Changed the nature of races from popularity contests to issue-based dialogues. Platforms have included supporting a living-wage campaign for campus workers, pushing for recruitment and retention of students and faculty of color, and instituting a university recycling policy. Can be linked to almost all other progressive organizations in town through members of DF. The center of progressive activism in Kansas.

WYANDOTTE INTERFAITH SPONSORING COUNCIL (WISC)

Contact: Shanta Bailey
Address: 2900 Minnesota Ave, PO Box 2817, Kansas City, KS 66110-0817
Phone: 913-281-0552
Founded: 1996
Budget: under 500k

The People's Rally, Kansas City, MO, May 13, 2000
© Laszlo Toth

Constituency Age: 13-25
Issues: Education, Youth Development,
Labor/Economic Justice, Media
Race: Multi-Racial
Profile: Using a faith-based community organizing model, the
Youth Campaign of WISC trains young people in public
speaking, issue analysis and research methods. The youth-led
steering committee then leads intergenerational campaigns
that address violence prevention, educational resources and
public space. A recent campaign successfully lobbied the city
council to open high school swimming pools to the community
for the summer. The Youth Campaign involves young people
from 15 different congregations.

KENTUCKY

APPALACHIAN MEDIA INSTITUTE/YOUTH BORED (APPALSHOP PROGRAM)
Contact: Nick Szeuperla
Address: 91 Madison Ave, Whitesburg, KY 41858
Phone: 606-633-0108
Email: nick@appalshop.org
Website: www.appalshop.org
Founded: 1988
Budget: under 250k
Constituency Age: 13-25
Issues: Youth Development, Media, Arts/Culture, Education
Race: White
Profile: AMI holds six-week summer media production training
programs for rural, low-income youth. Participants return to
their communities and train peers in video, radio and digital/
still photography with AMI equipment. Video projects have
screened at Sundance and include Because of Oxytocin, What
Does it Mean to be Gay or Lesbian in the Mountains? and
How Can Youth Organize? Music concerts bring together otherwise isolated young people-- sometimes attracting 600 or 700--
from rural communities in VA, WV, TN and KY.

BRYCC HOUSE
Contact: Jamie Prott
Address: 1055 Bardstown Road, Louisville, KY 40204
Phone: 502-456-1006
Email: brycc@brycchouse.org
Website: www.brycchouse.org
Founded: 1999
Budget: under 25k
Constituency Age: 13-25
Issues: Education, Women's Rights, Media, Arts/Culture
Race: Multi-Racial, White
Profile: The Bardstown Road Youth Cultural Center is the only
youth-operated center in the region that provides a community
space for concerts, art shows, poetry slams, political
conferences and festivals. Created a lending library of political

books, resources and independent magazines, offer a free
computer lab, program their own internet radio station
(including live concert broadcasts), and participate in various
local and national campaigns. Currently searching for a new
space, this activist hub will undoubtedly rebuild brick by brick.

DEMOCRACY RESOURCE CENTER
Contact: Greg King
Address: 253 Regency Circle, Suite A, Lexington, KY 40503
Phone: 859-276-0563
Email: info@kydrc.org
Website: www.kydrc.org
Founded: 1991
Budget: under 250k
Constituency Age: 13-30 and over
Issues: Racial Justice, Prisons/Criminal Justice,
Labor/Economic Justice, Youth Development, Welfare/Poverty
Race: Multi-Racial
Profile: The center of activism in Kentucky. Focus on
participatory action research in order to identify issues, popular
education to transform community experiences into action, and
general political education through networking and connecting
organizations from all over the state. Working in Hopkins
County to put discrimination on the agenda of local elected
officials. Has grown from a small, ignored movement to a large
coalition. Supporting Schools Not Jails and surveying youth in
Lexington about what issues they want addressed.

FAIRNESS CAMPAIGN
Contact: Carol Kramer
Address: 2263 Frankfort Ave, Louisville, KY 40206
Phone: 502-893-0788
Email: fairness@fairness.org
Website: www.fairness.org
Founded: 1991
Budget: under 1 million
Constituency Age: 13-30 and over
Issues: Women's Rights, Violence Prevention, Police
Accountability, LGBTTSQ/Queer
Race: Multi-Racial, White
Profile: The primary goal of the Fairness Campaign is to pass
comprehensive civil rights legislation prohibiting discrimination
on the basis of sexual orientation and gender. The Fairness
Campaign operates through public education and advocacy,
political activity, and reciprocal alliances with others in the
social justice community. Principle action committees include:
Community Building & Education, Discrimination Action
Response Team, Leadership Development & Operations, and
the Legislative Committee.

FROM HOLLER TO THE HOOD

Contact: Amelia Kirby
Address: c/o Appal Shop, 91 Madison Ave, Whitesburg, KY 41858
Phone: 606-633-0108
Email: h2h@appalshop.org
Website: ns.appalshop.org/h2h/
Founded: 2000
Budget: under 100k
Constituency Age: 12 and under-30 and over
Issues: Media, Hip Hop Activism, Prisons/Criminal Justice, Arts/Culture, Multi-Culturalism
Race: Multi-Racial
Profile: Broadcast from the Appalachians, this weekly Hip Hop radio show reaches out to young people throughout the region, particularly urban people of color imprisoned in rural areas. H2H works to build connections between rural and urban cultures, a division made visible with the rise of the Appalachian prison industry. Locating similarities between Hip Hop and traditional Appalachian cultures, H2H has initiated collaborative radio projects and community forums, creating a unique exchange and exploration in art and solidarity.

KENTUCKY ALLIANCE AGAINST RACIAL AND POLITICAL REPRESSION

Contact: Alice Wade
Address: 3208 West Broadway, Louisville, KY 40211
Phone: 502-778-8130
Email: kyall@bellsouth.net
Founded: 1972
Budget: under 250k
Constituency Age: 12 and under-30 and over
Issues: Youth Development, Racial Justice, Student Rights/Education Reform
Race: White, African-American/Black
Profile: Created by adult members who had been active in the Civil Right Movement after they realized nobody was telling young people about the rich history of youth organizing in Louisville. Students learn about the history of the Civil Rights Movement and research contemporary institutional inequality. Now four students are on the board of the organization and the young organizers have launched a campaign to include more African American history in the curriculum and to increase resources in their schools.

KENTUCKY REPRODUCTIVE HEALTH NETWORK

Contact: Sheila Sutton
Address: PO Box 995, Louisville, KY 40201
Phone: 502-589-6088
Email: krhn@bellsouth.net
Founded: 2001
Budget: under 50k
Constituency Age: 13-30 and over
Issues: Health Care, Youth Development, Reproductive Rights, Women's Rights

Race: White, African-American/Black
Profile: State-wide information dissemination and advocacy group for women's health and reproductive rights. Publish free resources guide with lists of clinics for STD screening, birth-control and abortion in KY and five surrounding states. Supports women through legal advocacy, letter writing and media campaigns, and by providing escorts for women encountering hostile protestors at clinics. Working to link campus activists across the state and currently advocating for a woman on trial for child abuse because she was a drug-user while pregnant.

LOUISVILLE YOUTH GROUP

Contact: Natalie Reteneller
Address: PO Box 406764, Louisville, KY 40204
Phone: 502-454-3300
Email: info@louisvilleyouthgroup.org
Website: www.louisvillyouthgroup.org
Founded: 1993
Budget: under 50k
Constituency Age: 13-21
Issues: Youth Development, Student Rights/Education Reform, LGBTTSQ/Queer, HIV/AIDS, Education
Race: Multi-Racial
Profile: A solid advocate and support for Louisville LGBTQ youth. Youth leaders organize and lead Friday night meetings and run LGBTG advocacy campaigns in public and Catholic schools. Work to familiarize residential treatment centers, conflict resolution agencies and school boards on LGBTQ youth issues. Working with the Hate-Free Schools Campaign, which gathers personal stories of discrimination and harassment to motivate the Board of Education to create anti-discrimination policies.

PROGRESS TRANSYLVANIA

Contact: Kristin Todd
Address: 300 N. Broadway, Lexington, KY 40508
Phone: 859-749-1196
Email: ktodd@mail.transy.edu
Founded: 1998
Budget: out of pocket
Constituency Age: 19-25
Issues: Women's Rights, Globalization, Health Care, Militarism, Labor/Economic Justice
Race: Multi-Racial, White
Profile: Progress Transylvania focuses on a wide range of issues while also serving as a local chapter of United Students Against Sweatshops. Recent efforts have included protests against the war in Afghanistan, organizing their annual walk-out for women's rights on International Women's Day, and a living wage and benefits campaign in alliance with solid waste workers in the community. Hosted a statewide forum with university professors on the history of US relations with Afghanistan and different perspectives within Islam.

LOUSIANA

CRITICAL RESISTANCE SOUTH

Contact: Melissa Burch
Address: PO Box 79123, New Orleans, LA 70179
Phone: 504-837-5348
Email: crsouth@criticalresistance.org
Website: www.criticalresistance.org
Founded: 2001
Budget: under 100k
Constituency Age: 13-30 and over
Issues: Racial Justice, Prisons/Criminal Justice, Human Rights, Drug Policy
Race: Multi-Racial
Profile: Building on the success of the groundbreaking Critical Resistance: Beyond the Prison Industrial Complex conference held in 1998 at UC Berkeley, CR South is organizing for an April 2003 gathering in New Orleans. The goal is to bring together prisoners, former-prisoners, their families, artists, organizers, and advocates from Alabama, Arkansas, Florida, Georgia, Kentucky, Louisiana, Mississippi, North Carolina, South Carolina, Tennessee, West Virginia and Virginia to network, build relationships, share skills and create strategies to counter the expanding prison industry.

LOUISIANA ENVIRONMENTAL ACTION NETWORK (LEAN) YOUTH ADVISORY COUNCIL

Contact: Wilbert Hasten
Address: PO Box 66323, Baton Rouge, LA 70806
Phone: 225-928-1315
Email: lean@leanweb.org
Website: www.leanweb.org
Budget: out of pocket
Constituency Age: 13-21
Issues: Youth Development, Student Rights/Education Reform
Race: Latina/o, African-American/Black
Profile: Founded in 1996, LEAN's Youth Advisory Council organizes around issues affecting them in their schools and their environment. Council youth attend protests, gather environmental samples and have testified before city council. Learn organizing skills an campaign development through workshops and by working alongside their elders in LEAN. Challenged the "No Braids" policy of their high schools, argued before the school board and won. Organize the annual Youth In Motion Conference.

PROJECT YES: YOUTH EXPLORING SOCIETY

Contact: Sammy Politziner
Address: 733 Marino St, Norco, LA 70079
Phone: 985-725-0949
Email: projectyesyellow@hotmail.com
Founded: 2000
Budget: under 25k
Constituency Age: 12 and under
Issues: Education, Youth Development, Multi-Culturalism
Race: Multi-Racial
Profile: With programs in NYC and Southeren Louisiana, Project YES is a summer program in which 3rd graders from underserved communities grapple with issues of race, class, segregation and equality of opportunity. Participating in Urban Expeditions, where they explore their neighborhoods, community organizations and cultural sites, students take on various community activities to become active parts of the solution. Last year they cleaned a park in Washington Heights, read to pre-schoolers at a homeless shelter and wrote letters to politicians.

TAMBOURINE AND FAN

Contact: Jerome Smith
Address: 1400 St Phillip, New Orleans, LA 70116
Phone: 504-565-7290
Budget: under 250k
Constituency Age: 12 and under-21
Issues: Welfare/Poverty, Student Rights/Education Reform, Labor/Economic Justice, Racial Justice, Prisons/Criminal Justice
Race: African-American/Black
Profile: Part of the living tradition of New Orleans Social Aid and Pleasure Clubs (and the only club to retain its focus on social justice) T&F members get down for Mardi Gras and organize direct actions targeting poverty and economic justice. Active for decades, protests have included delivering trash picked up from under-funded schools to school board meetings. With projects from needle exchanges to political education through football, T&F (located in the Treme, America's oldest African American neighborhood) is uniquely resourceful.

THE PEOPLE'S YOUTH FREEDOM SCHOOL

Contact: Joseph Parker
Address: PO Box 751208, New Orleans, LA 70175
Phone: 504-241-7472
Email: freedomschoolno@hotmail.com
Founded: 1997
Budget: under 25k
Constituency Age: 13-18
Issues: Youth Development, Racial Justice, Arts/Culture, Education, Hip Hop Activism
Race: Multi-Racial
Profile: An intergenerational group that runs a 6-week summer program (modeled after the Mississippi Freedom Schools of 1964) as well as year-round programs in anti-racist organizing, leadership development, self esteem and skills building. Work to build confidence through art, poetry and dance, and to creatively expose peers to historical analyses of African American, Latino, Asian American and Native American oppression. Uses local culture and Hip Hop as organizing tools.

MAINE

BEEHIVE DESIGN COLLECTIVE
Contact: Collective
Address: 3 Elm St, Machias, ME 04654
Website: www.beehivecollective.org
Founded: 2000
Budget: out of pocket
Constituency Age: 12 and under-30 and over
Issues: Arts/Culture, Globalization
Race: Multi-Racial
Profile: Creating the Biodiversity Crossroads Mural, an artistic
political history of agriculture and its potentials. Designs and
distributes original anti-copyright graphics filled with bug-based
images. Houses a lending library of street banners in an old
meeting hall which doubles as a community center and political
meeting space. Produces the super-sized Free Trade Areas of
the Americas and Plan Colombia posters. Runs an apprenticeship program in the rare craft of hand-cut stone mosaics.

BLUNT/YOUTH RADIO PROJECT
Contact: Claire Holman
Address: WMPG, PO Box 9300, Portland, ME 04104-9300
Phone: 207-767-1785
Email: cholman@usm.maine.edu
Website: www.wmpg.org
Founded: 1994
Budget: under 100k
Constituency Age: 13-18
Issues: Media
Race: White
Profile: An award-winning, entirely youth run radio program
empowering youth through direct media access. Topics run
from gun control to prisons, different forms of schooling to
self-managed teen bands. The students are fully responsible for
hosting, reporting, producing and engineering the show.

MAINE YOUTH CAMPFIRE COLLECTIVE
Contact: Matt Schlobohm
Address: 217 South Mountain Road, Greene, ME 04236
Phone: 207-946-4478
Email: emiller4@justice.com
Founded: 2000
Budget: out of pocket
Constituency Age: 13-30 and over
Issues: Corporate Accountability, Globalization
Race: White
Profile: Created at a campfire, this state-wide network of youth
activists mobilizes other young people to organize, educate and
take part in direct actions while keeping it all fun and festive.
Mass distribution of flyers against the FTAA and Fast-Track at
public events, manufacturing plants and in several cities.
Publish zines on trade and forest ownership. Compiled the
reader, "Resisting Coporate Globalization and Free Trade".
Plan trip to Brazil to strengthen global justice organizing work.

MILITARY TOXICS PROJECT YOUTH INITIATIVE
Contact: Steven Taylor
Address: PO Box 558, Lewiston, ME 04243
Phone: 207-783-5091
Email: mtp@miltoxproj.org
Website: www.miltoxproj.org
Founded: 2001
Budget: under 25k
Constituency Age: 13-25
Issues: Militarism, Environmental Justice
Race: People of Color
Profile: With its national office in Maine, MTP Youth Initiative
is a working group of youth from Memphis, San Antonio,
Los Angeles, Hawaii, and Vieques, Puerto Rico that work to
organize youth around the environmental assaults to
communities (mainly of color) perpetrated by the US military.
Youth Initiative members sit on the MTP board of directors,
significantly contribute to the overall national campaign, and
regularly participate in organizing trainings, national strategy
sessions and activities designed to build an intergenerational
network.

OUTRIGHT
Contact: Jayson Hunt
Address: PO Box 5077, Portland, ME 04101
Phone: 207-828-6560
Email: outright@outright.org
Website: www.outright.org
Founded: 1989
Budget: under 500k
Constituency Age: 13-25
Issues: LGBTTSQ/Queer
Race: Multi-Racial
Profile: A well-known youth/adult collaborative creating a safe
space for LGBT and questioning people ages 22 and under.
Six affiliated chapters state-wide (and five more throughout
New England). Weekly programs include support groups and
leadership workshops, while ongoing efforts include HIV/AIDS
education and advocacy in high schools. Hosts a LGBT Prom for
youth from all over the Northeast and winter holiday support
events. Serve thousands of youth annually through meetings
and a speaker's bureau.

YOUTH ACTIVIST GATHERING
Contact: Kal Clark
Address: RR2 Box 8049, Pittspan, ME 04345
Phone: 207-525-7776
Email: amongsttherubble@justice.com
Founded: 2001
Budget: out of pocket
Constituency Age: 13-21
Issues: Youth Development
Race: White
Profile: The only annual statewide gathering of young people
involved in and curious about political activism. Maintains an

email calendar of workshops on a wide range of topics, including globalization, education, community organizing, independent media work and environmental justice. An exciting forum for dialogue and a simple start to building a radical youth community in Maine.

YOUTH ADELANTANDO/PEACE THROUGH INTERAMERICAN COMMUNITY ACTION

Contact: Hannah Kates-Goldman
Address: 170 Park St, Bangor, ME 04401
Phone: 207-947-4203
Email: youthadelantando@pica.ws
Website: www.pica.ws
Founded: 1997
Budget: under 25k
Constituency Age: 13-21
Issues: Militarism, Labor/Economic Justice, Globalization
Race: Multi-Racial, White
Profile: A self-governed group of young people organizing to advance youth rights and participation in the community. Made a documentary featuring interviews with young people discussing how they are treated; almost everyone in the film agrees that youth are not taken seriously. Foster relationships with youth in their sister city in El Salvador and are building around issues of globalization. Sent a delegation of youth to El Salvador last summer and brought some young Salvadorenos to Maine in the Fall.

MARYLAND

CAGE– COALITION AGAINST GLOBAL EXPLOITATION

Contact: Penny Howard, Josh Brown
Address: 1443 Gorsuch Ave, Baltimore, MD 21218
Email: cage@mobtown.org
Website: www.mobtown.org/cage
Founded: 1998
Budget: out of pocket
Constituency Age: 13-30 and over
Issues: Corporate Accountability, Militarism, Globalization
Race: White
Profile: CAGE is all about non-violent direct action, running teach-ins and petitioning the Baltimore City Council to adopt anti-WTO resolutions. CAGE has organized and mobilized for anti-IMF/World Bank, anti-war, WEF, and post-9/11 pro Palestinian rights demonstrations as part of their ongoing campaign to educate people about globalization.

GLOBAL TOXINS

Contact: Ryan Harvey
Address: 21 Scottsdale Court, Lutherville, MD 21093
Email: globaltoxin@hotmail.com
Website: www.globaltoxin.org

Founded: 1999
Budget: out of pocket
Constituency Age: 13-18
Issues: Animal Rights, Militarism, Globalization, Housing/Gentrification
Race: White
Profile: Comprised mostly of high school aged organizers, Global Toxins is a collective fighting against local manifestations of globalization in the DC/Baltimore area. They protest military recruitment in high schools, run an anti-fur campaign targeting local fur stores (complete with street theater and leafleting), and conduct educational workshops on the global economy. As of June 2002, they had waged 26 anti-war demonstrations post-9/11. Currently organizing a squatter rights campaign in collaboration with the Homes not Jails movement in DC.

YOUTH WARRIORS

Contact: Lynn Pinder, Sierra Johnson
Address: 3011 Baker St, Baltimore, MD 21216
Phone: 410-233-0521
Email: ywaction1@yahoo.com
Website: www.youthwarriors.org
Founded: 1996
Budget: under 25k
Constituency Age: 13-21
Issues: Environmental Justice
Race: African-American/Black
Profile: Youth Warriors is a youth-led environmental justice organization focused in the African American community which does leadership development and environmental education (particularly around lead poisoning and asthma) combined with cultural and athletic activities. Their "Taking it to the Streets" campaign includes after school and apprenticeship programs, poetry slams, an annual Black Student Leadership Institute, technical and entrepreneurial training, environmental health workshops (focused particularly on teen mothers), community gardening and computer training. Founded by a 24 year old African-American woman.

MASSACHUSSETS

AFSC CRITICAL BREAKDOWN

Contact: Eric Wissa
Address: 2160 Massachusetts Ave, Cambridge, MA 02140
Phone: 617-661-6130
Email: criticalbreakdown@hotmail.com
Founded: 2000
Budget: under 25k
Constituency Age: 12 and under-21
Issues: Arts/Culture, Hip Hop Activism, HIV/AIDS, Multi-Culturalism, Racial Justice
Race: Multi-Racial

Profile: Created to bring diverse communities together through Hip Hop, spoken word and performance arts, Critical Breakdown has developed into a hub for local youth culture and politics. Hold monthly open mic events, provide free AIDS testing, and promote local/global political actions. Run a weekly young fathers support group and organize against both racist policing and the state-wide testing structure in public schools. Solid example of young leaders within an established intergenerational organization (American Friends Service Committee) creating an effective youth-led initiative.

BOSTON YOUTH ORGANIZING PROJECT

Contact: Janice Lee
Address: 485 Columbus Ave, Boston, MA 02118
Phone: 617-262-1895
Email: jnicelee@hotmail.com
Founded: 1998
Budget: under 250k
Constituency Age: 13-25
Issues: Campaign Finance, Public Space, Student Rights/Education Reform
Race: White, African-American/Black
Profile: With chapters in churches, synagogues and public schools, BYOP is a dynamic youth-led/adult-supported project of City Mission Society. Students elect their own leadership council, participate in organizing training and determine their campaigns. BYOP victories include convincing the city to extend student train pass hours and the mayor to allocate $2 million towards new text books. Also won voting rights for 17 year olds in Cambridge local elections. Current campaigns focus on violence, standardized testing and lowering the voting age nationally.

COALITION FOR ASIAN PACIFIC AMERICAN YOUTH (CAPAY)

Contact: Sophia Kim
Address: 100 Morrissey Boulevard, Boston, MA 02125
Phone: 617-287-5689
Email: capay@umb.edu
Founded: 1994
Budget: under 250k
Constituency Age: 13-21
Issues: Immigrant/Refugee, Racial Justice, Student Rights/Education Reform
Race: Asian/Pacific Islander
Profile: CAPAY works for racial justice, supports youth-led activism in schools and communities, and provides leadership training to API youth. Ongoing projects focus on issues such as API civil rights, history, culture, community organizing, and immigration. These projects include a leadership development summer program, the quarterly As.I.Am. Newsletter, Asian American studies workshops and the Annual Leadership Symposium, which provides educational resources on API history and heritage.

CUTTING EJ/COMMUNITIES UNITED TOGETHER FOR ECONOMIC JUSTICE

Contact: Mari Spira
Address: 49 Francesca St, Somerville, MA 02144
Phone: 617-627-4087
Email: maris@cuttingej.org
Website: www.cuttingej.org
Founded: 2000
Budget: under 1 million
Constituency Age: 13-25
Issues: Housing/Gentrification, Labor/Economic Justice, Welfare/Poverty
Race: People of Color
Profile: Cutting EJ is a grassroots organization working to build youth and low-income people led economic justice campaigns throughout Massachusetts. Through its summer institute, aims to recruit, train and mentor 80-100 interns for placement in organizations in 30 communities that are addressing welfare, housing and temporary/ low-wage worker rights. With its volunteer and host organization databases, listserv and staff work area within its website, Cutting EJ is creatively incorporating technology into its traditional grassroots strategy.

EL ARCO IRIS YOUTH AND COMMUNITY ARTS CENTER

Contact: Imre Kepes
Address: 60 Hamilton St, Holyoke, MA 01040
Phone: 413-532-2360
Founded: 1992
Budget: under 250k
Constituency Age: 12 and under-21
Issues: Arts/Culture, HIV/AIDS, Public Space, Racial Justice, Violence Prevention
Race: Latina/o
Profile: El Arco Iris is a multicultural community arts center that has been providing free after-school arts education and leadership development programming to Latino youth for more than 10 years. All of the organizing, classes and community service projects are designed and initiated by young people. Youth take part in trainings on violence, public speaking, problem solving, critical thinking, HIV /AIDS education and diversity, and, through the Youth Power project, work to address community issues using performance and visual arts.

GET UP GET DOWN/YOUTH ACTION COALITION

Contact: Sienna Baskin
Address: PO Box 747, Amherst, MA 01004-0747
Phone: 413-253-2158
Founded: 2000
Budget: under 25k
Constituency Age: 13-18
Issues: LGBTTSQ/Queer, Militarism, Youth Development
Race: White, Latina/o, African-American/Black
Profile: Get Up Get Down is a youth-led project of the Youth

Action Coalition promoting awareness and activism in Springfield, Holyoke and Amherst through conferences and concerts. Workshops and discussions include, "Transgender: Breaking, Bending, Playing with Gender," "The Truth About the Military," "Breakdancing," "What is Islam?" and "The Prison Industrial Complex." Facilitated by people under 25 using a popular education model, sessions are designed to spark ideas and projects that can be funded through Get Up Get Down mini-grants of $5-$300.

HYDE SQUARE TASK FORCE/YOUTH ORGANIZING INITIATIVE

Contact: Jesus Herena
Address: 375 Centre St, Jamaica Plain, MA 02130
Phone: 617-524-8303
Email: jesus@hydesquare.org
Website: www.hydesquare.org
Founded: 1999
Budget: out of pocket
Constituency Age: 13-18
Issues: Immigrant/Refugee, Public Space, Student Rights/Education Reform
Race: Latina/o
Profile: The HSTF provides educational programs and community organizing initiatives for people in theHyde/Jackson Square area of Roxbury. In HSTF's youth education program, teen leaders organize, mentor, and teach middle school students. The 15-member Youth Community Organizing Team actively learns how to participate in political decision-making processes. They attend community meetings and participate in neighborhood cleanups. Currently campaigning to get a recreational center built in Jackson Square and to resist a new proposal to end bilingual education.

NIA ACTION COLLECTIVE

Contact: Emery Wright
Address: PO Box 230039, Boston, MA 02123
Phone: 617-627-4159
Email: niaproject@hotmail.com
Founded: 1999
Budget: under 250k
Constituency Age: 13-18
Issues: Housing/Gentrification, Poverty/Welfare, Racial Justice
Race: Latina/o, African-American/Black
Profile: Nia (meaning "purpose" in Swahili) is a people of color organization working on multiple issues-- from education to workers rights-- with college students and surrounding communities. In Somerville they are creating a community center and a tenants association; in Roxbury, youth are mapping the assets of their neighborhood in an effort to close the digital divide. Broadcast a weekly internet show called Speak Truth to Power and travel to the Gullah Sea Islands in the Summer to support local organizing.

PRISON BOOK PROJECT

Contact: Kazu Haga
Address: POB 396, Amherst, MA 01004-0396
Phone: 413-584-8975 x208
Website: www.prisonbooks.org
Founded: 1998
Budget: out of pocket
Constituency Age: 13-25
Issues: Prisons/Criminal Justice, Arts/Culture
Race: Multi-Racial, People of Color
Profile: Prison Book Project is a non-profit, volunteer based collective working to distribute books free of charge to incarcerated people nationwide. Dedicated to offering the men and women behind bars the opportunity for self-empowerment, education, and growth, PBP uses this simple and direct strategy in its efforts to transform the criminal punishment sytem into a justice system that is interested in rehabilitaion and restoration.

PROJECT 10 EAST

Contact: Ashley Reed
Address: PO Box 382401, Cambridge, MA 02238
Phone: 617-864-GLBT
Website: www.project10east.org
Founded: 1988
Budget: out of pocket
Constituency Age: 13-18
Issues: LGBTTSQ/Queer
Race: Multi-Racial
Profile: Project 10 East works to start and sustain gay/straight alliances in high schools and communities throughout Massachusetts. Provide support for safe spaces, create opportunities for dialogue and exchanges for students, parents and educators, and offer technical assistance to emerging LGBTQ organizations. Launched the first gay/straight alliance in the Northeast, and increasingly developing leadership and organizing training for LGBTQ youth. "10" represents the estimated 10% of the US population that is openly gay, lesbian, bisexual or transgender.

PROJECT HIP HOP, INC.

Contact: Mariama White-Hammond
Address: 434 Massachusetts Ave, Suite 504, Boston, MA 02118
Phone: 617-262-2148
Email: hiphop@aclu-mass.org
Website: www.projecthiphop.org
Founded: 1993
Budget: under 250k
Constituency Age: 13-18
Issues: Hip Hop Activism, Media, Prisons/Criminal Justice
Race: People of Color, African-American/Black
Profile: This "rolling classroom" takes low-income, multicultural groups of teens on a journey through the South to study the Civil Rights Movement and racial oppression in the US. The trip

serves as a jumping off point: Project Hip Hop students have made presentations on their experiences in more than 220 schools, have created their own high school curriculum, produce a youth newspaper (Rising Times), and organize locally around issues impacting their communities. Dynamic, innovative and an important model of intergenerational work.

ROCA

Contact: Sandra L. Tacke
Address: 101 Park St, Chelsea, MA 02150
Phone: 617-889-5210
Email: info@rocainc.com
Website: www.rocainc.org
Founded: 1988
Budget: over 1 million
Constituency Age: 13-21
Issues: Youth Development
Race: People of Color, Asian/Pacific Islander, Latina/o
Profile: ROCA ("rock" in Spanish) is a multicultural community center that has served Chelsea, Revere, East Boston and Lynn, Massachusetts for almost 15 years. Main programs, all with intergenerational training components and activities, include the Lynn Cambodian Leadership Program, the Youth Star community involvement project, and the Environmental Health Project. ROCA is active in gang interventions, sponsors Hip Hop classes, and partnered with a local Muslim group to counter post-9/11 harassment. A solid merging of youth service, development and community organizing.

ROXBURY ENVIRONMENTAL EMPOWERMENT PROJECT (REEP)

Contact: Penn Loh
Address: 2343 Washington St, Second Floor, Roxbury, MA 02119
Phone: 617-442-3343
Email: info@ace-ej.org
Website: www.ace-ej.org
Budget: under 500k
Constituency Age: 13-18
Issues: Corporate Accountability, Environment, Environmental Justice
Race: African-American/Black
Profile: REEP, a project of Alternatives for Community Environment, develops environmental justice leadership through internships, community service initiatives and youth-led projects in low-income communities of color in Roxbury and Dorchester. Forced the Dept. of Environmental Protection to make Cruise Construction clean-up a lead and asbestos contaminated site and are currently researching the hazards of a diesel-powered bus depot. REEP members developed and teach a high school environmental justice curriculum.

STEPS-IT CONSORTIUM

Contact: Tyrone Wallace
Address: 97 Hawley St, Northhampton, MA 01060
Phone: 413-586-4900 x161
Email: steps@collaborative.org
Founded: 2000
Budget: out of pocket
Constituency Age: 13-30 and over
Issues: Racial Justice, Prisons/Criminal Justice
Race: Latina/o, African-American/Black
Profile: Tapping into 35 different companies and agencies STEPS, which is by and for young people who have been previously incarcerated, links people to employment opportunities while also politicizing the inmates in education workshops. Involved in the local chapter of Critical Resistance and is consistent with the more mundane activities of support for inmates through letters and visits. Currently seeking to increase their recruiting in women's prisons.

THE CITY SCHOOL

Contact: Justin Steil
Address: 74 Union-Park, Boston, MA 02118
Phone: 617-542-2489
Email: justin_steil@milton.edu
Website: www.thecityschool.org
Founded: 1995
Budget: under 100k
Constituency Age: 13-21
Issues: Prisons/Criminal Justice, Homelessness, Immigrant/Refugee, HIV/AIDS
Race: Latina/o, African-American/Black
Profile: TCS develops high school students into leaders through "out of school time" interdisciplinary programs that stress critical thinking and ethical reasoning. Participants volunteer and intern at local community organizations and are encouraged to think critically about the world around them in workshops on issues such as homelessness, community-building, immigration and AIDS. In the Prison Empowerment Project, students visit prisons and work to counter the expanding prison industry.

THE MIRROR PROJECT

Contact: Roberto Arevalo
Address: PO Box 1486, Somerville, MA 02144
Phone: 617-625-1690
Email: roberto@mirrorproject.org
Website: www.mirrorproject.org
Founded: 1992
Budget: out of pocket
Constituency Age: 13-18
Issues: Gang Issues, Media, Racial Justice, Housing/Gentrification
Race: White, Latina/o, African-American/Black
Profile: TMP was started in 1992 so that young people in

Protests of the FTAA, Quebec, April 2001
© Nick Cooper

WTO protests in Seattle, November 30, 1999
© Geoff Oliver Bugbee

underserved communities could create videos about their everyday experiences. Using their video work, participants lead media trainings and workshops on their experiences with public education, racism and police brutality. In neighborhoods like Boston's Villa Victoria and Somerville's Mystic Housing Projects, youth have documented gentrification and its effects. Videos are distributed within the community as well as to festivals, museums and TV stations. Thus far TMP has produced more than 150 videos.

THE STUDENT UNDERGROUND
Contact: Ethan Goldwater
Address: Box 373 BU Station, Boston, MA 02215
Phone: 617-230-9311
Email: gounderground@hotmail.com
Website: www.thestudentunderground.org
Founded: 1997
Budget: out of pocket
Constituency Age: 13-25
Issues: Media, Student Rights/Education Reform
Race: White, Latina/o, Asian/Pacific Islander
Profile: The Student Underground is a political newspaper at Boston University that works to raise student consciousness about local, national, and international justice struggles. Collectively run, the publication staff also organizes cultural events, supports local campaignss, and brings progressive speakers to campus. Recently won Campus Alternative Journalism Awards for "Publication of the Year"and for "Best Reporting on Gender and Sexism."

WHAT'S UP MAGAZINE
Contact: Amy Sussaman
Address: 23 Dartmouth St, Boston, MA 02116
Phone: 617-267-1575
Email: info@whatsupmag.org
Website: www.whatsupmagazine.org
Founded: 1997
Budget: under 250k
Constituency Age: 13-30 and over
Issues: Homelessness, Media, Arts/Culture
Race: Multi-Racial
Profile: What's Up brings local artists and homeless people together to create a street magazine and to throw regular community events. Homeless and low-income people join young artists in the production, sales and advertising of the magazine, as well as fundraisers and musical events. Issues covered range from community and public space to globalization, realities of Boston social service agencies to coverage of Boston's underground Hip Hop and rock scenes.

ZUMIX
Contact: Nick Richardson
Address: 202 Maverick St, Boston, MA 02128
Phone: 617-568-9777
Website: www.zumix.org
Founded: 1991
Budget: out of pocket
Constituency Age: 13-18
Issues: Arts/Culture
Race: Multi-Racial
Profile: Created in East Boston during a time of ethnic conflict, Zumix provides a safe space, music lessons and technical training for creative and motivated 8-18 year olds. Participants produce and record their own music, learn engineering and event production skills, and gain practical experience by working with community based organizations. Zumix folks are frequently found at local political organizing events providing technical and sound expertise. Founded by adults but, increasingly, young participants are beginning to run the show.

MICHIGAN

ARAB-AMERICAN ANTI-DISCRIMINATION COMMITTEE
Contact: Fadi Kiblawi
Address: 3909 Michigan Union, Room 4341, Ann Arbor, MI 48109
Phone: 734-717-5540
Email: fkiblawi@umich.edu
Website: www.umich.edu/~adcum/
Founded: 1996
Budget: out of pocket
Constituency Age: 12 and under-30 and over
Issues: Immigrant/Refugee, Racial Justice, Militarisn
Race: Middle Eastern, Multi-Racial
Profile: ADC is dedicated to promoting and increasing awareness about Arab-American cultures on the University of Michigan campus and the surrounding communities. They have created a support base for Arab-American youth, organizing, counseling and mentoring in local high schools. Post-9/11, their much needed educational presentations serve to counter circulating stereotypes about Arab and Muslim communities. They also work on the Blue Triangle campaign, which raises awareness about civil liberty violations.

DETROIT HIP HOP COALITION
Contact: Rob Gill
Address: PO Box 71694, Detroit, MI 48071
Phone: 810-394-7014
Email: scriptures2g@hotmail.com
Website: www.coalition.mainpage.net
Founded: 2000
Budget: out of pocket

Constituency Age: 13-25
Issues: Media, Hip Hop Activism, Arts/Culture
Race: Multi-Racial
Profile: With over 4,000 members, DHHC advocates for local and regional independent Hip Hop artists. Engaged in an ongoing media and direct action campaign against FM 98, the station that claims to be, "where Hip Hop lives," but does not play any local Hip Hop artists. Black-Out Fridays is the DHHC initiated weekly boycott of FM 98. Members also organize conferences and forums on topics such as the music industry, starting a company, being involved in community activism and Detroit-area issues.

DETROIT SUMMER
Contact: Shea Howell
Address: 4605 Cass Ave, Detroit, MI 48202
Phone: 313-832-2904
Email: detroitsummer@hotmail.com
Website: www.geocities.com/detroit_summer
Founded: 1992
Budget: under 50k
Constituency Age: 13-30 and over
Issues: Public Space, Racial Justice, Labor/Economic Justice, Youth Development
Race: Multi-Racial
Profile: A project of the Grace Boggs Institute, Detroit Summer is an activist training center which was created to empower young people to address multiple issues in their low-income urban communities. Programs are primarily youth-led and include community organic gardening, housing rehabilitation, transforming vacant lots into parks and painting public murals. Research projects focus on city infrastructure (like transportation and sanitation systems) and participants are consistently engaged in intergenerational dialogues with veterans of the labor, civil rights and Black Power movements.

GENDERFACTORY FIREHOUSE COLLECTIVE
Contact: Jessika Musinski
Address: c/o Idle Kids Books & Records, 4470 2nd Ave, Detroit, MI 48201
Phone: 313-832-7730
Email: typewritercore@hotmail.com
Website: www.genderfactory.batcave.net
Founded: 2002
Budget: out of pocket
Constituency Age: 13-25
Issues: LGBTTSQ/Queer, Arts/Culture
Race: White
Profile: Genderfactory Firehouse Collective is an art and community resource space started and run by young people to create a support base for LGBTQ youth in Detroit. They provide skills-building workshops on self-defense, music, visual and performance art and self-empowerment. Currently raising funds to create a permanent center where they plan to offer

child care, overnight accommodations for organizers, a recording studio, a darkroom, a café and a home for the local Food Not Bombs chapter.

STUDENTS ORGANIZING FOR LABOR AND EQUALITY
Contact: Jackie Bray
Address: 3909 Michigan Union, 530 S. South State St, Ann Arbor, MI 48109
Phone: 734-615-5221
Email: sole.steer@umich.edu
Website: www.umich.edu/~sole
Founded: 1998
Budget: out of pocket
Constituency Age: 13-25
Issues: Labor/Economic Justice, Corporate Accountability
Race: White, Multi-Racial
Profile: Based at the University of Michigan, SOLE advocates for worker health and safety standards, and against wage cuts linked to union activity. SOLE campaigns for the rights of all workers employed through the University-- teachers, janitors, security guards, service workers, as well as those overseas employed to manufacture merchandise sold through the school. They have organized several successful campaigns on campus in coalition with other groups, including a successful 3,000 student walkout in support of the graduate teachers union.

TRUMBULLPLEX
Address: 4210 Trumbull, Detroit, MI 48208
Phone: 313-832-1845
Email: trumbullplex@yahoo.com
Founded: 1993
Budget: out of pocket
Constituency Age: 13-30 and over
Issues: Housing/Gentrification, Arts/Culture
Race: Multi-Racial
Profile: A low-income anarchist housing collective near Detroit with three houses and a theatre, Trumbullplex hosts music and art events, operates an information center and cultivates several community gardens. Known by activists all over as an excellent place to organize, create community, work, play and eat GOOD FOOD. Their branch of Food Not Bombs serves free vegetarian meals in local parks on Saturdays and Sundays.

MINNESOTA

ARISE! BOOKSTORE AND RESOURCE CENTER
Contact: Amanda Luker
Address: 2441 Lyndale Ave, Minneapolis, MN 55405
Phone: 612-871-7110
Email: paarise@mtn.org
Website: www.arisebookstore.org
Founded: 1993

Budget: under 25k
Constituency Age: 13-30
Issues: Arts/Culture, Multi-Culturalism, Human Rights
Race: White
Profile: ARISE! Bookstore & Resource Center is a collectively run, indy information and activist hub that provides progressive and alternative media to the community as well as meeting space for local community groups. Their stock of books, magazines and videos offers alternative and multicultural viewpoints with focus on worldwide struggles for self-determination. ARISE! rents offices to local activist groups such as the Teenage Activist Network, Women's Prison Book Project, Sister's Camelot (food distribution), and the Youth Liberation Conference planning committee.

DIASPORA FLOW

Contact: Pradeepa Jeevamanaran
Address: 2311 W. 50th St, Apt 1, Minneapolis, MN 55410
Phone: 612-299-5852
Email: diasporaflow@yahoo.com
Website: www.diasporaflow.org
Founded: 2001
Budget: out of pocket
Constituency Age: 13-30 and over
Issues: Immigrant/Refugee, Arts/Culture, Racial Justice, Multi-Culturalism
Race: People of Color
Profile: Founded by two Sri Lankan women, DF works to support young artists of color that are committed to using their artistic expressions for social change. With members in both the Minneapolis-St.Paul area and NYC, DF organizes multimedia arts events that incorporate spoken word, Hip Hop, poetry slams, installation pieces, dance, theater and other visual/performing arts. Also conduct workshops and organize discussions groups on the how-to's of effective art-based social justice work in communities of color.

DISTRICT 202

Contact: Laura Ayers
Address: 1601 Nicollet Ave South, Minneapolis, MN 55403
Phone: 612-871-5559 x14
Email: youth@dist202.org
Website: www.dist202.org
Founded: 1993
Budget: under 500k
Constituency Age: 13-21
Issues: LGBTTSQ/Queer
Race: Multi-Racial
Profile: District 202 is a community center that provides a safe space for LGBT youth and their allies with emphasis on empowerment, risk-reduction and community building. From its youth speaker's bureau to employment opportunities, mentoring programs to theater productions, District 202 builds leadership, self-confidence and awareness through its

collaborative youth/adult leadership structure. Strives to build a diverse community throughout Minneapolis-St. Paul and its surrounding areas; also partners with social service agencies to provide information and resources to homeless LGBT youth.

FIRST AFRICAN THEN AMERICAN (FATA)

Contact: Jackie Byers
Address: 2880 James Ave South, Minneapolis, MN 55408
Phone: 651-641-1830
Email: jbyersoaproject@qwest.net
Founded: 2000
Budget: under 25k
Constituency Age: 13-21
Issues: Racial Justice, Violence Prevention
Race: African-American/Black
Profile: FATA (meaning "follow" in Swahili) is committed to addressing the many issues facing Afrikan youth in Minneapolis, from education to police brutality, violence prevention to self-esteem building. Teach African culture and history through intergenerational study groups, Hip Hop events and community service projects. Post 9/11, organized a unity group with Arab American students in Roosevelt High School to stop in-school violence and discrimination. Focused on developing young leaders of African descent.

GUERRILLA WORDFARE

Contact: Emmanuel Ortiz
Address: Minneapolis, MN
Phone: 612-729-6832
Email: guerrilla_wordfare@hotmail.com
Founded: 2001
Budget: out of pocket
Constituency Age: 13-30 and over
Issues: Arts/Culture, Hip Hop Activism, Multi-Culturalism, Racial Justice
Race: People of Color
Profile: Guerrilla Wordfare is a collective of young artists of color that produce awareness and fund raising events for organizations working to address a broad range of local and global issues. Events have included, "Creative Opposition to the Police State," and, "Arab American Artists in Support of Palestine." Other issues tackled have included discrimination against immigrants of color, worker rights and LGBTQ rights. Events merge spoken word, poetry, Hip Hop, music and dance. Revolutionary culture for inspiration and income.

INDIGENOUS ENVIRONMENTAL NETWORK (IEN) YOUTH COUNCIL

Contact: Heather Milton
Address: PO Box 485, Bemidji, MN 56619
Phone: 218-751-4967
Email: ienyouth@hotmail.com
Founded: 1999
Budget: under 100k

Constituency Age: 13-30 and over
Issues: Indigenous Rights, Environmental Justice, Environment
Race: Native American
Profile: IEN's Youth Council has built a network of Indigenous youth environmental activists and community representatives throughout the Americas, and is developing an environmental justice curriculum that features organizing training geared specifically towards Indigenous youth. While networking and skills sharing with other youth organizers nationwide, Youth Council members participate in IEN's eight ongoing,intergenerational organizing campaigns on climate, mining, healthcare, bio-diversity, persistent organic pollutants, occupational health, nuclear waste, and wolf and forest protection. IEN also works to bridge the digital divide.

IRON RANGE YOUTH IN ACTION

Contact: Ismil Chris
Address: Northland Office Center, 307 1st St South, Suite 114, Virginia, MN 55792
Phone: 218-749-7114
Email: ismilc@co.st-louis.mn.us
Website: www.co.st-louis.mn.us/partners
Founded: 1995
Budget: out of pocket
Constituency Age: 13-18
Issues: Youth Development
Race: Multi-Racial, White
Profile: Made up of 250 students from 14 high schools and 35 communities in St. Louis County, IRYA members identify community issues and develop youth-led campaigns. They have distributed the Youth Yellow Pages to 1300 young folks and hold regular Listening Lunches and an annual youth town meetings. Their mission is to build healthy communities, influence public policy to address the needs of young people, support and promote the positive development of youth and youth leadership, and create youth-friendly spaces.

STUDENT ASSOCIATION FOR THE ADVANCEMENT OF CHILDREN AS PEOPLE

Contact: Susie Oppenheim
Address: c/o Southside Family School, 2123 Clinton Ave South, Minneapolis, MN 55404
Phone: 612-872-8322
Email: eliza@southsidefamilyschool.org
Website: www.southsidefamilyschool.org
Founded: 1973
Budget: out of pocket
Constituency Age: 12 and under-18
Issues: Student Rights/Education Reform, Welfare/Poverty, Housing/Gentrification, Police Accountability, Militarism
Race: Multi-Racial
Profile: Based in Southside Family School, a K-8 alternative school teaching a social justice curriculum, SAACP is a student-led group that works to translate the principles they learn in

school into the lives of fellow students in and outside of school. The group researches and develops campaigns addressing welfare rights, housing issues and police brutality in their communities, which are largely low-income communities of color. SAACP also participated in anti-war activism and their school's annual Civil Rights History Trip through the South.

TEENS NETWORKING TOGETHER (TNT)

Contact: Jessie Ramirez
Address: 33 East George St, St Paul, MN 55107
Phone: 651-291-8575
Email: tnt55107@aol.com
Founded: 1990
Budget: under 250k
Constituency Age: 13-18
Issues: Racial Justice, Gang Issues, Violence Prevention
Race: Multi-Racial
Profile: TNT is a youth-led, multicultural community group in St. Paul, Minnesota where members actively pursue solutions to racism, neighborhood crime, gang violence, and negative attitudes towards teens. TNT is structured as an after-school program with recreational activities and peer mentoring. It has several focus groups such as Students Concerned About Racism, which does theater presentations to peers; Teens Running Our Own Streets, which addresses crime and violence prevention; and Sisters In Action, which focuses on the self-empowerment of young women.

YOUTH ORGANIZERS (YO!)

Contact: Anna Swanson
Address: 3019 Minnehaha Ave, Minneapolis, MN 55406
Phone: 612-276-0788
Email: yo@americas.org
Website: www.americas.org/youth
Founded: 1998
Budget: under 50k
Constituency Age: 12 and under-18
Issues: Labor/Economic Justice, Globalization, Corporate Accountability
Race: Multi-Racial, White
Profile: YO!, run by junior high and high school students, takes on sweatshops, child labor and global economic justice through grassroots organizing and peer education in schools, churches and community centers. Through a series of exercises at YO! in-school presentations, members raise awareness among their peers about the connections between child-labor exploitation and their own consumerism. YO! launched the highly successful "Sweatfree Schools" campaign in local districts to stop the buying of sweatshop-produced products.

© Pete Miser

© Mattie Weiss

© Josue Rojas, from YouthOulook.org

© Too Fly

Mississippi

Listing New Voices
Contact: Rodrick Moore
Address: PO Box 10433, Jackson, MS 39289
Phone: 601-352-1500
Email: souecho@bellsouth.net
Founded: 1989
Budget: under 50k
Constituency Age: 12 and under-30 and over
Issues: Welfare/Poverty, Racial Justice, Environmental Justice
Race: People of Color
Profile: Listing New Voices works to build a state-wide and regional cadre of youth organizers who strategically tackle environmental justice and juvenile justice issues through gatherings and youth-led trainings on leadership and organizational development. LNV is a project of Southern Echo, a model leadership development, political education and training organization that develops grassroots leadership across Mississippi and the Southeast. Since its inception, young people have been integrally involved in Southern Echo's organizing, providing a powerful model of intergenerational movement building.

NDN Rights Project
Contact: Charles Yow
Address: 302 Dunbar Ave, Bay St Louis, MS 39520
Phone: 228-467-3226
Email: director@ndnrights.org
Website: www.ndnrights.org
Founded: 1998
Budget: out of pocket
Constituency Age: 19-25
Issues: Indigenous Rights, Racial Justice
Race: Native American
Profile: The NDN Rights Project is a civil rights organization made up of Indigenous/American Indian students and student organizations across the country. The Project seeks to unite American Indian student organizations, support them in becoming effective on their campuses, and then link these campus chapters to local, national and international Indigenous/Indian struggles. They currently have about 4-5 affiliates and are working on campaigns to remove racist websites, school mascots and other media representations.

Tunica Teens in Action/Concerned Citizens for A Better Tunica
Contact: Melvin Young, Executive Director
Address: PO Box 2249, 1028 Prichard Road, Tunica, MS 38676
Phone: 662-363-1228
Founded: 2001
Budget: under 250k
Constituency Age: 12 and under-18
Issues: Environmental Justice, Student Rights/Education Reform
Race: African-American/Black
Profile: Founded in 1999, the 64 young people in Tunica Teens in Action prepare themselves to be community leaders through intergenerational work with Concerned Citizens for A Better Tunica and organizing and leadership trainings with Southern Echo. Currently campaigning to stop pesticide sprayings near their schools using door-to-door outreach, community forums and lobbying efforts. Successfully stopped the implementation of a dress-code in their schools and have plans for a state-wide youth gathering.

YAPS (Youth As Public Speakers)
Contact: Joyce Parker
Address: 526 W. Alexander St, Greenville, MS 38701
Phone: 662-332-4497
Email: jparker@bellsouth.net
Founded: 2002
Budget: out of pocket
Constituency Age: 12 and under-21
Issues: Arts/Culture, Racial Justice, Environmental Justice, Student Rights/Education Reform
Race: African-American/Black
Profile: YAPS is a youth-led project that uses art and popular education to teach peers about youth activism, African American culture and the legacy of young people in political movements. They are investigating and monitoring their school district and educating the community on local environmental justice, political and education issues. A dynamic and creative new project, YAPS recently combined cultural performances and a baby clothing drive with voter education and registration.

Youth Governance Initiative of Citizens for Quality Education
Contact: Ellen Reddy
Address: 109 Swinney Lane, Lexington, MS 39095
Phone: 662-834-0080
Email: cqe@tecinfo.com
Founded: 2001
Budget: under 100k
Constituency Age: 12 and under-18
Issues: Environmental Justice, Prisons/Criminal Justice, Campaign Finance
Race: African-American/Black
Profile: The Youth Governance Initiative engages young people in the political process through intergenerational and youth-led community organizing. Participants have campaigned to clean-up a contaminated dump site, organized around pesticide spraying, and are collaborating with Critical Resistance South on a juvenile justice initiative. YGI also hosts Democracy Summer, where young people convene with each other and meet with city and state legislators about critical community issues.

YOUTH INNOVATION MOVEMENT

Contact: Drewstella White
Address: 306 Main St, Duck Hill, MS 38925
Phone: 662-565-7004
Email: actionccmc@dixie-net.com
Founded: 1998
Budget: under 100k
Constituency Age: 12 and under-18
Issues: Youth Development
Race: African-American/Black
Profile: A project of Concerned Citizens of Montgomery County, YIM develops youth leadership by partnering young organizers with experienced adult mentors. Participants then design and implement campaigns that they feel will generate positive changes in their community. Organize community forums that have focused on issues such as welfare, police brutality and overcoming voting fears in the African American community. YIM also does voter outreach in rural areas to help elderly and illiterate people participate in elections.

MISSOURI

ARTISTS OF A NEW HORIZON/EARTH WALK

Contact: Drew Metcalf
Address: 6416 Nashville Ave, St Louis, MO 63139
Phone: 314-781-8095
Email: dub2love@yahoo.com
Founded: 2001
Budget: out of pocket
Constituency Age: 13-30 and over
Issues: Media, Arts/Culture
Race: African-American/Black
Profile: Earth Walk is an intergenerational collective that seeks to bring together artists committed to using their talents for their communities and for social justice movments. Produce a monthly public acess show, Artists of a New Horizon, which runs features on local issues, art centers, musicians, slam poets and anything else related to using artistic expression for social justice work. Though primarily focused on the St. Louis community, the program covers national and international developments as well.

COMMUNITY ARTS & MEDIA PROJECT (CAMP)

Contact: Katie Mack
Address: PO Box 63232, St Louis, MO 63163
Phone: 314-772-9178
Email: camp@stlimc.org
Founded: 2001
Budget: under 50k
Constituency Age: 13-30 and over
Issues: Youth Development, Media, Enviroment, Homelessness, Militarism
Race: Multi-Racial, White

Profile: CAMP is the new nexus and home of the radical community in St. Louis, including: Food Not Bombs, Center for Alternative Technology, Beehive Design Collective, Confluence, Southside University, and the St. Louis Independent Media Center. They just bought a 9,000 square-foot space that will house multiple organizations, community forums and cultural events; certain to remain an important resource and training ground for young organizers. Campaigns include public outreach and education on the FTAA, women's rights, the prison industry and more.

CONFLUENCE

Contact: Mark Bohnert
Address: PO Box 63232, St Louis, MO 63163
Phone: 314-771-2541
Email: markrobert@stlimc.org
Website: www.confluenceweb.org
Founded: 1995
Budget: under 25k
Constituency Age: 13-30 and over
Issues: Media, Student Rights/Education Reform
Race: White
Profile: Confluence is a free and independent bi-monthly journal, produced cooperatively and distributed throughout the Midwest. In addition to environmental and urban affairs, Confluence covers labor and social justice issues, the arts, race, gender and sexuality from an anti-authoritarian perspective. Delivering independent investigative news coverage, Confluence also provides a forum for critical essays, media reviews, art, poetry and humor aimed at inspiring social and political transformation.

ORGANIZE RESISTANCE

Contact: Michael McCormack
Address: PO Box 45613, Kansas City, MO 64171
Phone: 816-561-1908
Email: organizeresistancekc@hotmail.com, vietssarah@hotmail.com
Founded: 2000
Budget: out of pocket
Constituency Age: 19-30 and over
Issues: Prisons/Criminal Justice, Globalization, Welfare/Poverty, Hip Hop Activism
Race: White, Latina/o, African-American/Black
Profile: Organize Resistance (formerly called Solidarity and Unity Now) regularly packs 500 or more folks in at events about Mumia Abu-Jamal, the FTAA, welfare deform, environmental justice and prisons. OR also holds hip-hop battles, film screenings and study groups. Successfully fought to revise Kansas City's rally permit process, enabling grassroots organizations to more freely march and assemble. Current campaigns focus on improving public schools and ending police brutality. OR is one of the most effective youth-led organizations in the Midwest.

MONTANA

MONTANA HUMAN RIGHTS NETWORK

Contact: Betty Kijewski
Address: PO Box 1222, Helena, MT 59624
Phone: 406-442-5506
Email: betty@mhrn.org
Website: www.mhrn.org
Founded: 1991
Budget: out of pocket
Constituency Age: 13-30 and over
Issues: Racial Justice, Violence Prevention
Race: Multi-Racial, Native American
Profile: MHRN is a grassroots, membership based human rights organization with ten local groups throughout the state of Montana. They have two components, research and organizing; research includes monitoring hate groups; organizing includes speaking tours, lobbying, education, and legal strategies. Work to increase community support and legal protection for groups targeted by hate activity, namely Montana's religious (non-Christian) and people of color communities.

PROUD YOUTH RADICALLY ORGANIZING/PRIDE!

Contact: Karl Olsen
Address: PO Box 775, Helena, MT 59624
Phone: 406-442-9322
Email: pride123@aol.com
Website: www.gaymontana.com
Founded: 2000 (1994)
Budget: out of pocket
Constituency Age: 13-18
Issues: LGBTTSQ/Queer, Violence Prevention
Race: White
Profile: PYRO is a youth program of PRIDE!, a gay & lesbian rights advocacy group. Youth are involved in peer outreach and developed a how-to manual for folks interested in starting Gay/Straight Alliances. Their work has also led to the creation of a Safe Schools Coalition in Montana. PYRO annually hosts a Youth Summit conference designed to assist youth with accessing and creating support networks, understanding their rights, coming out and speaking out against violence and discrimination.

YOUTH FOR UNITY SPIDERWOMEN YOUTH ART INITIATIVE

Contact: Molly Madden
Address: 924 Butte Ave, Helena, MT 59601
Phone: 406-449-8790
Email: humanrightsmunky@hotmail.com
Founded: 1997
Budget: out of pocket
Constituency Age: 13-18
Issues: Arts/Culture, LGBTTSQ/Queer, Racial Justice, Women's Rights, Multi-Culturalism
Race: White, Native American
Profile: Now in transition, Youth For Unity held protests with hundreds of kids and were successful in getting condoms in high schools in this town of 50,000. Held vigils for Matthew Shepherd and organized for the National Day of Silence; lobbied on the state-level against the death penalty and for environmental justice. Created Spiderwoman to paint community murals with young women. Molly is a bad ass organizer-- whatever Youth for Unity transitions into will be worth checking out.

NEBRASKA

BOONDOGGLES

Contact: Angela Hatcher
Address: 122 N 14th St, Lower Level, Lincoln, NE 685
Email: boondoggle@ideviate.net
Website: www.ideviate.net
Founded: 1999
Budget: out of pocket
Constituency Age: 13-30 and over
Issues: Corporate Accountability, LGBTSTI/ Queer, Media, Women's Rights
Race: White
Profile: Boondoggles is an independent activist bookstore in Lincoln and a prime hub for activism in the area. They table at events to spread info about LGBTQ and women's issues. Boondoggles emphasizes distributing independently pressed books and donates a portion of all proceeds to other progressive groups.

SPECTRUM

Contact: Gina Matkin
Address: 234 Nebraska Union, 14th and R Streets, Lincoln, NE 68588-0455.
Phone: 402-472-5644
Email: gmatkin@unl.edu
Website: www.unl.edu/lambda
Budget: out of pocket
Constituency Age: 19-25
Issues: LGBTTSQ/Queer
Race: Multi-Racial, White
Profile: Spectrum, the Gay, Lesbian, Bisexual and Transgender Student Association at the University of Nebraska-Lincoln, works to build a safe and supportive campus environment for GLBT students. Primarily comprised of undergraduate students, Spectrum holds workshops, support groups and has a speaker's bureau. Spectrum also works with other organizations to combat racism, sexism, ableism and other forms of oppression.

NEVADA

NEVADA YOUNG ACTIVIST PROJECT

Contact: Inger McDowell
Address: 1101 Riverside Drive, Reno, NV 89503
Phone: 775-348-7557
Email: planinger@aol.com
Website: www.nyap-online.org
Founded: 2001
Budget: under 50k
Constituency Age: 13-25
Issues: Environmental Justice, Student Rights/Education Reform, Women's Rights, Racial Justice, LGBTTSQ/Queer
Race: Multi-Racial
Profile: Founded as a part of the Progressive Leadership Alliance of Nevada, NYAP organizes around multiple issues and provides peer leadership training. Current campaigns involve collecting and analyzing data to document racial profiling by police and they are lobbying to have a NYAP representative under 25 years old on the state-wide police monitoring committee. Also fighting an anti-gay legislation that will make all LGBT relationships illegal in the state of Nevada.

WESTERN SHOSHONE DEFENSE PROJECT

Contact: Lois Whitney
Address: PO Box 211308, Crescent Valley, NV 89821
Phone: 775-468-0230
Email: wsdp@igc.org
Website: www.alphacdc.com/wsdp
Budget: under 100k
Constituency Age: 13-30 and over
Issues: Militarism, Indigenous Rights, Racial Justice, Environment
Race: Multi-Racial, Native American
Profile: Currently focused on outreach and education related to preserving Western Shoshone culture and sovereignty, WSDP is an intergenerational project working to insure the long term health and integrity of the Western Shoshone Nation. In ongoing efforts to protect the environmental health of their traditional land base, WSDP is an active community voice in negotiations between the US government and the Western Shoshone Nation on resource use. No easy task given the US government's longstanding refusal to honor its own treaties.

NEW HAMPSHIRE

NEW HAMPSHIRE YOUTH MOBILIZATION

Contact: Steve Diamond
Address: PO Box 1497, Dover, NH 03821
Email: nhym@subdimension.com
Founded: 1995
Budget: out of pocket
Constituency Age: 13-25
Issues: Globalization, Human Rights, Militarism
Race: White
Profile: NHYM uses non violent direct action to address multiple issues, including the "war on terror," globalization, worker rights, the death penalty and the case of Mumia Abu Jamal. Organize teach-ins, community forums and demonstrations on both high school and college campuses. Work to build coalitions with the few politically progressive and radical groups in New Hampshire, including Amnesty International and the Student Environmental Action Center.

SEACOAST OUTRIGHT

Contact: Mim Easton
Address: PO Box 842, Portsmouth, NH 03802
Phone: 603-431-1013
Email: seacoastoutright@hotmail.com
Website: www.seacoastoutright.org
Founded: 1993
Budget: under 100k
Constituency Age: 13-30 and over
Issues: LGBTTSQ/Queer, Youth Development
Race: White
Profile: Seacoast Outright is a peer-led/adult facilitated support group and safe space for LGBTQ youth. Participants receive leadership and public speaking training; some speak to their schools and communities about prejudice and violence prevention while others get involved in community service projects addressing issues ranging from dating violence to AIDS. Work actively to transform seacoast New Hampshire and southern Maine into safe, healthy and welcoming communities for LGBTQ youth.

NEW JERSEY

BLACK NIA FORCE

Contact: Trevor Phillips
Address: 400 Highland Terrace, Apt 4H, Orange, NJ 07050
Phone: 973-495-0757
Email: tphillipscmts@yahoo.com
Budget: out of pocket
Constituency Age: 13-30
Issues: Labor/Economic Justice, Student Rights/Education Reform, Racial Justice
Race: African-American/Black
Profile: Black Nia FORCE (Freedom Organization for Racial and Cultural Enlightenment) works to empower African American youth and to fight racial and economic oppression. BNF has a monthly food and clothing drive, participates in statewide coalitions on public education, political prisoners and labor issues, and operates a Liberation School that teaches African and African American history, literacy and mathematics. BNF has actively supported Ras Baraka's campaigns for a city council seat in Newark in the last two elections.

© Margarita Garcia

© Bryan Iler

© Margarita Garcia

another world is possible

conversations in a time of terror

POWER TO THE YOUTH

Contact: Bill Wetzel
Address: 615 Little Silver Point Rd, Little Silver, NJ 07739
Phone: 732-530-1128
Email: info@youthpower.net
Website: www.youthpower.net
Founded: 1999
Budget: out of pocket
Constituency Age: 13-21
Issues: Student Rights/Education Reform
Race: White
Profile: Power to the Youth is a dynamic national organization of youth (and cool adults) who are taking charge of their schools. Their website offers all sorts of creative actions that every jr. high and high school student can and should take. Grade your school, organize a protest of a test (everyone leaves the test blank), commend creative teachers, plaster the school with posters (downloadable from the web), circulate a petition for peer-led classes. Mission: put mind-numbing schools out of business.

STUDENTS AGAINST TESTING

Contact: Dana Bennis
Address: 615 Little Silver Point Rd, Little Silver, NJ 07739
Phone: 210-224-7236
Website: www.nomoretests.com
Founded: 2001
Budget: out of pocket
Constituency Age: 13-18
Issues: Student Rights/Education Reform
Race: Multi-Racial
Profile: Related to Power to the Youth, Students Against Testing is focused on supporting student boycotts of standardized testing throughout the nation and promoting different forms of evaluation to replace these tests. Advocate boycotts of the ACT, SAT as well as the standardized testing mandatory for grade promotion that is sweeping the nation's public school system. Their informative website provides organizing materials as well as specific instructions on how to complete a test boycott.

NEW MEXICO

SAGE COUNCIL (SACRED ALLIANCES FOR GRASSROOTS EQUALITY)

Contact: Sonny Weahkee
Address: PO Box 82086, Albuquerque, NM 87198
Phone: 505-260-4696
Email: sage@sagecouncil.org
Website: www.sagecouncil.org
Founded: 1996
Budget: under 100k
Issues: Environmental Justice, Housing/Gentrification, Indigenous Rights, Public Space

Race: Native American, Latina/o, Asian/Pacific Islander
Profile: Run by Asian, Latina/o and Native American youth under 30, Sage Council built a strong political organizing coalition that successfully blocked one of the Southwest's biggest developers from building a highway over the Petroglyph National Monument, a sacred Native site. The Youth Involvement Program identifies youth of color for organizing and mobilization training, and then creates the space for these newly trained organizers to identify and run organizing campaigns in their communities.

SANTA FE MOUNTAIN CENTER (SFMC)

Contact: Sky Gray
Address: PO Box # 449, Tesuque, NM 87574
Phone: 505-983-6158
Email: sky@sf-mc.com
Website: www.sf-mc.com
Founded: 1979
Budget: under 1 million
Constituency Age: 13-30 and over
Issues: Indigenous Rights, Youth Development
Race: Native American
Profile: SFMC is an intergenerational organization providing adventure-based experiential education and leadership training opportunities for disenfranchised and incarcerated Native American youth. With 50% of nearby Zia Pueblo's population under 25, SFMC believes that training young organizers as community leaders is necessary to create social and political change. Central to SFMC's work is the belief that, "the wisdom of the elders, combined with the strength and savvy of the youth, will be a force to reckon with."

SOUTHWEST ORGANIZING PROJECT (SWOP)

Contact: Fernando Abeyta
Address: 211 10th St SW, Albuquerque, NM 87102
Phone: 505-247-8832
Email: swop@swop.net
Website: www.swop.net
Founded: 1980
Budget: under 25k
Constituency Age: 13-25
Issues: Environmental Justice, Police Accountability
Race: Latina/o
Profile: Organizing youth of color in primarily Mexicana/o and Chicana/o communities, SWOP works to create safe environments in the community and the workplace, and to increase community participation in decisions on the use of water and other natural resources. SWOP youth have successfully defeated the Albuquerque school superintendent's school "safety plan" and city-wide anti-youth ordinances with direct action and door to door campaigns. SWOP youth also created a youth organizing curriculum and promote collaboration with other organizations nationally and internationally.

TORTUGA PROJECT

Contact: Mike Ipiotis
Address: 915 Walter St Southeast #3C, Albuquerque, NM 87102
Phone: 505-766-5395
Email: mike3sixty@yahoo.com
Founded: 1998
Budget: out of pocket
Constituency Age: 13-18
Issues: Arts/Culture, Indigenous Rights, Public Space
Race: Native American
Profile: Tortuga Project is a collaborative youth group that works to create community self-sufficiency through art, education, cultural pride, community-controlled mediation and urban gardening. Tortuga travels the country leading workshops, presenting theater performances and painting murals that chronicle the continuum of traditional Indigenous culture and Hip Hop culture, while offering alternative approaches to dealing with gangs, substance abuse and violence. Creative, multifaceted and ambitious, Tortuga is a powerful example of youth organizing that opens minds and hearts.

YOUNG WOMEN UNITED

Contact: Ann Caton
Address: PO Box 12261, Albuquerque, NM 87195
Phone: 505-831-8930
Email: acaton@hotmail.com
Founded: 1999
Budget: under 250k
Constituency Age: 12-30
Issues: Violence Prevention, Reproductive Rights, Racial Justice, Women's Rights, Student Rights/Education Reform
Race: Multi-Racial
Profile: YWU is mobilizing and fighting against escalating violence in New Mexico, working to create spaces that support and empower women of color. Focusing on sexual violence, reproductive rights, and racial and economic injustice, YWU strives to educate and organize toward personal and community safety, health, happiness and freedom from fear. Activities include community education and forums, conducting a comprehensive survey of young women of color, improving sex education in public schools and fighting the arming of public-school security.

YOUTH ACTION

Contact: Patrick Masterson
Address: PO Box 12372, Albuquerque, NM 87195
Phone: 505-873-3345
Email: mastersonp@hotmail.com
Website: www.youthaction.net
Founded: 1987
Budget: under 500k
Constituency Age: 13-18
Issues: Student Rights/Education Reform, Racial Justice,

LGBTTSQ/Queer, Labor/Economic Justice, Environmental Justice
Race: Multi-Racial
Profile: YA creates regional and national leadership development and networking opportunities for youth organizers. Programs focus on political education, non-profit technical assistance (board development, fundraising, staff development, etc), networking opportunities for youth, and youth organizing training. YA also holds an annual national gathering, bringing together grassroots community groups to build a social justice network that empowers young people. Launching a national publication geared towards youth ages 13-19 and focused on discussions of local campaigns for social, economic, and environmental justice.

YOUTH ORGANIZING PROJECT OF THE COLONIAS DEVELOPMENT COUNCIL (YOP/CDC)

Contact: Ray Padilla
Address: 121 Wyatt Drive #5, Las Cruces, NM 88005
Phone: 505-647-2744
Email: cdcray@juno.com
Founded: 1994
Budget: under 500k
Constituency Age: 13-25
Issues: Immigrant/Refugee, Racial Justice
Race: Latina/o
Profile: YOP works along the US-Mexico border to improve daily living conditions or local residents. Much of the community lacks potable water, centralized sewers and/or decent housing. YOP organizes around issues including civil rights, immigrant rights, abusive border police and access to health care. Adults in CDC provide training and resources while the YOP members determine, design and implement their own campaigns.

NEW YORK

ABC NO RIO

Contact: Steven Englander
Address: 156 Rivington St, New York, NY 10002
Phone: 212-254-3697
Email: abc@abcnorio.org
Website: www.abcnorio.org
Founded: 1980
Budget: under 100k
Constituency Age: 13-30 and over
Issues: Arts/Culture, Housing/Gentrification
Race: Multi-Racial, White
Profile: ABC No Rio is an intergenerational, collectively-run center for artists and activists committed to sharing resources and ideas to impact society, culture and community. Members pursue social justice, equality, anti- authoritarianism, autonomous action, collective processes and alternative institutions. Shared resources include a darkroom, print shop,

library, computer center and performance space where music, poetry, visual art and other politically oriented events are hosted. Stated goal: to create cadres of actively aware artists and artfully aware activists.

ATREVETE

Contact: Angelines Mata
Address: 541 East 138th St, Bronx, NY 10451
Phone: 323-750-9087
Budget: out of pocket
Constituency Age: 13-18
Issues: Reproductive Rights
Race: Latina/o
Profile: Housed by the South Bronx Clean Air Coalition, Atrevete currently provides organizing training and leadership development for young women working on issues of reproductive freedom, public health issues and women's empowerment. They regularly work with other New York based organizations to provide week-long and on-going trainings to young women.

AYE - ARTISTS AND YOUTH EDUCATORS

Contact: Rhea Vedro
Address: 201 Ocean Ave, Brooklyn, NY 11225
Phone: 718-288-1923
Email: ayenyc@earthlink.net
Founded: 2000
Budget: out of pocket
Constituency Age: 13-30
Issues: Arts/Culture, Hip Hop Activism
Race: Multi-Racial
Profile: AYE is a network of youth workers, artists, and organizers seeking to incorporate visual and performing arts into political organizing. They simply ask, "how can I bring the arts into the work I do?" and, "how can we use the arts to inspire political activism?" Through their listserve, artists receive info about actions, campaigns and organizations looking for artists. Folks gather monthly in members homes for events ranging from Hip Hop showcases to political education meetings.

B-HEALTHY

Contact: Bryant Terry
Address: 260 St James Place #1D, Brooklyn, NY 11238
Phone: 877-295-4306
Email: b-healthy@onebox.com
Founded: 2002
Budget: out of pocket
Constituency Age: 13-21
Issues: Environmental Justice, Welfare/Poverty
Race: Multi-Racial
Profile: Through skills-building workshops, B-HEALTHY educates low-income youth and youth workers about healthy cooking, nutrition, and affordable alternatives to low-quality school lunches and fast food. B-HEALTHY also helps young people connect their personal health with the social and

economic health of their communities. Using this understanding as a foundation, the organization works to develop community organizers able to address issues related to health and well being.

BIG NOISE FILMS

Contact: Jackie Soohen
Address: 56 Walker St, New York, NY 10013
Email: web@bignoisefilms.com
Website: www.bignoisefilms.com
Founded: 1998
Budget: out of pocket
Constituency Age: 13-30 and over
Issues: Globalization, Corporate Accountability, Racial Justice, Media
Race: Multi-Racial, White
Profile: Working to, "democratize the cultural media-scape," the Big Noise Films collective shows up anywhere revolutionary activity jumps off, from Argentina to Afghanistan, Korea to Chiapas, documenting the critical political events often ignored or maligned by mainstream media. They have collaborated with the IMC and others to make important documentaries like Black and Gold (on the Latin Kings and Queens); Zapatista, This is What Democracy Looks Like (on Seattle) and a new film, 9.11.

BLACKOUT ARTS COLLECTIVE

Contact: Taij M
Address: 1576 Thomlinson Ave, Bronx, NY 10461
Email: taij23@hotmail.com
Website: www.blackoutartscollective.com
Founded: 2000
Budget: out of pocket
Constituency Age: 13-30 and over
Issues: Arts/Culture, Prisons/Criminal Justice, Racial Justice
Race: People of Color, African-American/Black
Profile: With bases in four cities, BAC is the most networked national collective of (mostly spoken word) artists of color. Committed to using artistic expression for community healing and liberation, BAC takes its Lyrics on Lockdown Tour to prisons and schools, holds a monthly showcase, and offers Hip Hop, spoken word, dance and interactive arts workshops for youth and artists. Comprised largely of artists under 30, BAC also supports a branch lead by and for teens (Junior BLACKOUT Arts Collective).

BLUESTOCKINGS WOMEN'S BOOKSTORE & CAFE

Address: 172 Allen St, New York, NY 10002
Phone: 212-777-6028
Website: www.bluestockings.com
Founded: 1999
Budget: out of pocket
Constituency Age: 12 and under-30 and over
Issues: Women's Rights, LGBTTSQ/Queer
Race: Multi-Racial, White
Profile: An indy women's bookstore & cafe of the Lower East

Side, promotes the empowerment of women through words, art and activism. An intersection of dialogue, info exchange, women-focused books, events, workshops, and a meeting place. Recognizing links between oppressions, BWBC's goal is to be trans-inclusive, multi-lingual, open to all sexualities, spiritualities, intergenerational and to challenge racism, classism, ablism, sexism, ageism and sizism.

CAAAV: ORGANIZING ASIAN COMMUNITIES

Contact: Jane Bai & Eric Tang
Address: 2473 Valentine Ave, Bronx, NY 10458
Phone: 718-220-7391
Email: justice@caaav.org
Website: www.caaav.org
Founded: 1986
Budget: under 500k
Constituency Age: 13-25
Issues: Housing/Gentrification, Welfare/Poverty, Racial Justice, Labor/Economic Justice, Immigrant/Refugee
Race: Asian/Pacific Islander
Profile: CAAAV has organized New York City's low-income Asian immigrant communities against racist violence, labor exploitation, police brutality, gentrification, environmental injustice and poverty for over 15 years. Their three community based programs include the Youth Leadership Project (based in the Southeast Asian community in the Bronx), the Racial Justice Committee (based in Chinatown), and the Women Workers Project. Recent accomplishments include producing Eating Welfare, a film documenting the struggle around welfare rights and injustices in the SE Asian community.

CASA ATABEX ACHE

Contact: Dayanara Marte
Address: 471 East 140th St, Garden Level, Bronx, NY 10454
Phone: 718-585-5540
Email: CasaAtabexAche@aol.com
Website: www.casaatabexache.org
Founded: 1994
Budget: out of pocket
Constituency Age: 13-18
Issues: Reproductive Rights, Women's Rights, Environmental Justice
Race: Latina/o, African-American/Black
Profile: Located in the Mott Haven community of the Southeast Bronx and serving a predominantly Latina and African American constituency, Casa provides health education, self-healing support groups and leadership training to women of all ages. Casa young women organize and educate on reproductive and community health issues, provide peer support, and are active in the Free Vieques! Campaign. Young women also participate in a 3-day retreat and a rites of passage ceremony, emphasizing the necessary balance between individual and community healing.

CONSCIOUS MOVEMENTS COLLECTIVE

Contact: Adrienne Brown
Address: 22 West 27th St, 5th Floor, New York, NY 10001
Email: gravityhiv@hotmail.com
Website: www.healinginnovations.net
Founded: 2000
Budget: out of pocket
Constituency Age: 13-30
Issues: Drug Policy, Racial Justice, Arts/Culture, HIV/AIDS, Human Rights
Race: Multi-Racial
Profile: Conscious Movements Collective uses art and entertainment to facilitate HIV/AIDS activism. CMC has three main objectives: to educate youth in New York City about protecting themselves from HIV/AIDS, to partner with grassroots organizations in Africa to help combat AIDS, and to help raise consciousness about HIV/AIDS among urban youth globally through Hip Hop culture. CMC's works specifically to empower LGBT youth, people of color and those below the poverty line.

DANCESAFE

Contact: Tim Santamour
Address: c/o HRC, 22 West 27th St, 5th Floor, New York, NY 10001
Phone: 510-834-7500
Email: tim@dancesafe.org
Website: www.dancesafe.org
Founded: 1999
Budget: under 250k
Constituency Age: 13-30
Issues: Drug Policy, Arts/Culture, LGBTTSQ/Queer
Race: White
Profile: With local chapters in twenty-six cities throughout the US and Canada, DanceSafe uses the harm reduction model for popular education at raves, nightclubs and other dance events. They staff booths on drugs, safer sex, and other health and safety issues concerning the electronic dance community while continually challenging city ordinances restricting public space and free assembly. A clever mixture of safety, youth culture and political education.

DESIS RISING UP & MOVING (DRUM)

Contact: Monami Maulik
Address: 73-16 Roosevelt Ave, 2nd Floor, Jackson Heights, NY 11372
Phone: 718-205-3036
Email: drum@drumnation.org
Website: www.drumnation.org
Founded: 2000
Budget: out of pocket
Constituency Age: 13-30
Issues: Globalization, Immigrant/ Refugee Rights, Women's Rights
Race: Asian/Pacific Islander

Close Spofford! Stop the criminalization of our generation!
© Christine Wong and Youth Force 2001

Self-Determination
© Christine Wong and CAAAV 2001

Profile: DRUM is a community-based collective organizing low-income South Asian immigrants for racial, economic, and social justice. DRUM's organizing campaigns foster the direct leadership of INS detainees and their families, undocumented immigrants, and Desi (of South Asian ancestry) youth in the struggle for human rights for immigrants and all oppressed people. In the aftermath of 9/11, DRUM launched two campaigns (STOP the Disappearances Campaign! and the 9/11 Community Self-Defense Project) in response to the attacks on immigrant communities.

EARTH YOUTH CREW PROJECT
Contact: Cecil Corbin-Mark
Address: 271 West 125th St, Suite 308, New York, NY 10027
Phone: 212-961-1000
Email: cecil@weact.org
Website: www.weact.org
Founded: 1994
Budget: out of pocket
Constituency Age: 13-18
Issues: Environmental Justice
Race: Latina/o, African-American/Black
Profile: WEACT's Earth Youth Crew develops the leadership potential of youth of color in Northern Manhattan by using the urban environment as a classroom. It provides a space to develop community organizing, critical thinking, writing, and public speaking skills. Youth Crew members devote 300 hours of work at a community organizing project related to environmental justice issues such as air monitoring and lead poisoning. Participate in national and international discussions on environmental racism.

EL PUENTE ACADEMY FOR PEACE AND JUSTICE
Contact: Frances Lucerna
Address: 211 South 4th St, Brooklyn, NY 11211
Phone: 718-387-0404
Email: egelpuente@aol.com
Founded: 1982
Budget: over 1 million
Constituency Age: 12-18
Issues: Arts/Culture, Environmental Justice
Race: Latina/o
Profile: El Puente (meaning "bridge") is a public high school dedicated to nurturing the next generation of community l eaders. While taking a full load of college preparatory and vocational courses, El Puente students are active in many local campaigns, ranging from post-9/11 peace and environmental justice organizing to police accountability and public education campaigns. With Hip Hop fully incorporated into their school curriculum, El Puente students integrate art and activism into their class assignments, community service projects and cultural events.

FIERCE
Contact: Jesse Ehrensaft-Hawley
Address: c/o Ella Baker Center for Human Rights, 437 W. 16th St, New York, NY 10011
Phone: 646-336-6789 x108
Website: www.ellabakercenter.org/fierce
Founded: 2000
Budget: under 100k
Constituency Age: 13-30
Issues: Police Accountability, LGBTTSQ/Queer, Violence/Abuse, Public Space, Housing/Gentrification
Race: Multi-Racial
Profile: FIERCE, based in NYC but a project of California's Ella Baker Center, is a youth-led organization working to end violence against LGBTQ youth of color. FIERCE is part of the No More Youth Jails campaign, fights to increase funding for community safe spaces and is addressing other issues such as gentrification, police brutality and profiling. Leads workshops and forums that explore LGBTQ civil rights at the intersection of racial and economic identity, employment and educational opportunities, and safety and health issues.

FILIPINO AMERICAN COALITION FOR ENVIRONMENTAL SOLUTIONS (FACES)
Contact: Angelica K. Jongco
Address: 16 West 32nd St, Suite 10B2, New York, NY 10001
Phone: 212-594-4021
Email: angelica@facessolutions.org
Website: www.facessolutions.org
Budget: out of pocket
Constituency Age: 19-30
Issues: Environmental Justice, Militarism
Race: Asian/Pacific Islander
Profile: FACES is a youth coalition of church, environmental, peace and justice groups and concerned individuals organizing to end toxic contamination at US military bases in the Philippines. Mobilizing grassroots support and educating US policymakers, they are addressing increased militarization in the Philippines following the deployment of thousands of troops post 9/11. They've organized letter-writing and chapter-building campaigns, participated in direct actions and visited and networked with the political and environmental struggles in Vieques, Puerto Rico and Memphis, TN.

GLOBAL KIDS
Contact: Michelle Luc
Address: 561 Broadway, 6th Floor, New York, NY 10012
Phone: 212-226-0130
Email: info@globalkids.org
Website: www.globalkids.org
Founded: 1989
Budget: over 1 million
Constituency Age: 13-21
Issues: Human Rights, Globalization, HIV/AIDS, Arts/Culture

Race: Multi-Racial

Profile: GK works in and out of schools, prioritizing leadership development, multicultural education, social action, peer education, academic enrichment and teacher training. GK participants are considered "at-risk" for academic failure, yet they design their community programs and initiate and lead political campaigns around human rights, environmental justice, prisons and education. Bringing together youth from all over the city, GK is a dynamic advocate for youth power and possibility.

GLOBAL YOUTH ACTION NETWORK

Contact: Benjamin Quinto
Address: 211 E. 43rd St, Suite 905, New York, NY 10017
Phone: 212-661-6111
Email: gyan@youthlink.org
Website: www.youthlink.org
Founded: 1995
Budget: under 250k
Constituency Age: 13-30
Issues: Human Rights
Race: Multi-Racial
Profile: The mission of GYAN is to unite the international youth-led movement by providing tools, resources and recognition for positive action. The Network also works to increase collaboration and resource-sharing among youth organizations in more than 165 countries and to connect, elevate and unite the voices of young people. Collaborate with TakingITGlobal and Youth In Action to create an on-line community that features a monthly newsletter, an idea bank and a global gallery.

HIP HOP LEADS (LEADING EFFORTS TO ADDRESS DISABLING SOCIAL CHALLENGES)

Contact: Marinieves Alba
Address: 159 E. 103rd St, Box 3A, New York, NY 10029
Email: HipHopLEADS@aol.com
Website: www.hiphopleads.org
Founded: 2001
Budget: under 25k
Constituency Age: 13-21
Issues: Women Rights, Student Rights/Education Reform, Hip Hop Activism, Arts/Culture, Racial Justice
Race: People of Color
Profile: Hip Hop LEADS is a progressive network for youth, youth activists and educators that uses Hip Hop culture as a bridge for political education, organizing and leadership training Holistic personal development is emphasized as a critical tool for collective consciousness building and community transformation. A speakers bureau and online resource center for educators and activists are in development. Hip Hop LEADS co-facilitates the International Hip Hop Exchange.

HIP HOP SPEAKS

Contact: Kevin Powell
Address: PMB 280, 138 Court St, Brooklyn, NY 11201
Phone: 718-399-0695
Email: Hiphopspeaks2001@aol.com
Website: www.hiphopspeaks.com
Founded: 2001
Budget: out of pocket
Constituency Age: 13-30 and over
Issues: Hip Hop Activism
Race: Multi-Racial, People of Color
Profile: HHS is a series of quarterly community forums and mc battles in NYC. While rhymers battle on the mic (with guidelines prohibiting excessive profanity or disrespecting of women in lyrical content), journalists, artists and community figures participate in dialogues on issues impacting youth of color. Forum topics have included 9/11, community activism, and a Father's Day discussion on manhood. HHS has plans to take this format for cultural and political dialogue on a ten city tour.

JUSTICE 4 YOUTH COALITION

Contact: Chino Hardin
Address: 388 Atlantic Ave, 3rd Floor, Brooklyn, NY 11217
Phone: 718-260-8805
Email: chino@nomoreprisons.org
Website: www.nomoreyouthjails.org
Founded: 2002
Budget: under 25k
Constituency Age: 12 and under-30
Issues: Racial Justice, Prisons/ Criminal Justice, LGBTTSQ/Queer, Women's Rights, Student Rights/ Education Reform
Race: Multi-Racial
Profile: The Justice4Youth Coalition spearheaded No More Youth Jails!, a two part campaign to 1) stop $64 million from being allocated to juvenile detention facilities, and 2) to reallocate those millions into NY communities most impacted by the criminalization of young people. Through intense lobbying, public education and demonstrations, the Coalition succeeded in the first and is pushing for the second. J4Y is made up of formerly incarcerated youth and adults, high school students, college students, parents, teachers and community members.

KOREAN YOUTH ACTION PROJECT

Contact: Wol-San Lim
Address: PO Box 540903, Flushing, NY 11354
Phone: 917-568-6347
Email: nodutdol@egroups.com
Website: www.nodutdol.com
Founded: 1999
Budget: under 25k
Constituency Age: 13-18
Issues: Youth Development
Race: Asian/Pacific Islander
Profile: A project of Nodutdol for Korean Community

Development, KYAP is a leadership program led by low-income Korean junior high and high school students. Through surveys, workshops and collective organizing projects, KYAP has campaigned around racism, bilingual education and the post-9/11 climate. With parent organization Nodutdol, KYAP seeks to bridge the divisions of war, nation, gender, class, language, and generation by creating a broader definition of what it means to be Korean and by building solidarity with the larger social change movement.

LA ABEJA OBRERA

Contact: Betsy Maclean
Address: c/o Center for Cuban Studies, 124 West 23 St, New York, NY 10011
Phone: 212-242-0559
Email: betsy@abejaobrera.org
Website: www.abejaobrera.org
Founded: 1999
Budget: under 25k
Constituency Age: 19-30 and over
Issues: Labor/ Economic Justice, Human Rights, Women's Rights
Race: Multi-Racial
Profile: La Abeja Obrera (the Worker Bee) aims to nurture and support global activism with local and international work projects that unite community members and foster learning about the process of transforming marginalized neighborhoods. Internationally, the Abejas use physical labor to express solidarity with the Cuban people and other revolutionary communities worldwide. In the US, Abejas use labor solidarity as a tool to support local community development. Abeja activities include collective fundraising, political education, volunteer work projects, and work brigade trips abroad.

MALCOLM X GRASSROOTS MOVEMENT

Contact: Monifa Akinwole
Address: 388 Atlantic Ave, 3rd Floor, Brooklyn, NY 11217
Phone: 718-254-8800
Email: mxgmny@hotmail.com
Founded: 1993
Budget: out of pocket
Constituency Age: 19-30 and over
Issues: Prisons/Criminal Justice, Racial Justice
Race: African-American/Black
Profile: Committed to ending the oppression of Afrikan people and building self-determined communities free of white supremacy and sexism. Organize bi-weekly feeding and clothing drives in Brooklyn and Harlem, participate in Brooklyn Cop Watch and are part of almost every important NYC political coalition. Ongoing work includes supporting US political prisoners/POWs, a prison book exchange, multiple campaigns through their New Afrikan Women's Caucus, and producing the pioneering Black August Hip Hop Benefit Concert series in the US, Cuba and South Africa.

NATIVE YOUTH MOVEMENTS

Contact: Tomas Shash
Address: 107 Giles St, Ithaca, NY 14850
Phone: 719-746-2400
Email: nymsavages@hotmail.com
Founded: 2002
Budget: out of pocket
Constituency Age: 12 and under-30
Issues: Environmental Justice, Indigenous Rights
Race: Native American
Profile: In 2002, two organizers traveled by foot (and greyhound) visiting fifteen Native territories across the country to establish independently-governed NYM chapters. While building relationships with local organizers and sharing their political work, groundwork was laid for a Freedom Tour that will bring Hip Hop, politics and a message of resistance to indigenous communities. The goal is to educate native youth about their history and power and the importance of indigenous unity through a model emphasizing Native culture and spirituality.

NEW YORK CITY INDEPENDENT MEDIA CENTER

Address: 34 East 29th St, 2nd Floor, New York, NY 10016
Phone: 212-684-8112
Email: imc-nyc@indymedia.org
Website: nyc.indymedia.org
Founded: 2000
Budget: under 25k
Constituency Age: 12 and under-30 and over
Issues: Media
Race: Multi-Racial
Profile: NYC IMC is a dynamic group of volunteers that has developed a popular website, a monthly free newspaper, community reporting workshops and other projects centered on reporting news ignored by mainstream media outlets. NYC IMC facilitates an open publishing space by inviting all local organizers and community members to contribute articles. NYC IMC also focuses on empowering young people with a philosophy of participatory media and encouraging them to be involved in print, radio, television and internet journalism.

NEW YORK PUBLIC INTEREST RESEARCH GROUP (NYPIRG)

Address: 9 Murray St, 3rd Floor, New York, NY 10007
Phone: 212-349-6460
Email: webmaster@nypirg.org
Website: www.nypirg.org
Founded: 1973
Budget: over 1 million
Constituency Age: 13-30
Issues: Environment
Race: Multi-Racial
Profile: One of the oldest and most effective grassroots youth-led organizations, they have maintained their consumer

protection base while branching into a range of issues from halting the end of recycling to rallying for public transportation with their straphangers campaign. They also focus on good government, monitoring the campaign finance laws, and operate an extensive campus network. Many activists have been in NYPIRG's unglamorous trenches-- the street canvassing work that has earned them a gritty reputation for rolling up their sleeves.

NKIRU CENTER FOR EDUCATION & CULTURE

Contact: Anjeanette Allen
Address: 732 Washington Ave, Brooklyn, NY 11238
Phone: 718-783-6306
Email: nkirucenter@nkirucenter.org
Website: www.nkirucenter.org
Founded: 1976
Budget: under 500k
Constituency Age: 13-30 and over
Issues: Hip Hop Activism, Education, Multiculturalism
Race: Multi-Racial, African-American/Black
Profile: Nkiru was created by Talib Kweli and Mos Def (of the popular Hip Hop duo Black Star) in order to continue the legacy of Nkiru Books, the oldest independent Black bookstore in Brooklyn. Now a not for profit organization, Nkiru promotes literacy and multicultural awareness for people of color through a free 12 week theatre and poetry workshop for teens, a storytelling program for preschoolers, a book club for adults, and FOUNDATIONS, an open mic Hip Hop and spoken word event.

PAPER TIGER TV

Contact: Carlos Pareja
Address: 339 Lafayette St, New York, NY 10012
Phone: 212-420-9045
Email: info@papertiger.org
Website: www.papertiger.org
Budget: out of pocket
Constituency Age: 13-25
Issues: Women's Rights, LGBTTSQ/Queer, Student Rights/Education Reform, Media, Arts/Culture,
Race: Multi-Racial
Profile: A pioneer in community controlled media, PTTV is a non-profit, volunteer video collective. Through production and distribution of public access programs, media literacy/video production workshops and community screenings, PTTV works to challenge and expose the corporate control of mainstream media. PTTV programs analyze and critique media, culture and politics. Shows feature scholars, community activists, critics and journalists covering a wide range of issues and international struggles, from Zapatistas to the Patriot Act, prisons to globalization, reproductive rights to independent media.

PRISON MORATORIUM PROJECT

Contact: Kate Rhee
Address: 388 Atlantic Ave, 3rd Floor, Brooklyn, NY 11217
Phone: 718-260-8805
Website: www.nomoreprisons.org
Founded: 1995
Budget: under 250k
Constituency Age: 13-30
Issues: Prisons/Criminal Justice, Labor/Economic Justice, Drug Policy
Race: Multi-Racial
Profile: The tiny organization behind three of the great success stories of the prison movement that has blossomed since 1998: the "Not With Our Money" campaign (college students forced Sodehxo-Marriott to sell its majority share in private prison corp CCA); blocking a $73 million upstate youth prison; and organizing the "No More Youth Jails" coalition that froze a $64 million expansion of the NYC juvenile detention system. Now convening a visionary 12 neighborhood assessment of what communities want instead of prisons.

PROJECT REACH

Contact: Don Kao
Address: 1 Orchard St, 2nd Floor, New York, NY 10002
Phone: 212-966-4227
Email: donkao@aol.com
Founded: 1970
Budget: under 500k
Constituency Age: 13-25
Issues: Arts/Culture, LGBTTSQ/Queer
Race: People of Color
Profile: Started in 1970 as a crisis center for Asian immigrant youth, Project Reach is an intergenerational, multiracial, multi-gender, anti-discrimination, grassroots youth organizing center with a commitment to challenging the destruction of New York City's youth communities. PR includes young women, LGBTQ youth, immigrant and undocumented youth, HIV+/ young people living with AIDS, young people who are differently-abled, teen mothers/fathers, gang-related/court-involved/ incarcerated youth, and runaway/foster care/homeless youth. Trainings on institutional discrimination and systemic oppression are at the core of its curriculum.

QUILOMBO COLLECTIVE NYC

Contact: Rosalyn Perez
Address: c/o The Brecht Forum, 122 27th St, 10th Floor, New York, NY 10001
Phone: 347-526-2889
Email: collective@quilombonyc.org
Website: www.quilombonyc.org
Founded: 1998
Budget: under 25k
Constituency Age: 13-30

Taxi Workers Alliance anti-war and post 9/11 immigrant repression protest in Flatbush, Brooklyn, June 9, 2002
© ramona photo

Issues: Prisons/Criminal Justice, LGBTTSQ/Queer,
Women's Rights, Student Rights/Education Reform,
Racial Justice
Race: Multi-Racial, People of Color
Profile: QCnyc is an intergenerational collective of teachers and
youth workers dedicated to social justice through popular
education. QCnyc works with youth and communities of color to
create spaces for dialogue, support and political education in
New York City. Quilombo Collective runs a popular education
experience for working class youth of color in NYC every
summer with the goal of building a broader base of youth
organizers and activists committed to local movements for
social justice.

RAPTIVISM RECORDS

Contact: Rishi Nath
Address: 61 E. 8th St #251, New York, NY 10003
Email: info@raptivism.com
Website: www.raptivism.com
Founded: 1998
Budget: out of pocket
Constituency Age: 13-30 and over
Issues: Arts/Culture, Racial Justice, Prisons/Criminal Justice,
Hip Hop Activism
Race: Multi-Racial
Profile: The leading independent, political Hip Hop label.
With the Prison Moratorium Project, Raptivism blew up
"No More Prisons," a benefit album addressing the expanding
prison industry and its impact upon communities of color.
Newly released projects include Tahir, Shabaam Sadeeq,
Danny Hoch and Akbar. Raptivism was the only label willing to
touch Dead Prez's song, "Cop Shot," a response to the murder
of Amadou Diallo.

RECLAIM THE STREETS

Phone: 212-539-6746
Email: rtsnyc@tao.ca
Budget: out of pocket
Constituency Age: 13-30
Issues: Public Space
Race: Multi-Racial
Profile: A broad coalition of environmentalists, students,
striking workers and ravers politicized by the creation of
draconian anti-assembly laws, RTS is about celebration as
direct action and dance as resistance. The model of protest
used is the reclamation of public space-- a street or road--
and transforming that stretch of asphalt into a place where
people gather together without cars, without shopping malls,
without permission from the state, with some music and some
ideas about transforming society. Making Golda Meir proud.

RED EYE

Contact: Johnathan Osler
Address: 116 Garfield Place, 4th Floor, Brooklyn, NY 11215
Phone: 917-288-7364
Email: editor@redeyemagazine.com
Website: www.redeyemagazine.com
Founded: 1999
Budget: out of pocket
Constituency Age: 13-30
Issues: Police Accountability, Media, Racial Justice,
Prisons/Criminal Justice, Hip Hop Activism
Race: Multi-Racial
Profile: Launched as a student publication at Wesleyan
University, the post-graduation Red Eye has become an
important youth-run political Hip Hop magazine (particularly
since Blu Magazine folded in 2000). The zine also teamed up
with Critical Breakdown (pg. 89) to form the Active Arts Project,
through which they do community outreach, community building
and event sponsorship in Boston and New York. Red Eye
believes Hip Hop can be a tool for critical thought and political
transformation; they publish quarterly to prove it.

SANGRE NUEVA

Contact: Hector Rivera
Address: 870 Manida Ave, Bronx, NY 10474
Phone: 917-704-0908
Email: photorican@yahoo.com
Founded: 2002
Budget: under 25k
Constituency Age: 13-30
Issues: Environmental Justice, Corporate Accountability,
Racial Justice
Race: Latina/o, African-American/Black, Middle Eastern
Profile: Led by teens in the South Bronx, Sangre Nueva draws
the cultural connections between Vieques, Puerto Rico and
Hunts Point in the Bronx. Youth are making a film and music
video on the relationships between the environmental hazards
suffered by both communities. They will use this video to
strengthen the talks they give throughout all of New York City
to raise awareness and inspire action about Hunts Point and
Vieques.

SISTA 2 SISTA

Contact: Loira Limbal
Address: 89 St Nicholas, Brooklyn, NY 11237
Phone: 718-366-2450
Email: info@sistaiisista.org
Founded: 1996
Budget: under 250k
Constituency Age: 13-18
Issues: Women's Rights, Violence Prevention,
Police Accountability, Housing/Gentrification
Race: People of Color

Profile: Through its Freedom School for Young Women of Color, SIIS offers political education, classes in creative self-expression and opportunities for self-development. Decisions are made collectively and work plans are created by members: the Action Squad develops and implements organizing strategies, while the Freedom Squad develops training and curricula for the Freedom School. Current campaigns include a fight against sexual harassment of young women by police, violence against women, racism, ageism, and gentrification. Among the most dynamic youth organizations nationwide.

SISTAS ON THE RISE

Contact: Yomara Velez
Address: 1384 Stratford Ave, Bronx, NY 10472
Phone: 718-328-5622
Email: yomarav@hotmail.com
Founded: 2002
Budget: out of pocket
Constituency Age: 13-25
Issues: Women's Rights, Reproductive Rights, Labor/Economic Justice
Race: People of Color
Profile: An emerging organization of young women of color in the Bronx, Sistas on the Rise seeks to build sisterhood between teen mothers and other young women of color. Programs include: SisterSoul, focused on emotional and spiritual wellness; SisterCypher, a peer and community education project using readings and video research that culminates in a campaign; and SisterSustain, an employment, economic justice and self-sufficiency project looking to increase skills and break cycles of dependency in the lives of women.

SLAM - STUDENT LIBERATION ACTION MOVEMENT

Contact: Rachel LaForest
Address: 695 Park Ave HN, Room 121, New York City, NY 10021
Phone: 212-772-4261
Founded: 1996
Budget: under 100k
Constituency Age: 13-25
Issues: Racial Justice, Student Rights/Education Reform, Prisons/Criminal Justice
Race: Multi-Racial
Profile: Among the most skilled youth orgs in the country, SLAM waged massive campaigns against tuition hikes and standardized admissions testing while engaging the national debate on the decreasing education/increasing prison budget corollary. Consistently working beyond campus issues, SLAM people of color affinity groups have been present at dozens of large national direct action protests and they run a high school technical/media literacy institute. When it finishes its current leadership transition, expect SLAM to be back on the front lines with women of color continuing to lead struggles for justice from the center.

STUDENTS FOR A FREE TIBET

Contact: Johnathan Hocevar
Address: 602 East 14th St, 2nd Floor, New York, NY 10009
Phone: 212-358-0071
Website: www.tibet.org/sft
Founded: 1994
Budget: under 250k
Constituency Age: 13-25
Issues: Human Rights, Immigrant/Refugee, Indigenous Corporate, Accountability
Race: Multi-Racial, Asian/Pacific Islander
Profile: With over 650 chapters in more than 30 countries, SFT may be the largest student-led human rights group in the world. Workshops, forums, publications, conferences, internet organizing and shareholder activism have proven to be effective means of raising awareness, creating international pressure and winning the release of political prisoners. A recent campaign lobbied investors to not participate in the Chinese Oil Company's initial public offering, dropping investment from an expected $10 billion to $2.8 billion.

THE NEUTRAL ZONE

Contact: Jennie Casciano
Address: 12 East 33rd St, 10th Floor, New York, NY 10016
Phone: 646-935-1943
Founded: 1992
Budget: under 250k
Constituency Age: 13-25
Issues: LGBTTSQ/Queer, Homelessness
Race: Multi-Racial, People of Color
Profile: Operates a drop in center for LGBTQ homeless youth (ages 15-22), offering walk-in counseling, referrals and support groups. They collaborated with FIERCE! and Paper Tiger TV to produce Fenced Out, a documentary about gentrification and its effect on youth in the West Village. An intergenerational organization, the Zone offers youth-led arts workshops and the active youth staff develops policies and programs in conjunction with adults.

THE POINT

Contact: Paul Lipson
Address: 940 Garrison Ave, Bronx, NY 10474
Phone: 718-542-4139
Website: www.thepoint.org
Founded: 1994
Budget: under 250k
Constituency Age: 12 and under-21
Issues: Youth Development, Hip Hop Activism, Arts/Culture, Environmental Justice
Race: People of Color, Latina/o, African-American/Black
Profile: No More Asthma Marches and Clean-Air Festivals are examples of an array of environmental justice organizing efforts 7-21 year olds at the Point use when fighting for justice through the arts. They do community economic projects, run an

international center of photography, a youth hosted micro-radio station, a dance studio and a performance company. Community gardening, canoe tours for visitors and EJ investigations and research address root causes of environmental ills in the battered South Bronx community.

UPROSE

Contact: Elizabeth Yeampiere
Address: 5417 Fourth Ave, Brooklyn, NY 11220
Phone: 718-492-9307
Email: UpRise99@aol.com
Budget: under 500k
Constituency Age: 13-21
Issues: Militarism, Women's Rights, Immigrant/Refugee, Environmental Justice
Race: People of Color
Profile: UPROSE works with high school age youth in the Sunset Park neighborhood comprised of 40% Palestinian, 40% Latino and 20% Asian and African-American youth. These environmental activists have been raising consciousness post 9/11 through rallies, panel discussions, and workshops. Past successes include halting a planned sludge treatment plant and a report documenting idling diesel truck violations. Currently opposing a major NY Power Authority proposal.
Youth initiatives include the Bring the Buya website and newsletter, Sistas Sol and the Environmental Enforcers.

UPTOWN FOR PEACE AND JUSTICE

Contact: Estevan Nembhard
Address: 11 Fort George Hill #18E, New York, NY 10040
Phone: 646-279-3205
Founded: 2001
Budget: out of pocket
Constituency Age: 13-25
Issues: Student Rights/Education Reform, Racial Justice, Public Space, Militarism, Hip Hop Activism
Race: Multi-Racial
Profile: UPJ is a grassroots organizing group of about 80 young people of color from the Harlem and Washington Heights neighborhoods working for peace and justice. They are waging anti-war and anti-violence campaigns that engage high school students in activism both in and outside the city. UPJ builds coalitions with youth organizations and local immigrant groups citywide dealing with the Patriot Act, organizes local open-mics and arts projects, and is campaigning against ongoing cuts to the education budget.

URBAN MINDZ

Contact: Kristian Bello
Address: 89 Crystal St, Brooklyn, NY 11208
Phone: 718-827-5577
Email: urbanmindz@hotmail.com
Founded: 2000
Budget: out of pocket
Constituency Age: 13-21

Issues: Student Rights/Education Reform, Racial Justice, Prisons/Criminal Justice, Police Accountability
Race: People of Color
Profile: Young people spreading strong organizing and leadership skills to other young people in order to transform the way the media, government, and schools criminalize youth. UM is campaigning against NY state legislation that tries juvenile offenders as adults, conducts community forums and has developed an incident report to monitor teachers, administrators and police in NYC public schools. UM is largely made up of high school students and "drop-outs" working together to address racism, homophobia and ageism.

VOICES UNBROKEN

Contact: Victoria Sammartino
Address: PO Box 342, Bronx, NY 10461
Phone: 718-239-0281
Email: voicesunbroken@yahoo.com
Founded: 1998
Budget: under 50k
Constituency Age: 13-21
Issues: Prisons/Criminal Justice, Arts/Culture
Race: People of Color
Profile: Based in the Bronx, Voices Unbroken conducts poetry workshops for under-heard populations throughout New York City, with an emphasis on working with prisoners, young women, and other youth that are outside of mainstream educational opportunities. Voices aims to provide its participants with the tools to explore their voice through poetry and creative writing. Literacy, political education, crisis prevention and mentorship are integrated into workshop offerings. Working to create artist residency programs in prisons throughout NYC.

YOUNG DEMOCRATIC SOCIALISTS

Contact: Erin Kaiser
Address: 180 Varick St, 12th Floor, New York, NY 10014
Phone: 212-727-8610 x24
Email: erin@dsausa.org
Website: www.dsausa.org/youth
Founded: 1983
Budget: under 50k
Constituency Age: 13-30
Issues: Welfare/Poverty, Racial Justice, Labor/EconomicJjustice, Globalization, Media
Race: Multi-Racial, White
Profile: YDS has 20 college chapters and played a key role in creating the campus anti-sweatshop, anti-war and anti-prison movements. Their publication, The Activist is smart, sassy and among the few non-annoying publications of the student socialist left. In addition to covering news from an anti-capitalist perspective, issues review online resources, discuss Hip Hop and other popular culture, evaluate organizer training schools and analyze the student movement. Making it safe for all the Socialists to come out of the closet.

YOUNG WOMEN OF COLOR LEADERSHIP PROGRAM/AUDRE LORDE PROJECT

Contact: Loyda Colon
Address: 85 South Oxford St, Brooklyn, NY 11217-1607
Phone: 718-596-0342
Email: alpinfo@alp.org
Website: www.alp.org
Founded: 1994
Budget: under 25k
Constituency Age: 13-25
Issues: Racial Justice, LGBTTSQ/Queer, Women's Rights
Race: People of Color
Profile: Creating a safe learning space for lesbian, gay, bisexual, two-spirit, transgender and questioning women of color, this youth leadership program introduces women 16-20 to direct action organizing, public speaking and grassroots campaign development. In the tradition of ALP, which has been on the frontlines of every social justice struggle in NYC since 1994, these young leaders are currently developing several local direct action campaigns. After age 20, participants move into ALP working groups, e.g., police violence, immigration and community outreach.

YOUTH BLOC

Contact: Libertad Gills
Address: 510 Prospect Ave, Brooklyn, NY 11215
Phone: 718-965-6039
Email: cubalibre@graffiti.net
Founded: 2002
Budget: out of pocket
Constituency Age: 13-21
Issues: Student Rights/Education Reform, Labor/Economic Justice, Immigrant/Refugee
Race: Multi-Racial
Profile: This high school coalition convened after the WEF protests. Working groups focus on creating local and global peace through justice, with the long-term aim of creating a model democracy that strives for the self-determination of oppressed communities. They coordinated a city wide high school walk out in solidarity with college students and collaborate with parents, teachers and communities to organize against education budget cuts. Regularly send a strong message to NYC that young people want edution to be a top priority.

YOUTH FORCE

Contact: Shirley Williams
Address: 320 Jackson Ave, Bronx, NY 10454
Phone: 718-665-4268
Email: msshirley@hotmail.com
Website: www.youthforcenyc.org
Founded: 1994
Budget: under 1 million
Constituency Age: 12 and under-25
Issues: Housing/Gentrification, Hip Hop Activism, Racial Justice, Prisons/Criminal Justice, Police Accountability
Race: Latina/o, African-American/Black
Profile: Youth founded and led, Youth Force fights the criminalization of youth in the South Bronx and advocates for education and housing reform. In 1997, they organized 20 groups to shut down Spofford, the worst of the city juvenile detention centers. Youth Force teaches community organizing and political education and administers a mini-grants program. They initiated the No More Youth Jails campaign, a NYC wide coalition seeking to stop juvenile detention expansion and reallocate $64.6 million to community based youth projects.

YOUTH INITIATIVE FOR SOCIAL ACTION (YOUTH IN ACTION)

Contact: Ana Liza Caraballes
Address: 122 W. 27th St, 10th Floor, New York, NY 10027
Phone: 212-741-6806
Website: www.philforum.org/youthinaction
Founded: 2000
Budget: under 100k
Constituency Age: 13-25
Issues: Labor/Economic Justice, Prisons/Criminal Justice, Globalization, Immigrant/Refugee, Racial Justice
Race: Multi-Racial, Asian/Pacific Islander
Profile: YIA's ongoing Youth Leaders Forum brings Filipino and Filipino American organizers in the tri-state together on a monthly basis to discuss their social, political and cultural work. YIA hosts a Community Organizers Summer Camp, a week long intensive where 25 youth learn history, culture, creative organizing skills, fundraising and team building while networking with other non-profit social justice organizations. In its 3-day Filipino American Youth Festival, YIA celebrates Filipino culture and gives awards to outstanding young community activists.

YOUTH MINISTRIES FOR PEACE AND JUSTICE

Contact: Yomara Velez
Address: 1384 Stratford St, Bronx, NY 10472
Phone: 718-328-5622
Founded: 1994
Budget: under 250k
Constituency Age: 13-21
Issues: Environmental Justice, Police Accountability, Youth Development
Race: Latina/o, African-American/Black
Profile: A faith-based organization dedicated to youth development and community organizing, YMPJ was founded in response to the attempted torching of a community church follwing an anti-drug rally. Based in and around the Bronx River Housing Projects, a cadre of 15-20 teenage organizers lead Project ROW (Reclaiming Our Waterfront) to restore the Bronx River and educate the community about high asthma rates. Their Campaign for Police Reform works to stop racial profiling and police brutality in their neighborhood.

FIERCE, NYC

Racial Justice Day image, NYC
© Too Fly

Youth Network & Artists Network of Refuse & Resist

Contact: Connie Julian
Address: 305 Madison Ave #1166, New York, NY 10165
Phone: 212-713-5657
Email: info@refuseandresist.org
Website: www.refuseandresist.org
Founded: 1996
Budget: under 25k
Constituency Age: 13-25
Issues: Militarism, Hip Hop Activism, Racial Justice, Prisons/Criminal Justice, Arts/Culture
Race: Multi-Racial
Profile: Fearlessly organizes young people and committed artists to connect with social and political movements. Projects include Philly Freedom Summer, where participants work on death penalty issues and the case of Mumia Abu Jamal, Act Your Rage, a lively open mic and political party, and Clinic Escorting, offering safety and support at health clinics that provide abortion. A project of Refuse & Resist, YN/AN has been a lead organizer in the Not in Our Name campaign against the "war on terrorism."

Youth Power Project

Contact: Oona Chaterjee
Address: 301 Grove St, Brooklyn, NY 11237
Phone: 718-418-7690 x204
Email: oona@maketheroad.org
Website: www.maketheroad.org
Founded: 1997
Budget: under 500k
Constituency Age: 13-21
Issues: Welfare/Poverty, LGBTTSQ/Queer, Labor/Economic Justice, Environmental Justice
Race: African-American/Black, Latina/o
Profile: Currently working with neighborhood residents aged 5-19, Youth Power fosters and sustains youth-driven community organizing in the Bushwick community. YP's main focus is drawing young people into organizing work that challenges police brutality, lack of funding for after-school programs, and increased city investment in juvenile prisons. Other activities include performing arts, radio documentary production, computer skills training and mural-making. Youth Power is a project of Make the Road By walking, one of the strongest grassroots community organizations in the country.

North Carolina

Duke Progressive Alliance

Contact: Natalie Lamela
Address: PO Box 90834, Durham, NC 27708
Email: nl12@duke.edu
Website: www.duke.edu/web/dpa
Founded: 2000
Budget: out of pocket
Constituency Age: 13-25
Issues: Racial Justice, Labor/Economic Justice, Globalization, Corporate Accountability
Race: Multi-Racial
Profile: DPA is a progressive coalition of campus groups ranging from Students Against Sweatshops to the Black Student Alliance, LGBTQ organizations to animals rights groups. They waged a campaign to prevent Aramark from outsourcing dining service work, losing the original battle but winning job protection and regulations for workers. DPA is taking a delegation to the Jobs with Justice Conference and is focused on launching its living wage campaign.

El Pueblo Youth Leadership Program

Contact: Jennifer Castillo
Address: 118 South Person St, Raleigh, NC 27601
Phone: 919-835-1525
Email: elpueblo@elpueblo.org
Website: www.elpueblo.org
Founded: 1994
Budget: under 25k
Constituency Age: 13-25
Issues: Student Rights/Education Reform, Education, Youth Development
Race: Latina/o
Profile: The Youth Leadership Program strives to empower Latinos, ages 13 –23, through advocacy, policy, leadership development, education and promotion of cross-cultural understanding at the local, state and national levels. The topics for El Pueblo's Spring and Summer Youth Forums are determined by the youth; past gatherings have focused on cultural identity, race relations, education and immigration. El Pueblo also makes mini-grants to youth initiated projects.

Garbage Liberation Front (GLF)

Contact: Jason Trashville
Address: 37 Mulberry St, Asheville, NC 28804
Phone: 828-773-0684
Email: trashio56@hotmail.com
Founded: 2000
Budget: out of pocket
Constituency Age: 12-30
Issues: Arts/Culture, Corporate Accountability, Environmental Justice, Genetic Engineering, Globalization
Race: White
Profile: The youth-led Garbage Liberation Front combines multi-

layered puppet shows on political and environmental issues with organizing workshops that teach concrete skills for sustainable living. Advocates for humanure composting, solar energy, and other strategies for living off the grid, they are active with the Ashville Bike Recyclery and Books for Prisons. If you can find the Ghetto Garden and Dumpsterland zines, both are great resources on GLF's work.

HILLSBOROUGH RD. CO-OP

Contact: Dawn Peebles
Address: 619/621 Hillsborough Rd, Carrboro, NC 27510
Phone: 919-942-7886
Email: dawn_aolani@hotmail.com
Founded: 2001
Budget: under 25k
Constituency Age: 19-30
Issues: Arts/Culture, Homelessness, Housing/Gentrification, Prisons/Criminal Justice, Welfare/Poverty
Race: White
Profile: An innovative affordable housing co-op model created by young people. Also publishing a book, Objective Collective, profiling radical kids who buy houses and live collectively nationwide. They are a wealth of information about activists buying houses, and do slide shows throughout the country. An emerging activist hub.

INTERNATIONALIST BOOKS & COMMUNITY CENTER

Contact: Darren Hunnicutt
Address: 405 W. Franklin St, Chapel Hill, NC 27516
Phone: 919-942-1740
Email: ibooks@mindspring.com
Website: www.internationalistbooks.org
Founded: 1981
Budget: under 25k
Constituency Age: 12 and under-30 and over
Issues: Corporate Accountability, Media
Race: Multi-Racial
Profile: I Books is the most important activist bookstore in the Southeast and a hub of youth organizing in Chapel Hill. Run by a volunteer collective mostly under 25, its members do crazy stuff like remove the books from the shelves on Buy Nothing Day and have a party in the store. The tiny store boasts dozens of amazing events, fascinating zines, stickers, a Food Not Bombs branch and a huge vision.

KNOW YOUR RIGHTS

Contact: Jess Fjeld
Address: Box 234-B Reynolds, Cullowhee, NC 28723
Phone: 828-227-6956
Email: info@studentactivism.org
Website: www.studentactivism.org
Founded: 1998
Budget: out of pocket
Constituency Age: 13-18

Issues: Student Rights/Education Reform
Race: Multi-Racial, White
Profile: KYR exists to promote student interest and participation in politics and the political process, and help educate youth about their rights as both students and citizens. Operate a useful website about civil liberties in high schools (touching topics like drugs, journalism and search & seizures) as well as a telephone hotline. KYR rose from the ashes of ISAA, a promising network of mostly suburban high school kids who fought their way onto local/state boards of education in the late 1990s.

NATIONAL CONFERENCE FOR COMMUNITY AND JUSTICE (NCCJ) – CHARLOTTE

Contact: Alex Wagaman, Jacotron Potts
Address: 4822 Albemarle Rd #240, Charlotte, NC 28205
Phone: 704-535-7277
Email: awagaman@nccj.org
Website: www.nccj.org
Founded: 1927
Budget: under 500k
Constituency Age: 14-21
Issues: Racial Justice, Youth Development
Race: Multi-Racial
Profile: With 60 regional offices, NCCJ works on an institutional level to eradicate bias, bigotry and racism. Through residential summer programs ("Anytown" and "Bring It On!") and skill building trainings during the school year, high school students learn how to be effective leaders for social justice. This local chapter of NCCJ also convenes a bi-monthly "Youth Empowerment Council" in the Charlotte-Mecklenburg region to consider and plan local projects that students initiate.

NORTH CAROLINA LAMBDA YOUTH NETWORK (NCLYN)

Contact: Paula Austin
Address: 115 Market St, Durham, NC 27701
Phone: 919-683-3037
Email: nclambda@aol.com
Website: www.nclambdayouth.org
Founded: 1996
Budget: under 250k
Constituency Age: 13-25
Issues: LGBTTSQ/Queer, Prisons/Criminal Justice, Racial Justice, Student Rights/Education Reform, Violence/Abuse
Race: Multi-Racial
Profile: NCLYN has become a critical model for multi-issue statewide LGBTQ youth organizing in the US. An outspoken voice for youth rights, NCLYN lobbies state legislators, builds coalitions, provides support services in and outside the school system and facilitates networking between gay/straight alliances. Mobilizing around issues ranging from prisons to the Patriot Act, they address economic and racial injustice within their analysis of homophobia and ageism, both in their organizing and within their own organization.

SOUTHERNERS ON NEW GROUND (SONG)

Contact: Kim Diehl
Address: PO Box 268, Durham, NC 27702
Phone: 919-667-1362
Email: kim@southnewground.org
Website: www.southnewground.org
Founded: 1994
Budget: under 500k
Constituency Age: 13-30
Issues: LGBTTSQ/Queer, Racial Justice, Violence/Abuse, Welfare/Poverty, Women's Rights
Race: Multi-Racial
Profile: SONG works in local communities in twelve states of the southeast, providing important regional infrastructure for building progressive LGBT, multi-issue organizing. They provide technical assistance to local community based organizations, run dismantling racism and homophobia workshops, and use art as a mode of liberation and activism through story circles, murals, quilting and theater projects. SONG focuses on people who want to move within an anti-racist, anti-sexist and anti-classist framework and are seeking skills and information on how to do that.

SURGE (STUDENTS UNITED FOR A RESPONSIBLE GLOBAL ENVIORMENT)

Contact: Stuart Davis, Kate Witchger
Address: PO Box 1188, Chapel Hill, NC 27514
Phone: 919-843-6548
Email: surgenc@yahoo.com
Website: www.surgenetwork.org
Founded: 1998
Budget: under 25k
Constituency Age: 18-25
Issues: Corporate Accountability, Environmental Justice, Globalization, Labor/Economic Justice, Militarism
Race: Multi-Racial
Profile: Based at the University of North Carolina, SURGE, "organizes to bring people together on all interconnected issues of social and environmental justice." Their listserv includes 400 people in NC, 300 nationwide and 30 globally. SURGE throws a major regional social justice conference and does local actions like Valentine's week-- collecting medicines that should be sent to Iraq (but are banned by sanctions) and symbolically mailing them to elected officials. They collaborate widely with other UNC students groups.

UNAMERICAN ACTIVITIES

Contact: Srini Kumar
Address: PO Box 2137, Asheville, NC 28801
Email: srini@unamerican.com, lupine@unamerican.com
Website: www.unamerican.com
Founded: 1994
Budget: out of pocket
Constituency Age: 13-30 and over
Issues: Media

Race: Multi-Racial
Profile: Creators of bumper stickers like Please Don't Start WWIII, This Town Kills Its Kids and Whitey Will Pay, these media rebel rousers have dozens of off-beat cultural/political campaigns such as Sticker Nation, where people create and disseminate their own stickers, encouraging free speech and political creativity nationwide. They work with the Asheville Free School to, "forge a generation where citizenship doesn't suck anymore."

YOUTH FOR SOCIAL CHANGE

Contact: Karen Hayes
Address: PO Box 240, Durham, NC 27702
Phone: 919-683-4310
Email: serejn@rejn.org
Website: www.rejn.org
Founded: 1997
Budget: under 100k
Constituency Age: 13-18
Issues: Environmental Justice, Student Rights/Education Reform
Race: Latina/o, African-American/Black
Profile: Youth for Social Change (YSC) is the youth training program of the Southeast Regional Economic Justice Net, a collective of 50 worker and community groups in the South. This program trains organizers and young people from 10 member organizations how to develop effective campaigns on educational and economic issues. YSC also provides internships and helps organize the Economic Justice for Youth Conference.

NORTH DAKOTA

BUILDING ROAD INTO DIVERSE GROUPS EDUCATING STUDENTS (BRIDGES)

Contact: Alva Irwin
Address: PO Box 8385, UND, Grand Forks, ND 58202
Phone: 701-777-2478
Email: alva_irwin@und.nodak.edu
Website: www.und.edu/org/span/bridges/main.html
Founded: 1971
Budget: out of pocket
Constituency Age: 19-30 and over
Issues: Indigenous Rights, Racial Justice
Race: Multi-Racial, Native American
Profile: BRIDGES, a student organization at the University of North Dakota, is committed to fighting racism and the systems that make it possible. They organize to eliminate UND's mascot, the "Fighting Sioux" and seek to replace it with imagery that all UND members, including the 300 Native American students on campus, can be proud of. They provide support and resources to students seeking to combat racism and run events encouraging diversity on campus.

CAMPUS COMMITTEE FOR HUMAN RIGHTS

Contact: Lucy Ganje
Address: University of North Dakota, PO Box 7035, Grand Forks, ND 58202
Phone: 701-777-2670
Email: lucy_ganje@und.nodak.edu
Founded: 1999
Budget: out of pocket
Constituency Age: 13-30 and over
Issues: Indigenous Rights, Racial Justice, Student Rights/Education Reform
Race: Multi-racial
Profile: CCHR works on a variety of local human rights issues (such as changing the University of North Dakota mascot), international human rights issues and peace activism. There are about 200+ people on the listserv which is used for action alerts, informational exchange and political discourse. The non-hierarchical steering committee of ten people includes faculty, staff and community members.

PROGRESSIVE STUDENT ALLIANCE

Contact: Sara Hallberg
Address: 1712 Continental Dr #209, Grand Forks, ND 58201
Phone: 701-777-5098
Email: sarapie1414@hotmail.com
Founded: 2002
Budget: out of pocket
Constituency Age: 19-22
Issues: Environmental Justice, Indigenous Rights, Labor/Economic Justice, Racial Justice, Student Rights/Education Reform
Race: Multi-Racial
Profile: PSA regularly puts out an educational/motivational zine designed to reach out to both the campus and local communities. They currently have about eighty students on their listerve and actively discuss racial, economic and social justice. Current campaigns focus on political education and outreach given the relatively limited progressive political activity in North Dakota. PSA is consensus based, i.e., everyone who comes to the meetings and is involved has equal say in decisions and discussions.

OHIO

ANTI-RACIST ACTION (ARA) COLUMBUS

Contact: Jerry Bellow
Address: PO Box 10797, Columbus, OH 43201
Phone: 614-596-7677
Email: aracolumbus@hotmail.com
Website: www.coil.com/~ara
Founded: 1988
Budget: out of pocket
Constituency Age: 13-30 and over
Issues: Racial Justice, Police Accountability

Race: Multi-Racial, White
Profile: The Columbus ARA works in mostly white, working-class communities to counter Neo-Nazis and other White Supremacist groups. ARA's grassroots, street level approach uses direct confrontation at rallies and demonstrations, abortion clinics, punk shows and other community venues. Responding to the resurgence of hate-group activity, ten members of the Columbus ARA are working to support chapters in Pennsylvania and other Mid-Atlantic states.

CINCINNATI COPWATCH

Contact: Gavin Leonard
Address: 1510 Elm St #3, Cincinnati, OH 45202
Phone: 513-241-1106
Email: copwatch513@hotmail.com
Website: www.cincinnaticopwatch.org
Founded: 2001
Budget: under 25k
Constituency Age: 13-21
Issues: Prisons/Criminal Justice, Police Accountability, Welfare/Poverty, Racial Justice, Labor/Economic Justice
Race: Multi-Racial
Profile: Cincinnati Copwatch uses direct monitoring of police activity as a tactic to create accountability and end the use of excessive force. Created after the April 1999 uprising that shut the city down, CC has launched an educational "know your rights" campaign in the community and set up a hotline for reports of police misconduct and abuse. CC participates in the Boycott Cincinnati campaign, an effort placing economic pressure on city officials for long-term political, economic and law enforcement reform.

CLAMOR MAGAZINE

Contact: Jason Kucsma
Address: PO Box 1225, Bowling Green, OH 43402
Phone: 419-353-7035
Email: jason@clamormagazine.org
Website: www.clamormagazine.org
Founded: 2000
Budget: out of pocket
Constituency Age: 13-30
Issues: Media
Race: White, Multi-Racial
Profile: The magazine most tapped-in to the global justice movement and punk/zine culture, Clamor is an open submission bi-monthly that covers culture, sex and gender, media, economics, and politics. Issue themes have included: "The Power of Youth," "New World Water," "Global Wealth Gap" and "Fashion for the Masses." Under the umbrella of Allied Media Projects, Clamor also publishes the Zine Yearbook, a yearly anthology of zine writing, and organizes the largest annual conference on underground publishing.

Taxi Workers Alliance anti-war and post 9/11 immigrant repression protest in Flatbush, Brooklyn, June 9, 2002
©ramona photo

YOUTH EMPOWEMENT PROGRAM OF THE COALITION ON HOMELESSNESS AND HOUSING IN OHIO

Contact: Angela Lariviere
Address: 35 East Gay St, Suite 210, Columbus, OH 43215
Phone: 614-280-1984 x17
Email: cohhio@aol.com
Website: www.cohhio.org/yep
Founded: 1999
Budget: under 100k
Constituency Age: 12 and under-25
Issues: Housing/Gentrification, Homelessness
Race: Multi-Racial
Profile: The Youth Empowerment Program (YEP) is comprised of seven councils of young people, both currently and formerly homeless, that focus on community service projects and direct outreach to local youth. YEP's state-wide support system enable council members to document the personal stories and battles of homeless youth and to challenge policies and laws that directly impact homeless children and youth.

OKLAHOMA

CHICKASAW NATION YOUTH COUNCIL

Contact: Sara Gibson
Address: 224 Rosedale Rd, Ada, OK 74820
Phone: 580-310-6620
Email: sara.gibson@chickasaw.net
Website: www.chickasaw.net
Founded: 1993
Budget: out of pocket
Constituency Age: 13-18
Issues: Youth Development, Arts/Culture, Indigenous Rights
Race: Native American
Profile: One of the strongest youth councils in the country with four branches in Oklahoma, CNYC is led by high school students with assistance from adults. The focus is raising consciousness, cultural awareness and pride through participation in workshops, traditional culture fairs and retreats. Students identify Indigenous rights issues they want to work on and define community service actions. Linked to United Indian Tribal Youth, CNYC serves as a vehicle for nationwide coalition building among young organizers within the Indigenous community.

SOULFORCE OKLAHOMA

Contact: Jake Reitan
Address: Rt 4 Box 3534, Stigler, OK 74462
Phone: 877-705-6393
Email: karen@soulforce.org
Website: www.soulforceinoklahoma.org
Founded: 1998
Budget: under 500k
Constituency Age: 21-25

Issues: Militarism, LGBTTSQ/Queer
Race: Multi-Racial
Profile: Interfaith group offering training in applying the principles of non-violence for direct action around LGBTQ issues. Participate in national conferences with a young adult caucus and offer unpaid internships across the country. Young people are trained to take leadership roles in protests, which take place both locally and nationally. With branches in Tulsa and Oklahoma City, recent actions include protests at the Southern Baptist National Conference in Saint Louis, and monthly vigils outside Village Baptist Church in Oklahoma City.

SOUTH CENTRAL OKLAHOMA ENVIRONMENTAL JUSTICE RESOURCE CENTER

Contact: John Ulrich
Address: East Central Oklahoma, Ada, OK 74820
Phone: 580-310-5507
Email: julrich@mailclerk.ecok.edu
Budget: out of pocket
Constituency Age: 19-30 and over
Issues: Environmental Justice
Race: Multi-Racial, White
Profile: Provides computer access to the community and offers youth training workshops and seminars. Publishes a newsletter connecting globalization with local issues such as the continuous industrial encroachment on Native American tribal lands, high levels of unemployment, and low income subsistence farming and ranching. Key campaigns include struggling against the placement of a new municipal land fill and a local firm trying to secure a permit to burn tires and other hazardous waste.

OREGON

ENVIRONMENTAL JUSTICE ACTION GROUP

Contact: Jeri Sundvall
Address: PO Box 11635, Portland, OR 97211
Phone: 503-283-6397
Email: ejag@teleport.com
Website: http://home.teleport.com/~ejag/
Budget: out of pocket
Constituency Age: 13-30 and over
Issues: Racial Justice, Militarism, Indigenous Rights, Environmental Justice, Women's Rights
Race: Multi-Racial
Profile: A community-based organization on the front lines, EJAG makes house calls to show people how to find asthma triggers, teaches community members to document their work as "air quality sniffers," and has a class-action suit against Oregon Steel Mills for 52 violations of the Clean Air Act (Oregon Steel conceded on 40). Partner with the Port Smith Middle School and (when funds are available) hold summer organizing institutes for girls 13-18. Currently fighting to prevent lane expansion of freeway I-5.

LATINOS UNIDOS SIEMPRE (LUS)

Contact: Abel Carbajal

Address: c/o Mano a Mano Family Center, 3545 Portland Rd
NE, Suite 220, Salem, OR 97303

Phone: 503-363-1895

Email: latinosunidossiempre@yahoo.comg

Budget: under 100k

Constituency Age: 12 and under-30

Issues: Immigrant/Refugee, Women's Rights, Welfare/Poverty,
Police Accountability

Race: Multi-Racial

Profile: LUS is an intergenerational organization that supports
Latina/o youth-led political, educational and cultural
development, with specific focus on public education and
immigrant rights. Youth-led initiatives include a prevention and
mediation project consisting of bilingual and bicultural youth
of color providing peer support to other young people involved
with gangs. LUS also organizes at the state and national levels
with campaigns on discrimination against youth of color in the
legal system, amnesty and welfare issues for immigrants, and
undocumented student rights.

SISTERS IN ACTION FOR POWER

Contact: Amara Perez

Address: 1732 NE Alberta St, Portland, OR 97211

Phone: 503-331-1244

Email: amarap@inetarena.com

Founded: 1999

Budget: under 250k

Constituency Age: 13-25

Issues: Women's Rights, Environmental Justice

Race: Multi-Racial

Profile: Sisters in Action for Power is a multi-racial,
intergenerational organization dedicated to strengthening low-
income communities and communities of color in Portland by
preparing young people ages 11-18 to organize. They are
currently organizing around the displacement, relocation, and
subsequent gentrification of low-income communities of color
as Portland prepares to tear down the last of the cities housing
projects. The Sisters engage in campaign planning, issue study
groups, self-defense classes, leadership trainings and an
intense leadership development program.

STUDENTS TRANSFORMING AND RESISTING CORPORATIONS (STARC)

Contact: Laura Close

Address: 831 North Watts, Portland, OR 97217

Phone: 503-247-5995

Email: staffer@starcalliance.org

Website: www.starcalliance.org

Founded: 1999

Budget: under 100k

Constituency Age: 13-25

Issues: Racial Justice, Labor/Economic Justice,
Environmental Justice, Globalization, Corporate Accountability

Race: Multi-Racial

Profile: Through public education and non-violent direct action
campaigns, STARC exposes corporate corruption, exploitation
and governmental manipulation. With 16 chapters and affiliates
spreading from campuses in the Pacific Northwest to the
Southeast, STARC is waging a major campaign against the Free
Trade Area of the Americas (NAFTA pt.2) and continues to
encourage shareholder activism as a socially responsible
investing strategy. Online archives also provide valuable information on the theory and practice of non-violent direct action.

PENNSYLVANIA

ACTION CENTER/PENNSYLVANIA ENVIRONMENTAL NETWORK

Contact: Mike Ewall

Address: 1434 Elbridge St, Philadelphia, PA 19149

Phone: 503-247-5995

Email: staffer@starcalliance.org

Website: www.starcalliance.org

Founded: 1997

Budget: out of pocket

Constituency Age: 13-25

Issues: Racial Justice, Labor/Economic Justice,
Environmental Justice, Globalization, Corporate Accountability

Race: White

Profile: The Action Center serves as a resource and organizing
center for environmental and social justice organizations
throughout Pennsylvania. In addition to housing the
Pennsylvania Environmental Network, the Action Center actively
supports the Energy Justice Network, Student Environmental
Action Coalition, NukeNet Anti-Nuclear Network and 180: the
Movement for Democracy & Education by coordinating
volunteers to do research, compile email lists and organize
gatherings. PEN projects include a Pollution Mapping Project
and a Corporate Dirt Archive Project.

AFROLEZ PRODUCTIONS

Contact: Aishah Shahidah Simmons

Address: POB 58085, Philadelphia, PA 19102-8085

Phone: 215-735-7372

Email: afrolez@aol.com

Founded: 1992

Budget: under 250k

Constituency Age: 13-30 and over

Issues: Women's Rights, LGBTTSQ/Queer, Arts/Culture

Race: Multi-Racial, African-American/Black

Profile: A multimedia arts company committed to using the
moving image and the written and spoken word to address the
impact of racism, sexism and heterosexism on the lives of Black
women and girls. Armed with an array of articles, films, videos,
and television/ radio programs, AfroLez has been teaching and

facilitating workshops, lectures, and seminars since 1992. Currently AfroLez is working on No!, a feature-length documentary focused on exposing the silence surrounding sexual assault in the Black community.

ASIAN AMERICANS UNITED/YOUTH INITIATIVE

Contact: Betty
Address: 913 Arch St, Philadelphia, PA 19107
Phone: 215-925-1538
Email: aaunited@critpath.org
Website: www.aaunited.org
Budget: out of pocket
Constituency Age: 13-25,
Issues: Violence Prevention, Housing/Gentrification
Race: Asian/Pacific Islander
Profile: AAU leads a variety of campaigns ranging from anti-Asian violence to quality of life issues and demands for social justice. AAU also offers summer enrichment camps and leadership training programs for high school youth. When plans were made to build a stadium in their neighborhood, AAU members decided to stop it. They organized the community and won. Currently engaged in the struggle to re-open Greenwich Library in South Philadelphia, AAU welcomes volunteers from all ethnic backgrounds.

ASIAN ARTS INITIATIVE

Contact: Catzie Vilayphonh
Address: 1315 Cherry St, 2nd Floor, Philadelphia, PA 19107
Phone: 215-557-0455
Email: info@asianartsinitiative.org
Website: www.asianartsinitiative.org
Founded: 1993
Budget: under 500k
Constituency Age: 13-and over
Issues: Arts/Culture, Violence Prevention, Immigrant/Refugee
Race: Asian/Pacific Islander
Profile: Offers an extraordinary array of artistic and educational programming with a political edge. Projects include the Artists in Communities training program, a monthly Rap Series, outreach to "Closet Artists," Speaking Pan Asian Mouths journal, youth arts video and sound training workshops, a community mural project, and the Gener-Asian Next Theatre. Committed to creating a safe space for cultural and political expression for young, diverse voices from within the Asian community.

AWOL MAGAZINE: REVOLUTIONARY ARTISTS WORKSHOP

Contact: Mario Hardy
Address: c/o CCCO, 1515 Cherry St, Philadelphia, PA 19102
Phone: 215-563-8787
Email: awol@objector.org
Website: www.awol.objector.org
Founded: 2001
Budget: under 25k
Issues: Media, Militarism
Race: African-American/Black, Asian/Pacific Islander
Profile: A project of the Central Committee for Conscientious Objectors (CCCO), AWOL Magazine offers revolution-minded musicians, writers, and visual artists a medium to express ideas ignored by the mainstream media. AWOL's main focus is anti-militarization and the heavy recruitment of youth of color into the US armed forces. Each issue includes a CD with politically conscious Hip Hop and spoken word. AWOL regularly participates in organizing events and rallies.

BOOKS THROUGH BARS/A-SPACE

Contact: Barbara Hirshkowitz
Address: 4722 Baltimore Ave, Philadelphia, PA 19143
Phone: 215-727-0882
Email: info@booksthroughbars.org
Website: www.booksthroughbars.org
Founded: 1989
Budget: under 50k
Constituency Age: 13-30 and over
Issues: Racial Justice, Prisons/Criminal Justice
Race: Multi-Racial, White
Profile: Started when a publishing employee began receiving and filling book requests from prisoners, BTB today fills 650 requests each month, publishes a calendar of inmate artwork, and works to develop the BTB network nationwide. BTB believes that social and economic inequality leads to a cycle of crime and incarceration, and they work to reverse the dehumanizing effects excessive punishment inflicts upon individuals, families and communities. BTB sends quality reading material to prisoners and encourages creative dialogue on the punishment system.

BROWN COLLECTIVE

Contact: Thoai Nguyen
Address: c/o AFSC, 1515 Cherry St, Philadelphia, PA 19102
Email: browncollective@yahoo.com
Founded: 2000
Budget: under 50k
Constituency Age: 13-30 and over
Issues: Globalization, Corporate Accountability
Race: Multi-Racial
Profile: A progressive people of color organization based out of Philadelphia that participates in direct action, the Brown Collective operated as an affinity group during the 2000 Republican National Convention. It is currently involved in the battle against school privatization, especially the Edison takeover of Philadelphia public schools. The Collective has also been advocating on the behalf of Miriam Wright, convicted of murder at the age of 13 and placed in solitary confinement 23 hours/day.

Empowerment Group

Contact: Peter Murray
Address: 2111 N Front St, Philadelphia, PA 19122
Phone: 215-427-9245
Website: www.empowerment-group.org
Founded: 1999
Budget: under 250k
Constituency Age: 12 and under-30
Issues: Labor/Economic Justice
Race: White, Latina/o, African-American/Black
Profile: Created and led by young people, EG uses an innovative combination of micro-enterprising, community education and leadership development to address poverty and limited opportunities in North Philadelphia. The Connections Project gives high school students creative writing, public speaking, and performing arts training that stress teamwork, creativity, self-esteem, critical thinking and expanding youth leadership for social change within urban communities. Empowered Painters, Kensington Driving Partners and the Self Initiated Employment Project create economic opportunities for low income and formerly incarcerated people.

Empty the Shelters

Contact: Sara Forgione
Address: 1014 S 47th St, Philadelphia, PA 19143
Phone: 215-724-1908
Email: etsphilly@igc.org
Founded: 1991
Budget: under 25k
Constituency Age: 13-30
Issues: Homelessness, Welfare/Poverty
Race: Multi-Racial
Profile: ETS combines education, direct action and community service in their work to address poverty and homelessness. In addition to holding an annual fundraisers to benefit the homeless, ETS raises public awareness through a five-part educational speaker series and a national speaking tour focused on sweatshop labor. They also coordinate Poverty Awareness Week activities and are collaborating with the Kensington Worker's Rights Union on a monthly newspaper and a political education campaign on no and low wage workers.

Hactivist.com/Carbon Defense League

Email: info@hactivist.com
Website: www.hactivist.com
Budget: out of pocket
Constituency Age: 19-25
Issues: Corporate Accountability
Race: White
Profile: Hactivist is a collective of media artists, technologists, activists and critical theorists working to explore the intersection between radical theory, traditional activism and technology. Tactical media projects, pager broadcasting, interactive wireless mapping servers, and several experimental interfaces are examples of tools that can benefit the next generation of political organizing. With the FBI's neo-Cointelpro activity and the expansive Homeland Security backlash sure to be felt on community organizers, Hactivists aim to even up the odds.

Mobilivre Bookmobile Project

Address: c/o Space 1026, 1026 Arch St, Philadelphia, PA 19107
Email: info@mobilivre.org
Website: www.mobilivre.org
Founded: 2000
Budget: out of pocket
Constituency Age: 13-30 and over
Issues: Media
Race: Multi-Racial
Profile: MBP is a community arts initiative that fuses artistic and literary production with political activism and community organizing-- on wheels. Traveling in a vintage Airstream to community centers, schools, festivals, and crazy remote towns where independent publications are impossible to get, MBP facilitates bookbinding and zine-making workshops, discussions, video screenings and related educational forums along the way. Committed to freeing information, literature, art and their production from corporate control.

National Council for Urban Peace and Justice

Contact: Khalid Raheem
Address: 711 Penn Ave, Suite 500, Pittsburgh, PA 15222
Phone: 412-261-1312
Email: ncupj@aol.com
Website: www.ncupj.org
Founded: 1991
Budget: out of pocket
Constituency Age: 19-30 and over
Issues: Welfare/Poverty, Racial Justice, Prisons/Criminal Justice
Race: African-American/Black
Profile: Like many organizations where activism is more about survival than ideology, NCUPJ is a small organization trying to fill a lot of big holes. Founded as a gang-truce initiative, their programs and campaigns now include a mentoring program for 11-18 year old, a youth employment program, an urban gardening initiative, violence and crisis intervention, and the quarterly Movement Magazine. Part youth service, part youth development, part youth organizing, NCUPJ is tackling racism and violence with everything it's got.

Philadelphia Student Union

Contact: Eric Braxton
Address: 1315 Spruce St, Philadelphia, PA 19107
Phone: 215-546-3290
Email: ebrax@phillystudentunion.org
Website: www.phillystudentunion.org
Founded: 1995
Budget: under 250k

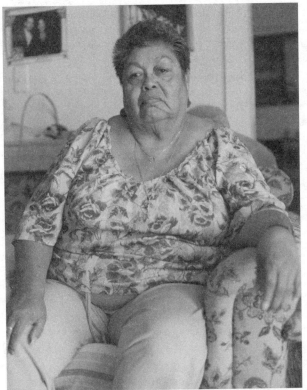

Delano, CA
Prison Town, USA

In the last decade, California has built 8 new prisons in the Central Valley within a 150-mile radius. The City of Delano, about 20 miles from Bakersfield, currently holds one prison, and is slated to build another one in the next few years. Delano is typical of central valley prison towns: agricultural, immigrant, rural, poor, and high school educated or less, with unemployment three times the state average.

Delano is best known for birthing Caesar Chavez's United Farm Workers in the 1950s. Like many rural communities, it has suffered due to the economic restructuring of agricultural America that started in the 1980s. The decline in agricultural related industries can be correlated to the increase in prisons in rural communities.

Delano is predominantly Mexican-American, but has a significant Filipino American, Asian American, African American, Southeast Asian American, and European American population. As a small rural town, it lacks sufficient political power and strong represen-tation with powerful interest groups who have access to state decision makers, complicating efforts to resist construction. Without political leverage, decisions are made without sufficient community input.

This photo essay strives to make visible some of the people of these rural prison towns. As Delano awaits a second prison, the people wait to be noticed.

©Robyn Twomey, 2001

Clockwise from upper left:
Louisa, disabled farm worker
Luis and friends
James, Manager, Best Western Liberty Inn

Constituency Age: 13-18

Issues: Student Rights/Education Reform

Race: White, African-American/Black

Profile: With six chapters, PSU organizes high school students around the belief that quality public education is necessary for the creation of a more accessible and just society. Founded and led by young people, students work to increase school funding, ensure school safety without criminalization, create space for student participation in school governance, and to resist the privatization of their schools by Edison. PSU, known for organizing massive rallies and press conferences, recently led 1,300 students in a school walk-out.

PROMETHEUS RADIO PROJECT

Contact: Petri Dish

Address: PO Box 42158, Philadelphia, PA 19101

Phone: 215-727-9620

Email: petri@prometheusradio.org

Website: www.prometheusradio.org

Founded: 1998

Budget: under 100k

Constituency Age: 13-30 and over

Issues: Media

Race: White

Profile: Committed to freeing the radio airwaves, Prometheus practices a mixture of research, advocacy, activism and direct services in the name of media democracy. Prometheus offers technical assistance to organizations that want to start independent community radio stations and produces educational tours, conferences, events and literature on the growing micro-radio movement. Offers internships to other youth. In 2000, played a key role in a victory that made it legal to broadcast 100 watt community radio stations in towns and rural areas.

REACHING ADOLESCENTS VIA EDUCATION (RAVE)

Contact: Louis Ortiz

Address: 1233 Locust St, 3rd Floor, Philadelphia, PA 19107

Phone: 215-985-3382

Website: www.critpath.org/galaei

Founded: 1989

Budget: under 250k

Constituency Age: 13-25

Issues: Violence Prevention, LGBTTSQ/Queer, HIV/AIDS

Race: African-American/Black, Latina/o

Profile: A project of the Gay and Lesbian Latino AIDS Education Initiative, RAVE is a peer-led and peer-run sexual health education program for Latino/a LGBTQ youth. RAVE addresses self-esteem issues, mental health, preventive health, HIV/AIDS, STDs, substance abuse, homophobic violence, and conflict resolution/mediation through peer mentoring and interactive workshops. Youth are organizing to create safe environments both in and out of school as well as speaking out about violence and discrimination.

SELF EDUCATION FOUNDATION

Contact: Emily Nepon

Address: PO Box 30790, Philadelphia, PA 19104

Phone: 215-386-6081

Email: info@selfeducation.org

Website: www.selfeducation.org

Founded: 2000

Budget: under 50k

Constituency Age: 12 and under-30 and over

Issues: Racial Justice, Prisons/Criminal Justice, Student Rights/Education Reform

Race: Multi-Racial

Profile: A unique foundation created by six young women who fund, connect, and organize on multiple issues. SEF has four programs: Grantmaking (to underfunded community-based education initiatives); Unlocked Minds (supporting self-educating prisoners); Student-led School Reform (currently fighting Philly school privatization); and BUILD, a self-education resource center for teenagers. SEF also published a resource guide for Philly dropouts, produced a video called "60%" about sentencing laws, and will be collaborating with other organizations to publish a book written by incarcerated women.

SANKOFA COMMUNITY EMPOWERMENT

Contact: Lurie Daniel

Address: 328 S. Mathilda St #2, Pittsburgh, PA 15205

Phone: 412-687-1823

Email: sankofaempowerment@yahoo.com

Founded: 2000

Budget: under 100k

Constituency Age: 13-30

Issues: Education, Racial Justice, Arts/Culture, Prisons/Criminal Justice

Race: African-American

Profile: Growing out of the successful 2001 struggle to increase Black studies and retention of Black students and faculty at the University of Pennsylvania (in which they occupied the administration building), Sankofa has built an impressive statewide network with chapters at five PA colleges. Currently developing a slew of community-based programs aimed at building the political leadership of young African-Americans on and off campus.

STUDENT ENVIRONMENTAL ACTION CENTER (SEAC)

Contact: Jason Fults

Address: PO Box 31909, Philadelphia, PA 19104

Phone: 215-222-4711

Email: seac@seac.org

Website: www.seac.org

Founded: 1990

Budget: under 25k

Constituency Age: 13-25

Issues: Environmental Justice, Globalization

Race: White, Multi-Racial

Profile: SEAC is a national network that supports solidarity work on environmental justice issues between communities of color and predominately white students. They have campaigned nationally against dioxins in tampons, for clean energy legislation, and to oppose reliance on nuclear energy, oil, and coal. In addition to numerous regional campaigns on industrial pollution and misuse, they have advocated for schools to comply with international recommendations on global warming through their national Kyoto Now! campaign.

THE ATTIC

Contact: Chy Spain
Address: 419 South 15th St, Philadelphia, PA 19146
Phone: 215-545-4331
Email: theatticyouthcenter@aol.com
Website: www.angelfire.com/pa2/youthcenter or
www.atticyouthcenter.org
Founded: 1994
Budget: out of pocket
Constituency Age: 13-25
Issues: Health Care, Arts/Culture, HIV/AIDS, LGBTTSQ/Queer
Race: Multi-Racial
Profile: The Attic is completely youth-run and the largest LGBTQ youth center in Philadelphia, providing peer-counseling, a safe space for social activities, sexual education, psychological services and crisis intervention. Organize Pride events, alternative proms, have an active speaker's bureau and educate peers through Thesbians & Drama Queens, an improvisational theater troupe that uses interactive social-drama-comedy to advocate for tolerance and respect. Attic members have testified before the Philadelphia School Board in their efforts to create safe educational environments for LGBTQ youth.

WHAT COLLECTIVE

Contact: Etta Cetera
Address: PO Box 71357, Pittsburgh, PA 15213
Phone: 412-802-8575
Email: de_tritus@yahoo.com
Founded: 2000
Budget: out of pocket
Constituency Age: 13-30
Issues: LGBTTSQ/Queer, Labor/Economic Justice, Public Space, Prisons/Criminal Justice
Race: Multi-Racial, White
Profile: One of the most radical young activist groups in Pittsburgh, WHAT Collective is a direct action group with a broad focus. In addition to campaigns & demonstrations, WHAT is involved in community gardens, public access TV, a books to prisoners program, and a recycle-a-bike program. Its latest, most significant project was to buy a space and create an activist warehouse greenhouse to serve as the mainframe for WHAT's activities.

YOUTH FOR MUMIA

Contact: Kevin Price
Address: PO Box 19709, Philadelphia, PA 19143
Phone: 215-476-8812
Email: icffmaj@aol.com
Website: www.mumia.org
Founded: 1981
Budget: out of pocket
Constituency Age: 13-30 and over
Issues: Prisons/Criminal Justice, Police Accountability, Racial Justice
Race: Multi-Racial
Profile: Organized to free journalist and former black panther Mumia Abu Jamal, YFM is affiliated with International Concerned Friends and Family of Mumia Abu Jamal. Convicted and sentenced to death for murdering a Philadelphia police officer, many believe he was framed for his political work and support for the MOVE family (think Waco, TX but African Americans in 1985). The Free Mumia campaign has been instrumental in politicizing a generation about the death penalty, US political prisoners and the prison industry.

YOUTH HEALTH EMPOWERMENT PROJECT

Contact: Jacqui Ambrosini
Address: JFK Building, 112 N Broach St, 9th Floor, Philadelphia, PA 19102
Phone: 215-476-8812
Email: icffmaj@aol.com
Website: www.fight.org/yhep.asp
Founded: 1994
Budget: under 50k
Constituency Age: 13-30 and over
Issues: Health Care
Race: People of Color
Profile: A project of Philadelphia Fight, YHEP is a highly successful, youth-led peer education program that provides teens with life-saving information in a language and style they can relate to. Following intensive peer advocacy and leadership training, outreach team members work primarily in the neighborhoods and schools they come from, adding to their effectiveness in building trust. The result is 15,000 "high-risk, hard-to-reach, and out-of-school" youth turned into health-wise and sexually responsible young adults every year.

YOUTH UNITED FOR CHANGE

Contact: Rebecca Rathje
Address: 2810 Frankford Ave, Suite 1111, Philadelphia, PA 19134
Phone: 215-423-9588
Email: yuc@mindspring.com
Website: www.yucyouth.org
Founded: 1990
Budget: under 250k
Constituency Age: 13-18
Issues: Youth Development

Race: White, Latina/o, Asian/Pacific Islander, African-American/Black

Profile: YUC is dedicated to developing young leaders in Philadelphia and empowering them to improve their communities and schools. Central to this strategy is the bringing together of diverse groups of teenagers to identify common concerns and take collective action through community organizing. YUC members create chapters in their high school, establishing networks and relationships within their schools and work collectively to address issues such as school privatization, standardized testing, school resources and police harrassment.

RHODE ISLAND

BROAD STREET STUDIO

Contact: Sam Seidel

Address: 790 Broad St, Providence, RI 02909

Phone: 401-831-9327

Email: youth@as220.org

Website: www.as220.org/broadSt/

Founded: 2001

Budget: under 250k

Constituency Age: 13-21

Issues: Welfare/Poverty, Hip Hop Activism, Arts/Culture, Racial Justice, Prisons/Criminal Justice

Race: White, Latina/o, African-American/Black

Profile: A local arts, culture and politics incubator. Young artists produce a bi-monthly youth magazine, have access to a recording studio and artist studios to create, market and produce their own small businesses in the arts. Many of the youth come from under-resourced communities and work closely with youth at local juvenile prisons. They orchestrate monthly youth open mic performances and host monthly dinners dubbed Food for Thought.

PROVIDENCE YOUTH STUDENT MOVEMENT (PRYSM)

Contact: Kagnaone Som

Address: 22 Miller Av, Providence, RI 02905

Phone: 401-286-0573

Email: pryouthsm@hotmail.com

Founded: 2000

Budget: out of pocket

Constituency Age: 13-25,

Issues: Women's Rights, Racial Justice, Police Accountability

Race: Multi-Racial, Asian/Pacific Islander

Profile: PrYSM, primarily led by high school students, focuses on racial justice and other issues facing South East Asian youth. With shifts in law enforcement tactics, such as the institution of the gang database, racial profiling has become an even more serious issue in Providence, making PrSYM's work crucial. They also organize a politically directed arts committee and a

women's group, Seacret Expressions, where participants find support for personal struggles.

SEEDS OF CHANGE/DIRECT ACTION FOR RIGHTS AND EQUALITY

Contact: John Mahone

Address: 340 Lockwood St, Providence, RI 02907

Phone: 401-351-6960

Website: www.daretowin.org

Founded: 1986

Budget: under 500k

Constituency Age: 13-18

Issues: Student Rights/Education Reform, Public Space

Race: Latina/o, African-American/Black

Profile: Seeds of Change, the youth component at D.A.R.E., is engaged in a campaign to secure free public transportation for students. In a city with a dropout rate just above 60% for 9th graders and high unemployment, they feel that a recent fare increase will only exacerbate an already serious situation. They have also been active in the fight against racial profiling after the highly publicized shooting of black police officer Cornell Young Jr.

YOUTH IN ACTION

Contact: Tamica Ramos

Address: 393 Broad St, Providence, RI 02907

Phone: 401-751-4264

Email: yia@ids.ne

Founded: 1997

Budget: under 500k

Constituency Age: 13-21

Issues: Arts/Culture, HIV/AIDS, Public Space

Race: Latina/o, African-American/Black

Profile: YIA connects teens to decision-making processes and uses workshops, peer leadership trainings, and health education to empower young people. The youth have sponsored poetry and Hip Hop nights and participated in policy agenda sessions that have improved public transportation in the state. Their weekly door to door outreach CAT teams reach out on the anti-violence and HIV/AIDS tip. YIA also works in conjunction with other youth organizing initiatives in the area.

YOUTH PRIDE INC.

Contact: Berto Galvao

Address: 134 George M. Cohan Blvd, Providence, RI 02903

Phone: 401-421-5626

Email: youth_pride@yahoo.com

Founded: 1998

Budget: under 25k

Constituency Age: 13-25

Issues: LGBTTSQ/Queer

Race: Multi-Racial

Profile: Youth Pride, Inc. is a 21 group coalition of Gay/Straight Alliances statewide. They provide collaborative trainings on issues of racial and economic justice, LGBT youth, gender and identity. Their summer project is designed by youth and they coordinate ongoing speak outs and community forums for youth 13 to 23 years old. Trainers support and urge political action toward the creation of more GSA's and for anti-discrimination policies in schools.

South Carolina

Carolina Alliance for Fair Employment (CAFE)

Contact: Carol Bishop
Address: 1 Chick Springs Road, Suite 110-B, Greenville, SC 29609
Phone: 864-235-2926
Email: cafesc@earthlink.net
Website: www.cafesc.org
Founded: 1980
Budget: under 500k
Constituency Age: 13-21
Issues: Youth Development, Racial Justice, Labor/Economic Justice, Environmental Justice, Student Rights/Education Reform
Race: Multi-Racial
Profile: CAFE's two youth chapters, led predominantly by Latino and African American youth, are working to build a multiracial alliance in South Carolina for economic and racial justice. They've registered people from remote areas to vote, have lead rallies at their city hall, and lobbied legislators about labor, housing discrimination and environmental justice. Responding to violent police activity in schools and violence in their communities, CAFE has launched a new campaign around the criminalization of youth and domestic violence.

South Carolina Advocates for Pregnant Women

Contact: Wyndi Anderson
Address: PMB 243, 164-D Market Street, Charleston, SC 29401-1984
Phone: 843-579-0637
Email: scapw@scapw.org
Website: www.scapw.org
Founded: 1999
Budget: under 50k
Constituency Age: 13-30 and over
Issues: Racial Justice, Drug Policy, Women's Rights, Welfare/Poverty, Reproductive Rights
Race: Multi-Racial
Profile: In 1997, South Carolina Supreme Court declared that fetuses are children and that it is attempted homicide for women to use illegal drugs while pregnant (though studies indicate that cigarettes and alcohol are more dangerous). This statute was used to incarcerate poor women and take away their children. SCAPW organized criminalized moms to argue on their own behalf, ultimately winning a victory before the Supreme Court in 2000. Exemplary among reproductive rights groups for kicking ass and being inclusive of race and class issues.

Vanguard for Total Liberation

Contact: Ja'maal Mosley
Address: 2441 Lang Rd, Columbia, SC 29204
Phone: 803-731-2637
Email: scvanguard@blackplanet.com
Founded: 2000
Budget: out of pocket
Constituency Age: 13-30
Issues: Racial Justice, Violence Prevention
Race: African-American/Black
Profile: The mission of the Vanguard is to promote political, social and intellectual development in the most racist, economically depressed and underrepresented communities of South Carolina. Strategies include community education forums, grassroots literature and door-to-door community building. Direct actions have included breaking up Klan rallies and recruitment sessions, and burning Confederate Flags in protest of the State flag. Young folks ain't afraid to represent!

South Dakota

Lakota Student Alliance

Contact: Robert Quiver
Address: PO Box 225, Kyle, SD 57752
Phone: 605-867-1507
Founded: 1994
Budget: out of pocket
Constituency Age: 26-30
Issues: Racial Justice, Welfare/Poverty, Indigenous Rights
Race: Native American
Profile: LSA organizes around land issues and gang prevention. Community members run a large-scale gardening project, where people grow and buy cheap organic produce; this helps combat high diabetes and heart disease rates while teaching traditional farming. In 1999, LSA camped outside of Rep. Tom Daschell's office for a year (12-200 people at a time) to demand the repeal of a bill transferring reservation land to the state. The bill was repealed for 3 months but then re-passed; the fight continues.

Los Angeles, August 15, 2000
© Geoff Oliver Bugbee

May Day in Portland, 2002
© Geoff Oliver Bugbee

YOUTH ADVISORY COUNCIL

Contact: Sharon Asetoyer
Address: PO Box 572, Yankton Sioux Reservation, Lake Andes, SD 57356-0572
Phone: 605-487-7072
Email: nativewoman@igc.org
Website: www.nativeshop.org/nawherc.html
Founded: 1988
Budget: under 100k
Constituency Age: 13-21
Issues: Women's Rights, Violence Prevention, Environmental Justice
Race: Native American
Profile: YAC, a component of the Native American Women's Health Education Resource Center, meets weekly to address community issues and hosts dances to provide safe spaces for youth to gather. Located on the 62 square mile Yankton Sioux Reservation, the youth organize community service work and are beginning to address the environmental contamination and health issues on their land. They also do peer counseling on HIV, smoking and substance abuse.

TENNESSEE

CONTACT COUNCIL

Contact: Camille Carter
Address: 115 Mulberry St, Newport, TN 37821
Phone: 423-623-3700
Website: www.easttncontact.org
Founded: 1996
Budget: under 250k
Constituency Age: 13-18
Issues: Public Space, Racial Justice, Police Accountability, Environment
Race: African-American/Black
Profile: Working to clean up the Pigeon River, where companies, including Champion Paper, have been dumping industrial waste for over 50 years. Young folks are also questioning why their schools look like jails and how they are profiled by the Cott County police. The are organizing against the Ku Klux Klan, which is planning to march on ML King Day-- their campaign is called, "When Hate Comes to Town." Their "Pizza and Poetry" night evolved into JustUs, a performance/workshop youth group.

MID-SOUTH PEACE AND JUSTICE CENTER

Contact: Julie Rogers
Address: 1000 S. Cooper St, Memphis, TN 38104
Phone: 901-725-4990
Email: center@midsouthpeace.org
Website: www.midsouthpeace.org
Founded: 1982
Budget: under 50k

Constituency Age: 19-25
Issues: Militarism, Labor/Economic Justice, Indigenous Rights, Immigrant/Refugee, Environmental Justice
Race: Multi-Racial
Profile: MSPJC is the major multi-racial/multi-issue org in Memphis, they organize Bike Cooperative Revolutions, where they collect bikes, recycle them, and distributes them to the community. Started the Orange Mound community garden and an Oral History Project, where young organizers tape their elders, transcribe and then create something-- this year they will do a play of monologues, all within a human rights framework. Regularly involved in campaigns for women's rights, environmental justice, immigrant rights and indigenous people's rights.

PROGRESSIVE STUDENT ALLIANCE

Contact: Cameron Brooks
Address: 1718 Melrose Place, Knoxville, TN 37916
Phone: 304-325-6105
Budget: out of pocket
Constituency Age: 18-25
Issues: Labor/Economic Justice
Race: White
Profile: Based at the University of Tennessee- Knoxville, PSA is working in solidarity with the United Campus Workers fighting for a living wage. They helped campus workers get free vaccinations and changed the grievance procedure at their college so workers can't get fired without having a hearing. They also helped hourly workers on campus form a union. Started a living wage campaign on campus; work in conjunction with Jobs for Justice.

THE deCLEYRE CO-OP

Contact: Shawn
Address: 787 Ellsworth St, Memphis, TN 38111
Phone: 901-458-9907
Email: cic@tao.ca
Website: www.tao.ca/~cic/collective.htm
Founded: 1998
Budget: out of pocket
Constituency Age: 13-30 and over
Issues: LGBTTSQ/Queer, Environment
Race: White
Profile: A focal point of progressive and creative organizing in Orange Mound, Memphis near the University of Memphis. Includes a community garden, a media co-op, the Constructive Interference Collective, a bike co-op, food co-op, and a Food Not Bombs chapter. Allied with the Mid-South Peace and Justice Center.

THE YOUNG AND THE RESTLESS PROGRAM OF THE HIGHLANDER CENTER

Contact: Paulina Hernandez Gomez
Address: 1959 Highlander Way, New Market, TN 37820
Phone: 865-933-3443
Email: hrec@highlandercenter.org
Website: www.highlandercenter.org
Founded: 1998
Budget: under 100k
Constituency Age: 13-21
Issues: Indigenous Rights, Women's Rights, Racial Justice, Prisons/Criminal Justice, Labor/Economic Justice
Race: Multi-Racial
Profile: An initiative of the revered Highlander Center, YRP is a two year organizing training for 30 youth from a variety of community groups all over the South. The goal is to strengthen youth leadership within social justice organizations. The YRP team networks with other youth organizers, trains in popular education and organizing strategies in intensive week-long workshops, uses the Center as an educational resource and then creates organizing projects addressing issues in their respective communities.

YOUTH TERMINATING POLLUTION

Contact: Marquita & Isis Bradshaw
Address: 1000 South Cooper St, Memphis, TN 38104
Phone: 901-942-0329
Email: quitabrad@hotmail.com
Budget: under 25k
Constituency Age: 19-30
Issues: Women's Rights, Violence Prevention, Environmental Justice, Hip Hop Activism
Race: African-American/Black
Profile: With an army depot a few miles up creek from the biggest Black high school in Memphis and high teenage cancer rates throughout the community, Youth Terminating Pollution organized in 2000, pushing the Army to stop polluting their neighborhood and holding teach-ins. YTP is currently organizing around the development of a youth sports complex on contaminated land. While developing a website, newsletter and documenting their work, YTP is working on fighting domestic violence, and trying to do environmental health testing.

TEXAS

ACCION ZAPATISTA

Contact: Manuel Callahan
Address: 312 East 43rd #203, Austin, TX 78751
Phone: 512-302-9547
Email: tamara@inlex.net
Website: www.utexas.edu/students/nave
Founded: 1996
Budget: out of pocket
Constituency Age: 19-30 and over

Issues: Human Rights, Indigenous Rights
Race: Latina/o
Profile: Accion Zapatista organizes in solidarity with EZLN and the Zapatistas communities fighting for indigenous sovereignty in Chiapas, Mexico. Through solidarity gatherings, demonstrations and workshops Accion Zapatistas works to generate both campus and international support for the international struggle for indigenous rights.

AUSTIN LATINO/LATINA LESBIAN, GAY, BISEXUAL & TRANSGENDER ORGANIZATION (ALLGO)

Contact: Martha Duffer
Address: 701 Tillery St, Box 4, Austin, TX 78702
Phone: 512-472-2001
Email: allgoinc@aol.com
Website: www.allgo.org
Founded: 1985
Budget: out of pocket
Constituency Age: 13-30 and over
Issues: Health Care, HIV/AIDS, Racial Justice, LGBTTSQ/Queer, Labor/Economic Justice
Race: People of Color, Latina/o, Native American
Profile: ALLGO is a multigenerational community organizing group advocating for the rights of the Latino/a LGBTQ community in Austin. Work to empower LGBT people of color and connect their struggle to other struggles for liberation. ALLGO has implemented four projects as part of its work to build community, to combat the effects of inequitable access to health care and health information, to generate awareness and response to structured inequality and social injustices, and to celebrate and create LGBT culture.

BIKES ACROSS BORDERS/CYCLE CIRCUS

Contact: Beth Ferguson
Address: 300 Allen St, Austin, TX 78702
Phone: 512-385-3695
Email: cyclecircus@riseup.net
Website: www.rhizomecollective.org
Founded: 2001
Budget: out of pocket
Constituency Age: 12 and under-30 and over
Issues: Environmental Justice, Genetic Engineering, Globalization, Immigrant/Refugee, Arts/Culture
Race: Multi-Racial
Profile: Bikes Across Borders is a collective of environmental and social justice activists, radical puppeteers, youth, Mexican artists, bicycle mechanics, journalists and circus performers that have organized 400-mile tours and created a bike shop for Maquiladora workers along the Mexican border. Setting up shop anywhere, swinging from trapezes and using direct action, political puppet shows, and free public political workshops, they address the struggles of Maquiladora workers along the border and combat racism, NAFTA, globalization, the prison industrial system and biotechnology.

CALPULLI TLAPALCALLI

Contact: Elga Garza
Address: 27712 FM 803, San Benito, TX 78586
Phone: 956-748-9159
Email: tlacalli@aol.com
Founded: 1996
Budget: under 50k
Constituency Age: 13-30 and over
Issues: Indigenous Rights, Police Accountability,
Immigrant/Refugee, Environment
Race: Native American, Latina/o
Profile: Calpulli Tlapalcalli isn't so much a community organiza-
tion as it is the community itself. With a community center and
seven organic gardens where food, medicine, and herbs for
shampoo and body oils are grown, youth are the backbone of
the organization and at the forefront of every effort. Projects
include educating and organizing surrounding communities
about the environment and brutality and harassment by the
border patrol. The Chale Patrol is a copwatch they established.

CENTER FOR CREATIVE AUTONOMY

Contact: Louis Chatos
Address: 2014 Washington Ave, Houston, TX 77007
Phone: 713-864-0972
Email: creative_autonomy@hotmail.com
Founded: 2002
Budget: out of pocket
Constituency Age: 22-30 and over
Issues: Indigenous Rights, Labor/Economic Justice,
Homelessness
Race: White, Native American, Asian/Pacific Islander
Profile: CCA is a radical grassroots community center seeking
to create communities based upon principles of community
building, mutual aid and skill sharing. Run by twenty and
thirty-somethings, its current efforts include a gardening
project, dumpster diving, a barter café (where things like
coffee, soil, services, and clothes are traded), and a campaign
against gentrification in the 4th and 5th wards of Houston.

DEMON KILLER COMMITTEE

Contact: Charles "Nook" Byrd
Phone: 512-563-5519
Founded: 1996
Budget: out of pocket
Constituency Age: 13-25
Issues: Hip Hop Activism, Police Accountability
Race: Multi-Racial, African-American/Black
Profile: Born out of a highly publicized incident of police
brutality on Valentine's Day, 1995 at a Hip Hop show,
DKC is dedicated to police accountability and community
empowerment. Its main project is a series of summer concerts
called "Jump On It," which focuses on combining
entertainment with education. The DKC successfully banned
police from these events and use their own security team.
Result: five years of "Jump On It" with no violent incidents.

FUERZA UNIDA

Contact: Viola Casares
Address: 17 New Laredo Highway, San Antonio, TX 78211
Phone: 210-927-2294
Email: fuerzaunid@aol.com
Website: www.fuerza-unida.org
Founded: 1990
Budget: out of pocket
Constituency Age: 13-30
Issues: Environmental Justice, Labor/Economic Justice,
Militarism
Race: Latina/o
Profile: Run by low-income women of color, Fuerza Unida
advocates for workers rights in the face of globalization and
runs a summer program for San Antonio youth that provides
cultural history and organizing training. In addition to a sewing
co-operative, family wellness program and educating on
women's rights, they lead border tours in coalition with
Southwest Workers Union which expose the environmental
justice hazards and human rights violations caused by US
Border policy and post-NAFTA industrial practices.

HOUSTON AMERICAN INDIAN MOVEMENT (AIM)

Contact: Tristan Ahtone
Address: PO Box 541242, Houston, TX 77254-1242
Phone: 832-594-6510
Email: houstonaim@yahoo.com
Website: www.aimovement.org
Founded: 2002
Budget: out of pocket
Constituency Age: 13-30 and over
Issues: Racial Justice, Indigenous Rights
Race: Native American
Profile: Part of the long tradition of intergenerational,
Indigenous struggle in the Americas, AIM-Houston promote
indigenous sovereignty, land rights, water rights and the
protection of elders, women, children and tradition. Hold huge
marches in support of political prisoner Leonard Peltier and
regularly bring truth to Columbus Day celebrations across the
country. Host First Nations Radio on KPFT and its Pacifica
Network affiliates.

HOUSTON INDEPENDENT MEDIA CENTER

Contact: Nick Cooper
Address: PO Box 2318-A, S. Shepard # 403, Houston, TX 77019
Email: imc-houston@listindymedia.org
Website: www.houston.indymedia.org
Founded: 2001
Budget: under 25k
Constituency Age: 13-30 and over
Issues: Media
Race: Multi-Racial
Profile: The Houston IMC website features openly submitted
news articles and information on current political and social
events. They hold monthly documentary screenings, host a

weekly radio show and avidly use their press passes to document demonstrations and other political events. They run educational presentations in high schools and colleges to emcourage young people to counter media consumerism with the power of their own critical voices. Motto: "Don't hate the media-- become the media."

MEXICAN AMERICAN YOUTH ALLIANCE (MAYA)

Contact: Francisco Martinez
Address: 608 South St Vrain, El Paso, TX 79901
Phone: 915-532-6953
Email: maya@lafeclinic.org
Website: www.lafeclinic.org
Founded: 1960's
Budget: out of pocket
Constituency Age: 13-18
Issues: Youth Development
Race: Latina/o
Profile: Young people participate in a variety of activities, determining activities and campaigns on their own. Cesar Chavez's birthday was celebrated with an educational cookout and basketball tournament while MLK's was commemorated with a food-drive and volleyball tournament. They also recently completed a PSA in English and Spanish about underage drinking which was aired around the city. All production on the PSA, except for the editing, was done by the youth. Currently designing political and cultural education outreach programs.

MOVIMIENTO ESTUDIANTIL CHICANO DE AZTLAN (MEChA)

Contact: Juan Rodriguez
Address: 1201 W. University Dr, UC 205, Edinburg, TX 78539
Phone: 956-583-2659
Email: ollintzin@hotmail.com
Website: www.panam.edu/orgs/mecha/nat.html
Founded: 1968
Budget: out of pocket
Constituency Age: 13-25
Issues: Racial Justice, Labor/Economic Justice, Indigenous Rights, Immigrant/Refugee
Race: People of Color, Latina/o, Native American
Profile: MEChA is the key network of Chicana and Chicano high school and college students nationwide. These chapters, at Edinburg Memorial Middle School and University of Texas-Pan American, work to inform their peers about Aztlán history, culture and global struggles for indigenous sovereignty. UT-Pan American also hosts the national MEChA website. MEChA won major victories for Chicano studies, affirmative action, bilingual education etc. In the 70's, the huge annual MEChA conference is an important opportunity to learn about the ongoing struggle for indigenous rights.

PROGRESSIVE VOTERS IN ACTION

Contact: Gretchen Himsl
Address: PO Box 667307, Houston, TX 77266
Phone: 713-302-8676
Website: www.votepva.org
Founded: 1999
Budget: under 250k
Constituency Age: 19-25
Issues: Racial Justice, Reproductive Rights, LGBTTSQ/Queer
Race: White, Latina/o, African-American/Black
Profile: PVA is a grassroots organization run by youth with adult allies aiming to create a progressive voter block of 100,000 in Houston. The goal is to impact local and state politics by injecting racial and economic justice, gender equality and reproductive freedom into the mainstream political debate. Through topical workshops and voter preference surveys, PVA works to foster a more politically educated and active community. They were instrumental in the election of a former Black Panther member to city council.

RADICAL ENCUENTRO

Contact: Chickpea
Address: PO Box 541242, Houston, TX 77254-1242
Phone: 214-642-6580
Email: radicalencuentro@yahoo.com
Website: www.radicalencuentro.org
Founded: 2002
Budget: under 25k
Constituency Age: 19-25
Issues: Corporate Accountability
Race: White, Latina/o, African-American/Black
Profile: Through its training camps, Radical Encuentro builds solidarity between diverse grassroots community organizations and activist throughout Texas. Their activist camps provide hands-on workshops on media messaging, campaign organizing and direct action strategies. Political education workshop topics have ranged from the Zapatistas and Women in the Black Panthers to the death penalty and globalization. Timed the first camp to coincide with ExxonMobil's annual shareholder meeting; needless to say theory quickly became practice.

RHIZOME COLLECTIVE

Contact: Scott Kellogg
Address: 300 Allen St, Austin, TX 78702
Phone: 512-385-3695
Email: rhizomecollective@earthlink.net
Website: www.rhizomecollective.org
Founded: 2000
Budget: under 25k
Constituency Age: 22-30 and over
Issues: Immigrant/Refugee, Environment
Race: White, Latina/o
Profile: Striving for urban sustainability, the Rhizome Collective has torn up the asphalt surrounding its warehouse and started

gardens that include fruit trees and edible plants. Its efforts and gardens have expanded into neighboring low-income communities with the goal of creating "edible neighborhoods." The Collective's other projects include rain catching, water recycling, bike building, a Holistic Healthcare Resource Center, a Foods Not Bombs chapter (run out of the RC kitchen), and a Single Parents Resource Network.

SAN ANTO CULTURAL ARTS

Contact: Manuel Castillo
Address: 1300 Chihuahua, San Antonio, TX 78207
Phone: 210-226-7466
Email: sanantoarts@aol.net
Founded: 1997
Budget: out of pocket
Issues: Youth Development
Race: Latina/o
Profile: SACA organizes eye opening field trips for young people, challenge them, "to think outside of their neighborhoods." They also organize huge Mural Blessing celebrations after a mural gets painted, complete with dancing and poetry. Also an important aspect of SACA is El Placazo newspaper, a monthly publication run totally by youth. The publication gets a lot of contributions from inmates. SACA is also expanding into other forms of media and plans to concentrate on video and documentary production.

SOUTHWEST WORKERS UNION

Contact: Che Lopez
Address: PO Box 830706, San Antonio, TX 78283-0706
Phone: 210-299-2666
Email: info@swunion.org
Website: www.swunion.org
Budget: under 25k
Constituency Age: 12 and under-30
Issues: Militarism, Labor/Economic Justice, Immigrant/Refugee, Racial Justice, Environmental Justice
Race: Multi-Racial, Latina/o, African-American/Black
Profile: SWU is committed to leadership training for low-income workers in communities of color and to grassroots advocacy for environmental and economic justice. SWU's Youth Leadership Organization, founded in 1997, runs the Organizing Training School, a year-long program to provide young adults with daily hands-on organizing skills and trainings on the EJ movement, border issues, globalization and electoral politics. YLO's organizers collaborate widely with other organizations in the southwest and nationally, broadening their political and movement analysis and exchanging strategies.

STAMINA

Contact: Clayton McCook
Address: PO Box #12062, Fort Worth, TX 76110
Phone: 817-875-7826
Email: stamina@yahoo.com
Founded: 2000
Budget: out of pocket
Constituency Age: 19-30
Issues: Arts/Culture, Hip Hop Activism
Race: Multi-Racial
Profile: Stamina is a grassroots organization made up of a diverse group of young artists and activists committed to using their talents for social justice work. As an intergenerational collective, Stamina focuses on nurturing artists who are newly discovering the role their work can play in social change, and trains folks on artist economics so they can, "eat, live, work and pursue justice all at the same time." Currently developing an interdisciplinary communal studio and performance space.

UNITED PEOPLE RESISTING OPPRESSION AND RACISM (UPROAR)

Contact: Scott Crow
Address: 902 Wayne St, Dallas, TX 75223
Phone: 214-642-6580
Email: info@uproarnow.org
Website: www.uproarnow.org
Founded: 2001
Budget: out of pocket
Constituency Age: 19-25
Issues: Racial Justice, Prisons/Criminal Justice, Globalization
Race: Multi-Racial, White
Profile: UPROAR is an intergenerational collective that is committed to using non-violent direct action on a wide range of issues. Current campaigns focus on racial justice, globalization and the expanding prison industry/police state. UPROAR also trains other organizations how to effectively use direct action, civil disobedience and media strategies. Specialties include blockades, banners, puppets and "urban climbing." An eclectic, energetic training ground for anyone committed to non-violent direct action.

UNIVERSITY OF TEXAS GREEN PARTY

Contact: Bob Libal
Address: University of Texas, Austin, TX 78712
Phone: 512-419-9641
Email: UTGreens@yahoo.com
Website: www.utexas.edu/students/utgreens
Founded: 2000
Budget: out of pocket
Constituency Age: 13-30 and over
Issues: Animal Rights, Globalization, Racial Justice, Militarism, Labor/Economic Justice
Race: White

Profile: Beyond its work in supporting the national political party, University of Texas Green Party organizes on campus for peace and worker rights and against prisons and globalization. They coordinate speakers and events, participate in the Taco Bell Boycott, and organize protests against the American Correctional Association. They are currently campaigning against a planned merger between University of Texas and Sandia, a giant nuclear weapons development corporation.

XICANA/XICANO EDUCATION PROJECT

Contact: Alejandro Perez
Address: PO Box 37105, San Antonio, TX 78237
Phone: 210-437 5196
Email: xicano68@hotmail.com
Founded: 1999
Budget: under 25k
Constituency Age: 13-25
Issues: Indigenous Rights, Police Accountability
Race: Latina/o, Native American
Profile: XEP is an emerging intergenerational organization that has developed a 'know your rights' campaign to address racial profiling and police brutality in San Antonio. Currently planning to begin a copwatch program, an abuse hotline and a community magazine. Their Annual Youth Conference, modeled after the Xicano Liberation Conference in the 1960's, presents workshops on a wide range of issues, ranging from understanding capitalism to Chiapas, worker rights to domestic violence.

YOUNG SCHOLARS PROGRAM OF PEOPLE ORGANIZED IN DEFENSE OF EARTH AND HER RESOURCES (PODER)

Contact: Susana Alamanza
Address: 55 North IH 35 #205B, Austin, TX 78702
Phone: 512-472-9921
Email: poder@gbronline.com
Website: www.gbronline.com/poder
Founded: 1991
Budget: under 100k
Constituency Age: 13-21
Issues: Student Rights/Education Reform, Racial Justice, Prisons/Criminal Justice, Environmental Justice
Race: Latina/o, African-American/Black
Profile: The Young Scholars Program is a leadership development project launched by PODER, one of the most effective grassroots environmental justice groups in the country. PODER successfully shut down a 52-acre tank farm owned by 6 major oil companies, had a 7-acre recycling center relocated, and waged successful campaigns for new street-lights, street signs, bus shelters and sidewalks. In addition to continued environmental justice campaigns, young organizers are working to create a bus rider's union and address the crimininalization of youth.

YOUNG TEXANS AGAINST GUN VIOLENCE

Contact: Florinda Garcia
Phone: 713-521-7921
Website: www.texansforgunsafety.org/ytagv.htm
Budget: out of pocket
Constituency Age: 13-21
Issues: Violence Prevention, Corporate Accountability
Race: Multi-Racial
Profile: Following violence at Columbine High School in 1999, a group of students formed YTAGV, one of the first youth-led gun violence prevention organizations in the country. YTAGV, now a project of Texans for Gun Safety, works to prevent gun violence through community education and advocacy. Its two executive councils in Dallas and Houston are governed by 8-12 high school students from diverse backgrounds. YTAGV initiatives include petitions for sensible gun laws and an informative website with facts, events and links.

UTAH

FOOD NOT BOMBS

Contact: Richard Hurst
Address: 735 South 400 West, Salt Lake City, UT 84101
Phone: 801-355-7044
Email: richardh@uarc.com
Website: www.foodnotbombs.net
Founded: 1995
Budget: out of pocket
Constituency Age: 13-30 and over
Issues: Welfare/Poverty, Public Space, Militarism, Homelessness
Race: White
Profile: Didn't know there was one in Utah, did you? Basic strategy: recover food that would otherwise be thrown out, make fresh hot vegetarian meals and serve them in city parks to anyone who is hungry. The groups also serve free vegetarian meals at protests and other events. FNB is a great portal to youth activism in Utah and, with its collective leadership structure, one of the most accessible ways for young people to get involved.

UTAH ANIMAL RIGHTS COALITION

Contact: Sean Diener
Address: PO Box 6762, Salt Lake City, UT 84110
Phone: 801-321-8272
Email: sdiener@uarc.com
Website: www.uarc.com
Founded: 1998
Budget: out of pocket
Constituency Age: 13-30
Issues: Animal Rights
Race: White

Profile: An intergenerational organization that aggressively and effectively advocates for veganism and animal rights. Staged protest at the 2002 Winter Olympic Rodeo, actively educate in public schools about animal cruelty and veganism, and have ongoing campaigns against a local fur store, horse drawn carriages and animal testing done at the University of Utah. UARC also regularly collaborates with human rights and labor groups at protests, activist convergences and trainings.

UTAH YOUTH ADVOCACY COUNCIL

Contact: Jeremy Van Wagenen
Address: 361 North 300 West, Salt Lake City, UT 84101
Phone: 801-299-9296
Email: envy42@models.com
Website: www.glccu.com
Founded: 1999
Budget: out of pocket
Constituency Age: 19-25
Issues: LGBTTSQ/Queer
Race: White
Profile: A project of the Gay and Lesbian Community Center of Utah (GLCCU), UYAC is a statewide outreach program that brings together LGBTQ youth and provides leadership and organizational development training. Youth work to identify ways to address issues and concerns of LGBTQ youth living in Utah including school violence and discrimination, safe social spaces, HIV/AIDS education and homelessness. GLCCU's Youth Activity Center serves as UYAC's base, providing a range of other services, activities and learning opportunities for LGBTQ youth.

VENCEREMOS

Address: 200 South Central Campus Drive, Room 240, Salt Lake, UT 84112
Phone: 801-587-9751
Email: Venceremos@chronicle.utah.edu
Founded: 1993
Budget: under 25k
Constituency Age: 19-30 and over
Issues: Racial Justice, Globalization, Arts/Culture, Prisons/Criminal Justice, Labor/Economic Justice
Race: Multi-Racial
Profile: This quarterly student paper covers topics about the local and global economy, the Zapatistas, the struggle of undocumented workers, indigenous peoples rights as well as resistance through arts and culture. They distribute 8,000-10,000 copies throughout Salt Lake City and Salt Lake Valley. Though principally committed to educating the community about Xicano/a culture and politics, Venceremos is produced by a multicultural collective that actively seeks coalitions with other youth activists on and off campus.

WESTMINSTER STUDENTS FOR PEACE AND JUSTICE

Contact: Richard Wagner
Address: Westminster College, 1840 South 300 East, Salt Lake City, UT 84105
Phone: 801-412-0176
Email: rww0714@westminstercollege.edu
Founded: 2000
Budget: out of pocket
Constituency Age: 19-25
Issues: Environmental Justice, Globalization, Student Rights/Education Reform, Militarism, Racial Justice
Race: White
Profile: Westminster Students for Peace and Justice works to educate the public about the horrors of war, the injustice of globalization, and the necessity of local activism. In addition to organizing panels, films, and demonstrations, they recently organized and hosted the Wasatch Activist Convergence Training, and supplied a contingent of Salt Lake City activists for the April 20, 2002 IMF/ World Bank protest. They are currently working on building an even stronger local network of activists.

VERMONT

BASTA!

Contact: Lindsay Ryan
Address: Putney School, Putney, VT 05346
Email: basta@mail.putney.com
Founded: 1998
Budget: out of pocket
Constituency Age: 13-18
Issues: Globalization, Labor/Economic Justice
Race: White
Profile: Basta! ("enough" in Spanish) is a group of high school organizers based at Putney School who use political education and non-violent direct action to protest globalization. They publish a monthly newsletter, run workshops and organize the Our Future is Not for Sale-- Youth Mobilized for Global Justice conference. Basta! does banner drops and stuffs pamphlets into merchandise at department stores. Imagine trying on that Nike sweatshirt and finding info on the child labor used to make it in the pocket!

CHILD LABOR EDUCATION AND ACTION PROJECT

Contact: John Ungerleider
Address: Kipling Road, PO Box 676, Brattleboro, VT 05302-0676
Phone: 802-258-3334
Email: clea@sit.edu
Website: www.clea.sit.edu
Founded: 1998
Budget: under 25k
Constituency Age: 13-18

Issues: Human Rights, Labor/Economic Justice, Welfare/Poverty

Race: White

Profile: CLEA is a partnership between the School for International Training and Brattleboro Union High School. The chapter has been active in a wide variety of activities in Vermont, speaking on labor issues, marching against sweatshops with 1,000 other youth, and bringing together 250 students for a conference-- Taking Action: Youth Responses to Child Labor. CLEA is a training ground for future college activism. This statewide youth coalition against sweatshops and oppressive labor practices is the strongest in the country!

CLUB YOUTH SPEAK OUT

Contact: Betsy Rosanzky

Address: 82 South Winooski Ave, Burlington, VT 05401

Phone: 802-865-7178

Email: cysovt@sover.net

Founded: 1997

Budget: out of pocket

Constituency Age: 13-18

Issues: HIV/AIDS

Race: White

Profile: A project of the Community Justice Center, CSYO was started by youth who felt that the Burlington community ignored the input, experiences and rights of young people. Currently organizing social events, advocating for youth positions on Burlington boards and commissions, and working to create drug and alcohol-free spaces for entertainment and mentoring. Through newsletters, event calendars, parties and an annual community speak-out, CYSO members work to build their vision of a safe, just and diverse community.

OUTRIGHT VERMONT

Contact: Chistopher Kaufman

Address: PO Box 5235, Burlington, VT 05402

Phone: 802-865-9677

Email: info@outrightvt.org

Website: www.outrightvt.org

Founded: 1989

Budget: under 250k

Constituency Age: 13-25

Issues: LGBTTSQ/Queer

Race: White

Profile: Outright Vermont is an intergenerational organization offering a safe space and supportive environment for youth under 22. Through education and outreach, OV actively challenges stereotypes, prejudice and violence both in and out of school. OV provides education and HIV/AIDS services, runs a library, a drop-in center and weekly support groups, and has a speaker's bureau that educates the broader Vermont community. Every year OV organizes a speak-out and a youth pride march.

STUDENT POLITICAL AWARENESS AND RESPONSIBILITY COALITION (SPARC)

Contact: Erin Hawley

Address: c/o SGA Billings Student Center, Burlington, VT 05405

Phone: 802-865-7706

Website: www.uvm.edu/sparc

Budget: out of pocket

Constituency Age: 13-25

Issues: Genetic Engineering, Police Accountability, Globalization, Environment

Race: Multi-Racial, White

Profile: For decades, SPARC has been active on the UVM campus, operating as an alternative speaker's bureau and film forum, serving as a central organizer and portal for student/faculty/community activism and involvement, and working on both local and global issues. Current activities and campaigns include operating the Vermont Indymedia Center, protesting the School of the Americas and the IMF/World Bank/FTAA, and calling for student oversight of the UVM police. SPARC's rich non-violent direct-action tradition continues today, stronger than ever.

VIRGINIA

COMMUNITY SPACE PROJECT

Contact: Greg Well

Address: PO Box 5021, Richmond, VA 23220

Phone: 804-644-2544

Email: gregwells36@hotmail.com

Founded: 2001

Budget: out of pocket

Constituency Age: 19-25

Issues: Environmental Justice, Public Space

Race: White

Profile: The Community Space Project is a coalition of young people working on environmental justice issues, queer youth activism, homeless organizing, corporate accountability and living wage campaigns. Collectively, they work to build partnerships between the African and Anglo American communities in Richmond and to create "oppression-free" community structures. The long term goal of the Project is to establish a communal space that will house initiatives focused on education, creative expression, networking, dialogue, and alternative forms of resource distribution.

RICHMOND ANTI-GLOBALIZATION NETWORK/FOOD NOT BOMBS

Contact: Jason Guard

Address: PO Box 5688, Richmond, VA 23220

Phone: 804-359-4880

Email: a16rva@hotmail.com

Website: http://foodnotbombsrva.8m.com

Budget: out of pocket

WTO protests in Seattle, November 30, 1999
© Geoff Oliver Bugbee

Constituency Age: 13-30
Issues: Police Accountability, Homelessness, Militarism,
LGBTTSQ/Queer, Environment
Race: White
Profile: These folks are into puppet making, street theater,
direct action and organizing protesters to attend and support
large anti-globalization demos internationally. Back in
Organizing Richmond they have launched Caroling for the
Campaign of Labor Rights-- they sing fun, anti-globalization
songs in malls and other public places! Members have also
practiced successful jail solidarity. Merged with the Richmond
Food not Bombs, which has been organizing enormous weekly
meals, gardening projects and homeless/low-income solidarity
campaigns for 9 years.

RICHMOND BICYCLE LIBRARY

Contact: Greg Will
Address: 325 South Carry St, Richmond, VA 23220
Phone: 804-644-2544
Email: s3glwill@atlas.vcu.edu
Founded: 2000
Budget: out of pocket
Constituency Age: 13-30
Issues: Youth Development, Environment
Race: White
Profile: Creative yet simple, The Bike Library lends bikes.
Going to the root of pollution and environmental responsibility,
these folks make it easy for community members to get to
work, school, events or wherever without using gas-guzzlin',
air-pollutin', resource gluttons, a.k.a, cars. The Library also
donates or sells bikes and parts on a sliding scale. Mechanics
help repair bikes and teach bike repair, both one-on-one and in
semi-regular workshops. Tools and repair stands are available
for use. Fun, cheap, informative.

VEGAN ACTION

Contact: Krissi Vandenberg
Address: PO Box 4288, Richmond, VA 23220
Phone: 804-254-8346
Email: information@vegan.org
Website: www.vegan.org
Budget: under 25k
Constituency Age: 13-30 and over
Issues: Animal Rights, Environment
Race: White
Profile: Promotes the vegan option, awareness of animal cruel-
ty and public accountability for the meat industry. With a
national network of campus chapters, Vegan Action has won
campaigns for vegan dorm food, runs a vegan food certification
program and launched a clever parody of McDonald's: "No, this
isn't McDonalds. It's McVegan. Our motto 'billions and billions
saved' is recited by Ronald McDonald's compassionate twin
brother, Reggie McVeggie." Mickey D's sued, then backed
down, which got lots of publicity-- which was the point!

VIRGINIA ORGANIZING PROJECT

Contact: Joe Szakos
Address: 703 Concord Ave, Charlottesville, VA 22903
Phone: 434-984-4655
Email: szakos@virginia-organizing.org
Website: www.virginia-organizing.org
Founded: 1995
Budget: under 100k
Constituency Age: 13-25
Issues: LGBTTSQ/Queer, Racial Justice,
Labor/Economic Justice, Environment, Immigrant/Refugee
Race: Multi-Racial
Profile: With three people under 30 on their statewide board
and nine young interns involved in all their organizing efforts,
VOP has trained and educated, politicized, and organized
thousands throughout Virginia. High school organizers
successfully added sexual orientation to a non-discrimination
policy for students in the Charlottesville and Albemarle county
school boards. The interns also work on a living wage
campaigns in Charlottesville in solidarity with city employees
and contract workers. Their efforts have inspired similar
campaigns across the state.

WASHINGTON

ANAKBAYAN

Contact: Freedom Siyam
Address: PO Box 80064, Seattle, WA 98108
Phone: 206-763-9611
Email: anakbayan206@hotmail.com
Website: www.anakbayan206.cjb.net
Founded: 1995
Budget: out of pocket
Constituency Age: 19-30
Issues: Human Rights, Environmental Justice, Racial Justice,
Militarism, Globalization
Race: Asian/Pacific Islander
Profile: AnakBayan-- "sons and daughters of the country" in
Tagalog-- is a Filipino student and youth organization that
characterizes the 103 year relationship between the US and the
Philippines as neocolonialist and exploitative. Through public
education campaigns, coalition-building and direct action,
AnakBayan has focused on labor and globalization.
They organized the first North American Filipina Women's
Conference in 2001 and have had a contingent at every global
justice action since the 1999 WTO protests. Publish the radical
zine .45 Caliber Proof.

ENVIRONMENTAL JUSTICE YOUTH ADVOCATES

Contact: Yolanda Sinde
Address: 105 14th Ave, Suite 2D, Seattle, WA 98122
Phone: 206-720-0285
Email: justice@ccej.org
Budget: under 100k
Constituency Age: 13-30 and over
Issues: Environmental Justice, Corporate Accountability,
Racial Justice
Race: Multi-Racial
Profile: A project of the Community Coalition for Environmental
Justice, EJYA is a leadership development and internship
project through which young people of color address the
economic and environmental health issues that
disproportionately impact their refugee, indigenous, immigrant,
and low income communities. Victories include shutting down a
medical waste incinerator and a paint factory in a residential
neighborhood. Youth are involved in public outreach on indoor
air pollution and organizing low-income communities displaced
by gentrification and the federal Hope VI program.

JASIRI MEDIA GROUP

Contact: Johnathan Moore AKA Wordsayer
Address: 1122 E. Pike St #913, Seattle, WA 98122
Phone: 206-559-2767
Email: jasiri@speakeasy.org
Website: www.jasirimusic.org
Founded: 1993
Budget: out of pocket
Constituency Age: 12 and under-30 and over
Issues: Hip Hop Activism, Racial Justice, Arts/Culture
Race: Multi-Racial
Profile: The original political, cultural and entrepreneurial
Seattle Hip Hop family, JMG is a community-based arts
collective that divides its time between the underground music
scene, youth education programs and political events.
Throws weekly events, including Sure Shot Sundays, an all-age,
no smoking/alcohol show in downtown Seattle, and is involved
in anti-gentrification campaigns. Groups include Source of
Labor, Piece of Sol, Beyond Reality and Maktub; when not
making music, members teach at Franklin High School,
Miller Community Center and Experience Arts Camp.

NORTHWEST COALITION FOR HUMAN DIGNITY/CLUB COALTION PROJECT

Contact: Eric Ward
Address: PO Box 21428, Seattle, WA 98111
Phone: 206-762-5627 x13
Email: nwchd@nwchd.org
Website: www.nwchd.org
Founded: 1987
Budget: under 500k
Constituency Age: 13-21
Issues: Labor/Economic Justice, Racial Justice,
Environmental Justice, Arts/Culture

Race: Multi-Racial
Profile: A coalition of young people, musicians, artists and
performers working to counter the rise of white power music
and increasing bigotry in the music scene. Distributed their
Postive Power magazine to over 30,000 young people while on
organizing tours with major music acts like Blink 182. Well-
connected and innovative programs such as CREATE!, an
organizer training conference, and the YOUNG AMERICANS -
Do It Yourself Revolution Tour, where young people learn to
organize a musical event, fundraise and build coalitions.

PEACE FOR THE STREETS BY KIDS FROM THE STREETS

Contact: Elaine Simons
Address: 1411 E. Olive Way, Seattle, WA 98122
Phone: 206-726-8500
Email: peacehype@msn.com
Founded: 1995
Budget: under 100k
Constituency Age: 13-30
Issues: Arts/Culture, Welfare/Poverty, Police Accountability,
Housing/Gentrification, Homelessness
Race: Multi-Racial
Profile: PSKS works with a volunteer staff of homeless and
street-involved youth to provide assistance and address
community misconceptions about homelessness. The PSKS
model empowers youth to design programs and participate in
decision-making while promoting dialogue between
street-involved youth and other community members, from
business owners to police to state government officials.
Produce a monthly public access television program (now in
its 3rd season), participate in social service coalitions and offer
stipends to homeless youth.

PEOPLE'S COALITION FOR JUSTICE (PCJ)

Contact: Dustin Washington
Address: 1140 18th Ave, Seattle, WA 98122
Phone: 206-632-0500 x14
Founded: 1998
Budget: out of pocket
Constituency Age: 12 and under-30 and over
Issues: Racial Justice, Police Accountability
Race: Multi-Racial
Profile: PCJ is an intergenerational, people of color
organization working to build a community-wide campaign
against racial profiling and police violence. PCJ orchestrated a
"counter" vote in high schools and colleges throughout Seattle
in response to a police union's internal "vote of confidence"
for department heads that have a history of racist policing.
Currently campaigning for a civilian review board, community
monitoring and anti-racist workshops for police officers. Also
organizing around the criminalization of young people and the
growing prison industry.

RED CURSOR COLLECTIVE/RISEUP.NET

Contact: Elijah Saxon
Address: 1309 13th Ave South, Seattle, WA 98144
Phone: 206-324-6822
Email: redcursor@riseup.net
Website: www.riseup.net
Founded: 2000
Budget: out of pocket
Constituency Age: 13-30
Issues: Media
Race: White
Profile: The emerging favorite activist internet service provider, riseup.net is a project of the Red Cursor Collective , a 100% volunteer effort of young activists using technology for radical social change. RCC provides training, web hosting, listservs, email accounts, and any kind of tech support needed by the activist community. Future projects include spearheading a tech activist federation and creating an online toolbox designed to meet online communication and collaboration needs of activist organizations.

SEATTLE INDEPENDENT MEDIA CENTER

Contact: Daniel Hannah
Address: 1415 Third Ave, Seattle, WA 98101
Phone: 206-262-0721
Email: imc-seattle@indymedia.org
Website: www.seattle.indymedia.org
Founded: 1999
Budget: under 25k
Constituency Age: 13-30 and over
Issues: Globalization, Media
Race: Multi-Racial, White
Profile: A simple but brilliant idea: "um, no, we're not going to let the corporate media cover our protest. We're the media too." When they launched in preparation for the WTO protest, they received millions of visits in one week. Now there are more than 80 IMCs around the world from Nigeria to Colombia to Jerusalem and the IMC sites serve as vital discussion centers for young activists globally. A good example of both the potential and limitations of internet organizing.

SEATTLE YOUNG PEOPLE'S PROJECT

Contact: Dustin Washington
Address: 123 21st Ave, Seattle, WA 98122
Phone: 206-860-9606
Email: sypp@drizzle.com
Website: www.sypp.org
Founded: 1992
Budget: under 100k
Constituency Age: 13-21
Issues: Women's Rights, LGBTTSQ/Queer, Student Rights/Education Reform, Racial Justice, Corporate Accountability
Race: Multi-Racial

Profile: SYPP is an umbrella organization that urges Seattle youth to address issues affecting their lives through education and activism. Their programs, led by high-school-age youth, include fighting corporate exploitation, developing LGBT initiatives and coordinating conferences. Their Youth Undoing Institutionalized Racism (YUIR) project advocates for truly multicultural history in public schools, created a resource center for out-of-school youth, and works to end military recruitment on campuses. YUIR also created a 9/11 CD featuring Hip Hop and spoken-word artists.

STRONGHOLD PROJECT

Contact: Randy Engstrom
Address: 3046 Beacon Ave S, Seattle, WA 98144
Phone: 206-721-7506
Email: vitalproducts@hotmail.com
Website: www.strongholdcollective.org
Founded: 2000
Budget: under 100k
Constituency Age: 13-30
Issues: Housing/Gentrification, Hip Hop Activism, Public Space, Prisons/Criminal Justice, Arts/Culture
Race: White
Profile: A unique nine-member collective of young artists that purchased a four house compound, Stronghold seeks to create by-artists-for-artists sustainable spaces. Stronghold collaborates and provides support for numerous politically active and conscious arts organizations in Seattle including the Fremont UNconventional Center, Emergence Gallery and ArtWorks. Lends space and talent to campaigns around the prison industry, gentrification and globalization.

West Virginia

Junior Cooperative Action Program
Contact: Raina Branham
Address: PO Box 134, Panther, WV 24872
Phone: 304-938-3199
Founded: 2000
Budget: out of pocket
Constituency Age: 12 and under-18
Issues: Youth Development
Race: White
Profile: JCAP is the youth-led component of the Cooperative Action Program, a successful grassroots organization that works with low income families on multiple issues. Campaigns include welfare and worker rights, educational and technological access, and the Democracy Education project, which provides local residents with leadership training. JCAP members also design and implement their own initiatives. Whether working with coal miners or emergency workers during a recent flood, the Juniors make sure young people have a positive presence in Panther, WV

South Central Educational Development
Contact: Darryl Cannady
Address: PO Box 4322, Bluefield, WV 24701
Phone: 304-325-6105
Email: sced@stargate.net
Founded: 1992
Budget: under 100k
Constituency Age: 13-30
Issues: HIV/AIDS, Student Rights/Education Reform
Race: African-American/Black
Profile: This intergenerational HIV/AIDS service organization has several leadership training programs focused on peer education and outreach. Through skits, puppet shows and a speaker's bureau, young people reach out to other teens in high schools in six counties. Youth are also developing a high school sex education curriculum designed to make schools healthy environments for open, honest discussions about sex. All education and outreach programs are developed with young people and youth also serve on the SCED board of directors.

Wisconsin

Asian Freedom Project
Contact: Kabzuag Vaj
Address: 601 Bayview, Madison, WI 53715
Phone: 608-256-7808
Email: refugeeproject@hotmail.com
Founded: 2000
Budget: out of pocket
Constituency Age: 13-30
Issues: Prisons/Criminal Justice, Police Accountability, Immigrant/Refugee, Welfare/Poverty, Racial Justice
Race: Multi-Racial
Profile: The intergenerational Asian Freedom Project promotes political activism as a means of youth empowerment within a diverse Asian community. Young people have identified issues in their communities that need attention that include, immigration, bi-lingual education and the post-9/11 climate. Reforming the prison system, welfare, loitering ordinances and racial profiling of people of color are also core concerns, for which AFP has provided education, resources and a community space to organize campaigns.

Hip Hop Generation
Contact: Matt Temkin
Address: 731 State St, Madison, WI 53703
Phone: 608-256-1607
Email: bennyblanco@hiphopgeneration.org
Website: http://wiscinfo.doit.wisc.edu/
soo/pages/organiza1.asp?RegHistoryID=4929
Founded: 1999
Budget: under 50k
Constituency Age: 13-30
Issues: Racial Justice, Prisons/Criminal Justice, Student Rights/Education Reform, Hip Hop Activism, Arts/Culture
Race: Multi-Racial
Profile: HHG is a student organization at U. of Wisconsin-Madison dedicated to youth empowerment and social change through Hip Hop Culture. Its core effort is an annual three-day Hip Hop as a Movement conference featuring panels addressing issues ranging from The Prison Industrial Complex to Sexuality and Homophobia in Hip Hop to The Impact of Guerilla Radio and the Internet on Music. As a result, some of Hip Hop's most respected performers, journalists and activists converge on Madison every year.

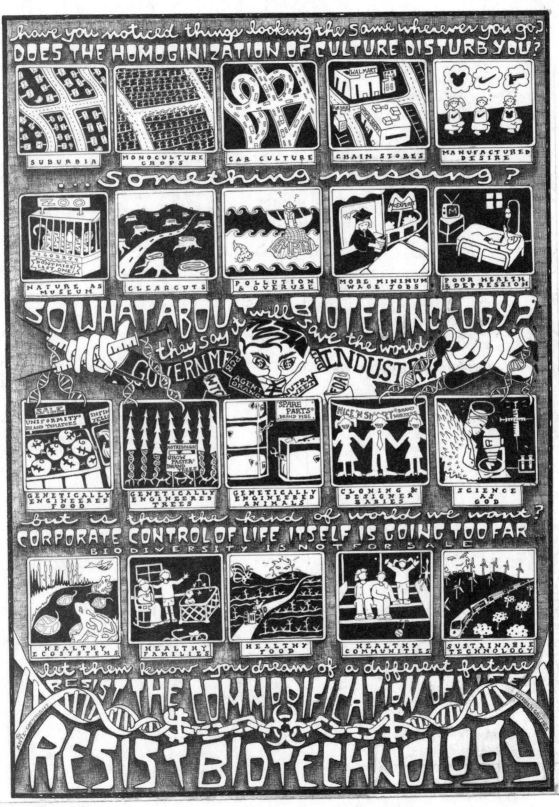

Resist the Commodification of Life
© Beehive Design Collective

MULTICULTURAL STUDENT COALITION

Contact: Peter Moran
Address: 2nd Floor Red Gym, 716 Langdon St,
Madison, WI 53706
Phone: 608-262-5131
Email: pgmoran@students.wisc.edu
Founded: 1999
Budget: under 1 million
Constituency Age: 19-30
Issues: Racial Justice, Immigrant/Refugee,
Prisons/Criminal justice
Race: Multi-Racial
Profile: Student group extraordinaire at the University of
Wisconsin, MSC does all the diversity training for the university
while connecting and supporting many student groups on
campus. Major Fall orientation program for incoming students
with BBQs, DJ battles and introductions to administrators.
Educate campus on student government politics and
candidates. Pushing the Plan 2008 diversity initiative to
increase number of faculty and students of color on campus.
A strong web of student activism and education.

MILWAUKEE BICYCLE COLLECTIVE

Contact: Ian Fritz
Address: 929 N. 33rd St, Milwaukee, WI 53208
Phone: 414-264-7211
Email: info@bikecollective.org
Website: www.bikecollective.org
Founded: 2001
Budget: out of pocket
Constituency Age: 12 and under-30 and over
Issues: Arts/Culture, Labor/Economic Justice,
Housing/Gentrification, Public Space
Race: Multi-Racial
Profile: MBC is a newly formed resource for people that are
creatively pursuing alternatives to polluting forms of
transportation. MBC offers free space, parts and tools to local
cyclists through a work-trade system. By helping people learn
to repair and create their own modes of transportation, and
connecting bike mechanics and recreation to environmental and
economic issues, MBC has become a community organizing
hub. Currently planning to create a full resource library on
sustainable development, alternative energy sources and
environmental activism.

URBAN UNDERGROUND

Contact: Reggie Moore
Address: 231 W. Wisconsin Ave #500, Milwaukee, WI 53203
Phone: 414-225-8995
Email: moore4youth@yahoo.com
Website: www.urbanunderground.org
Founded: 1999
Budget: under 100k
Constituency Age: 13-18
Issues: Student Rights/Education Reform, Racial Justice,
Public Space, Police Accountability
Race: People of Color
Profile: Emphasizing the role that young people can play in
changing unjust social and educational policies, Urban
Underground amplifies the voices and actions of teens
addressing racism, welfare, crime, and education. Through the
Youth Empowerment Project, UU trains young people to
research and address social issues affecting their lives;
the mainly high school age participants then lead workshops
training middle and elementary schoolers. On "The Other
America Tour," students give presentations on awareness,
accountability, and activism against racism and oppression.

UW GREENS

Contact: John Peck
Address: 31 University Sq, Madison, WI 53715
Phone: 608-262-9036
Email: infoshop@eudoramail.com
Founded: 1988
Budget: under 50k
Constituency Age: 19-25
Issues: Public Space, Student Rights/Education Reform,
Police Accountability, Globalization, Corporate Accountability
Race: White
Profile: UW Greens (not affiliated with the Green Party) is a
major nerve center for activism at one of America's most
consistently active campuses. The group publishes an annual
"disorientation manual," which offers students information on
campus activism and alternatives to corporate buying. An
all-student consensus organization that includes several task
groups focusing on environmental, social, economic and
anti-corporate issues, UW Greens are currently organizing
demonstrations against the National Mayor's Summit, as well
as fighting post 9/11 police brutality.

WYOMING

LGBT ASSOCIATION AT UNIVERSITY OF WYOMING

Address: PO Box 3625, Laramie, WY 82071
Phone: 307-766-6340
Email: lgbta@uwyo.edu
Website: www.uwyo.edu/lgbta
Founded: 1980
Budget: under 25k
Constituency Age: 13-30
Issues: LGBTTSQ/Queer
Race: White
Profile: The only youth LGBT group in the state, the Association
serves primarily as a safe social and educational space for
students. Sponsor panels, movies, speakers, brown-bag
lunches and are becoming more involved in actions against
discriminatory and exclusionary policies. Organize Gay

Awareness Week around National Coming Out Day, including a memorial for LGBTA member Matthew Shepherd. Communicate with LGBT groups at other schools in the region and connect people to the Rainbow Resource Center on campus.

WIND RIVER COUNTRY INITIATIVE FOR YOUTH

Contact: Debra East
Address: 484 N. 3rd St, Lander, WY 82520
Phone: 307-332-2890
Email: wrcyouthinitiative@yahoo.com
Founded: 2000
Budget: under 100k
Constituency Age: 12 and under-30 and over
Issues: LGBTTSQ/Queer
Race: Multi-Racial, White, Native American
Profile: WRCTY is an intergenerational advocacy group working to create safe spaces for all queer people in a large frontier region in Wyoming. Making sure there is a queer presence in the area, WRCTY representatives regularly communicate with 36 regional organizations to, "integrate, not assimilate" a queer voice and to focus on bias crime legislation. Recognizing the complexity of queer identity, they train through their parent organization, National Coalition Building Initiative to address race and class issues.

YOUNG WARRIORS SOCIETY

Contact: Martin Blackburn
Address: PO Box 128, Stephens St, WY 82524
Phone: 307-857-0545
Email: youngwarriors@hotmail.com
Founded: 1997
Budget: out of pocket
Constituency Age: 12 and under-30 and over
Issues: Arts/Culture, Violence Prevention, Indigenous Rights, Environmental Justice
Race: Native American
Profile: Young people work with the elder keepers of the Arapahoe and Eastern Shoshone cultures to learn the warrior tradition: to provide, to protect, to lead spiritually. Weekly meetings include guest speakers, arts and crafts projects, helping out an elderly member of the community. Young people are learning about water culturally, politically and scientifically and have participated in water quality testing with the Tribal Waters Engineers Office. Also involved with anti-violence prevention work and the Eastern Shoshone diabetes summer camp.

National Resources and Networks

We debated whether to even have a national list. Challenges: comprehensiveness, groups fitting into multiple categories, many strong national youth resources are housed within adult organizations, many have no central office (some well-known groups like MEChA and Radical Cheerleaders don't even have centralized websites or stable phone numbers). But for all its flaws, this is by far the most comprehensive list to date of youth organizing and activism in the US. We need you to help us keep it fresh. If you see groups missing, go to www.Future500.com, and add 'em.

We offer this list of 100 groups as a resource and as an imaginative exercise. Consider: Which groups are able to maintain strong, consistent networks and which aren't? Why? Where are the gaps in issues, constituencies, strategies, geography? Where are the opportunities for unlikely collaboration? What are the groups you'd like to create a chapter of in your neighborhood or campus? What national networks would you like to tap into? Help create?

Culture and Media

Obviously this list could go on forever with websites, zines, etc. We tried to choose a representative handful of the most useful ones that are truly national in scope.

33 1/3 Gallery & Books: Hip Hop activism hub and maverick gallery that created the Unbound Project (anti-prison compilation). www.revolutions-per-minute.net;1200 N. Alvarado Blvd, Los Angeles, CA 90026; 323-662-9463.

Art and Revolution: Could be listed under radical franchises or global justice. A loose seven city network of political creatives. www.artandrevolution.org (See CA).

AWOL Magazine: In the tradition of Blu, geared to young people of color with an anti-military edge and comes with a CD. www.awol.objector.org (See PA)

Bitch: The most feminist, cleverest popular young women's zine. www.bitchmagazine.com; 2765 16th St, San Francisco, CA 94103; 510-625-9390.

BlackOut Arts Collective: The closest thing to a national network of political and community-oriented spoken word artists. www.blackoutartscollective.com (See NY)

Clamor: The independent magazine of culture and activism, especially the punk/global justice side. www.clamormagazine.com (See OH)

Colorlines: Key publication of the racial justice movement. Multi-generational with a strong community-organizing bent. www.colorlines.org; 3781 Broadway, Oakland, CA 94611; 510-653-3415.

Colours of Resistance: A virtual North America-wide community of writers, organizers, and strategists building an anti-racist global justice movement. www.tao.ca/~colours; c/o Student-Worker Solidarity, QPIRG-McGill, 3647 University St 3rd Floor, Montreal, QC, H3A 2B3, Canada; colours@tao.ca.

DanceSafe/Late Night Coalition: The most politically conscious network in the rave scene. Many local chapters do work around de-criminalization. www.dancesafe.org (See NY, CA)

DaveyD.com: An invaluable one-man effort to cover Hip Hop and politics, Davey D is the popular Bay Area DJ fired by Clear Channel after interviewing Rep. Barbara Lee.

Free Speech TV: A media treasure chest for the movement and a hub of independent media. Daily broadcasts on Satellite Dish TV. www.fstv.org

Hip Hop Congress: The only attempt at creating a network of campus-based Hip Hop groups. www.hiphopcongress.org (see IN)

Hip Hop Generation: Based in Madison WI, the major national political Hip Hop conference three years running. www.hiphopgeneration.org (See WI)

Independent Media Center: With 90+ offices in 3 years, their global reach rivals CNN. Log on to Indymedia.org-- 'nuff said! (See NY, TX)

Protest.net: A collective of activists who run a website that lists protests from around the world.

Raptivism: The most successful independent political rap label to date. www.raptivism.com (See NY)

Red Cursor Collective: The people behind radical Internet Service Provider, Riseup.net. (See WA)

Red Eye: The most promising new political Hip Hop magazine, consciously seeks to support movement-building. www.redeyemagazine.com (See NY)

ReGeneration TV: Hip Hop, politics, interviews, seditious media-- among the first folks to grasp the democratic potential of the web and to use it as an archive of global political action... and DJ contests. www.regenerationtv.org; 4477 Hollywood Blvd #213, Los Angeles, CA 90027; 323-906-8651.

Skatepark.com: Young people often have to fight for skateparks so they're sometimes the one sign of activist life in many suburbs and small towns.

The Activist: Doesn't come out often, but when it does, it's one of the best mags on the movement, especially the student side. www.theactivist.org (See YDS in NY)

Tree of Knowledge: One of the few independent publishers and distributors of zines and books in the South with an anarchist/punk focus. treeofknowledge@yahoo.com; PO Box 251766, Little Rock, AR 72225; 501-590-3849.

Youth Speaks: The closest thing we have to a national teenage network of spoken word artists. www.youthspeaks.org (See CA)

Wiretap.org: The best weekly digest and reporting on alternative youth cultural and political news and lit. www.wiretapmag.org (See CA)

Zines: Informally networked via the Underground Publishing Conference www.clamormagazine.org (See OH).

Radical Franchises

These tend to appeal mainly to white youth in their teens and 20s. They're non-hierarchical (at least in theory), a strong link in many movements, and you gotta love 'em because they run on little to no money and are the only thing happening in a lot of small towns.

Anarchist Black Cross (ABC): Supports political prisoners. Gaining support as political dissent is criminalized. www.anarchistblackcross.org; PO Box 19733, Austin, TX 78760; 512-497-5975

Anti-Capitalist Convergence: Ad hoc group that mobilizes for mass demonstrations and civil disobedience. www.abolishthebank.org (See DC)

Anti-Racist Action (ARA): Fights overt racist groups. www.azone.org/ara (See IL, OH)

Books to Prisoners Programs: There are about 15 now. Books Through Bars in Philadelphia is an unofficial hub. www.booksthroughbars.org (See PA)

Collective houses: There's not even an informal network of the hundreds that exist but Hillsborough Rd. Co-op in Chapel Hill has compiled a slide show on how punks can buy houses and make collectives work. (See NC)

Copwatch: Autonomous chapters loosely affiliated with one another, often connected to ARA. (See AZ, OH)

Critical Mass: Bike activism in hundreds of cities worldwide connected via www.critical-mass.org and www.criticalmasshub.com. Sometimes connected to Earn-A-Bike programs for kids.

Direct Action Network: Formed around WTO protests, has loose affiliates in a dozen cities. http://riseup.net/cdan/, www.anotherworldispossible.com (See IL)

Food Not Bombs: Hundreds of chapters networked via listserve and www.foodnotbombs.org. (See UT, VA)

Infoshops: Informally networked through The Long Haul Infoshop in Berkeley. www.Infoshop.org; 3124 Shattuck Ave, Berkeley, CA 94705; 510-540-0751.

Microradio broadcasters: Informally networked via Prometheus Radio Project in Philly. www.prometheusradio.org (See PA)

Radical Cheerleaders: Dozens of squads, very informally networked. (See FL)

Reclaim the Streets: Autonomous chapters informally networked via www.reclaimthestreets.net. (See NY)

Refuse and Resist: Mainly does prison, police, repro-rights and anti-militarism work. www.refuseandresist.org (See HI, NY)

Student Networks

180 Movement for Democracy and Education (180 MDE): Global justice, campus democracy, and corporate issues. www.corporations.org/180mde (See AR)

By Any Means Necessary (BAMN): Campus-based group focusing mainly on affirmative action. Has a loose national network. www.bamn.com; 3430 East Jefferson Ave, Suite 545, Detroit, MI 48207; letters@bamn.com.

Campus Greens: Loosely affiliated with the Green Party, but separate. Works on eco, global justice, and democracy issues. www.campusgreenparties.org; 3411 West Diversey Blvd, Suite 5, Chicago, IL 60647-1125. (See also DE)

MEChA (Movimiento Estudiantil Chicano de Aztlan): The primary Latino (especially Chicano) student activist org at high schools as well as colleges. Has huge annual gathering. www.panam.edu/orgs/mecha/nat.html (See TX)

Muslim Student Association (MSA): Has been forced to become much more active post September 11. www.msa-natl.org; Altaf Husain, PO Box 18612, Washington, DC 20036; 703- 820-7900.

National Youth and Student Peace Coalition (NYSPC): Remarkable new coalition post-Sept 11. www.nyspc.net (See CT)

Sierra Student Coalition: Liberal eco group. Some chapters do creative public education about global warming, etc. www.ssc.org (See DC).

Student Action Network: a collaborative between the major campus environmental groups. www.studentactionnetwork.org; Joshua Sage; sage@rightonthe.com.

Student Alliance with Farmworkers (SAF): Works with the Coalition of Immoklee Workers on the No Quiero Taco Bell Campaign supporting tomato workers. www.ciw-online.org; Brian Payne, c/o Coalition of Immokalee Workers, PO Box 603, Immokalee, FL 34143; 941-657-8311; sfw_alliance@hotmail.com. (see FL)

Student Environmental Action Center (SEAC): The major environmental justice network on campuses. Many chapters partner with local EJ groups. www.seac.org (see PA)

Student Labor Action Project (SLAP): Housed within Jobs with Justice, winning major living wage campaigns nationwide. www.jwj.org/SLAP/slap.htm (see DC)

Student Peace Action Network (SPAN): A tiny group started before September 11, which supports the NYSPC (above). www.gospan.org (See DC)

Students for a Free Tibet (SFT): One of the biggest networks with hundreds of chapters, notable corporate victories. www.tibet.org/sft (see NY)

Students for Justice in Palestine (SJP): Started at UC Berkeley before September 11, spreading quickly. www.justiceinpalestine.org; 2425 Channing Way PMB #572, Berkeley, CA 94704; 866-841-9139 x1752; justiceinpalestine@yahoo.com.

Students for Sensible Drug Policy (SSDP): The fastest growing group of 2000/2001, campaign against the Higher Education Act which cuts financial aid for students with drug convictions. www.ssdp.org (See DC)

Students Transforming and Resisting Corporations (STARC): The major multi-issue global/local justice network on campuses. Does a road show. www.starcalliance.org (See OR)

Students United for a Responsible Global Environment (SURGE): www.surgenetwork.org (see NC)

United Students Against Sweatshops (USAS): One of the most successful student groups. Currently widening its focus to include local labor issues. www.usasnet.org (See DC)

United States Student Association (USSA): The major liberal to progressive alliance of college students, representing millions. www.usstudents.org (See DC)

Young Democratic Socialists (YDS): The only Socialist group that consistently works well with other student groups. A key early force in the anti-prison, sweatshop, and living wage campaigns. www.dsausa.org/youth (See NY)

Issue-Based Groups

This list could go on forever; below is a sampling of groups we found with significant national presence. Many of these groups don't fit narrowly into a single issue. And within each issue, many groups are culturally divided between white liberal groups, white radical groups, and people of color-based groups. We mix them together here.

American Friends Service Committee (AFSC): Quaker organization that includes people of various faiths committed to issues related to economic justice, peace-building and demilitarization, social justice, and youth. Key branch in Iowa. www.afsc.org; 4211 Grand Ave, Des Moines, IA 50312; 515-274-4851.

American Indian Movement: Network of autonomous chapters that support each other in local mobilizations. www.dickshovel.com/AIMIntro.html or www.aimovement.org

Atrevete (formerly Muevete): The largest gathering/training of Latino youth on the East Coast. Pan Latino, mainly Puerto Rican. (See NY)

Black Radical Congress (BRC): A critical national network of black activists and scholars, includes young people. www.blackradicalcongress.org; National Office, Columbia University Station, New York, NY 10025-1509; 212-969-0348.

Black Youth Vote: The major group educating and mobilizing Black youth voters nationwide. www.bigvote.org (See DC)

Critical Resistance: The major national network, campaign hub, and gathering around prison issues. www.criticalresistance.org; Rose Braz, 1212 Broadway Suite 1400, Oakland, CA 94612; 510-444-0484; crnational@criticalresistance.org.

Earth First!: The major network of radical enviros. www.earthfirst.org

Ella Baker Center: Based in NY and CA, national Books Not Bars Campaign is highly strategic. www.ellabakercenter.org (See CA)

Families Against Mandatory Minimums (FAMM): Works with many young people nationwide whose parents have been taken away. www.famm.org (See DC)

Free the Planet!: Works to hold polluters and politicians accountable for enviromental protection. Helps launch campaigns at colleges and runs a speaker trainings. www.freetheplanet.org; 218 D St SE, Washington, DC 20003; 202-547-3656.

Gay/Lesbian and Straight Education Network (GLSEN): National network of LGBT teachers and GSAs. www.glsen.org

Gay Straight Alliance Network: California focused, a network of GSAs with a progressive bent. www.gsanetwork.org; Carolyn Laub, 160 14th St, San Francisco, CA 94103; 415-552-4229; carolyn@gsanetwork.org.

Grassroots Leadership: Hired key leadership of the Prison Moratorium Project to run a national anti-private prison campaign, focused in the Northeast and Southeast. www.grassrootsleadership.org

Greencorps: The major post-college, liberal, eco-organizing training program. www.greencorps.org; 29 Temple Place, Boston, MA 02111; 617-426-8506.

Indigenous and Non-Indigenous Youth Alliance (INIYA): A loose hemisphere-wide network. www.iniya.org (See CA)

Indigenous Environmental Network (IEN): Has a youth leadership program and a youth-led petroleum land use campaign. (See MN)

International People's Democratic Uhuru Movement (INPDUM): Founded in the tradition of the Panthers, has strong chapters in several cities. www.inpdumchicago.com (See IL)

Malcolm X Grassroots Movement (MXGM): Cultural and political activism in the Black community, from Copwatch and feeding programs to Black August. Also strong in the South and in Cali. (See NY)

Military Toxics Project Youth Initiative: A few youth groups, but very spread out: Vieques, Hawaii, Memphis, San Diego. www.miltoxproj.org (See ME)

NAACP Youth: Generally disappointing but on many historically black campuses, they're the best thing going. www.naacp.org

National Abortion and Reproductive Rights Action League (NARAL): Not especially diverse or youth-friendly but the major national group fighting to protect repro rights. 462 Broadway, Suite 540, New York, NY 10013; 212-343-0114.

National Coalition to Abolish the Death Penalty (NCADP): Has several youth chapters. www.ncadp.org/html/youthpage.html; 1436 U St NW, Suite 104, Washington, DC 20009; 202-543-9577.

National Council of La Raza: Same as NAACP, but for Latinos. www.nclr.org

National Youth Advocacy Coalition (NYAC): The major national network of community-based LGBT youth groups. www.nyacyouth.org; 1638 R St, Suite 300, Washington, DC 20009; 202-319-7596.

New Black Panther Party: From reparations to police abuse, a hub with several loosely affiliated chapters nationwide. www.newblackpanther.net; nbppheadquarters@aol.com

People of Color Environmental Leadership Summit: Multi-generational, currently developing its youth track. www.weact.org; c/o WE ACT Inc, 271 West 125th St, Suite 308, New York, NY 10027-4424; (212) 961-1000.

Prison Activist Resource Center (PARC): The best general resource for prison activists in the US. www.prisonactivist.org (See CA)

Prison Moratorium Project (PMP): The key group organizing on campuses nationwide, now focused primarily in New York. www.nomoreprisons.org (See NY)

Rainforest Action Network (RAN): Key group behind international solidarity with indigenous people in rainforests. www.ran.org (See CA)

Southern Girls Convention: An informal, mainly white, but large and kick ass gathering. www.infoshop.org/southerngirls (See AL)

Youth for Environmental Sanity! (YES): Holds numerous summer retreats, trainings, and camps for youth and young activists, domestic and international. www.yesworld.org (See CA)

Global Justice/International Solidarity

Includes US-based groups only. Some are country-specific, some global in scope. We tried to pick a spectrum of the most active and youth-oriented groups.

50 Years is Enough: Major network challenging global financial institutions. www.50years.org

Campaign for Labor Rights: Supports key labor campaigns in the US and abroad.www.summersault.com/~agj/clr; Daisy Pitkin, 1247 E St, SE, Washington, DC 20003; 202-544-9355; clrdc@afgj.org.

Chiapas Support Committee: Exposes human rights abuses, supports local projects, and educates the US public. www.chiapas-support.org; PO Box 3421, Oakland, CA 94609; 510-271-0349.

Eactivist.org: A useful general resource, especially for international stuff. Informally run out of the International Development Exchange (www.idex.org). www.eactivist.org

Estacion Libre: The major group sending people of color in the US to Chiapas. e-libre@tao.ca (See CA)

Fair Trade Resource Network: Has a student network, a speakers bureau and sends action packets. www.fairtraderesource.org; PO Box 33772, Washington, DC 20033; 202-302-0976.

Free Burma Coalition: Won major divestment victories against Burma's dictatorship. www.freeburmacoalition.org (See DC)

Free the Children: Based in Toronto, the largest international organization of children helping children around the world. Focused on child labor, health, and building schools. www.freethechildren.com

Global Exchange: Huge clearinghouse and innovative action center for progressive international issues. www.globalexchange.org; 2017 Mission Street #303, San Francisco, CA 94110; 415-255-7296; info@globalexchange.org.

International Solidarity Movement: Organizes a Freedom Summer program sending Americans to Israel and Palestine and other actions. www.palsolidarity.org

Jewish Social Justice Network: Emerging network with a handful of affiliates. jsjn@jfjustice.org

JustACT, Youth Action for Global Justice: Key group connecting young people of color in the US to the global justice movement. www.justact.org (See CA)

National Labor Committee (NLC): Helped incubate the student sweatshop movement along with UNITE. www.nlcnet.org

Project Underground: Supports local struggles against mining, oil drilling and other environmental violence worldwide. www.moles.org (see CA)

School of the Americas Watch: Mobilizes tens of thousands, including youth, to protest the US Army School of Americas. www.soaw.org; PO Box 4566, Washington, DC 20017; 202-234-3440.

TransAfrica Forum: The major progressive pan-African policy organization, starting a student organizing component. www.transafricaforum.org; 1426 21st St, NW, 2nd Floor, Washington, DC 20036; 202-223-1960.

U'wa Defense Project: Solidarity with an Indigenous people in the rainforest whose life is threatened by oil companies. (see CA)

Vieques Support Campaign: Connects US-based efforts to support people of Vieques against bombing and imperialism. http://palfrente.tripod.com; 402 West 145th St, New York, NY 10031; viequessc@hotmail.com. Also see dynamic youth organization Comite Pro-Rescate e Desarollo de Vieques/Juventud Viequense Unida: PO Box 1424, Vieques, PR 00765; 787-741-2461; Bieke@prdigital.com

Foundations

The following is a listing of some foundations (and a collaborative) that have committed funds specifically to youth organizing over the last two years. This list is far from comprehensive, but it will give a grant seeking organization some sense of which foundations may be interested in their work. Below is a combination of foundations that have explicit youth organizing programs as well as foundations that have funded organizing through their youth development programs; some are regional, most are national. Many of the trainings, workshops, and organizations listed in the Allies section on pg. 158 can help organizations better navigate the grant proposal process.

21st Century Foundation	www.21cf.org	212-662-3700
A Territory Resource Foundation	www.atrfoundation.org	206-624-4081
Active Element	www.activelement.org	212-283-8272
Appalachian Community Fund	www.appalachiancommunityfund.org	865-523-5783
Arthur M. Blank Family Foundation	www.blankfoundation.org	404-239-0600
Beldon Fund	www.beldon.org	212-616-5600
Ben & Jerry's Foundation	www.benjerry.com/foundation	802-846-1500
Boston Foundation	www.tbf.org	617-338-1700
Boston Women's Fund	www.bostonwomensfund.org	617-725-0035
Bread & Roses Community Fund	www.breadrosesfund.org	215-731-1107
California Wellness Foundation	www.tcwf.org	818-593-6600
Catholic Campaign for Human Development	www.nccbuscc.org/cchd	202-541-3000
Charles Hayden Foundation	www.fdncenter.org/grantmaker/hayden	212-785-3677
Charles Stewart Mott Foundation	www.mott.org	810-238-5651
Chinook Fund (FEX)	www.chinookfund.org	303-455-6905
Common Counsel	www.commoncounsel.org	510-834-2995
Cowell Foundation	www.shcowell.org	415-397-0285
Diana Fund-US	www.usdianafund.org	n/a
East Bay Community Foundation	www.eastbaycf.org	510-836-3223
Edward W. Hazen Foundation	www.hazenfoundation.org	212-889-3034
Evelyn and Walter Haas Jr.	www.haasjr.org	415-856-1400
Ford Foundation	www.fordfound.org	212-573-5000
French American Charitable Trust	www.factservices.org	415-288-1305
Fund for Southern Communities	www.fund4south.org	404-292-7600
Funders' Collaborative on Youth Organizing	www.fcyo.org	212-213-2113
Gill Foundation	www.gillfoundation.com	303-292-4455
Girls Best Friend Foundation	www.girlsbestfriend.org	312-266-2842
Haymarket People's Fund	www.haymarket.org	617-522-7676
Hyams Foundation	www.hyamsfoundation.org	617-426-5600
Irvine	www.irvine.org	415-777-2244
Jewish Fund for Justice	www.jfjustice.org	212-213-2113
Levi Strauss & Co.	www.levistrauss.com/responsibility/foundation	415-501-6000
Liberty Hill Foundation (FEX)	www.libertyhill.org	310-453-3611
Mary Reynolds Babcock	www.mrbf.org	336-748-9222
McKay Foundation	www.mckayfund.org	415-288-1313
McKenzie River Gathering Foundation	www.mrgfoundation.org	503-289-1517
Merck	www.merckff.org	617-696-3580
Needmor Fund	www.fdncenter.org/grantmaker/needmor	303-449-5801
New World Foundation	www.newwf.org	212-249-1023
New York Community Trust	www.nycommunitytrust.org	212-686-0010
New York Foundation	www.nyf.org	212-594-8009
New York Women's Foundation	www.nywf.org	212-414-4342
Norman Foundation	www.normanfdn.org	212-230-9830
North Star Fund (FEX)	www.northstarfund.org	212-620-9110

Open Society Institute	www.soros.org	212-548 0153
Peace Development Fund	www.peacefund.org	212-256-8306
Public Welfare Foundation	www.publicwelfare.org	800-275-7934
RESIST, Inc.	www.resistinc.org	617-623-5110
Rockefeller Brothers Fund	www.rbf.org	212-812-4200
San Francisco Foundation	www.sff.org	415-733-8500
Scherman Foundation	www.scherman.org	212-832-3086
Southern Partners Fund	www.spfund.org	404-873-0014
Surdna Foundation	www.surdna.org	212-557-0010
Third Wave Foundation	www.thirdwavefoundation.org	212-675-0700
Tides Foundation	www.tidesfoundation.org	415-561-6400
Unitarian Universalist Funding Program	www.uucsr.org	516-627-6576
Vanguard Public Foundation	www.vanguardsf.org	415-487-2111
W. K. Kellogg Foundation	www.wkkf.org	616-968-1611
Walter S. Johnson Foundation	www.wsjf.org	650-326-0485
William Penn Foundation	www.wpennfdn.org	215-988-1830

These are organizations that are not youth groups but can provide support.

ARIZONA

EARTH FIRST! JOURNAL
Address: PO Box 3023, Tuscon, AZ 85702
Phone: 520-620-6900
Website: www.earthfirstjournal.org
Profile: Earth First!, a "no compromise" environmental movement which publishes a quarterly journal, believes in using everything in the toolbox, ranging from grassroots organizing and involvement in the legal process to civil disobedience and monkeywrenching.

ARKANSAS

ACORN
Contact: Zach Polett
Address: 2101 South Main St, Little Rock, AR 72206
Phone: 501-376-7151
Email: poldirect@acorn.org
Website: www.acorn.org
Profile: ACORN, the nation's largest community organization of low and moderate-income families (120,000 member families organized into 600 neighborhood chapters in 45 cities), has been advocating for fair wages, affordable housing and quality public education through direct action and lobbying for over 30 years.

CALIFORNIA

AGENDA
Contact: Munia Bhaumik
Address: 2826 South Vermont, Suite 940, Los Angeles, CA 90007
Phone: 323-730-4950
Email: munib@earthlink.net
Profile: Currently working in a joint organizing project with Service Employees International Union, Locals 660 and 347, to organize people on public assistance.

APPLIED RESEARCH CENTER
Contact: Gary Delgado
Address: 3781 Broadway, Oakland, CA 94611
Phone: 510-653-3415
Email: arc@arc.org
Website: www.arc.org
Profile: The Applied Research Center is a public policy, educational, and research institute whose work emphasizes issues of race and social change.

BRIDGES
Contact: Viviana Rennella
Address: 1203 Preservation Park #301, Oakland, CA 94612
Phone: 510-271-8286
Email: info@grassrootsbridges.org
Website: www.grassrootsbridges.org
Profile: Connects young social justice activists in the Bay to grassroots communities in the Global South (Africa, Asia and Latin America) to make tangible connections between global and local issues.

CENTER FOR THIRD WORLD ORGANIZING
Contact: Dan HoSang
Address: 1218 East 21st St, Oakland, CA 94606
Phone: 510-533-7583
Email: ctwo@ctwo.org
Website: www.ctwo.org
Profile: CTWO has been at the forefront of developing organizers and organizations of color for 20 years, with its essential publication, Colorlines, a commitment to creating an active progressive network, and its excellent Minority Activist Apprenticeship Program (MAAP).

COMMUNITY SELF-DETERMINATION INSTITUTE
Contact: Sean Emerson
Address: 9101 South Hooper, Los Angeles, CA 90002
Phone: 323-586-8791
Email: aqeelas@dot.com
Profile: CSDI runs a three-pronged program: drop-out prevention and retrieval, gang intervention, and life skills and literacy education. Recognized for its gang truce negotiations, CSDI also supports individuals in a goal-oriented life management plan.

CORPWATCH
Contact: Nadia Khastagir
Address: PO Box 29344, San Francisco, CA 94129
Phone: 415-561-6568
Email: corpwatch@corpwatch.org
Website: www.corpwatch.org
Profile: A leader in the corporate accountability movement and excellent resource for activists, CorpWatch's online magazine carries much useful information on democratic reform of corporations. Bridging gap between domestic and international groups working on the same issues.

DATA CENTER
Contact: Ryan Pintado-Vertner
Address: 1904 Franklin St, Suite 900, Oakland, CA 94612
Phone: 510-835-4692
Email: terry@datacenter.org
Website: www.datacenter.org
Profile: DataCenter provides strategic information to social justice organizations, specializing in research that supports informed action.

INSTITUTE FOR MULTIRACIAL JUSTICE/YOUTH OF COLOR FILM FESTIVAL

Contact: Elizabeth Martinez
Address: 522 Valencia St, San Francisco, CA, 94110
Phone: 415-701-9502
Email: i4mrj@aol.com
Website: www.multiracialjustice.org
Profile: IMRJ holds the Shades of Power film festival and publishes an influential multi-racial justice movement newsletter. Primarily a resource center.

LONG HAUL INFOSHOP

Contact: Collective
Address: 3124 Shattuck Ave, Berkeley, CA 94705
Phone: 510-540-0751
Email: slingshot@tao.ca
Website: www.tao.ca/~slingshot
Profile: One of the longest standing and best networked infoshops in the US. Publishes Slingshot magazine and the fat little organizer (calendar) used by activists everywhere.

MEDIA ALLIANCE

Contact: Jeff Perlstein
Address: 814 Mission St #205, San Francisco, CA 94103
Phone: 415-546-6491
Email: info@media-alliance.org
Website: www.media-alliance.org
Profile: Supports media activism including a new national campaign with the Hip Hop community to challenge Clear Channel's stranglehold on radio.

MEDICAL STUDENTS FOR CHOICE

Contact: Lois Bachus
Address: PO Box 70190, Oakland, CA 94612
Phone: 510-238-5210
Email: msfc@ms4c.org
Website: www.ms4c.org
Profile: As medical students, members of MSFC work to make reproductive health care, including abortion, a part of standard medical education and residency training and are dedicated to ensuring that women receive the full range of reproductive health care choices.

MOVEMENT STRATEGY CENTER

Contact: Taj James
Address: 1611 Telegraph Ave, Oakland, CA 94612
Phone: 510-444-0640
Email: taj@movementstrategy.org
Website: www.movementstrategy.org
Profile: MSC is a movement building intermediary that engages youth and adults across issues and regions through a collective visioning and mapping process that encourages collaboration and joint strategizing in order to develop stronger, more effective movements for democracy and social change.

ROCK THE VOTE

Contact: Mario Velasquez
Address: 10635 Santa Monica Blvd, Mail Box 22, Los Angeles, CA 90025
Phone: 310-234-0665
Email: mail@rockthevote.org
Website: www.rockthevote.org
Profile: Besides getting presidential candidates to say what style underwear they prefer, Rock the Vote raises political awareness of young people and organizes massive voter registration campaigns.

CONNECTICUT

ADAM KREIGER ADVENTURE PROGAM (AKAP)

Contact: Joey Gonzalez
Address: 986 Forrest Rd, New Haven, CT 06515
Phone: 760-634-3604
Email: sofrito4life@aol.com
Profile: AKAP provides leadership development and outdoor skills training for grassroots organizations throughout the Connecticut region seeking to strengthen their critical thinking, problem solving, and conflict resolution skills.

COLORADO

AMERICAN INDIAN MOVEMENT/FOURTH WORLD CENTER

Contact: Glenn Morris
Address: 201 West 5th Ave, Denver, CO 80204
Phone: 303-556-6243
Website: www.aimovement.org
Profile: Goal is to help Native Americans regain their human rights and achieve restitutions and restorations; a national network of autonomous chapters that support each other in local mobilizations.

COLORADO PROGRESSIVE COALITION

Contact: Soyun Park
Address: 1420 Ogden St, 1st Fl, Denver, CO 80218
Phone: 303-866-0908
Email: coprogressive@aol.com
Website: www.progressivecoalition.org
Profile: Colorado Progressive Coalition is one of Colorado's leading voices for civil rights, racial justice, public school accountability, and high quality, affordable health care for all.

Police brutality protest outside Rampart station in LA, August 2000
© ramona photo

FREE SPEECH TV

Contact: Nancy Harvey
Address: PO Box 6060, Boulder, CO 80306
Phone: 303-442-8445
Email: sten@atombom.com
Website: www.fstv.org
Profile: The only nationwide progressive TV channel broadcast to 11 million homes via sattelite dish and cable access stations. Lots of young staff, videographers, "stringers," and coverage of youth movements.

ROCKY MOUNTAIN CENTER FOR PEACE AND JUSTICE

Contact: Christie Donner
Address: PO Box 1156, Boulder, CO 80306
Phone: 303-444-6981
Website: www.rmpjc.org
Profile: Created in the spirit of unconditional nonviolence, the Rocky Mountain Peace and Justice Center is dedicated to research, education, and action in nonviolence as a way of life and as a means for personal and social change.

DELAWARE

GREEN DELAWARE

Contact: Alan Muller
Address: PO Box 69, Port Penn, DE 19731
Phone: 302-834-3466
Email: greendel@dca.net
Website: www.greendel.org
Profile: Green Delaware is a grassroots organization that advocates policies consistent with good health, preservation of biodiversity, and long term sustainability.

PUBLIC ALLIES DELAWARE

Contact: Patrick Carroll
Address: 100 West 10th St #812, Wilmington, DE 19801
Phone: 302-573-4438
Email: Delaware@publicallies.org
Profile: This branch of an excellent Americorps-funded leadership program places young people in local non-profits. They're connected to a lot of what's going on in Wilmington.

DISTRICT OF COLUMBIA

50 YEARS IS ENOUGH NETWORK

Contact: Njoki Njehu
Address: 3628 12th St, NE, Washington, DC 20017
Phone: 202-463-2265
Email: 50years@50years.org
Website: www.50years.org
Profile: Coalition of over 200 grassroots, women's, solidarity, faith-based, policy, social justice, youth, labor, and development organizations dedicated to the profound transformation of the World Bank and the International Monetary Fund.

CENTER FOR COMMUNITY CHANGE (CCC)

Contact: Pedro Aviles
Address: 1000 Wisconsin Ave, NW, Washington, DC 20007
Phone: 220-342-0567
Website: www.communitychange.org
Profile: CCC believes low income people are best equipped to address poverty; its strategy is to strengthen community based organization in low income areas by providing on-site technical assistance, connecting groups to additional resources, and encouraging coalition work with other organizations.

CENTER FOR YOUTH AS RESOURCES

Contact: Kelly Nagy
Address: 1000 Connecticut Ave NW, Suite 1204, Washington, DC 20036
Phone: 202-261-4131
Email: yar@ncpc.org
Website: www.cyar.org
Profile: Serves as an umbrella organization for local Youth as Resources programs whose principles are: youth-adult partnership in governance, youth as grantmakers, and youth-led service.

ECONOMIC POLICY INSTITUTE

Address: 1660 L St, NW, Suite 1200, Washington, DC 20036
Phone: 202-775-8810
Email: epi@epinet.org
Website: www.epinet.org
Profile: Very academic, but highly useful resources providing both economic critiques and proposed solutions; focus areas include sustainable economics, education, social security, globalization, living standards, wages, government expenditures and much more.

FAMILIES AGAINST MANDATORY MINIMUMS

Contact: Julia Stewart
Address: 1612 K St, NW, Suite 700, Washington, DC 20006
Phone: 202-822-6700
Email: famm@famm.org
Website: www.famm.org
Profile: A lobbying and public education organization working to change mandatory sentencing laws and promote alternatives.

LEADERSHIP CONFERENCE ON CIVIL RIGHTS

Contact: Donna Wilson
Address: 1629 K St, NW, Suite 1000, Washington, DC 20006
Phone: 202-466-3311
Email: lccr@civilrights.org
Website: www.civilrights.org/programs

Profile: For half a century, the Leadership Conference on Civil Rights has led the fight for equal opportunity and social justice.

NATIONAL COALITION BUILDING INSTITUTE
Address: 1120 Connecticut Ave, NW, Washington, DC 20036
Phone: 202-785-9400
Email: ncbiinc@aol.com
Website: www.ncbi.org
Profile: NCBI is a leadership training organization that has been working to eliminate prejudice and intergroup conflict in communities throughout the world; have trained leadership teams in a variety of settings, including schools, corporations, foundations, correctional facilities, and labor unions.

NATIONAL COUNCIL OF LA RAZA
Contact: Marco Davis
Address: 1111 19th St, NW, Washington, DC 20036
Phone: 202-785-1670
Website: www.nclr.org
Profile: NCLR is the largest constituency-based national Latino organization, serving all Latino nationality groups in all regions of the country to reduce poverty and discrimination and to increase opportunities.

PROGRESSIVE TECHNOLOGY PROJECT
Contact: Julio Dantas
Address: 1436 U St, NW, Suite 201, Washington, DC 20009
Phone: 202-387-9960
Website: www.progressivetech.org
Profile: Provides tech support to grassroots community organizations nationwide.

SENTENCING PROJECT
Address: 514 10th St, NW, Suite 1000, Washington, DC 20004
Phone: 202-628-0871
Email: staff@sentencingproject.org
Website: www.sentencingproject.org
Profile: The Sentencing Project promotes decreased reliance on incarceration and increased use of more effective and humane alternatives. It is a good source of criminal justice policy analysis, data and program information.

YOUTH TODAY
Contact: Bill Treanor
Address: 1200 17th St, NW, 4th Fl, Washington, DC 20036
Phone: 202-785-0764
Email: info@youthtoday.org
Website: www.youthtoday.org
Profile: Youth Today is the only independent, national newspaper geared towards people who work with youth.

FLORIDA

COALITION OF IMMOKALEE WORKERS
Contact: Lucas Benitez
Address: PO Box 603, Immokalee, FL 34142
Phone: 850-434-3456
Email: CoaImmwkr@aol.com
Website: www.ciw-online.org
Profile: Main goal is to bring growers to the table to change the imbalance of power between the agricultural workers and growers. Also going after consumers in struggle targeting Taco Bell.

MIAMI WORKERS CENTER
Contact: Gihan Perrera
Address: 6127 NW 7th Ave, Miami, FL 33127
Phone: 305-759-8717
Email: info@theworkerscenter.org
Website: www.theworkerscenter.org
Profile: MWC provides needed support to workers, including assistance on immigration matters and organizing workers to fight for better working and living conditions.

ONWARD
Contact: Dan Berger
Address: PO Box 2671, Gainsville, FL 32602
Email: info@onwardnewspaper.org
Website: www.onwardnewspaper.org
Profile: This quarterly anarchist newspaper is a forum for anarchist news and radical history, theory, and opinion; not only critiques existing social and political relationships, but also presents a viable and logical future based on voluntary cooperation, direct and participatory democracy, mutual aid, solidarity and freedom.

GEORGIA

AFRICAN–AMERICAN ENVIRONMENTAL JUSTICE ACTION NETWORK
Contact: Tanisa Foxworth
Address: PO Box 10518, Atlanta, GA 30310
Phone: 404-755-2855
Email: aaejan@yahoo.com
Profile: An inter-generational organization, AAEJAN provides resources and technical assistance to their emerging network in the Southeast of 86 member organizations across 11 states.

ENVIRONMENTAL JUSTICE RESOURCE CENTER

Contact: Robert Bullard

Address: 223 James P. Brawley Drive, Atlanta, GA 30314

Phone: 404-880-6911

Email: ejrc@cau.edu

Website: www.ejrc.cau.edu

Profile: EJRC is a research, policy, and information clearinghouse on issues related to environmental justice, race and the environment, civil rights, facility siting, land use planning, brownfields, transportation equity, suburban sprawl and Smart Growth.

GARAL

Contact: Ebony Barley

Address: PO Box 5589, Atlanta, GA 31107

Phone: 404-875-6338

Email: info@garal.org

Website: www.garal.org

Profile: GARAL protects women's right to make personal decisions regarding the full range of reproductive choices through lobbying, education and political action.

PROJECT SOUTH

Contact: Jerome Scott

Address: 9 Gammon Ave SW, Atlanta, GA 30315

Phone: 404-622-0602

Email: jerome@projectsouth.org

Website: www.projectsouth.org

Profile: Project South is a community-based membership institute that develops and conducts political and economic research and workshops created by and for grassroots activists, scholars, organizers, and youth.

SOUTHERN ORGANIZING COMMITTEE FOR ECONOMIC AND SOCIAL JUSTICE

Contact: Connie Tucker

Address: PO Box 10518, Atlanta, GA 30310

Phone: 404-755-2855

Email: socejp@igc.apc.org

Website: www.igc.org/socejp

Profile: The Southern Organizing Committee for Economic & Social Justice is a multi-issue, multi-racial network of people working against racism, war, economic injustice, and environmental destruction.

IDAHO

IDAHO MEDIA PROJECT

Contact: Jeremy Maxand

Address: PO Box 2194, Boise, ID 83701

Phone: 208-385-0611

Email: info@idahomediaproject.org

Website: www.idahomediaproject.org

Profile: The principal objectives of IMP are to systematically monitor local and regional mass media, to analyze local media content, and to call attention to cases of inaccurate or biased reporting.

ILLINOIS

CHICAGO PUBLIC ART GROUP

Contact: John Pounds

Address: 1259 S Wabash Ave, Chicago, IL 60605

Phone: 312-427-2724

Email: cpag@mindspring.com

Website: www.cpag.net

Profile: One of the key public art groups nationwide, CPAG supports artists, community dialogue, public artworks, and is actively involved in the shaping of the international community arts movement by participating in project and artist exchanges.

GUILD COMPLEX

Contact: Ellen Placey Wadey

Address: 1212 North Ashland, Chicago, IL 60622

Phone: 773-227-6117

Website: www.guildcomplex.com

Profile: A cultural center and forum for literary cross-cultural expression, discussion, and education in combination with other arts to reach broad, multi-ethnic audiences with quality arts programming including spoken word, art shows, workshops and literary festivals.

NATIONAL TRAINING & INFORMATION CENTER

Contact: Joe Mariano

Address: 810 North Milwaukee Ave, Chicago, IL 60622

Phone: 312-243-3035

Website: www.ntic-us.org

Profile: Connected to National People's Action (www.npa-us.org), NTIC trains and supports a national network of neighborhood groups to fight on local and national issues.

KANSAS

LEONARD PELTIER DEFENSE COMMITTEE

Contact: Denis Moynihan

Address: PO Box 583, Lawrence, KS 66044

Phone: 785-842-5774

Email: lpdc@freepeltier.org

Website: www.freepeltier.org

Profile: LPDC is an international group campaigning for the immediate release of politcal prisoner Leonard Peltier,and serves as the center of communication between Leonard Peltier, his supporters, his family, the media, and key government officials.

KENTUCKY

KENTUCKIANS FOR THE COMMONWEALTH
Contact: Burt Lauderdale
Address: PO Box 1450, London, KY 40743
Phone: 606-878-2161
Email: stonehouse@kih.net
Website: www.kftc.org
Profile: Strong network of social, economic and environmental activists across Kentucky. Members form chapters in their counties and focus on local issues, ranging from coal-mining and forestry to rights of solid-waste workers and police brutality.

LOUISIANA

CONCERNED CITIZENS OF IBERVILLE PARISH
Contact: Albertha Hasten
Address: 32365 Doc Dean St, White Castle, LA 70788
Phone: 225-545-8917
Profile: CCIP is a grassroots organizing group working on environmental justice issues and how they affect poor people in Louisiana.

NEW ORLEANS COMMUNITY BIKE PROJECT (PLAN B)
Contact: Yoni Mazuz
Address: PO Box 72581, New Orleans, LA 70172
Phone: 504-947-0982
Email: nolabike@yahoo.com
Profile: A volunteer-run bicycle workshop, offering free access to manuals and tools, free help with repairs, and inexpensive used parts and bikes.

PEOPLE'S INSTITUTE FOR SURVIVAL AND BEYOND
Contact: Ron Chisom
Address: 7166 Crowder Blvd, Suite 100, New Orleans, LA 70127
Phone: 504-241-7472
Email: PISAB@thepeoplesinstitute.org
Profile: National anti-racism training network that is reportedly rigid but highly useful; committed to the idea that the kind of coalition building that social movements require can only happen if organizers go beyond learning mere tactics and begin to challenge their own assumptions, work patterns and internalized issues.

PEOPLE'S INTER-COMMUNAL RESISTANCE MOVEMENT (PICRM)
Contact: Shana Griffin
Address: PO Box 51325, New Orleans, LA 70151
Phone: 504-827-5620
Email: ambakeysha@yahoo.com

Profile: Builds alliances locally, nationally, and internationally for direct actions aimed at self-sufficient, autonomous communities. PICRM's Fred Hampton Youth Education Committee has residencies and members at local high schools as well.

MARYLAND

NAACP
Contact: Jamal Bryant
Address: 4805 Mt Hope Dr, Baltimore, MD 21215
Phone: 877-NAACP-98
Website: www.naacp.org
Profile: The NAACP works at the national, regional, and local level to secure civil rights through advocacy for supportive legislation and by the implementation of strategic initiatives.

MASSACHUSSETS

ARISE FOR SOCIAL JUSTICE
Contact: Michaelann Bewsee
Address: 94 Rifle St, Springfield, MA 01105
Phone: 413-734-4948
Email: michaelannb@hotmail.com
Profile: A low-income rights organization which is active in a number of social causes related to poverty.

CITY YEAR
Contact: Jeff Paquette
Address: 285 Columbus Ave, Boston, MA 02116
Phone: 617-927-2600
Website: www.cityyear.org
Profile: City Year seeks to demonstrate, improve and promote the concept of youth service as a means for building a stronger democracy.

POLITICAL RESEARCH ASSOCIATES
Address: 1310 Broadway, Suite 201, Somerville, MA 02144
Phone: 617-666-5300
Email: pra@igc.org
Website: www.publiceye.org
Profile: PRA is an independent, nonprofit research center that studies antidemocratic, authoritarian, and other oppressive movements, institutions, and trends; an invaluable source of accurate, reliable research and analysis for activists, journalists, educators and the public.

UNITED FOR A FAIR ECONOMY
Address: 37 Temple Place, 2nd Fl, Boston, MA 02111
Phone: 617-423-2148
Email: info@faireconomy.org
Website: www.ufenet.org
Profile: UFE puts a spotlight on the dangers of growing income,

wage and wealth inequality in the US and seeks to reduce the gap by providing popular education resources, working with grassroots organizations, conducting research, and supporting creative and legislative action.

MICHIGAN

LABOR NOTES
Contact: Marsha Niemeijer
Address: 7435 Michigan Ave, Detroit, MI 48210
Phone: 313-842-6262
Profile: Labor Notes aims ,"to put the movement back in labor movements," by publishing a magazine, putting on conferences, and advocating projects that support organizing for economic justice and worker rights.

SOUTHWEST MICHIGAN COALITION AGAINST RACISM & POLICE BRUTALITY
Contact: JoNina Abron
Address: PO Box 19962, Kalamazoo, MI 49019
Phone: 423-622-7614
Email: banco_midwest@hotmail.com
Profile: A project of BANCO (Black Autonomy Network of Community Organizers), this group campaigns against racism and for police accountability through education and advocacy.

MINNESOTA

HONOR THE EARTH
Contact: Winona LaDuke
Address: 2801 21st Ave South, Minneapolis, MN 55407
Phone: 800-327-8407
Email: contact@honorearth.org
Website: www.honorearth.com
Profile: Organizing against the US Department of Energy (DOE) and corporations that want to turn the Yucca Mountains in Nevada, a sacred site for the Western Shoshone Pauite tribes, into a radioactive parking lot for more than 70,000 metric tons of nuclear waste

NORTHLAND POSTER COLLECTIVE
Contact: Ricardo Morales
Address: 1613 E. Lake St, Minneapolis, MN 55407
Phone: 612-721-2273
Email: info@northlandposter.com
Website: www.northlandposter.com
Profile: Northland Poster Collective is dedicated to promoting a socially just world through the use of art. They create, find, distribute, and encourage art that will make a positive contribution.

ORGANIZING APPRENTICESHIP PROJECT
Contact: Beth Newkirk
Address: 1885 University Ave West, Suite 95, St Paul, MN 55104
Phone: 651-641-1830
Email: oaproject@queStnet
Profile: OAP is an intergenerational grassroots organizer training program whose participants work on range of social justice initiatives, in particular, immigration and education.

RESOURCE CENTER OF THE AMERICAS
Contact: Pam Costain
Address: 3019 Minnehaha Ave, Minneapolis, MN 55406
Phone: 612-276-0788
Email: info@americas.org
Website: www.americas.org
Profile: The Resource Center of the Americas is devoted to the notion that every person in this world is entitled to the same fundamental human rights and focuses on education and global justice in the Americas.

MISSISSIPPI

SOUTHERN ECHO
Contact: Leroy Johnson
Address: PO Box 2350, Jackson, MS 39255
Phone: 601-352-1500
Profile: Focused in Mississippi, supports multi-generational grassroots (especially rural) organizing throughout the deep South. Oustanding model of organizational development.

MISSOURI

COALITION AGAINST POLICE CRIMES AND REPRESSION
Contact: Jamala Rogers
Address: PO Box 9226, St Louis, MO 63117
Phone: 314-454-9005
Email: capcr_cob@hotmail.com
Profile: Fights to end police brutality, bringing awareness about the prison industrial complex and the criminalization of a generation to its community. Also developed a proposal for a Civilian Oversight advisory board to monitor police culture.

RECYCLED SOUNDS/FREE SPEECH COALITION/CULTURE UNDER FIRE
Contact: Ann Winter
Address: 3941 Main St, Kansas City, MO 64111
Phone: 816-531-4890
Email: rcyclsnd@sounds.net
Website: www.kcfreespeech.org
Profile: Growing out of the music censorship fights of the early

90s, Free Speech Coalition created "Culture Under Fire," an annual festival of underground culture and social issues.

Montana

Northern Plains Resource Council
Contact: Steve
Address: 2401 Montana Ave #200, Billings, MT 59101
Phone: 406-248-1154
Email: info@ncrpmt.org
Website: www.northernplains.org
Profile: The Northern Plains Resource Council is committed to land stewardship, the preservation of family farms, ranches, and small businesses, and providing the information and tools necessary to give citizens an effective voice in decisions that affect their lives.

Nebraska

Nebraska Farmers Union
Contact: John Hanson
Address: PO Box 22667, Lincoln, NE 68542
Phone: 402-476-8815
Email: nefu@nebraskafarmersunion.org
Website: www.nebraskaframersunion.org
Profile: Largely because of NEFU, Nebraska has the strongest anti-corporate farm laws in the country. They fight not only for farm subsidies and rural infrastructure, but for protection of soil and water resources, rural health care, farmer-owned cooperatives, labor rights, and healthy democratic government.

Nevada

Progressive Leadership Alliance of Nevada (PLAN)
Contact: Bob Fulkerson
Address: 1700 E Desert Inn Road, Suite 113, Las Vegas, NV 89109
Phone: 702-791-1965
Email: planvegas@aol.com
Website: www.planevada.org
Profile: PLAN is the key multi-issue progressive organization in the Casino state.

New Mexico

Interhemispheric Resource Center
Address: PO Box 2178, Silver City, NM 88062
Phone: 505-388-0208
Email: irc@irc-online.org
Website: www.irc-online.org

Profile: IRC seeks to educate policymakers and influence public debates on the U.S. role in global affairs, change public opinion, inform activists, and foster strategic dialog among progressives planet-wide on key issues like economic globalization, sustainable development, peace and security.

Soltari
Contact: Eli Lee
Address: 202 Central Ave, SE, Suite 100B, Albuquerque, NM 87102
Phone: 505-842-5539
Email: eli@soltari.com
Website: www.soltari.com
Profile: Founded by Eli Il Young Lee (former head of Youth Action), Soltari does strategy with local and national political campaigns, nonprofit organizations, and small businesses interested in creating justice.

Southwest Network for Environmental and Economic Justice
Contact: Richard Moore
Address: PO Box 7399, Albuquerque, NM 87194
Phone: 505-242-0416
Email: sneej@igc.org
Profile: Current work includes the Border Justice Campaign, their Youth Leadership Development campaign, EPA Accountability, Sovereignty, dumping on Native people/lands, and a technology project.

New York

Alianza Dominicana
Contact: Moises Perez
Address: 2410 Amsterdam Ave, New York, NY 10033
Phone: 212-740-1960
Email: mguerrero@alianzadom.org
Website: www.alianzadom.org
Profile: Alianza Dominicana is a community development organization that partners with youth, families, and public and private institutions to revitalize economically distressed neighborhoods, especially the largely Dominican Washington Heights area of Manhattan.

Center for Constitutional Rights (CCR)
Address: 666 Broadway 7th Fl, New York, NY 10012
Phone: 212-614-6464
Email: info@ccr-ny.org
Website: www.ccr-ny.org
Profile: CCR uses litigation to empower poor communities and communities of color, guarantee the rights of those with the fewest protections and least access to legal resources, train the next generation of constitutional and human rights attorneys, and strengthen the broader movement for constitutional and human rights.

National day of solidarity with Muslim and Arab communities, outside the INS in NYC, February 20, 2002
© ramona photo

Police brutality protest outside Rampart station in LA, August 2000
© ramona photo

COALITION FOR THE HUMAN RIGHTS OF IMMIGRANTS

Address: 339 Lafayette St, New York, NY 10012
Phone: 212-254-2591
Email: chri@itapnet.org
Website: www.itapnet.org/chri
Profile: Confronting anti-immigrant policies through grassroots education and action, the coalition focuses on the way in which immigration policies discourage undocumented immigrants from defending their labor rights, including the right to organize.

ENVIRONMENTAL DEFENSE ACTION NETWORK

Contact: Gina Blue
Address: 257 Park Ave South, New York, NY 10010
Phone: 212-505-2100
Email: bensmith@environmentaldefense.org
Website: http://actionnetwork.org
Profile: The Environmental Defense Action Network is funded by Environmental Defense, which links science, economics, and law to create innovative, equitable, and cost-effective solutions to the most urgent environmental problems.

GAY LESBIAN AND STRAIGHT EDUCATION NETWORK (GLSEN)

Address: 121 W 27th St, Suite 804, New York, NY 10010
Phone: 212-727-0135
Email: glsen@glsen.org
Website: www.glsen.org
Profile: GLSEN is the leading national organization fighting to end anti-gay bias in K-12 schools.

INTERNATIONAL ACTION CENTER

Contact: Ramsey Clark
Address: 39 West 14th St, New York, NY 10011
Phone: 212-633-6646
Email: iacenter@action-mail.org
Website: www.iacenter.org
Profile: Information, activism, and resistance to US militarism, war, and corporate greed. Linking these battles with the struggles against racism and oppression in the US.

JEWISH SOCIAL JUSTICE NETWORK

Contact: Cynthia Greenberg
Address: c/o Jewish Fund for Justice, 260 Fifth Ave, Suite 701, New York, NY 10011
Phone: 212-213-2113 x23
Email: jsjn@jfjustice.org
Profile: A consortium of Jewish organizations working to promote the involvement of Jews in social justice work through a variety of methods, including community organizing, advocacy, activism, training & education.

JFREJ– JEWS FOR RACIAL AND ECONOMIC JUSTICE

Contact: Sarah Eisenstein
Address: 140 West 22nd St #302, New York, NY 10011
Phone: 212-647-8966
Email: jfrej@igc.org
Website: www.jfrej.org
Profile: JFREJ provides an opportunity for all Jews-- young and old, secular and religious, lesbian, gay, and straight-- to explore issues of racial and economic justice and to shape a collective Jewish response.

LIVING WAGE CAMPAIGN ONLINE RESOURCE CENTER

Address: 88 3rd Ave, Brooklyn, NY 11217
Phone: 877-55ACORN
Website: www.livingwagecampaign.org
Profile: Starting point for anyone wanting to create a living wage campaign; this site, sponsored by ACORN, contains a history of living wage organizing, resource guides, statistics, talking points and links to other resources.

NEW YORK CITY ORGANIZING SUPPORT CENTER

Contact: Rachel Pfeffer
Address: 180 Varick St, 12th Fl, New York, NY 10014
Phone: 212-627-9960
Email: info@nycosc.org
Website: www.nycosc.org
Profile: Seeks to strengthen use of community organizing as a tool to build power for justice in New York City, offering a program of technical support, training, and other forums for grassroots community organizers and leaders to build their skills and strengthen their strategies and alliances.

ROOTS/WAR RESISTERS LEAGUE

Contact: Asif Ullah
Address: 339 Lafayette St, New York, NY 10012
Phone: 212-228-0450
Email: roots@warresisters.org
Website: www.rootsnet.org
Profile: Have been around for a long time as an ally of war resisters and peace activists. Publishes Non-Violent Activist magazine and a peace calendar.

SCALE/NATIONAL LABOR COMMITTEE

Contact: Mieke
Address: 275 7th Ave, 15th Fl, New York, NY 10001
Phone: 212-242-3002
Email: nlc@nlcnet.org
Website: www.nlcnet.org
Profile: The National Labor Committee's mission is to educate and actively engage the US public on human and labor rights abuses by corporations. They house a high school student project, Student Committee Against Labor Exploitation (SCALE).

TRAINING INSTITUTE FOR CAREERS IN ORGANIZING (TICO)
Contact: Norma Jackson
Address: 109 East 196th St, Bronx, NY 10468
Phone: 212-608-6365
Email: tico@igc.org
Profile: TICO is a unique program for NYC students and others who want to learn how to organize that holds a 12 week full-time training program open to college students.

UNITE (UNION OF NEEDLETRADES, INDUSTRIAL AND TEXTILE EMPLOYEES)
Contact: Chris Chafe
Address: 1710 Broadway, New York, NY 10019
Phone: 212-265-7000
Website: www.uniteunion.org
Profile: Formed by the merger of two of the nation's oldest unions, UNITE is one of the fiercest unions. Helped train and spawn the student sweatshop movement.

VIEQUES SUPPORT CAMPAIGN
Address: 402 W 125th St, New York, NY 10031
Phone: 212-677-0619
Email: viequessc@hotmail.com
Website: http://palfrente.tripod.com
Profile: The VSC is an anti-imperialist, anti-colonialist organization in the US looking to build support for the people's struggle on the island municipality of Vieques, Puerto Rico.

YA-YA NETWORK
Contact: Amy Wagner
Address: 250 West 57th Street, New York, NY 10107
Phone: 212-581-6922
Email: yayanetnyc@aol.com
Profile: A network of youth workers and organizations that aid each other's projects. Also circulates an email bulletin with updates on jobs, events, trainings and actions.

NORTH CAROLINA

DEMOCRACY SOUTH
Address: 105 West Main St, Carrboro, NC 27510
Phone: 919-967-9942
Email: info@democracysouth.org
Website: www.democracysouth.org
Profile: For those who see an important relationship between electoral and grassroots politics, DS is a valuable non-partisan, non-profit research, organizing and advocacy resource committed to campaign finance reform and to building progressive multi-issue coalitions to address issues of social, environmental, and economic justice.

FARM LABOR ORGANIZING COMMITTEE (FLOC)
Contact: Kevin Pentz
Address: 503 Solomon St, Faison, NC 28341
Phone: 910-296-1910
Email: mariaalapisco@hotmail.com
Website: MR82780@hotmail.com
Profile: For almost 30 years, FLOC, a farmworker union affiliated with the AFL-CIO, has fought for better wages, safer work and living conditions, against gender discrimination and exploitation of undocumented workers, and for recognition of non-English languages.

GRASSROOTS LEADERSHIP
Contact: Si Kahn
Address: PO Box 36006, Charlotte, NC 28236
Phone: 704-332-3090
Email: info@grassroots.org
Website: www.grassrootsleadership.org
Profile: Grassroots Leadership is a multiracial team of organizers who help Southern community and labor organizers think critically, work strategically, and take direct action to end oppression, gain power, and achieve justice and equality.

INSTITUTE FOR SOUTHERN STUDIES
Address: PO Box 531, Durham, NC 27702
Phone: 919-419-8311
Email: info@i4south.org
Website: www.southernstudies.org
Profile: Throughout its 32 year history, ISS has maintained a strong commitment to developing research and publication projects that directly support grassroots organizing; its journal Southern Exposure provides excellent regional statistics and analysis on a wide range of issues.

OREGON

WESTERN PRISON PROJECT
Contact: Brigette Sarabi
Address: PO Box 40085, Portland, OR 97240
Phone: 503-335-8449
Email: info@westernprisonproject.org
Website: www.westernprisonproject.org
Profile: Western Prison Project builds the prison activist movement in seven western states by bringing prisoners, prisoners' families, and grassroots activists together.

WESTERN STATES CENTER
Contact: Tarso Ramos
Address: 310 SW 4th Ave #1140, Portland, OR 97204
Phone: 503-228-8866
Email: info@wscpdx.org
Website: www.westernstatescenter.org
Profile: The key progressive multi-issue training, coalition

building, and political power building network organization of the eight Northwest States: Oregon, Washington, Utah, Idaho, Nevada, Montana, Wyoming, and Alaska.

PENNSYLVANIA

CAMPUS ACTIVISM (CAMPUSACTIVISM.ORG)

Contact: Aaron Kreider
Address: Philadelphia, PA
Email: akreider@nd.edu
Website: www.campusactivism.org
Profile: Campusactivism.org is designed to facilitate networking between student activists in the US and Canada through the sharing of contacts, ideas and resources.

KENSINGTON WELFARE RIGHTS UNION

Contact: Cheri Honkala
Address: PO Box 50678, Philadelphia, PA 19132
Phone: 215-203-1945
Email: kwru@kwru.org
Website: www.kwru.org
Profile: The Kensington Welfare Rights Union (KWRU) is a multi-racial organization for, of, and by poor and homeless people.

TALLER PUERTORRIQUENO

Contact: Dora Viacava
Address: 2721 N. 5th St, Philadelphia, PA 19133
Phone: 215-426-3311
Email: info@tellerpr.org
Website: www.tallerpr.org
Profile: Taller Puertorriqueno is a Puerto Rican cultural arts center in the heart of North Philly, one of the nation's most economically depressed neighborhoods. It provides an after-school creative arts program for youth and houses an art gallery and bookstore of progressive books·in English and Spanish.

SOUTH CAROLINA

SOUTH CAROLINA PROGRESSIVE NETWORK (SCPN)

Contact: Brett Bursey
Address: PO Box 8325, Columbia, SC 29202
Phone: 803-808-3384
Email: network@scpronet.com
Website: www.scpronet.com
Profile: SCPN is a strong network whose members have mobilized in support of the Charleston 5 and helped organize 70,000 people to rally against the state flag. Big campaigns on clean elections, racial profiling, gender equity, and DHEC (enviromental) reform.

SOUTH DAKOTA

DAKOTA RURAL ACTION

Contact: John Bixler
Address: PO Box 549, Brookings, SD 57006
Phone: 605-697-5204
Email: action@dakotarural.org
Website: www.dakotarural.org
Profile: Through community organizing efforts works to achieve and create a sustainable society which will guarantee freedom of choice for future generations.

TENNESSEE

ALTON PARK–PINEY WOODS NEIGHBORHOOD IMPROVEMENT CORP.

Contact: Debra Williams
Address: PO Box 2485, Chatanooga, TN 37409
Phone: 423-266-2751
Email: debapp@vol.com
Profile: Grassroots African-American environmental justice group works with residents to take ownership of their community and hosts an intergenerational summer conference, "Making the Link," where they run environmental justice workshops for 200 youth.

CITIZENS FOR JUSTICE, EQUALITY AND FAIRNESS (CJEF)

Contact: Calvin Ballinger
Address: PO Box 536, Dandridge, TN 37725
Phone: 865-397-4693
Email: losborne@cn.edu
Profile: This historically Black organization's works lies in opposing oppression, especially the effects of racism in the public school system and other county functions.

HIGHLANDER CENTER

Contact: Ron Davis
Address: 1959 Highlander Way, New Market, TN 37820
Phone: 865-933-3443
Website: www.highlandercenter.org
Profile: Over its 70 year history, Highlander has housed many historic meetings and retreats. Today, it remains relevant by providing conference space and workshops for organizations that are: 1) composed of and led by the people most affected by oppressive structures, 2) democratically organized, and 3) addressing fundamental issues of power and inequality.

TEXAS

ESPERANZA PEACE AND JUSTICE CENTER

Contact: Graciela Sánchez
Address: 922 San Pedro San Antonio, TX 78212
Phone: 210-228-0201
Email: esperanza@esperanzacenter.org
Website: www.esperanzacenter.org
Profile: The Esperanza Center advocates for women, people of color, lesbians and gay men, youth, the working class and poor. EC promotes building bridges and honest and critical dialogue through its diverse programming that includes film festivals, art exhibitions, writer's forums, a youth media program, leadership workshops, technical assistance, and marches and rallies.

NATIONAL HISPANIC INSTITUTE

Contact: Dominic Gonzales
Address: PO Box 220, Maxwell, TX 78656
Phone: 512-357-6137
Email: domenic@nhimail.com
Website: www.nhi-net.org
Profile: NHI's main focus is to teach high school students organizational and leadership skills. Recently put together a successful Ozomatli concert and hopes to continue use of popular mediums to educate youth on organizing.

UTAH

SHUNDAHAI NETWORK

Contact: Pete Litster
Address: PO Box 1115, Salt Lake City, UT 84110
Phone: 801-359-2614
Email: shundahai@shundahai.org
Website: www.shundahai.org
Profile: Founded to resist nuclear waste violations on Western Shoshone tribal land, the network lobbies, advocates, and organizes direct action around issues of nuclear pollution and testing.

UTAH INDEPENDENT MEDIA CENTER

Contact: Johnny Jemming
Address: PO Box 2891, Salt Lake City, UT 84110
Phone: 801-328-0831
Email: imc-utah-features@lists.indymedia.org
Website: www.utah.indymedia.org
Profile: The most important clearinghouse of alternative information in Utah where anyone can post an article on the site and the editorial staff selects the "front-page" news.

UTAH PROGRESSIVE NETWORK (UPNET)

Contact: Lorna Vogt
Address: PO Box 521391, Salt Lake City, UT 84152
Phone: 801-466-0955
Email: info@upnet.org
Website: www.upnet.org
Profile: Offers political education, leadership development training, and technical training to the members of the network's organizations. Recent work has focused on anti-immigrant issues.

VERMONT

INSTITUTE FOR SOCIAL ECOLOGY

Contact: Claudia Bejiakas
Address: 1118 Maple Hill Road, Plainfield, VT 05667
Phone: 802-454-8493
Email: info@social-ecology.org
Website: www.social-ecology.org
Profile: ISE is committed to the social and ecological transformation of society, offering intensive summer programs, a year-round BA degree program, workshops on issues such as biotechnology, fall and winter lecture series, internship opportunities, and a speakers bureau.

WEST VIRGINIA

OHIO VALLEY ENVIRONMENTAL COALITION

Contact: Dave Cooper
Address: PO Box 6753, Huntington, WV 25773
Phone: 304-522-0246
Email: ohvec@ezwv.com
Website: www.ohvec.org
Profile: Oppose mountain-top removal coal mining and are trying to raise community and media awareness about environmental justice issues in Appalachia. Working on clean-money campaign reform to get big political donations out of election campaigns.

WEST VIRGINIA ENVIRONMENTAL COUNCIL

Contact: Denise Poole
Address: 1324 Virginia St East, Charleston, WV 25301
Phone: 304-346-5905
Email: deniseap@earthlink.net
Website: www.wvecouncil.org
Profile: WVEC's mission is to facilitate communication and cooperation among citizens in promoting environmental protection, to assist in organizing grassroots groups, and to correspond with all appropriate local, state, and federal agencies involved in the management of West Virginia's environment.

WISCONSIN

MIDWEST ENVIRONMENTAL ADVOCATES

Contact: Melissa Scanlan
Address: 22 East Mifflin St, Madison, WI 53703
Phone: 608-251-5047
Email: scanlan@chorus.net
Website: www.midwest-e-advocates.org
Profile: Midwest Environmental Advocates provides legal and technical assistance to Native Americans and environmental groups working for environmental justice in the Western Great Lakes. Hopes to inspire a multi-cultural coalition of Native and non-Native people working to solve environmental problems and reduce pollution, poverty and racism.

WELFARE WARRIORS

Contact: Pat Gollins
Address: 2711 West Michigan Ave, Milwaukee, WI 53208
Phone: 414-342-6662
Website: www.execpc.com
Profile: The Welfare Warriors are low-income mothers and children working to make their voices heard in all policies affecting families in poverty through activism, advocacy, and their newspaper, The Mother Warriors Voice.

WYOMING

EQUALITY STATE POLICY CENTER

Contact: Tom Phroop
Address: 304 Main St #8, Lander, WY 82520
Phone: 307-332-0156
Email: tpespc@wyoming.com
Website: www.equalitystate.org
Profile: On the cutting edge of progressive work in Wyoming, ESPC builds coalitions and provides organizational support. Helping to start a women's, Latino/Latina, young people's and Native American policy organization in addition to a new youth organization, Students for Progressive Action.

UNITED GAYS AND LESBIANS OF WYOMING

Contact: John Little
Address: PO Box 6837, Cheyenne, WY 82003
Phone: 307-778-7645
Email: info@uglw.org
Website: www.uglw.org
Profile: UGLW seeks to enhance the lives of gay, lesbian, bisexual, and transgender people through education, advocating the protection and promotion of civil rights, and the establishment of a statewide network.

Racial Composition of Future 500

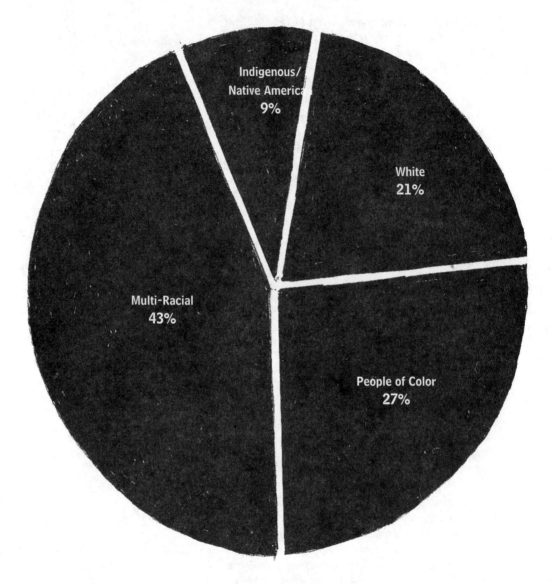

Indigenous/
Native America
9%

White
21%

Multi-Racial
43%

People of Color
27%

- Multi-Racial refers to groups that are comprised of White, People of Color and/or Indigenous/Native American organizers or constituents.
- Indigenous/Native American groups are distinguished from People of Color groups as a means of encompassing some of the additional geographic and national characteristics of these organizations.
- People of Color is being used to refer to African American/African, Latino/a, Asian/Pacific Islander and/or Arab/Arab American organizers or constituents.
- White refers to European American organizers or constituents.

Organization Needs of Future 500

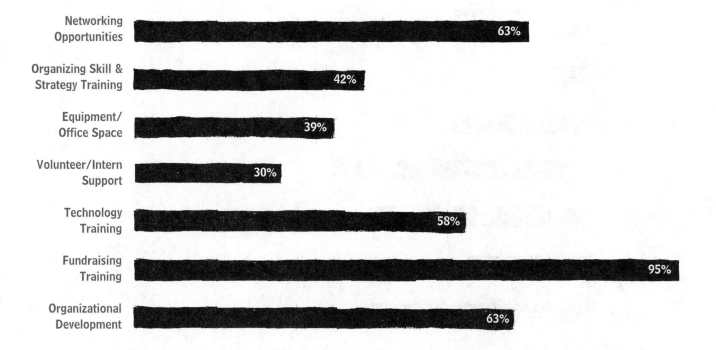

- **Organizational Development** includes developing personnel policies, keeping financial records, creating and working with a board of directors or advisors, securing tax-exempt status and/or mastering strategic planning.
- **Fundraising Training** includes proposal writing, cultivating foundation and individual donor relationships and/or plannning and executing fundraising events.
- **Technology Training** includes securing computer access, creating internal computer networks, establishing a web presence and/or utilizing databases for organizing purposes.
- **Volunteer/Intern Support** includes identifying and recruiting volunteer/intern support for daily opearations, securing pro bono professional services and/or learning how to effectively utilize existing volunteers/interns.
- **Equipment/Office Space** includes meeting spaces, copiers/faxes, phone systems, vehicles and other tangible tools needed to successfully complete a group's work.
- **Organizing Skill & Strategy Training** includes learning how to effectively design a lobbying campaign, conduct civil disobedience or other direct actions, design an effective media campaign and or recruit and train members.
- **Networking Opportunities** include spaces for local, regional and international groups to share experiences and resources, exchange strategies and common challenges, and/or develop unified campaigns.

* Data is based upon 326 respondents; groups were permitted to select as many areas of need as they felt necessary.

Budget Size of Future 500

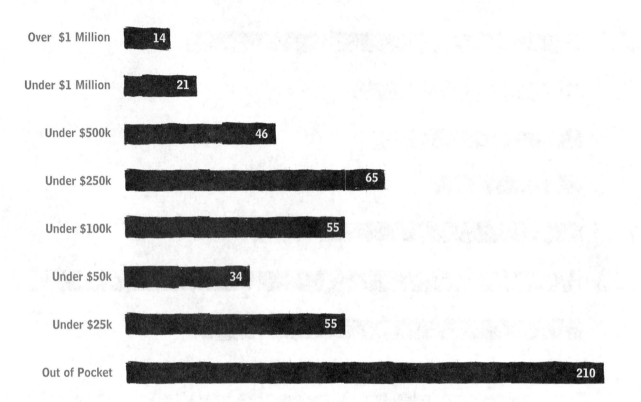

Over $1 Million	14
Under $1 Million	21
Under $500k	46
Under $250k	65
Under $100k	55
Under $50k	34
Under $25k	55
Out of Pocket	210

* This graph illustrates the annual budgets of 500 youth organizations, the majority of which are profiled in the Future 500. "Out of Pocket" refers to groups that are primarily volunteer efforts, with members providing the majority of operating resources. As this chart indicates, 354 of the groups surveyed (71%) have annual budgets of less than $100,000. Bottom bar is not to scale because of overwhelming majority of groups whose budget is out of pocket.

15 Leading Issue Areas of Future 500

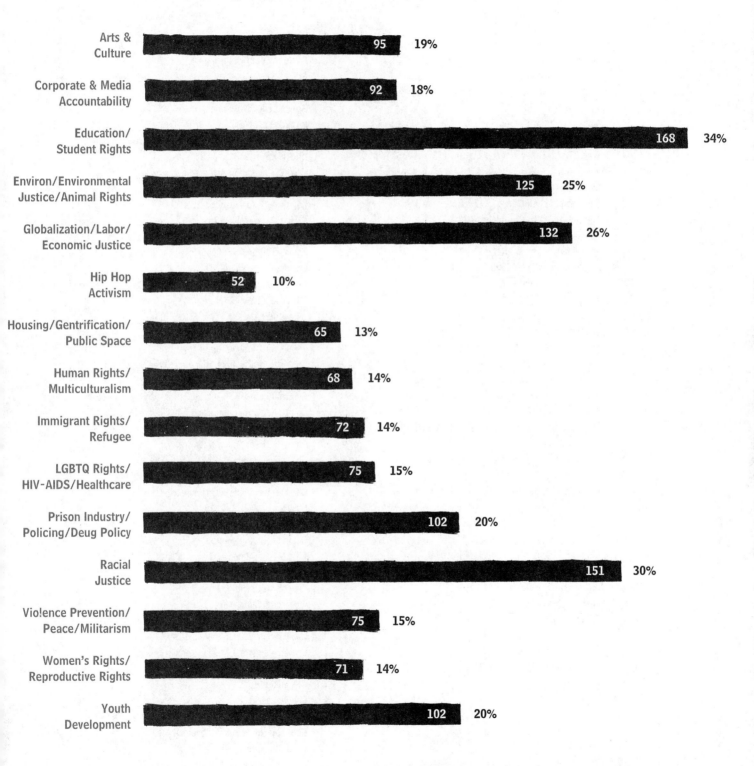

Issue Area	Count	Percent
Arts & Culture	95	19%
Corporate & Media Accountability	92	18%
Education/ Student Rights	168	34%
Environ/Environmental Justice/Animal Rights	125	25%
Globalization/Labor/ Economic Justice	132	26%
Hip Hop Activism	52	10%
Housing/Gentrification/ Public Space	65	13%
Human Rights/ Multiculturalism	68	14%
Immigrant Rights/ Refugee	72	14%
LGBTQ Rights/ HIV-AIDS/Healthcare	75	15%
Prison Industry/ Policing/Deug Policy	102	20%
Racial Justice	151	30%
Violence Prevention/ Peace/Militarism	75	15%
Women's Rights/ Reproductive Rights	71	14%
Youth Development	102	20%

* Data is based upon 500 respondents; groups were permitted to select as many issue areas as they felt necessary (though in their profiles, groups were limited to five issue areas). Related issues were collapsed together but filtered out for duplicate respondents. The relatively even distribution across issue areas indicates both the diversity of the contemporary youth organizing landscape and how common it is for individual groups to be engaged in multiple issue organizing.

Arts/Culture

Animal Cruelty

Campaign Finance

Corporate Accountability

Drug Policy

Education

Environment

Environmental Justice

LGBTTSQ/Queer

Police Accountability

Prisons/Criminal Justice

Public Space

Racial Justice

Reproductive Rights

Student Rights/Education Reform

Youth Development

Credits

Compiled by: Jee Kim, Mathilda de Dios, Pablo Caraballo, Manuela Arciniegas, Ibrahim Abdul-Matin, Kofi Taha
Project Manager: Jee Kim
Design: Tyler Askew (www.tyleraskew.com)
Photo Editors: Jee Kim, Emily Kramer
Assistant Photo Editors: Ricardo Cortez (www.magicpropagandamill.com), Rhea Vedro (rheavedro@yahoo.com)
Website Design: Ian Spalter (www.rootzero.com)
Website Programming: David Jacobs

Writers

Amy Sonnie, Chhaya Choum, Chisun Lee, Lester Garcia, Jamel Brinkley, rashid kwame shabazz, walidah imarisha, Malachi Larrabee-Garza, Supriya Pillai, Brooke Lehman, Nell Geiser, Jackie Vélez, Natalie Avery, Mangala Manju Rajendran, Gina Arias

Photo/Illustration Credits

ramona photo (ramona_ramona@yahoo.com), Mattie Weiss (mattiemartha@hotmail.com), Jee Mee Kim (kimjeemee@mail.com), Robyn Twomey (robyntwomey.com), Steve Meslemka, Rhea Vedro, Christine Wong (info@christinewong.org), Hans Bennet (PO Box 30770, Phila, PA 19104), Bryan Iler (bryan.iler@verizon.net), Steve Marcus (smarcus.com), Laszlo Toth, Beehive Collective (beehivecollective.org), Nick Cooper (nickcooper.com), Pete Miser (pete@petemiser.com), Too Fly (TOOFLYDESIGN@aol.com), Josue Rojas, Margarita Garcia, Amy Woloszyn (amymade.com), Geoff Oliver Bugbee (geoffbugbee.com)

Acknowledgements

We have so much appreciation for the folks who tackled the tedium and logged crazy long hours to make this directory a tangible reality. There is not enough gratitude to honor the dedication and vision of: Ibrahim Abdul-Matin, Manuela Arciniegas, Tyler Askew, Terry Bailey, Max Benitez, Jamel Brinkley, Harriet (Happy) Burbeck, J-Love Calderon, Mahealani Campbell, Pablo Caraballo, Jeff Chang, Ricardo Cortez, Eric Denby, Mathilda de Dios, Gita Drury, Desiree Evans, Katie Gunther, Mia Herndon, Danny Hoch, Jeff Hull, David Jacobs, Jee Kim, Emily Kramer, Nupur Modi, Bernadette Moreno, Emily Nepon, Christina Sandoval, Jamie Schweser, Shawnta Smith, Amy Sonnie, Ian Spalter, Adam Stenftenagel, Kofi Taha, Carver Tate, Meghan Tauck, Rhea Vedro, Mattie Weiss, Billy Wimsatt, Amy Woloszyn, and Asia Wong.

Matching this human effort with the resources necessary to sustain a two-year project was a challenge. AEF is indebted to the faith and support of the Hull Family Foundation and the community building vision of Ellen Furnari and Suresh Subramanian at the Waitt Family Foundation. Additional support from the following made this directory possible:

Blessing Way Foundation
Dobkin Family Foundation
Joshua Mailman Charitable Trust
New World Foundation
Rachel Dobkin Tzedakah Fund of The Shefa Fund
Three Bridge Trust
Underdog Fund of the Tides Foundation

We want your feedback-- your honest, straight-up, constructive criticism. It will help us make future editions even better. Thank you.

Future 25

Likes:

Dislikes:

Who would you recommend for the Future 25?

Future 500

Likes:

Dislikes:

Groups you would recommend for the Future 500:

Resources (National Networks, Foundations, Allies, Graphs)

Likes:

Dislikes:

Other resources you'd like to see:

Overall

Likes:

Dislikes:

Suggestions:

Please cut this form out along perforation and send it back to:
Active Element Foundation
532 La Guardia Place, #510 New York, NY 10012